FEMINIST THEOLOGY
a reader

FEMINIST THEOLOGY
a reader

edited by Ann Loades

SPCK   W/JKP

First published in Great Britain 1990
SPCK
Holy Trinity Church
Marylebone Road
London NW1 4DU

First published in the USA 1990
Westminster/John Knox Press
Louisville, Kentucky

British Library Cataloguing in Publication Data
Feminist theology: a reader
  1. Christian feminism
I. Loades, Ann, 1938–
  261.83442
  ISBN 0-281-04450-3

Library of Congress Cataloguing in Publication Data
  Feminist theology : a reader / edited by Ann Loades.
       p.   cm.
  Includes bibliographical references.
  ISBN 0-664-25129-3

  1. Feminist theology. I. Loades, Ann.
  BT83.55.F45 1990
230′.082—dc20   89-77155
                                               CIP

Typeset by Goodfellow and Egan, Cambridge
Printed in Great Britain by
Biddles Ltd, Guildford and Kings Lynn

Contents

Acknowledgements

I am deeply grateful to a number of friends and colleagues for drawing attention to material I might not have found myself. I hope that the selections I have made from the vast range of possibilities will provide stimulating reading and enable us to engage for ourselves with the opportunities presented to us by feminist theology. I am especially grateful to Philip Law of SPCK who patiently endured the sorting out of the first edition of this book, and contributed judiciously to the decisions about what should and not be included. Any remaining errors are of course my own.

Permission to reprint is acknowledged as follows:

- Some of my own writing is reworked from an essay, 'Feminist Theology', in D. Ford (ed.) *The Modern Theologians: An Introduction to Christian Theology in the Twentieth Century*, vol. 2 (Oxford, Blackwell, 1989), pp. 235–52.
- Ruth Page's essay first appeared as 'Re-Review: Elizabeth Cady Stanton's *The Woman's Bible*' in *MC* (The Journal of the Modern Churchpeople's Union) 29:4 (1987), pp. 37–41 and is reprinted by permission of the editor.
- Phyllis Trible's essay, 'Feminist Hermeneutics and Biblical Studies', is reprinted from *The Christian Century*, 3–10 February 1982, pp. 116–18, by permission of *The Christian Century*. Copyright © 1982 The Christian Century Foundation.
- Toni Craven's essay, 'Tradition and Interpretation in the Book of Judith', is reprinted from M.A. Tolbert (ed.), *The Bible and Feminist Hermeneutics* (a special number of *Semeia*; Atlanta, Scholars Press, 1983), pp. 49–61, by permission of Scholars Press.
- Nicola Slee's essay, 'Parables and Women's Experience', is reprinted from *MC* 26:2 (1984), pp. 20–31 by permission of the editor.
- Sharon Ringe's essay, 'A Gentile Woman's Story', is reprinted from L.M. Russell (ed.) *Feminist Interpretation of the Bible* (Oxford, Blackwell; Philadelphia, Westminster, 1985), pp. 65–72, by permission of Blackwell and Westminster Press.
- Elisabeth Schüssler Fiorenza's essay, 'Missionaries, Apostles, Co-workers: Romans 16 and the Reconstruction of Women's Early Christian History', is reprinted from *Word and World* 6:4 (1986), pp. 420–33 by permission of Professor Schüssler Fiorenza and the editor.

- Angela West's essay, 'Sex and Salvation: a Christian Feminist Bible Study on 1 Cor. 6, 12—7, 39', is reprinted from *MC* 39:3 (1987), pp. 17–24 by permission of the editor.
- Karen Armstrong's treatment of 'The Acts of Paul and Thecla' was first published in her book, *The Gospel According to Woman* (London, Elm Tree, 1986; New York, Anchor Pr., Doubleday, 1987), pp. 125–30, copyright © 1986 by Karen Armstrong, and is reprinted by permission of Hamish Hamilton Ltd and Doubleday, a division of Bantam, Doubleday, Dell Publishing Group Inc.
- The material by Genevieve Lloyd is reprinted from the chapter, 'The Divided Soul: Manliness and Effeminacy' in her *The Man of Reason: 'Male' and 'Female' in Western Philosophy* (Minneapolis, University of Minnesota Press, 1984), pp. 28–37, copyright © 1984 by Genevieve Lloyd, by permission of the University of Minnesota Press and Methuen and Co.
- Eleanor McLaughlin's essay, 'Women, Power and the Pursuit of Holiness in Medieval Christianity', is reprinted from R.R. Ruether and E. McLaughlin (eds.), *Women of Spirit: Female Leadership in the Jewish and Christian Traditions* (New York, Simon & Schuster, 1979), pp. 99–130, copyright © 1979 by Rosemary Radford Ruether and Eleanor McLaughlin, by permission of Simon & Schuster Inc.
- Merry Wiesner's essay, 'Luther and Women: The Death of Two Marys', is reprinted from Jim Obelkevich, Lyndal Roper and Raphael Samuel (eds.), *Disciplines of Faith: Studies in Religion, Politics and Patriarchy* (London, Routledge & Kegan Paul, 1987), pp. 245–308 by permission of Routledge and the History Workshop Centre for Social History.
- Rosemary Radford Ruether's essay, 'The Liberation of Christology from Patriarchy', is reprinted from *New Blackfriars* 66 (1985), pp. 324–35 and 67 (1986), pp. 92–3 by permission of Professor Radford Ruether and the editor.
- Sara Maitland's essay, 'Ways of Relating' is reprinted from *The Way*, 26:2 (1986), pp. 124–33 by permission of Sara Maitland and the editors.
- Janet Morley's essay, 'I Desire Her with My Whole Heart', is reprinted from *The Month* 21:2 (1988), pp. 541–4 by permission of Janet Morley and the editor.
- Gail Ramshaw-Schmidt's 'Letters for God's Name: "Q" and "W"' are reprinted from *Letters for God's Name*, (Minneapolis, Seabury/Winston Press New York, Harper & Row, 1984), pp. 51–3, copyright © 1984 by Gail Ramshaw-Schmidt, by permission of Harper & Row, Publishers, Inc.). Her Essay 'De Divinis Nominibus: the Gender of God' (which is published by

'Gail Ramshaw') is reprinted from *Worship* 56 (1982), pp. 117–31 by permission of the editor.
* The concluding pages of Mary Daly's *Beyond God the Father* are reprinted from the 1986 edition (The Women's Press, London), pp. 195–8 by permission of Professor Mary Daly.
* Beverly Wildung Harrison's essay, 'The Power of Anger in the Work of Love: Christian Ethics for Woman and Other Strangers', is reprinted from C.S. Robb and B. Wildung Harrison (eds.), *Making the Connections: Essays in Feminist Social Ethics* (Boston, Beacon Press, 1985), pp. 3–21, copyright © 1985 by Beverly Wildung Harrison and Carol Robb), by permission of Professor Wildung Harrison and Beacon Press.
* Daphne Hampson's essay, 'Luther on the Self: a Feminist Critique', is reprinted from *Word and World* 7:4 (1988), pp. 334–42 by permission of the editor.
* Letty M. Russell's 'Good Housekeeping' is a chapter of her *Household of Freedom: Authority in Feminist Theology* (Philadelphia, Westminster Press, 1987), pp. 84–114, and is reprinted by permission of Westminster.
* Margaret A. Farley's essay, 'Theology and Bioethics', is reprinted from Earl E. Shelp (ed.), *Theology and Bioethics: Exploring the Foundations and Frontiers* (Dordrecht, D. Reidel, 1985), pp. 163–85, by permission of Kluwer Academic Publishers, Dordrecht, Holland, and is © D. Reidel Publishing Company, 1985.
* The material by Sallie McFague is reprinted from her *Models of God: Theology for an Ecological, Nuclear Age*, (London, SCM; Minneapolis, Augsburg, Fortress, 1987), copyright © 1987 by Fortress Press, pp. 116–23, 146–55 and 174–80 by permission of SCM and Fortress Press.
* Ursula King's essay, 'Women in Dialogue: a New Vision of Ecumenism', is reprinted from *The Heythrop Journal*, 26 (1985), pp. 125–42 by permission of the editor.

Contributors

RUTH PAGE University of Edinburgh
PHYLLIS TRIBLE Union Theological Seminary, New York
TONI CRAVEN Brite Divinity School, Texas Christian University
NICOLA SLEE Whitelands College, London
SHARON H. RINGE Methodist Theological School, Ohio
ELISABETH SCHÜSSLER FIORENZA Harvard Divinity School
ANGELA WEST Freelance author, Oxford

KAREN ARMSTRONG Freelance author, London
GENEVIEVE LLOYD Australian National University
ELEANOR MC LAUGHLIN Andover Newton Theological Seminary
MERRY WIESNER University of Wisconsin, Milwaukee
ROSEMARY RADFORD RUETHER Garrett Evangelical Seminary,
Evanston, Illinois
SARA MAITLAND Freelance author, London
JANET MORLEY Freelance author, London
GAIL RAMSHAW Freelance author and liturgist, Philadelphia

MARY DALY Boston College, Mass.
BEVERLY WILDUNG HARRISON Union Theological Seminary,
New York
DAPHNE HAMPSON University of St Andrews
LETTY M. RUSSELL Yale Divinity School
MARGARET FARLEY Yale Divinity School
SALLIE MC FAGUE Vanderbilt University, Nashville
URSULA KING University of Bristol

Introduction

□ 'Feminist theology' is a phrase that shelters many different positions, as do the words 'feminism' and 'theology' taken separately. Broadly speaking, there are three main types of feminism.[1] The liberal tradition has been concerned with equality of civil rights for women as for men, with access to educational and professional opportunities, reproductive self-determination, and equal pay for comparable work. Marxist feminism has been concerned with economic autonomy. Finally, there is romantic feminism, which celebrates the emotional and the natural, to counteract the prevailing emphasis on the rational and the technical; this includes the radicals who want to reject the male world altogether, as well as those who want mutuality between women and men, and a balance of the masculine and feminine in everyone.

At its most minimal, then, feminism is a movement that seeks change for the better for women, for justice for them; thus feminism can mean a doctrine of social and political rights, an organization for working for those rights, the assertion of the claims of women as a group and the body of theory they have created, and the recognition of the necessity of long-term social change (to draw on Gerda Lerner's definitions).[2] So what is the problem for theology? The feminist argues that our culture, and Christian theology as one manifestation of that culture, is in fact riddled with what Gerda Lerner herself calls 'a conceptual error of vast proportion'.[3] For where the male has been thought to represent the *whole* of humanity, the half has been mistaken for the whole, so that what has been described has been distorted in such a way that we cannot see it correctly. As long as men believe that their experiences, viewpoint, and ideas represent all of human experience and all of human thought, abstract definition and description of the real will alike be inaccurate.[4]

What she calls this 'androcentric fallacy' has been built into all the mental constructs of western civilization, and it cannot be put right merely by 'adding women' (for instance, by saying 'brothers and sisters' in the liturgy, leaving everything else as it is). We require a radical restructuring of thought and analysis which comes to terms with the reality that humanity consists of women and men; that 'the experiences, thoughts and insights of both sexes must be represented in every generalization that is made about human beings'. In other words, only half the story has been told. The half that now needs to be given prominence concerns women: their contribution to and share in the world and its work, and their centrality in making society and building civilization.

The story about women has been thoroughly obscured by the ways in which women have been excluded from the processes by which cultures find meaning, interpret and explain their past and present, and orientate themselves to the future, as all this is expressed in *texts*, which may simply represent the views of the most privileged and atypical members of a given community of language users.[5] The most minimal attention to the history of the fight for education for women, and especially for education for the professions, illustrates the point. Exclusion from *theological* education, in particular, has been contingent upon exclusion from leadership roles as 'ordained' ministers in Christian communities, and therefore from the forms of educational preparation associated with those roles.

Not every feminist is female by sex, and not every female theologian is a feminist theologian. The major feminist theologians at the present time are female, however, because a primary need for women is being expressed in this form of theology. Feminist theologians want to eliminate the androcentric fallacy, and rely on themselves for understanding the God they have found to be theirs, though mediated to them by a religious tradition which causes them profound problems as one powerful form of mediating that fallacy. It is arguable that as Christianity has been understood, it has had some disastrous consequences for women's self-understanding and self-esteem, and at the high price of neglecting important elements in men's lives too. What has been thought to be 'universal' theology has excluded women and their insights, and there is no reason to suppose that either sex can monopolize alleged truths about God and what it is to be human in our many different ways.

It is not to my purpose here to rehearse Gerda Lerner's account of the historical process by which women were excluded from the contribution to the formation of cultural meaning, including theological meaning, and from recognition of their creativity in society, as agents in their own histories, maintaining a cultural expression too often regarded by men as marginal, not least in religion. What does need emphasizing here is her point that there is no *one* simple or single cause to explain the complexities of women's relationships to men in different societies over five millennia. It also needs to be emphasized that our present state of affairs is the result of a long historical *process*. There is, in other words, however complex the causes, nothing inevitable, fixed in advance for ever, about our present situation, in culture or religious tradition. Historical processes that are ongoing can be shaped and changed for the better as we discern it, though it will not, one hopes, take another five millennia. Another point that I think continues to merit close scrutiny, is just how women's co-operation was and still is secured in a pattern of relationships which has served to marginalize them and to allow androcentric error. Educational deprivation has already been mentioned. We must add 'gender indoctrination' (to which I will return), of which religious traditions are one vehicle within a culture.[6] As difficult to confront as any feature of our situation is the division of women from one another by defining 'respectability' and 'deviance' according to women's sexual activities in relation to men; and the control of women by restraint and outright physical coercion.[7] Women have been discriminated against in access to economic resources (Diane Pearce coined the phrase 'the feminization of poverty'),[8] and discriminated against in access to political power. Class privileges have been awarded to conforming women.[9] Any combination of these factors has hindered the development of a feminist perspective, but reflection, including theological reflection, must now include the particular variable of women's experience. This must continue to affect an evaluation of our religious traditions too, for they also are the result of a long historical process, which merits reconsideration without predetermined immunity of any kind.

I have found when trying to discuss feminist theology with people, that some of them have great difficulty in seeing that women need have any great problem with the Christian tradition. After all, as one of my friends has recently written:

> If we try to describe the Christian understanding of the whole person, then, we describe a person who fully embodies a sense of the common good that includes the broader culture, but is not limited to it. For her ends are informed by something more ultimate and her talents developed in accordance with those ends. She draws life and inspiration from her culture, but her ultimate source of light would come from God. Her service to her community would be her witness to the fulness of life.[11]

It sounds admirable enough, but compare it with an example given by Nelle Morton,[11] the first woman in the USA to teach a university course (at Drew) on women, theology and language. She describes in one of her essays a sculpture in wood outside a church building, a sculpture on the theme of vocation taken from 1 Corinthians 10.31, 'Whether therefore ye eat, or drink, or whatsoever ye do, do all to the glory of God.' The sculpture shows thirty individual forms representing nineteen different kinds of work. Only seven of the thirty figures are women, represented as nursing a baby, on knees scrubbing a floor, serving a man seated at table, assisting a male doctor, feeding chickens, pounding a typewriter, and teaching children. All these figures represent tasks that need doing, but it is absurd to associate that necessity with women alone, and absurd to exclude them from connection with the other twenty-three figures representing nineteen kinds of work. It needs little imagination to think out the likely roles of the male figures in the sculpture.

The basic point is that the Christian tradition is fundamentally ambivalent for women. We might like to think that it has offered women only what my friend describes as the Christian understanding of the whole person, but what is represented on the sculpture described by Nelle Morton is only too depressingly familiar. The Christian tradition has not only urged some version of what my friend commends, but all too strongly the one represented by the sculpture, which systematically undercuts the former. And worse, too many women exhibit what Anne Wilson Schaef[12] calls the symptoms of co-dependence, that is, low self-esteem, an inability to take care of themselves, whether physically, emotionally, spiritually or psychologically. They spend much of their time trying to work out what *others* want, so they can deliver it to them, believing that whatever goes wrong is their fault, and it is their responsibility to put it right. They are trained *not* to form boundaries, not to know what *they* think and feel from the inside. They cannot possibly become the whole persons of the ideal.

Our tradition has in fact fostered sexism, that is, the belief that persons are superior or inferior to one another on the basis of their sex. And sexism, as Margaret Farley points out, includes the attitudes, value systems and social patterns that express or support this superiority/inferiority.[13] The Christian tradition has too frequently, predominantly and insistently offered women a particularly disabling gender construction, which critical appropriation of our inheritance seeks to remedy. The word 'theology' itself is one such gender-related term, coming from the Greek word for god-male, constantly signalling to those alert to the problem the unease in the Christian tradition about the association of the female and the feminine with the godlike (the*a*logy). Put more precisely, and following Margaret Farley again, the central stumbling blocks to attributing the full 'image of God' to women have been four in number: (1) the failure to find femininity in God; (2) the insistence that woman is derivative from and hence secondary to man; (3) the assumption that woman is characterized by passivity; and (4) the tendency to identify woman with bodiliness as opposed to transcendent mind.

Before thinking what needs to be done about the problem, it is worth clearing up the distinction between 'sex' and 'gender' – at any rate, as *I* employ them. 'Sex' has to do with basic biological differences, such as that men ejaculate, women ovulate, gestate and lactate. Until about the sixth week of development, human embryos (eggs fertilized by sperm and beginning to develop) are anatomically identical. Then, those eggs fertilized by Y-chromosome-bearing sperm will after six weeks develop into males, and those fertilized by X-chromosome-bearing sperm will develop into females. 'Gender' refers to what a particular society makes of the relationships between males and females. One example of gender construction is the nursery rhyme which asks the question, 'What are little girls made of?' and replies in terms of sugar and spice and all things nice. To the question, 'What are little boys made of?', the reply is couched in terms of slugs ('snips' in the USA!) and snails and puppy dog tails. In terms of Nelle Morton's example, it can be argued that the dominant gender construction of Christian culture for men has been that they are active, independent, intelligent, brave, strong, good and, needless to say, godlike. God in turn is male-like, but is also *all*-powerful and *all*-knowing, as well as having some peculiarly godlike characteristics, like being present everywhere, being eternal. Males are *always* more godlike than females could ever be, even when they try to approximate to males, and small wonder when their religiously sanctioned gender construction has been that they are passive, dependent, bodily, emotional, weak, peculiarly responsible for evil and sin (though not for pride, the sin of the intellect!) and childlike.

Tangled up in all this is a fundamental assumption which is now wholly at odds with reality; it is counter-factual, but pervades doctrines, liturgies and institutions. This assumption is not unique to the Christian tradition, but is well worked into it, and is that males are primarily creative, that a child originates essentially from only one source, that the male has the primary and essential role in reproduction.[14] The appropriate metaphor is found at least as early as Athenian marriage contracts, and is that the male plants the seed and the woman is like the field. It connects neatly with belief in one god, understood and signified primarily by male metaphor and appellation, notwithstanding the variety and richness of female-related metaphor for God in both Scripture and tradition. Why else deny women the vote, deprive them of access to education, to theological education, to the ordained ministry, unless they are deemed to be *merely*

nurturant and non-essential, except as aids to male procreators?

Of course, every intelligent believer may learn to say that
whatever is meant by God, God transcends both sex and
gender, but our present symbol system works by giving pride
of place to male-related appellation and metaphor, since
males are godlike procreators. Not surprisingly, this is also
expressed in some familiar analogies, such as that men are to
women as culture is to nature; or woman is to man as the
created, natural world is to God (reconsider Cinderella, Snow
White and Sleeping Beauty). Or we can construct a hierarchy
rather than attend to identifying relevant analogies, and
notice that the order is God, men, women, children, animals,
earth. There is of course no necessary connection whatsoever
between the perception of *differences* and the construction of
the analogies or the hierarchy, so to dislodge the analogies
and to dismantle that whole way of thinking and replace it
with something that does justice to the life-giving contribution of women as well as men in our religious tradition and
culture, does not require that we pretend that we can
obliterate sex or gender difference. It is simply, but painfully, to acknowledge that in so far as we have ordered our
traditions and societies, explicitly or implicitly, by means of
such constructs, and whatever function they may possibly
once usefully have served, now we are increasingly conscious
of the damage they do, and of our responsibility to do
something about it.

My friend who writes about the Christian understanding
of the whole person rightly says that a culture embodies
many diverse elements, and that not all of them are equally
worthy. He urges us to apply 'a critical knife to prejudice', to
develop the capacity to distinguish gods from idols, not just
our finite cultural idols, but our religious ones too.[15] We can
already see that some branches of the Christian Church are
appreciating the importance of the feminist critique. For
instance, there exists a thoroughly orthodox and correct brief
statement of faith drawn up in draft by the Presbyterian
Church of the USA.[16] It is orthodox in that it concludes with
the *gloria* in the familiar, all-male language characteristic of
an earlier period of doctrinal formulation. Liturgy and

doctrine need change, but cannot be changed too precipi-
tously, at least for those who want to continue ecumenical
conversations, in which women have only recently been
permitted to participate.[17] At least, however, the statement
talks of Christ as God with us in *human* flesh, as one who
proclaimed the *reign* of God, a God *sovereign in love*, whom
Jesus called Abba, Father. This is a God who created all
things good, and made us equal in God's image, male and
female, every race and people. God remains faithful still,
'like a mother who will not abandon the child in her arms,
like a father who runs to welcome the prodigal home', and
who calls both women and men to all the ministries of the
Church. The Spirit gives us power 'to smash the idols of
church and culture, and to claim all of life for Christ'. It is in
its own way a good example of the linguistic shift, indicating
the real change in the nature of community that needs to be
made if becoming a whole person, embodying a sense of the
common good, is to become a genuine and authentic possibility for women as well as men in Christian institutions.
Another example could be taken from the writing of Roman
Catholic theologian Monika K. Hellwig, writing on the role
of the theologian as mythmaker. Here is one such 'myth':

> God creates human persons in the divine image by awakening
> them into freedom, self-determination, and creativity, in which
> they discover that they are essentially relational and that their
> humanity is realized in the ways they shape the earth, them-
> selves, one another, and their societies; in this they are fulfilling
> and realizing the creativity of God; when they shape communi-
> ties which offer liberation, happiness and fulfilling relationships
> to all, they fulfil the purpose of creation; then all creation is
> drawn into a great harmony and returns to the Creator in peace,
> and God is glorified.[18]

Feminist theology offers the Christian tradition a major
challenge from within, but also, inside the feminist theologist
movement there is a crucial confrontation that has to be
made – that is, with the matters not only of gender construction and class privilege, but also with the ways these are
complicated by our incapacity to deal with the question of
racism. If 'feminist theology' were to mean only the theology
of white Western privileged women, deluding themselves

that they spoke for *all* women, this would be a catastrophic mistake. The language may seem to be the same, but the realities to which it refers may be profoundly different. Mercy Amba Oduyoye writes powerfully of feminism as a precondition for a Christian anthropology, but adds that Christian feminists dramatize the plight of all the underprivileged and the loss to the community of their gifts and experiences; and that 'The separate development to which the church has resorted only helps to reinforce the vested interest apparent in the rest of the human community, and thus contributes to the mutilated relations and identities that are inimical to the building up of a community unashamed before God'.[19] She can make that claim with a strength which others cannot make for her, and it would be presumptuous for them to attempt to do so. Earlier ventures by individual women theologians now are coming together in sets of essays by women from Africa, Asia and Latin America, much of it explicitly feminist.[20] In the USA , the issues are certainly sharp, as Ada María Isasi-Díaz points out to 'Anglo feminists', urging that 'Mutuality asks us to give serious consideration to what the other is saying, not only to respect it but to be willing to accept it as good for all.' If the word 'woman' refers only to middle- and upper-strata white women, then it shows us who decides what is normative. 'All the rest of us, in order not to be totally invisible, have to add adjectives to the word: *poor* women, *Black* women, *Hispanic* women.' Letty Russell's edition of *Inheriting our Mothers' Gardens: Feminist Theology in Third World Perspective* represents a recent attempt at such mutuality, as does *God's Fierce Whimsy: Christian Feminism and Theological Education* by the Mud Flower Collective.[21] That apart, as one analogy runs that purple is to lavender as womanist is to feminist, then feminist theologians have much to learn from the priorities of womanist theologians, their concern for liberation from white–male–white–female domination,[22] the way it affects their reflection on Scripture (for instance in the work of Renita J. Weems and Sheila Briggs), and in the resources they find in Afro-American women's literature, of which Alice Walker's *The Color Purple* is the most brilliant example.[23]

Since I write as a white feminist theologian, then, I acknowledge the challenge that is internal to this movement in theology; at the moment, though, I can do little more than respect it, and focus on the major task of evaluating those forms of thought and expression that are determined by and reflect 'the needs of the socially powerful gender group and where, consequently, the needs and experiences of women are often forgotten, ignored, or at best, subsumed under categories created by and appropriate to men.'[24] What it is to be embodied as female or male, to survive childhood and adolescence, to flourish as an adult, connects with varying social, political and religious constructs, worldviews and concepts, depending on how human beings classify things and sort them out and make them more or less manageable and enjoyable. What it is to be a male or female is astonishingly variable in different contexts, since human beings and their perceptions and evaluations of one another are surprisingly malleable. Religious traditions do not escape gender constructions, so feminist theologians are particularly concerned with the way these traditions work, the symbolism they use, the characteristics of roles within them, the way the traditions reflect social assumptions and shape and reshape those assumptions, and especially the gender-related way in which we talk about God.[25] Feminist theologians are optimists, in the sense that they hope that old stories can be retold and new ones invented to 'verbalize' God in an inclusively human manner, which takes account of women (and their insights) as well as men. The languages that mediate divine reality to us have differed depending on their relationship to shifting contexts, and we can learn that even biblical language for God may be more gender-inclusive than we at first supposed, though there are clear limitations to this. Feminist theologians want to see if we can make an imaginative, moral and theological shift, so that we come to share a new vision of goodness and be given and gain access to it.

The material that follows is a *selection* from the vast range of what is now available, and it is all the work of those who are explicitly feminist in their theology. This is not in any way to deny that male theologians can be feminist, only that given the limitations of a selection in an introductory volume, their work is not included here, though some valuable material is referred to in the Notes. And it should be noted that I have throughout restricted myself to discussion of the Christian tradition, though I would like to express my gratitude to those who are so rapidly interpreting for us women's relationships to non-Christian religious traditions and to the feminist theologies appropriate to them.[26]

PART ONE
Biblical Tradition and Interpretation

☐ Whatever valuable resources for theology and thealogy are now being recovered by research in forgotten or neglected writing by and about women in the Christian tradition,[1] there is no problem about identifying the doyenne of the present movement. Elizabeth Cady Stanton was a daughter in a Presbyterian family who tried endlessly to make up to her father for the loss of his male children. No college in the USA admitted women until Oberlin began to do so in 1834, and Elizabeth ran full tilt into the problems of securing an adequate education – so typical of women like her for many generations to come. She married Henry Stanton, and her honeymoon trip included the Anti-Slavery Convention of June 1840, in London, the famous convention at which almost all the men refused to allow the women delegates to be seated. Tucked away in a curtained-off space to one side, and allowed to attend business sessions as a concession, she came to know well Lucretia Mott, one of the distinguished Quakers of her day. She too became a campaigner for women, and when she moved out to the country – to Seneca Falls in 1847 with her growing family, – she and Mrs Mott and others booked the Wesleyan Methodist chapel in the village, and advertised a meeting for women. Paraphrasing the American Declaration of Independence, they produced a Declaration of Principles, and one of their resolutions was simply that 'woman is man's equal – was intended to be so by the Creator, and the highest good of the race demands that she should be recognized as such'.[2] Elizabeth Cady Stanton herself made a speech on this famous day (19 July 1848), in which she urged:

> Let woman live as she should. Let her feel her accountability to her maker. Let her know that her spirit is fitted for as high a sphere as man's, and that her soul requires food as pure and exalted as his. Let her live *first* for God, and she will not make imperfect man an object of reverence and awe. Teach her her responsibility as a being of conscience and reason, that all earthly support is weak and unstable, that her only safe dependence is the arm of omnipotence, and that true happiness springs from duty accomplished. Thus will she learn the lesson of individual responsiblity for time and eternity. That neither father, husband, brother, or son, however willing they may be, can discharge her high duties of life, or stand in her stead when called into the presence of the great Searcher of Hearts at the last day.[3]

One of the women present was Charlotte Woodward, then aged only nineteen, who alone lived to be able to vote for President in 1920. Although less electrifying than the speech of Sojourner Truth ('And a'n't I a woman?' (29 May 1851)),[4] Elizabeth Cady Stanton's speech launched her into a whole series of campaigns, and, for the purposes of this *Reader*, that associated with *The Woman's Bible* is the most important. She published it just two weeks after her eightieth birthday in 1895, a birthday celebrated at the Metropolitan Opera House in New York. One of the tributes she received on that occasion said:

> Every woman who seeks the legal custody of her children; who finds the door of a college or university open to her; who administers a post-office or a public library; who enters upon a career of medicine, law or theology; who teaches school or tills a farm or keeps a shop or rides a bicycle – every such woman owes her liberty largely to yourself and to your earliest and bravest co-workers.[5]

Elizabeth Cady Stanton had had an adolescent rebellion against Presbyterianism and revivalism, but had kept reading theology off and on all her life, and with the publication of the Revised Version in 1881, she seized the opportunity to establish her own team of scholars to comment on the parts of the Bible that referred to women. The basic point was to attack all those who used the Bible to condemn women to secondary status. She and her commentators did not reject the Bible wholesale, but, even so, the publication of the first volume in 1895 caused a tremendous split in the party of those still fighting for the vote for women – for many thought that it would now be better to steer clear of any association with her. The book was a best-seller, however, running through seven printings in six months, and translated into other languages. By the time of the second volume in 1898, she had some thirty members on her team of collaborators. One indication of the journey from Elizabeth Cady Stanton to our own time is that Elisabeth Schüssler Fiorenza in 1987 became the first woman President of the Society of Biblical Literature.[6]

With all its limitations, *The Woman's Bible* is still worth reading for Elizabeth Cady Stanton's perception of the way in which an amalgam of canon and civil law, Church and state, priests and legislators, political parties and religious denominations had inculcated in women a fundamental conviction of their inferiority, conveyed to them not least by their alleged incapacity to 'image' God. The first essay to be included in this *Reader* is an assessment of *The Woman's Bible*, together with some material drawn from the latest and major biography by Elisabeth Griffith, *In Her Own Right: The Life of Elizabeth Cady Stanton* (Oxford, OUP, 1984), which puts *The Woman's Bible* into relationship with the other fruits of a long and productive life. The essay was written by Ruth Page, and from reading it we can move on to look at the impact of feminism on biblical studies. Katharine Doob Sakenfeld has recently given us a kind of rubric to bear in mind as we read, which is that 'Feminist scholars in all fields have a high level of investment in the relationship between their work and social change, no matter how arcane their subject may seem.'[7] To be self-critical and reflective about our response is to stand in the tradition inaugurated by Elizabeth Cady Stanton, listening to *all* the voices of those whose viewpoint has too often been disregarded, hoping that in hearing them there is the greater likelihood of encountering the God who seeks to encounter us. First, however, Ruth Page's assessment of the importance of Elizabeth Cady Stanton.

RUTH PAGE
Elizabeth Cady Stanton's *The Woman's Bible*

In 1869, Hester Vaughan was a twenty-year old woman, deserted by her husband, who had become a servant in a Philadelphia household. She had been seduced, become pregnant, and was dismissed. Destitute, she delivered the baby alone in an unheated garret and collapsed. Twenty-four hours later mother and child were discovered. The baby was dead and Vaughan was charged with infanticide. Tried without counsel, forbidden to testify, she was found guilty and sentenced to hang.[1]

The aggregate of female misery in a world whose laws and standards were made by men illustrates graphically the problems Elizabeth Cady Stanton grappled with all her life. In this case, Vaughan was pardoned after women's protests and publicity, while typically Stanton used the case to further her attack on the prevailing double standard of morality and the denial to women of such legal rights as taking the stand in their own defence or serving as jurors. From the moment when, as a child, she had observed that five daughters, however gifted, were no consolation to her adored father after the death of her last brother, Stanton set herself to acquire learning, then political judgement, in order to change attitudes and overcome legal, social and ecclesiastical constrictions on women. This ebullient, articulate, unofficially educated woman spent her life in passionate engagement for every form of female emancipation from suffrage to the experiment with 'bloomers'.

She was too much even for some of her fellow reformers, male and female. Those, for instance, who belonged to the Women's Christian Temperance Union wished to narrow their sights to suffrage alone, and hoped to be rewarded with the vote on account of their seemliness and capable assistance to men from their home sphere. Stanton, on the other hand, fought all her adult life against notions of divinely ordained separate spheres for men and women. The vote was not some hoped-for reward from magnanimous males to be received with meek gratitude, but a right of women because of their humanity, just as it had been for male slaves when they were emancipated. She won some battles and lost others, but by 1895, when she was eighty, Stanton had earned this tribute: 'Every woman who seeks the legal custody of her children; who finds the door of a college or university open to her; who administers a post-office or a public library; who teaches school or tills a farm or keeps a shop or rides a bicycle – every such woman owes her liberty largely to yourself!'[2] That has not been achieved without reasoned, articulate perseverance in the face of ridicule and slander, and an increasing network of support as the unthinkable became, after all, a possible goal. Although the biography by Elisabeth Griffith is rather dominated in the first third by the explanation of action in terms of 'role models' (which can seem too deterministic for an innovator like Stanton), it gives an admirable account of her varied interests, the quirks of her personality, the gains and losses of the reform movement in the midst of other historical events, the joys and sorrows of Stanton's home life (with a largely unsympathetic husband and seven children) in tension with her public work.

Plus ça change, plus c'est la même chose. Even today women may be placed on a spectrum ranging from those who believe that the most appropriate place for the whole sex is the home, through those who want moderate change without rocking too many boats, to those for whom any perceived inequality is a trumpet call to action. And again, although there are far more men who are sympathetic on at least some issues, the 'separate spheres' argument is still with us in the guise of 'equal but complementary', a proposition which continued to be legitimated by appeal to the Bible. It seems very odd to women that biblical exhortations to be good slaves and masters are now universally seen to be a reflection of first-century conditions addressed in the expectation of the End, while similar exhortations concerning the respective roles of women and men are still held by some to be timelessly binding whatever social conditions prevail. Indeed the depressing observation on reading Griffith's biography is that although many of Stanton's actual objectives have been achieved, this has not generally speaking resulted in a change of attitude. If attitudes had truly changed it would no longer be remarkable or newsworthy for a woman to enter politics, engineering or the ministry of word and sacrament (or, for that matter, for a man to keep house). But, as things are, each issue involving women and each new career possibility has to be broached almost from scratch with the same old arguments on female ability rehearsed yet again.

Nevertheless, the actual conditions in which women find themselves today are incomparably better than those against which Elizabeth Cady Stanton fulminated. The courage, vigour and success of her 'immodest, inappropriate behaviour' (which she more often than not enjoyed) qualify her for a place in any woman's pantheon. Yet her last essay in defence of woman's status brought her more opprobrium and less sympathy from younger women than any other. This was *The Woman's Bible*, which after its *succès de scandale* was quickly buried and has only recently been reissued in America and Britain. Stanton found it necessary to engage in interpretation of the Bible because it was used as the ultimate sanction against any change in conditions for women. 'Whatever advances women tried to make – in education, or employment, or political rights – were held to contradict the will and word of God as revealed in the Scriptures and interpreted by ministers.'[3] As Stanton herself wrote:

> The chief obstacle in the way of women's elevation today is the degrading position assigned to her in the religion of all countries – an afterthought in Creation, the origin of Sin, cursed by God, marriage for her a condition of servitude, maternity a degradation, unfit to minister at the altar and in some churches even to sing in the choir. Such is her position in the Bible and religion.[4]

Some of this may seem crudely negative today but had point in its time. When women could not control their own property, could not sue for divorce on the grounds of drunkenness or violence, and had no income or prop but their husband, marriage indeed could be 'a condition of servitude' legitimated by biblical texts.

Stanton was brought up a Presbyterian but found its Calvinist teachings too gloomy and its God too punitive. In 1831, when she was fifteen, she attended one of C.G. Finney's crusades and, in what seems to be the most emotional moment of her religious life, was briefly 'converted'. What was of lasting significance to her from the experience was that at the camp meetings she had seen people being summoned to make a choice about God rather than having their status fixed *a priori* by election. Moreover, she had heard *women* on *public* platforms testifying and praying. In fact, revival meetings led to women being called on not only to speak but to serve the Lord in charity and philanthropy. This they did by banding into societies which in turn cultivated their organizational experience and political skills. Women came to be part of nation-wide campaigns on issues like temperance and the abolition of slavery, so that many of those who demanded female emancipation had had their training in revival circles. But Stanton moved on to much more rational religion. In Boston she admired the Unitarian transcendalist Theodore Parker, who preached an androgynous

God and refused to take Scripture literally. Although she was always interested in religious matters, they appear in her later life to be issues of intellectual stimulation rather than personal engagement.

For this reason, *The Woman's Bible*, many of whose commentaries she wrote herself, is a work of intellectual and rationalist criticism, like many productions of its time. 'The object is to revise only those texts and chapters directly referring to women, and those also in which women are made prominent by exclusion.'[5] Such passages, in the editor's estimation, amounted to about one-tenth of Scripture, and the pattern adopted was to set out the text involved and then comment on it. A committee of men had just revised the Authorized Version of the Bible, and what men could do with Scripture women could do also.

Stanton and her team were formidably well read in the scholarship of the time (1895). For the creation stories they could put the Yahwist and Elohist accounts in parallel columns and conclude: 'it is manifest that both of these cannot be true'.[6] They are aware that these are 'fables' and opt for the story which represents the equality of man and woman in creation and dominion (Gen. 1. 27f.). Here, as often in *The Woman's Bible*, there is a concern to meet point for point the interpretations that were used to subject women.

New perceptions and values abound in the book also. Job's wife, for instance, receives perhaps her first kindly comment. 'Poor woman, she had scraped lint (as American women did in the Civil War), nursed him and waited on him to the point of nervous exhaustion – no wonder she was resigned to see him pass to Abraham's bosom.'[7] Vashti, who refused the bidding of the drunken King Ahasuerus in the book of Esther, becomes a heroine. 'Rising to the heights of self-consciousness and of self-respect, she takes her soul into her own keeping.'[8] To the male-determined women of the nineteenth century that represented liberation. On the other hand, there is also fresh vision on what is *not* said in the Bible. Concerning Deuteronomy 28.56,64, Stanton writes: 'In enumerating the good things that would come to Israel if the commandments were obeyed, nothing is promised to women, but when the curses are distributed woman comes in for her share.'[9] Biting modern applications are often made: in this case woman 'is given equal privileges with man in being imprisoned and hung, but unlike him she has no voice in the laws, the judge, the jury'. Clearly, this is not dispassionate exegesis, but there is only an occasional sense of the wrenching of a text to fit a commitment. At the same time, male exegesis of certain passages could scarcely be called dispassionate either.

The New Testament is in general more thinly dealt with except for objections to female roles in the Epistles. There are some surprising omissions including the declaration of freedom in Galatians, especially 3.28: 'there is neither male nor female' in Christ. The status of women in the early Church has received scholarly treatment recently, but the conclusions are largely those of *The Woman's Bible* in 1898 lost for so long. 'To one who uses unbiased common sense in regard to the New Testament records, there can be no question of women's activity and prominence in the early ministry.'[10] Phoebe and Priscilla in Romans 16 are given their place, while a male exegete (Chalmers) is quoted as saying that if Priscilla really did help Paul it must have been as 'a teacher of women and children', which is hardly what 'unbiased common sense' would suggest from reading Acts 18.26.

What kind of people must wise virgins be? They are 'summoned to the discharge of an important duty at midnight, alone, in darkness, and in solitude. . . . They must depend on themselves, unsupported, and pay the penalty for their improvidence and unwisdom'.[11] Self-abnegation in the service of men clearly will not fit women for such a role. 'The wise virgins are those . . . who have secured a healthy, happy, complete development . . . so that when the opportunities and responsibilities of life come, they may be fully fitted to enjoy the one and ably to discharge the other.'[12] As this quotation illustrates, the book has little spiritual tone; but within its rationalist frame it is perceptive. Perhaps spiritual books written by devout ladies would have been less threatening. Much of the historical exegesis, however, is now dated, and many of the discoveries have been taken up and made properly public by female biblical scholars.

The Women's Bible, and all that lies behind it, is a clear outcome of the perennial difficulty in using the Bible to guide life and morality in changing societies. To apply texts and prescriptions directly, in a quasi-literal and supposedly timeless manner is the easiest method and has the appearance of a faithfulness. But that may in fact, as in the case of the treatment of women, work in a contrary direction to the love, reconciliation and justice which are key themes of the Bible. What is called for instead, in this as in so many other cases, is the much more demanding and sensitive 'running conversation' which Paul Lehmann recommends between instructions for biblical situations and the always contemporary ethical context.[13]

☐ Those who want to follow up the connection between 'women's studies and biblical studies' could usefully read the essay by Dorothy C. Bass in the special issue of the *Journal for the Study of the Old Testament* (22, February, 1982), pp. 6–12. The issue was concerned with the effects of women's studies on biblical studies and contains introductory essays by a series of familiar names in this field. And two valuable collections are those edited by Adela Yarbro Collins, *Feminist Perspectives on Biblical Scholarship* (Chico, CA, Scholars, 1985) and Letty Russell, *Feminist Interpretation of the Bible* (New York and Oxford, Basil Blackwell, 1985).

As in Elizabeth Cady Stanton's day, it is vain to belittle the influence of the biblical tradition, depending on how it is evaluated and used. The political context has changed, from that of the anti-slavery campaign and the fight for the vote, education for girls and women, to the campaign for peace, and assessment of artificially assisted human reproduction, for instance, and of 'abortion rights'.[8] But the problem of the use of the Bible in influencing what are deemed to be appropriate possibilities for women in social, ecclesiastical and educational contexts continues to need the most careful attention.[9] So far as feminist theologians are concerned, therefore, it is not just the biblical texts, but what, as it were, surrounds them, such as centuries of habits of exegesis, ecclesiastical practice and tradition which are now ripe for scrutiny, all alike without immunity of any kind. It could be said that whatever seems to propose or to be used for what women discern to be a means of 'oppression' in relation to their lives is likely not to carry 'authority' as 'divine revelation' for them, although they may still find their resources within the tradition, notwithstanding its ambiguity. For the moment, we need to look at some developments in biblical studies, following on from the impetus provided by Elizabeth Cady Stanton and her friends.[10]

Of feminist scholars of the Old Testament, Phyllis Trible is clearly outstanding,[11] and as early as 1973 she had claimed that 'Hebrew Scriptures and Women's Liberation do meet and . . . their encounter need not be hostile.' In her paper to the American Academy of Religion,[12] she admitted that 'patriarchy' referred appropriately to the male-dominated society and the God of the fathers to be found in Scripture, but argued that the *intentionality* of biblical faith is neither to create nor to perpetuate such patriarchy, but rather to function as salvation for both women and men. Her two major books illustrate the difficulties and the promise. *Texts of Terror: Literary Feminist Readings of Biblical Narratives* (Philadelphia, Fortress Press, 1984) speaks all too powerfully of the present, in its study of the stories of Hagar, Tamar and Amnon, Jephthah's daughter, and the unnamed concubine of Judges 19. (And, incidentally, one way of getting into Phyllis Trible's treatment of these stories is to treat her chapters in effect as scripts for voices, for reading out loud, with some 'editing out' of the technicalities. It is not necessary to know Hebrew to be able to get into her presentations.) Her other major work, *God and the Rhetoric of Sexuality* (Philadelphia, Fortress Press, 1978), represents 'promise'. While it is not difficult to find texts indicating women's inferiority, subordination and abuse in Scripture, those same Scriptures also contain challenges to such devaluation, not only in the figures of some of the magnificent women of the Jewish tradition, but, importantly, in the unlikely source of Genesis 2 and 3. Phyllis Trible's interpretation of Genesis becomes a key to unlock some of the meaning of the Song of Songs; and she pays a great deal of attention to some of the metaphors for God in whose image female and male are made. Her major theological clue comes from Scripture itself, and she traces the journey of a single metaphor (womb/compassion) which highlights female/feminine-related imagery for God.

A particular example from the 'lexicon of birth' is that of Deuteronomy 32.18, which uses two figures of speech for God. One is that of 'rock', which can relate to the one who bears or the one who begets. The other is that of the labour pains of birth, so in the RSV, 'You were unmindful of the Rock that begot you/and you forgot the God who gave you birth.' Mayer I. Gruber[13] is not alone in thinking that she may have pressed her case for female/feminine-related imagery for God too hard at certain points, so that references to the compassion of God are not necessarily references to God-feminine as it were. That would be to make too much of the etymological relationship of the word for 'womb' and the verb 'to be compassionate'. But Mayer Gruber goes on to reinforce her major point about figures of speech for God being more 'feminine' than we are sometimes in the habit of highlighting, when he undertakes his own critique of maternal expressions for God to be found in second and third Isaiah. The most extraordinary of these is the juxtaposition in Isaiah 42.13–14 of God as a man of war and as a woman in labour. Scholars (male) have suggested that a warrior is 'active' and a woman in childbirth is 'passive', forgetting that in 'natural' childbirth at least, the woman is active, as God in Isaiah: 'I will scream like a woman in labour/I will inhale, and I will exhale simultaneously.' Mayer Gruber indeed concludes that prophets such as Jeremiah and Ezekiel failed to put an end to idolatry in Israel, whereas second Isaiah could commend God to non-Jews precisely because the prophet could show that a positive-divine value is attached to *both* sexes.

Included here is a complete short essay by Phyllis Trible.

2 PHYLLIS TRIBLE
Feminist Hermeneutics and Biblical Studies

Born and bred in a land of patriarchy, the Bible abounds in male imagery and language. For centuries interpreters have explored and exploited this male language to articulate theology: to shape the contours and content of the Church, synagogue and academy; and to instruct human beings – female and male – in who they are, what rules they should play, and how they should behave. So harmonious has seemed this association of Scripture with sexism, of faith with culture, that only a few have even questioned it.

Within the past decade, however, challenges have come in the name of feminism, and they refuse to go away. As a critique of culture in light of misogyny, feminism is a prophetic movement, examining the status quo, pronouncing judgement and calling for repentance. In various ways this hermeneutical pursuit interacts with the Bible in its remoteness, complexity, diversity and contemporaneity to yield new understandings of both text and interpreter. Accordingly, I shall survey three approaches to the study of women in Scripture. Though these perspectives may also apply to 'intertestamental' and New Testament literature, my focus is the Hebrew Scriptures.

When feminists first examined the Bible, emphasis fell upon documenting the case against women. Commentators observed the plight of the female in Israel. Less desirable in the eyes of her parents than a male child, a girl stayed close to her mother, but her father controlled her life until he relinquished her to another man for marriage. If either of these male authorities permitted her to be mistreated, even abused, she had to submit without recourse. Thus, Lot offered his daughters to the men of Sodom to protect a male guest (Gen. 19.8); Jephthah sacrificed his daughter to remain faithful to a foolish vow (Judg. 11.29–40); Amnon raped his half-sister Tamar (2 Sam. 13); and the Levite from the hill country of Ephraim participated with other males to bring about the betrayal, rape, murder and dismemberment of his own concubine (Judg. 19). Although not every story involving female and male is so terrifying, the narrative literature nevertheless makes clear that from birth to death the Hebrew woman belonged to men.

What such narratives show, the legal corpus amplifies. Defined as the property of men (Exod. 20.17; Deut. 5.21), women did not control their own bodies. A man expected to marry a virgin, though his own virginity need not be intact. A wife guilty of earlier fornication violated the honour and power of both her father and husband. Death by stoning was the penalty (Deut. 22.13–21). Moreover, a woman had no right to divorce (Deut. 24.1–4) and most often, no right to own property. Excluded from the priesthood, she was considered far more unclean than the male (Lev. 15). Even her monetary value was less (Lev. 27.1–7).

Clearly, this feminist perspective has uncovered abundant evidence for the inferiority, subordination and abuse of women in Scripture. Yet the approach has led to different conclusions. Some people denounce biblical faith as hopelessly misogynous, although this judgement usually fails to evaluate the evidence in terms of Israelite culture. Some reprehensibly use these data to support anti-Semitic sentiments. Some read the Bible as a historical document devoid of any continuing authority and hence worthy of dismissal. The 'Who cares?' question often comes at this point.

Others succumb to despair about the ever-present male power that the Bible and its commentators hold over women. And still others, unwilling to let the case against women be the determining word, insist that text and interpreters provide more excellent ways.

The second approach, then, grows out of the first while modifying it. Discerning within Scripture a critique of patriarchy, certain feminists concentrate upon discovering and recovering traditions that challenge the culture. This task involves highlighting neglected texts and reinterpreting familiar ones.

Prominent among neglected passages are portrayals of deity as female. A psalmist declares that God is midwife (Ps. 22.9–10): 'Yet thou art the one who took me from the womb; thou didst keep me safe upon my mother's breast.'

In turn, God becomes mother, the one upon whom the child is cast from birth: 'Upon thee was I cast from my birth, and since my mother bore me thou hast been my God.' Although this poem stops short of an exact equation, in it female imagery mirrors divine activity. What the psalmist suggests, Deuteronomy 32.18 makes explicit: 'You were unmindful of the Rock that begot you and you forgot the God who gave you birth.'

Though the RSV translates accurately 'The God who gave you birth', the rendering is tame. We need to accent the striking portrayal of God as a woman in labour pains, for the Hebrew verb has exclusively this meaning. (How scandalous, then, is the totally incorrect translation in the Jerusalem Bible, 'You forgot the God who fathered you'.) Yet another instance of female imagery is the metaphor of the womb as given in the Hebrew radicals *rḥm*. In its singular form the word denotes the physical organ unique to the female. In the plural, it connotes the compassion of both human beings and God. God the merciful (*raḥum*) is God the mother. (See, for example, Jer. 31.15–22.) Over centuries, however, translators and commentators have ignored such female imagery, with disastrous results for God, man and woman. To reclaim the image of God female is to become aware of the male idolatry that has long infested faith.

If traditional interpretations have neglected female imagery for God, they have also neglected females, especially women who counter patriarchal culture. By contrast, feminist hermeneutics accents these figures. A collage of women in Exodus illustrates the emphasis. So eager have scholars been to get Moses born that they pass quickly over the stories that lead to his advent (Exod. 1.8–2.10). Two female slaves are the first to oppose the Pharaoh; they refuse to kill newborn sons. Acting alone, without advice or assistance from males, they thwart the will of the oppressor. Tellingly, memory has preserved the names of these women, Shiprah and Puah, while obliterating the identity of the king so successfully that he has become the burden of innumerable doctoral dissertations. What these two females begin, other Hebrew women continue:

> A woman conceived and bore a son and when she saw that he was a goodly child she hid him three months. And when she could hide him no longer, she took for him a basket made of bulrushes . . . and she put the child in it and placed it among the reeds at the river's bank. And his sister stood at a distance to know what would be done to him (Exod. 2.2–4).

In quiet and secret ways the defiance resumes as a mother and daughter scheme to save their baby son and brother, and this action enlarges when the daughter of Pharaoh appears at the riverbank. Instructing her maid to fetch the basket, the princess opens it, sees a crying baby, and takes him to her heart even as she recognizes his Hebrew identity. The daughter of Pharaoh aligns herself with the daughters of Israel. Filial allegiance is broken; class lines crossed; racial and political difference transcended. The sister, seeing it all from a distance, dares to suggest the perfect arrangement: a Hebrew nurse for the baby boy; in reality, the child's own mother. From the human side, then, Exodus faith originates as a feminist act. The women who are ignored by theologians are the first to challenge oppressive structures.

Not only does this second approach recover neglected women but also it reinterprets familiar ones beginning with the primal woman in the creation story of Genesis 2–3. Contrary to tradition, she is not created the assistant or subordinate of the man. In fact, most often the Hebrew word 'ezer ('helper') connotes superiority (Ps. 121.2; 124.8; 146.5; Exod. 18.4; Deut. 33.7, 26, 29), thereby posing a rather different problem about this woman. Yet the accompanying phrase 'fit for' or 'corresponding to' ('a helper corresponding to') tempers the connotation of superiority to specify the mutuality of woman and man.

Further, when the serpent talks with the woman (Gen. 3.1–5), he uses plural verb forms, making her the spokesperson for the human couple – hardly the pattern of a patriarchal culture. She discusses theology intelligently, stating the case for obedience even

more strongly than did God: 'From the fruit of the tree that is in
the midst of the garden, God said: "You shall not eat from it, and
you shall not touch it, lest you die."' If the tree is not touched, then
its fruit cannot be eaten. Here the woman builds 'a fence around
the Torah', a procedure that her rabbinical successors developed
fully to protect divine law and ensure obedience.

Speaking with clarity and authority, the first woman is theologian, ethicist, hermeneut and rabbi. Defying the stereotypes of
patriarchy, she reverses what the Church, synagogue and academy
have preached about women. By the same token, the man 'who was
with her' (many translations omit this crucial phrase) throughout
the temptation is not morally superior by rather belly-oriented.
Clearly this story presents a couple alien to traditional interpretations. In reclaiming the woman, feminist hermeneutics gives new
life to the image of God female.

These and other exciting discoveries of a counter literature that
pertains to women do not, however, eliminate the male bias of
Scripture. In other words, this second perspective neither disavows
nor neglects the evidence of the first. Instead, it functions as a
remnant theology.

The third approach retells biblical stories of terror *in memoriam*,
offering sympathetic readings of abused women. If the first
perspective documents misogyny historically and sociologically,
this one appropriates such evidence poetically and theologically. At
the same time, it continues to look for the remnant in unlikely
places.

The betrayal, rape, murder and dismemberment of the concubine in Judges 19 is a striking example. When wicked men of the
tribe of Benjamin demand to 'know' her master, he instead throws
the concubine to them. All night they ravish her; in the morning
she returns to her master. Showing no pity, he orders her to get up
and go. She does not answer, and the reader is left to wonder is she
is dead or alive. At any rate, the master puts her body on a donkey
and continues the journey. When the couple arrive home, the
master cuts the concubine in pieces, sending them to the tribes of
Israel as a call to war against the wrong done to *him* by the men of
Benjamin.

At the conclusion of this story, Israel is instructed to 'consider,
take counsel and speak' (Judg. 19.30). Indeed, Israel does reply –
with unrestrained violence. Mass slaughter follows; the rape,
murder and dismemberment of one woman condones similar

crimes against hundreds and hundreds of women. The narrator (or editor) responds differently, however, suggesting the political solution of kingship instead of the anarchy of the judges (Judg. 12.25). This solution fails. In the days of David there is a king in Israel, and yet Amnon rapes Tamar. How, then, do we today hear this ancient tale of terror as the imperatives 'consider, take counsel and speak' address us? A feminist approach, with attention to reader response, interprets the story on behalf of the concubine as it calls to rememberance her suffering and death.

Similarly, the sacrifice of the daughter of Jephthah documents the powerlessness and abuse of a child in the days of the judges (Judg. 11). No interpretation can save her from the holocaust or mitigate the foolish vow of her father. But we can move through the indictment of the father to claim sisterhood with the daughter. Retelling her story, we emphasize the daughters of Israel to whom she reaches out in the last days of her life (Judg. 11.37). Thus, we underscore the postscript, discovering in the process an alternative translation.

Traditionally, the ending has read, 'She [the daughter] had never known man. And *it* became a custom in Israel that the daughters of Israel went year by year to lament the daughter of Jephthah the Gileadite four days in the year' (11.40). Since the verb *become*, however, is a feminine form (Hebrew has no neuter), another reading is likely: 'Although she had never known a man, nevertheless *she* became a tradition [custom] in Israel. From year to year the daughters of Israel went to mourn the daughter of Jephthah the Gileadite, four days in the year.' By virtue of this translation, we can understand the ancient story in a new way. The unnamed virgin child becomes a tradition in Israel because the women with whom she chooses to spend her last days do not let her pass into oblivion; they establish a living memorial. Interpreting such stories of terror on behalf of women is surely, then, another way of challenging the patriarchy of Scripture.

I have surveyed three feminist approaches to the study of women in Scripture. The first explores the inferiority, subordination and abuse of women in ancient Israel. Within this context, the second pursues the counter-literature that is itself a critique of patriarchy. Utilizing both of these approaches, the third retells sympathetically the stories of terror about women. Though intertwined, these perspectives are distinguishable. The one stressed depends on the occasion and the talents and interests of the interpreter. Moreover, in its work, feminist hermeneutics embraces a variety of methodologies and disciplines. Archaeology, linguistics, anthropology and literary and historical criticism all have contributions to make. Thereby understanding of the past increases and deepens as it informs the present.

Finally, there are more perspectives on the subject of women in Scripture than are dreamt of in the hermeneutics of this essay. For instance I have barely mentioned the problem of sexist translations which, in fact, is receiving thoughtful attention from many scholars, male and female. But perhaps I have said enough to show that in various and sundry ways feminist hermeneutics is challenging interpretations old and new. In time, perhaps, it will yield a biblical theology of womanhood (not to be subsumed under the label humanity) with roots in the goodness of creation female and male. Meanwhile, the faith of Sarah and Hagar, Naomi and Ruth, the two Tamars and a cloud of other witnesses empowers and sobers the endeavour.

☐ Following Phyllis Trible's essay, I have included here one example of feminist exegesis that illustrates Elisabeth Schüssler Fiorenza's comment that we should not picture Jewish women in primarily negative terms (*In Memory of Her*, p. 118). The essay by Toni Craven is about continuity and change in the beliefs and practices of a covenant community.

3 TONI CRAVEN
Tradition and Convention in the Book of Judith

In an article entitled 'Life, Faith, and the Emergence of Tradition',[1] Walter Harrelson maintains that continuity and change are the hallmarks of the traditions of Israel. He posits that each generation shapes tradition in ways appropriate to its own experence: 'Tradition does not remain fixed: it grows.'[2] Thus, women and men in ancient Israel preserved, challenged, and appropriated the religious beliefs and practices of their society.[3]

Among those who radically reinterpreted traditions forcing certain conventions to give way, are Ruth, Esther and Judith.[4] They are the only women whose names are titles of biblical books. Canonical status indicates that the community accepted their stories as valid, authoritative interpretations of the covenant relationship. Comparison of the stories illuminates the participation of these women in the hermeneutical process of continuity and change, as well as highlights the singular contribution of Judith.

Canonical counterparts

As skilfully constructed short stories,[5] the tales of Ruth, Esther and Judith are remarkably similar. The plot of each moves from tragedy to triumph through the resolute acts of the female character.[6] No miracles or promises from God assure success for the women. They are victorious because they use well the human resources available to them. In a situation of famine and death, Ruth heeds the advice of her mother-in-law Naomi about securing a spouse and a home (Ruth 3.1–5). With annihilation threatening the Jewish people, Esther brings about the downfall of their enemy by persuading the Persian king to act according to her desires (Esth. 5.1—7.10). When the Israelites are about to surrender to the Assyrians, Judith delivers her community by first beheading the enemy general and leading a military counter-offensive (Judith 8—13). Each of these females is subject, not object, of her own story.

The societal hierarchies in these stories, however, are male dominated. Independence and decision-making belong to men. For example, in Ruth, the elders of Bethlehem decide the future of Naomi and Ruth (4.1–12). In Esther, men have the king decree that women of the Persian empire must honour and obey them (1.15–22). In the opening chapters of Judith, men in Jerusalem and Bethulia control all political and religious offices and make all decisions. Without question, Ruth, Esther and Judith are stories of 'women in a man's world'.[7]

None the less, within this patriarchal milieu, the three women emerge as independent, making their own decisions and initiating actions in unconventional ways. When widowed, Ruth rejects Naomi's instruction that she return to her own family (1.8); but at the time of the barley harvest, she accepts her mother-in-law's advice that she 'uncover the feet' of Boaz and propose to him (3.6–9). Both Ruth and Naomi act in ways that radically defy traditional standards of patriarchy. Esther's behaviour is also irregular. As a candidate for the Persian king's harem, she obeys Mordecai's charge that she keep her Jewish identity secret (2.20); but as queen, she refuses his first request that she entreat King Ahasuerus to forbid the destruction of the Jews (4.8–11). Eventually, Esther does agree to go unbidden before the king, but she declares that such an act is unlawful and may cause her to perish (4.16). Although Judith punctiliously obeys religious regulations, fasting only when the law allows (8.6) and eating and drinking only ritually pure food even when in the enemy camp (12.2–4.19), she rejects male authority as absolute. When Uzziah tells her to pray for rain, she responds by upbraiding his lack of faith, urging him and the other officials of Bethulia to listen to her voice (8.32; cf. 8.11). She decides for herself that she will go against the enemy with planned deceit that culminates in an assassination (Judith 9—13). Unconventional conduct is not only permitted these women, but it is approved because through their acts tradition is being served.[8]

Theological motives lie behind the telling of each story. Even though God is not mentioned in the Hebrew text of Esther, the narrative is a rescue story in which a woman mediates continued freedom for the covenant people.[9] The feast of Purim, which develops out of this story (9.1–28), celebrates God's deliverance of the Jews. Hence by extension, the story functions theologically. In Ruth, the narrator and the community more explicitly credit God with a causative role as the one who blesses and curses in hidden ways.[10] For instance, though God does not appear personally, Naomi charges that the Almighty is the one who has caused her grief (2.13,20–21), and the narrator acknowledges God as granting conception to Ruth (4.13). The women of Bethlehem make the startling declaration that the Lord has restored the fortunes of Naomi by giving her a daughter-in-law whose love is of greater value than seven sons (4.14–15). In Judith, too, God is presented as the one behind the scene who gives and takes away blessing. This story is a contest between rivals who champion the causes of opposing gods. Holofernes claims Nebuchadnezzar as the one to whom allegiance is owed; Judith defends Yahweh as the protector of Israel. The covenant people must decide which God better gives and takes away life. Thus the whole book addresses the question of the identity of the true God for Israel. In sum, then, explicit theological concerns are peripheral in Esther, hidden in Ruth, but central in Judith.

Comparison of Ruth, Esther and Judith shows tradition under-

going modification in similar ways through reinterpretation. Each
story is a vehicle for change. But whereas alteration of theological
understanding occurs as a byproduct of the stories of Ruth and
Esther, it is a primary objective in the book of Judith. This woman
unequivocally declares the theology of the establishment invalid.[11]
Like Ruth, Judith knows a God who acts in hidden ways; unlike
Ruth, she speaks openly and directly about this God. Like Esther,
Judith uses her sexuality to her own advantage; but unlike Esther,
Judith preserves her purity while still winning the favour of those
whom she wishes to beguile.[12] Of all women in Scripture, Judith
alone says that theological misrepresentations cannot be tolerated.
Thus the particularities of her story merit further attention.

Narrative counterpoints

The Book of Judith is a narrative about faith lost and found by a
people sorely tested. Judith herself does not appear nor is she even
mentioned until the second half of the story. The book, which is
sixteen chapters long in its Greek version, is structured in two
parts. Nebuchadnezzar, king of Assyria, governs the actions of
Part I (chs. 1—7); Judith, a widow of Bethulia, leads the way in
Part II (chs. 8—16). In a story whose details are fanciful overlays of
geograhical and historical data, [13] a contest is struck to prove who is
the true God, the true Lord of all the Earth. The contest is played
out in a life or death situation in which Holofernes, who is leading
punitive forces against the nations that refused to aid Nebuchadnezzar in battle, claims that his king is the sovereign God (3.8; 6.2).
Israel, one of the nations attacked by Holofernes, is ready to
surrender when Judith appears and risks her life and reputation by
making the counter-claim that Yahweh is the one true God (cf.
8.20). Part I narrates the military aggression of the Assyrian enemy
and Israel's near submission to their rule and claim that Nebuchadnezzar is God. Part II records Judith's triumph over the Assyrian
enemy and the consequent transformation of the fear that paralysed
the covenant community. Together, Parts I and II disclose what is
involved in knowing the covenant God, Yahweh.

Literary artistry and theological concerns work together in the
Book of Judith to produce a finely crafted narrative which checks
the human tendency to bind the purposes of God.[14] The entire first
half of the book builds sympathy for the frightened people of Israel
who cry passionately to a God who seems to have failed them.
Despite numerous prayers and pious acts, the covenant people are
dying of thirst as Part I ends. They know only terror and the

feeling of abandonment. These seven chapters prompt the consideration: What more or what else could the people of Israel have done? When Judith appears in Part II, she unhesitatingly assumes control of the situation and the story.[15] She knows no agony or doubt as she chastises the leaders of Bethulia and then destroys the enemies of Israel. Her heroism and triumph prompt the consideration: Why did God grant her such success, and how did Judith know what to do?

Traditional practice would suggest it fitting for the Israelites and Judith to take their distressful situation before God. Models abound in psalms and narratives for the community or one of its members to protest oppression and call God to action.[16] Such models of lament regularly contain elements of (1) an address to God; (2) a complaint; (3) a petition; (4) an expression of trust; (5) a word of assurance; and (6) a vow.[17] In both Parts I and II, these components appear as first the community and then Judith act out laments to God. Examination of the laments, element by element, illuminates the turns at which the practices of the community do not measure up to those of Judith.

Lament components appear in Part I as follows:

Address to God

The covenant people appear for the first time in the narrative in chapter 4. This entire section is given over to public acts which draw God's attention to the plight of the people of Israel. Upon hearing that Holofernes has destroyed the temples of their neighbouring nations, the Jerusalem high priest, Joakim, orders the Israelites to seize all the passes that lead to their hilltop towns. Then in a public ceremony, all in Israel cry out to God with great fervour, fast, put ashes on their heads and cover everything with sackcloth.[18] The test records that 'the Lord heard their prayers and looked upon their affliction' (4.13). As the situation worsens, the people repeat their cries to the Lord (6.18–19,21; 7.19,29).

Complaint

In Part I, the complaint is first expressed as concern for Jerusalem and the temple (4.2). But as the enemy approaches, the terrified Israelites say to one another: 'These men will now lick up the face of the whole land; neither the high mountains nor the deep ravines nor the hills will bear their weight' (7.4). As thirst overcomes the Israelites, their courage fails, their self-interest becomes central, and they complain: 'We have no one to help us; God has sold us into their hands' (7.25). Thus a complaint which first identified the Assyrians as the enemy shifts as the crisis becomes acute to identify God as the one who does terrible things to Israel (7.28).

Petition

At first, the request is simply that the 'Lord look with favour upon the whole house of Israel' (4.15). When the people believe that Yahweh is on their side, they ask that God take pity on them because of the arrogance of their enemies (4.12;6.19). But when the covenant people lose heart, their petition changes to a request for surrender. Believing that God has sold them into the hands of the enemy to be slaughtered, they decide that capture by the Assyrians is preferable to death (7.23–28).

Expression of trust

Nowhere in Part I do the people of Israel express trust in their God. Neither explicit words of trust nor passages recounting God's past deeds of protection appear. The closest the narrative comes to expressing trust in Yahweh is the half-hearted statement of Uzziah that God 'will not forsake us utterly' (7.30c).

Word of assurance

In Part I, this element takes the form of the compromise proposed by Uzziah that the covenant people allow God five more days to deliver them before surrendering to the Assyrians (7.30–31). That the people are not comforted is evident in their reaction of great depression (7.32).

Vow

The only promise made in Part I is the five-day postponement of surrender which Uzziah pledges (7.30–31). He agrees that if in five days God has not come to the help of the people of Israel, then he will hand over the town of Bethulia to the enemy.

In sum, then, as a lament Part I is sadly lacking. Ironically, the public actions that the people perform to get God's attention are successful; God does hear their prayer and does see their affliction (4.13). But because God does not act in the way that the people desire, they turn against the very one whose protection earlier they begged in their complaint and petition. Trust is entirely wanting, and the word of assurance offered by the community leaders is hollow and empty. The vow is surely not a promise to praise God, but rather an ultimatum to coerce the deity's action.

False guilt seems to have brought about confusion for the people of Israel. When they ask the town leaders to surrender their city because they fear God wills them evil, the people say that God is punishing them according to their sins and the sins of their fathers (7.28). The officials make no attempt to dissuade them from this interpretation of the Assyrians' apparent success. The leaders, too, are disoriented by crisis. Their faith, as well as that of the people, is found wanting when tested. Insufficient, indeed, is their trust in God.

Judith now enters the story as theologian and hermeneut. Before she addresses God, she has her maid summon Uzziah, Chabris and Charmis to her house. She soundly upbraids them for promising to surrender the city. In the first section (8.11–17) of a long speech to the town officials, she declares that what they have done is wrong. She charges that they have exceeded their authority by 'putting God to the test' (8.12). She insists that they, who are unable to plumb the depths of the human heart, are surely unable to search out the ways of God. She argues that God has the power to protect or to destroy (8.15). Judith defends God's freedom, saying: 'Do not try to bind the purposes of the Lord our God; for God is not like a man to be threatened, nor like a human being to be won over by pleading' (8.16).

The Assyrians had threatened the covenant people with a great display of military might; the Israelites had pleaded with God by numerous acts of penitence. And now the town officials have failed to understand that faith means 'waiting for deliverance' (8.17), not coercing God.

In the second section of her speech (8.18–27), Judith reminds the officials that since their generation has not sinned by knowing other gods, they have every reason to hope that God will not disdain them (8.18–20). She points out that capture would mean the desecration and plunder of the sanctuary (8.21) and that slavery would mean dishonour (8.23). Therefore, she urges the officials to set an example for the townspeople (8.24). She argues that they are being tested (8.25), just as Abraham, Isaac and Jacob were tested (8.26).

Judith is convinced that to God alone belongs the right to test. She calls for a reversal in the thinking of officials who have put God to the test with their five-day plan. But they do not understand her words. Still looking for a miracle, Uzziah responds by asking her to pray for rain (8.31)! Ignoring his request, she tells the officials to meet her at the town gate that night. Though she does not explain exactly what she plans, she does claim that within the days in which they have said that they would hand over the town, the Lord will look with favour on Israel in an act accomplished through her hand (8.33). The officials bless her and take their leave (8.35). At this point in Part II the components of a lament appear, but in striking contrast to their use in Part I.

Address to God

Alone, Judith turns to God and begins a lengthy prayer which occupies the whole of chapter 9. Using ashes and sackcloth and crying out in a loud voice, she implores God to listen to her, a widow (9.4). Again before the gate of Bethulia is opened for Judith and her maid to leave for the Assyrian camp, she will raise her voice to God (10.8). And when with the enemy general, she describes herself as one who is 'religious and serves the God of heaven day and night' (11.17). She claims prophetic foreknowledge, explaining to him that she needs to go outside the camp each night to pray so that God can tell her when the time is right for Holofernes to attack the Israelites (11.18–19). Thus her habit of prayer provides the ruse that permits her escape from the enemy camp. When she has chopped off the general's head, she simply walks out of the camp. Holofernes's attendant assumes that she has gone out to pray as usual (13.3).

Words addressed to God appear on Judith's lips at literally every turn in the narrative. She prays twice before killing Holofernes (13.4b–5, 7b); she praises God as she asks the Bethulians to open the gate upon her return to the town (13.11); and she leads a triumphant prayer of thanksgiving to God at the conclusion of the narrative, in which she and the people of Israel address a new song to the Lord who crushes wars (16.1–17). In addition to all these explicit words of address to God the narrative states that Judith had been involved with private devotions for the three years and four months of her widowhood (8.4–8). At the end of the story, she returns to this solitude, living as a woman accustomed to prayer and strict religious observance until her death at 105 years of age (16.23).

Complaint

Judith's complaint is not with God, but rather with the town officials who have struck the compromise with the people of Bethulia, postponing surrender for five days. She has told the officials that what they have said is not right (8.11b). They have put themselves in the place of God, and their promise to surrender may mean the destruction of the sanctuary itself (8.21). Judith defends both God's freedom and the people's innocence as she laments the actions of the town's officials (see 8.11–34).

Petition

In her opening prayers (chapter 9),[19] Judith asks three things of the Lord: (1) that God hear her widow's prayer (9.4); (2) that God break the strength of the Assyrians (9.8); and (3) that God give to her, a widow, the strength to crush the arrogance of the Assyrians by the deceit of her lips (9.10).[20] She desires these things so that the whole nation and every tribe will know that Yahweh is the God of all power and might and that there is none other who protects Israel (9.14). Vulnerability does not concern Judith for the power of her God does not depend upon numbers or strength; Yahweh is the 'God of the lowly, helper of the oppressed, upholders of the weak, protector of the forlorn, saviour of those without hope' (9.11). She closes her requests with a repeated entreaty that God hear her prayer and make her 'word and deceit for the wound and bruise of those who have purposed hard things' against Israel (9.13). As Judith readies to chop off Holofernes' head, she once again asks God to look on the work of her hand and grant her strength (13.4b–5,7b).[21]

Expression of trust

Unlike the community of Israel, nowhere does Judith express anything except complete trust in God. She says explicitly that to God alone belongs the right to protect or destroy (8.15). Implicit in her every action is the conviction that God will hear her voice and the voice of her people, if God so pleases (cf. 8.17). Because her trust does not depend on visible results, she is more optimistic than the townspeople who despair and Uzziah who grows faint-hearted when the situation worsens. She unreservedly argues that since neither she nor the people know other gods their hope is that Yahweh will not disdain them (8.20).

Word of assurance

Because Judith's trust is so complete, all of her actions in the narrative function to convince the covenant people that faithfulness is the proper way of life for them. She says to Uzziah, Chabris and Charmis that the lives of the people depend on the kind of example they set for them (8.24). The rightness of her assurance is made clear in her triumph. When she returns to Bethulia after beheading the enemy, she cries to those who open the gate that God is still with the covenant people, that God's strength has vanquished the enemy (13.11b). She sweeps the people into her prayer of praise as she ecstatically declares that God has not withdrawn mercy from the house of Israel but has destroyed their enemy by her hand (13.14). She is an exemplary model of faith, and in her the covenant people are loosed from their fears. Their cowardice and desire for surrender are transformed by her triumph. As Achior the Ammonite is converted to Judaism on her account (14.10), so too are the covenant people converted to right fear of the Lord. Uzziah says to Judith, 'Your hope will never depart from human hearts, as they remember the power of God' (13.19). In Judith, all have come to the assured knowledge that the one 'who fears the Lord shall be great for ever' (16.16b).

Vow

The success of Judith's promise that God would deliver the people by her hand before the five days of compromise had passed is celebrated in a triumphant liturgical procession which she leads to Jerusalem. Her song in chapter 16 is now not only her own. Shifts from first-person narration to third-person description of her deeds indicate that other voices have joined Judith's.[22] She and her community feast in Jerusalem before the sanctuary for three months (16.20). Judith and the people give back to God all the spoils of the great victory which the Almighty has won for them through the hand of the woman Judith.

Thus in Part II, God grants the prayer of a pious, wealthy widow and brings down the arrogance of the enemy of the covenant people. To this woman who trusts wholly in the Lord is granted triumph such as the armies and leaders of Israel were unable to achieve. Because Judith did not hold the covenant relationship a guarantee to victory, she did not despair when God seemed to have given the people over to slaughter. Because she believed in a God whose success did not depend on might, she was free to act according to a plan of her own making. Clearly, Judith understood lament more authentically than did her community. Trust, not manipulative demands, marks her faith.

Work suited to the female charism[23]

At the close of the book, the text records that many desired to marry Judith; yet she remained a widow all the days of her life

(16.22). Her fame increased, and she grew old alone with her favourite maid. Before her death, she distributed her wealth and freed the faithful woman who had accompanied her to the enemy camp (16.23–24). The story concludes, 'No one ever again spread terror among the people of Israel in the days of Judith, or for a long time after her death' (16.25).

For a total of only sixty-four days does Judith publicly participate in a battle that has raged for close to seven years (cf. 1.1,13; 2.1,21; 7.20). Since most of her life is devoted to private religious observances, the community finds in her not a permanent leader, but rather a model of how to acquire permanent freedom. She embodies the ancient truth that by vocation the covenant people are freed to choose life if they rely wholly on their God.

Judith works to conserve traditions as old as the Exodus. By her own example, she makes the covenant community of her narrative world mindful that they must serve only one God, turn to this God for an easing of their plight, and trust God to free them from bondage. She communicates these fundamental truths through actions which shatter narrow orthodoxy. It is indeed exceptional in ancient Israel that a woman chop off a man's head, lie for the sake of her people and the sanctuary of their God, upbraid the theological posture of community leaders, delegate the management of her household to another woman, and refuse to marry. Yet the high priest and senators of the holy city itself say of this woman:

> You are the exaltation of Jerusalem, you are the great glory of Israel, you are the great pride of our people! By your hand you have done all this; you have done a great deed for Israel, and God is well pleased with it. May you be for ever blessed in the eyes of the Lord! (15.9b–10a)

If Judith had believed that status and gender excluded her from responsibility for the community, then she would have allowed the town officials to surrender Bethulia. Had she not understood that authentic lament requires unquestioning trust, then the religious heritage of Israel might have ceased. Because this servant of the Lord was convinced that God upholds all, she was free to say to the men who governed Bethulia: 'Let *us* show an example to our people, for their lives depend on *us*, and the sanctuary and the temple and the altar rest upon *us*' (8.24). Faith makes this childless woman a mother to Israel[24] and a model of true freedom.

Judith and her canonical sisters Esther and Ruth conserve ancient religious truths and preserve the life of the covenant community in ways suitable to their times. Each woman does her

own kind of work in a man's world. In Ruth and Judith, women
bind together for mutual support. Ruth has the counsel of Naomi;
Judith has the help of her favourite maid. In Esther and Judith,
political concerns motivate sexual involvements. Esther wins the
favour of Ahasuerus as the most pleasing maiden in the Persian
empire; Judith dares much with Holofernes as a daughter of Israel
feigning escape. Ruth, Esther and Judith teach that certain conventions may be forced to give way so that tradition can be faithfully
preserved. No unalterable set of prescriptions regarding appropriate female behaviour forbids their participation in the process of
modifying tradition. And no small debt is owed these women of
Scripture for their part in the hermeneutical process of continuity
and change.[25]

☐ From the wealth of material on the Christian Scriptures, I
have selected an essay by Nicola Slee on parables and
women's experience, to which I referred towards the end of
the Introduction. She has written to call part of the gospel
tradition of the teaching of Jesus of Nazareth into dialogue
with women's experience as an experiment in the reclamation
of tradition with which at any rate some forms of feminist
theology is concerned. She points out that at the heart of the
parabolic method 'lies a recognition of the power of language
in our lives, to awaken the imagination, to stir the will, to
shape our very understanding of reality and to call us into
being and response'. She claims too that a second crucial
characteristic of the parabolic method is that 'it reconciles the
secular, humdrum, everyday world of realism with the
unexpected, the extraordinary, the realm of the transcendent
and the divine'. She believes that the parables can speak to
women's quest for wholeness and also that they suggest the
need for attention to 'the power and politics of language'. As
she queries: 'could there not be a much wider recognition of
the power of the kind of language and method employed by
the parables in feminist thinking and theology, and a reclamation of this language and method as our own?' We need to
find new ways of doing theology in symbol and metaphor,
poetry and narrative, using all the creative and imaginative
skills we have, and use shock, humour and surprise in order

to disarm opposition and provoke perception. Or, as the Mud Flower Collective wrote in *God's Fierce Whimsey* (p. 158), 'Feminist theology must be inductive, synthetic, and imaginative. Its primary values include perceptiveness, insight, depth and breadth of critical illumination, and respect for the diversity of experiences of persons in different social locations.' So to the last part of Nicola Slee's essay.

4 NICOLA SLEE
Parables and Women's Experience

The male characters in the parables cover a wide range: farmers, builders, merchants, kings, judges, stewards, doctors, bridegrooms, servants, sons, fathers, priests, publicans, rich men, poor men, thieves, fools, scoundrels and more. The women featured in the parables can be listed exhaustively as: ten bridesmaids, a woman searching for a lost coin, a widow seeking justice, and a handful of unspecified wives, mothers and daughters mentioned in general terms (e.g. Matt. 18.23–25, Luke 12.51–53).

This surface dominance of male characterization amd the anonymity of women in the parables must not be brushed aside too easily. The need for women to experience and express pain at the sign of our invisibility in Scripture must be recognized and affirmed. However, I suggest that it is possible to find beneath the surface invisibility of women a host of images and situations in the parables which are uniquely evocative of women's lives and experiences, and speak deeply to them. I would like to identify five groups of themes running through the parables which may have a particular relevance to women's lives.

1 Parables set in the domestic sphere

Many of the parables are set in the context of Palestinian domestic and familial life and speak of situations intimately familiar to many women: sewing patches (Mark 2.21), baking bread (Matt. 13.33), making wine (Mark 2.22), sending for the doctor (Luke 5.31), serving meals (Luke 22.27), sweeping the house (Luke 15.8–10), children playing in the market (Matt. 11.16–19), and so on. Yet within the familiar domestic scene, the unexpected erupts, the absurd in postulated. The patch tears the cloth, the wine bursts the skins, the action of yeast in the dough transforms the lump, the lamp is put under the bed, the master serves the meal to his servant, the friend calls at midnight. The realism is fractured by this element of extravagance which causes it to burst out of its framework of the ordinary, everyday world. What this might mean for women's lives is neither a tacit acceptance of our place in the domestic sphere nor a rejection of the mundane and domestic. The parables suggest that within the context of the domestic the unexpected, the wholly gratuitous and unlooked for, erupts – but in so doing, the very world of the everyday is irretrievably shattered, irreversibly transformed. This provides no easy solution to the conflicts women experience between the domestic and the professional, home and work, family and society, and others, but it does hint that to discover the presence of God within the confines of the mundane and domestic is radically and explosively to transform these realties – and this may be as uncomfortable as it is unexpected.

2 Parables of growth

A second dominant motif in the parables is the image of growth and rhythm in the natural world. There are images of the growth of seed to good and bad crops (Mark 4. 3–8, Mark 4, 30–32), trees producing good and bad fruit (Matt. 7.15–20), nature's provision for the birds of the air and the lilies of the field (Matt. 6. 26–28), the signs of the seasons and the sky (Matt. 16.2–4), the secret action of yeast in the dough (Matt. 13.33) and sap in the wood (Luke 23.31). Underlying these parables is a deep attentiveness to the secret yet strong rhythm of the natural world, the cycle of growth from the sown seed to the gathered crop, the movement of the seasons and the endless process of life and death at the heart of creation. Are these not images which strike resonant chords in woman hearers, whose lives and bodies share uniquely in creation's rhythm, the cycle of labour and birth and growth, the mysterious, hidden action of generation and regeneration? Yet as with the domestic parables, this emphasis on cyclical growth, continuity and the natural process is only half the story. As Dodd has argued, the parables of growth are closely related to a crisis, a moment of denouement and judgement. If there is growth, it is growth to a crisis. The harvest is a time of decision when the good crop is stored and used and the bad destroyed; the tree which does not bear fruit is chopped down; the signs of the times declare the crisis of the kingdom.

I do not read this note of crisis and judgement as a denial of women's intimate awareness of rhythm and cycle, but as a word which both affirms that experience and calls constantly to submit to judgement the goals and aims of all our growing. Perhaps, too, it affords a context for wrestling with the perpetual crises, whether they be domestic, emotional or spiritual, which disrupt and disturb our sense of rhythm and pace.

3 Parables of celebration and feasting

A third theme runs through many of the parables, as a dominant image in some and a significant motif in others. This is the theme of celebration, banqueting, feasting and fêting which crops up in parables about a king throwing a wedding party for his son (Matt. 22.1–14), the heavenly banquet of the kingdom (Matt. 8.11–12), a master feasting his faithful servants (Luke 12.35–38), where to sit when invited to a supper party (Luke 14.7–11), whom to invite when giving a party (Luke 14.12–14), and the joyful festivities which celebrate the recovery of a lost sheep (Luke 15.4–7), a lost coin (Luke 15.8–10), and, most memorable of all, a lost and rebellious son (Luke 15.11–32). The theme is a peculiarly Lukan one, affirming his sense of the joyful news of the Kingdom and the worth of human action and history.

The banquet image is, of course, a symbol of the eschatological Kingdom deeply embedded in the Old Testament and the intertestamental literature. But again, it does speak to women whose lives are very much bound up with the rituals of feeding and feasting, which take on special significance at the celebration of births, marriages, anniversaries and achievements, and at the more sombre times of death and departure, but can also have a treasured place in the rhythm of daily life. In the recent collection of essays from the federation of L'Arche communities, Sue Mosteller[1] gives a beautiful description of the meanings hidden in the preparation and sharing of daily food. She speaks of the time of preparation of food as a time in which 'we try to become conscious of the act of preparing for those we love, conscious that we can give life through this act of preparing the meal'. She goes on:

> the meals themselves are a time of utmost importance, for the bodily nourishment and for all it signifies. We discover that it is also a time for our deeper hungers to find satisfaction. Perhaps here, at the table, our strongest experience is the taste of our solidarity. The stories, the bantering, the remarks about the cooking, the serving and passing of the food, the arguments, the broken diets and the sharing of the last piece of cake all give the same message to my hungry heart: the message

that I belong to this people and I am acceptable, as I am here: that this is my home.

This space for the sharing and the kindling into celebration of the simple necessities of life is a quality of living which women may be able to affirm in a special way because of its place in our family and social lives. The banquet parables call us to create this space of celebration, with room for all, in our families, our various social groupings and, most of all, in the Eucharistic community of the Church, where so often the table seems so bare, the occasion so devoid of festivity, the community so impoverished of love.

4 Parables of relationship

A further prominent theme in the parables is that of relationship. There are images of fidelity and irresponsibility in relationships between master and servants (Mark 13.34–37, Matt. 24.43–51), king and debtors (Matt. 18.23–35, Luke 7.41–43), disciple and teacher (Matt. 10.24), employer and employee (Matt. 20.1–16), and father and son (Matt. 21.28–31). Other parables trace the pattern of brokenness and conflict in relationship (Mark 3. 24–25, Luke 16.19–31), which sometimes leads to restoration and healing, between two opponents going to court (Matt. 5.25–26), between a rich man and his crafty steward (Luke 16.1–8) and between a father and his rebellious son (Luke 15.11–32). Finally, there are vivid images of trust (Matt. 7.9–11), service (Mark 9.37, 41, Luke 10.30–37), persistence (Luke 11.5–8, Luke 18.1–6), need (Luke 10.30–37, Luke 11.5–8, Luke 18.9–14) and suffering love (Luke 15.11–32, Matt. 23.37) in relationship.

Of course these pictures of relationship do not speak exclusively to women. I do not wish to suggest a simple dichotomy between women whose lives are rooted to the relational sphere and men whose lives are not. One of the main struggles of the women's movement is surely to invite men and women to share equally the responsiblity for relationships. Nevertheless, as women are traditionally said to enjoy greater space and skills in relationship than men, by virtue of spending a great deal of their lives restricted to the relational sphere of the home and in the nurture and care of other people, perhaps it is likely that women may 'hear' the deeper demands and calling of these parables. This is something which can then be shared with and offered to others (perhaps largely, but not exclusively, men) whose lives are oriented towards activity outside the relational sphere, towards professional achievement which may have to be won at the expense of personal relationship, for example.

What, then, do these parables seem to be saying? Traditionally the values of unassuming service and dedicated Christian charity have been stressed in the exegesis of these relationship-oriented parables. We are called to emulate the humility of the sinful publican, the charity and generosity of the good Samaritan, the faithful and undemonstrative obedience of the trusty servant and the dutiful son, the abundant forgiveness of the king towards his debtors. Yet, again, this emphasis on the denial of self and the service of others, with all the attendant traditional Christian virtues, is only half the truth. There is also, in these parables, a strong affirmation of other more forceful and self-assertive human qualities. They commend the initiative and forethought shown by the one who makes peace with his opponent on the way to court, the widow's persistence in demanding the justice which is rightfully her own, the steely attentiveness of the servant during long hours of waiting, and even the steward's use of craft and cunning to extricate himself from a sticky situation. The totality of these parabolic images suggests the possibility of a way of relationship which finds room for both a compassionate orientation towards others, with the willingness to be at their disposal, and the assertion and affirmation of one's own needs and claims. This reconciliation of the needs of self and others in these relational parables is surely a word of hope for women who often experience the conflicting demands of self and others in a peculiarly acute way because of their role as carers and carriers in personal and familial relationships. As Christian feminists struggle to find authentic modes of relationship in the light of the gospel which are both self-fulfilling and affirmative of others, these parables can provide images which speak to this struggle.

5 Parables of violence

Finally, there is an unmistakable strand of violence and harshness running through the parables which is sometimes quite grotesque. There are many images of physical violence and bodily mutilation: the plank in the eye (Luke 6.42), the self-mutilation of cutting off hand and foot and plucking out the eye (Mark 9.43–49), being thrown into the sea with a millstone around the neck (Mark 9.42), the binding of the strong man (Mark 3.27), the beating and killing of servants and the vineyard owner's son (Mark 12.1–9), the beating and stripping of the man on the road to Jericho (Luke 10.30–37), the casting into outer darkness with weeping and gnashing of teeth (Matt. 8.11–12, Matt. 22.1–14), and the call to take up the cross or, literally, to face the agony and brutality of death by crucifixion. Other images of judgement, violence and destruction are those of burning by fire (Matt. 3.12, Matt. 7.15–20), the axe laid to the roots of the tree (Matt. 3.10), the plant pulled up by its roots (Matt. 15.13), being thrown into jail (Matt. 18. 23–35), the image of war and fighting (Matt. 10.34), possession by evil spirits (Matt. 12.43–45), hatred and conflict within families (Mark 3.24–25, Luke 12.52–53) and the gathering of vultures by the dead body (Luke 17.37).

In what ways can these hard, almost repulsive, images speak to women? Can they not speak to us of our own experience of violence, conflict, anger, self-disgust and loathing? I am not thinking here primarily of battered wives or physical violence of other kinds, nor of the emotional conflicts and ravages which we share with men simply by virtue of our common human condition of fallenness, though doubtless these parables may speak to such experience. What I have in mind here is the violence, the struggle and the pain that women experience *as women*, and particularly as women within the Christian community, as unequal partners in God's world, as those committed to the struggle to obtain 'the glorious liberty of the children of God' (Rom. 8.21) which is our heritage, and yet is denied us. Surely one of the things we are learning from the secular feminist movement is that we must find a voice for this pain, this sense of rejection and denial, and our own deep sense of inadequacy, frustration and self-rejection which is fostered by it. If we cannot name our experience of pain and anger, we cannot release the sources of energy and vision within us. Part of our struggle as Christian feminists is to find a way of naming this pain and desire which is at once constructive and prophetic, healing and releasing for the *whole* Christian community. Yet this search for a language in which to name our experience can often seem a peculiarly desolate task, as we find that the very language of our Christian tradition is part of the thing that pains and restrains us:

> There is no word in any tongue,
> Can make clear to one and all,
> My strange hunger, or that fight
> My back against a wall.[2]

But perhaps these harsh and violent parables are part of the Gospel tradition which can be reclaimed as words to give voice to our experience of pain, to release the anger and reshape our lives.

Conclusion

In the attempt to engage in the dialogue between the Gospel parables and women's experience, the preceding reflections have emerged as fragmentary, imagistic and episodic, personal and subjective rather than general and detached, suggestive of possibilities rather than descriptive of actualities. Perhaps this is not entirely inappropriate in the light of the nature of the parables themselves, which defy all attempts at systematization and finality and invite the hearer perpetually to renew thought and experience in the dynamic and potent parabolic images and narratives of the gospel.

☐ If we take seriously Nicola Slee's last words about the dynamic and potent parabolic images and narratives of the gospel, then we need to attend more closely to some parts of Scripture that we easily neglect. Elisabeth Schüssler Fiorenza's major book takes its title from an incident involving an unnamed woman. *In Memory of Her* has a immensely powerful introduction, by way of reconsidering the story in the second Gospel of the woman who anoints Jesus' head,[14] a prophetic sign-action which, despite Jesus' words, did not become part of our inheritance in the way other Gospel stories have done. It is something that it stayed as part of the canonical text, but whereas the name and more of the story of the disciples who betrayed Jesus are retold, not so that of this faithful woman. 'And truly I say to you, wherever the gospel is preached in the whole world, what she has done will be told in memory of her.'

And yet, as Elisabeth Schüssler Fiorenza remarks, 'Both Christian feminist theology and biblical interpretation are in the process of rediscovering that the Christian gospel cannot be proclaimed if the women disciples and what they have done are not remembered' (p. xiv). So she wants to reconstruct early Christian history as *women*'s history, thus restoring women's stories, and also to reclaim this history as the

history of both women and men. We need not at this point
engage with her critique of other feminist theologians to
appreciate the point that her method makes room for 'an
often mixed, confused, inarticulate, and only partially feminist historical consciousness and agency of women' living still
within the boundaries and mechanisms of what oppresses
them, and for the recovery of history as inclusively *human*
history (p. 25).

Thus she writes:

> Though the twelve are identified as men, through the list of
> names taken over by Mark from tradition, the wider circle of
> disciples are not identified as males. That Mark's androcentric
> language functions as inclusive language becomes now apparent
> in the information that women disciples have followed Jesus
> from Galilee to Jerusalem, accompanied him on the way to the
> cross, and witnessed his death. Just as in the beginning of the
> Gospel, Mark presents four leading male disciples who hear
> Jesus' call to discipleship, so at the end s/he presents four
> leading women disciples and mentions them by name. The four
> women disciples – Mary of Magdala, Mary, the daughter or wife
> of James the younger, the mother of Joses and Salome – are
> preeminent among the women disciples who have followed
> Jesus, just as Peter, Andrew, James and John are preeminent
> among the twelve. Though the twelve have forsaken Jesus,
> betrayed and denied him, the women disciples, by contrast, are
> found under the cross, risking their own lives and safety. That
> they are well aware of the danger of being arrested and executed
> as followers of a political insurrectionist crucified by the Romans
> is indicated in the remark that the women 'were looking from
> afar'. They are thus characterized as Jesus' true 'relatives'
> (p.320).

They, like the woman who anointed Jesus, understood that
Jesus' Messiahship meant suffering and death. Their own
understanding of discipleship means that they follow him,
minister to him and themselves become apostolic eye-
witnesses of his resurrection, as well as of his death and
burial. Elisabeth Schüssler Fiorenza's discussion of the
fourth Gospel is specially rewarding. Much more of her book
explores what may have happened to the movement initiated
by Jesus of Nazareth and the women and men associated
with him, both sexes indispensable to the early missionary

activity of the movement, and its attempt to make its way in a slave-owning society living by certain household codes. (See the essay by Sheila Briggs cited in note 23 of the Introduction.) Limitation of women's roles, despite the alternative character of what was originally on offer to them, gradually restricted what they could do in the religious as well as in the social context.

In representing the discipleship and apostolic leadership of women, Elisabeth Schüssler Fiorenza helps us to see that in their appropriation of Jesus' practice of love and service, women too may be seen as 'the image and body of Christ'. One very important section of her book is that on 'The Sophia-God of Jesus and the Discipleship of Women', the grace and goodness of the divine indicated by means of Jewish 'wisdom' theology, which arguably used elements of the feminine-divine to speak of God, and made possible Jesus' invitation of women into his discipleship in a way in which their role could be central.[15]

Those like her who want to reclaim biblical material, may of course be expressing, despite themselves, not so much recovery of what has been lost from the original community around Jesus, as *hope* for new possibilities in a still-alive tradition. One such example, inspired both by Phyllis Trible and by Elisabeth Schüssler Fiorenza is by Sharon Ringe, 'A Gentile Woman's Story'. From her reinterpretation of the story of this particular 'uppity woman' we can move to an essay by Elisabeth Schüssler Fiorenza[16] on some more 'uppity women' mentioned by Paul in Romans 16; then we conclude Part One of this *Reader* with an essay by Angela West, which discusses very well some of the problems women have in reading at least one text of Paul's!

5 SHARON RINGE
A Gentile Woman's Story

The Church has trouble with uppity women. Such women are co-opted, ridiculed, ignored, condemned – one way or another gotten out of the way of the important business of the church and of theology. The Gentile woman whose story is told in Mark

7.24–30 and Matthew 15.20–28 has been dealt with in all these ways at various times in the church's history and in modern critical and theological interpretation. This study is presented *in memoriam*[1] – in memory of her and of her fate and for the encouragement of her sisters.

The church has trouble with uppity women. Like the woman in this story, they have shown a knack for confronting pretence, predictability, and easy solutions when these are presented as a way of domesticating the offence and liberating the power of the gospel. This study is presented in celebration of the gifts and ministry of this woman and for the encouragement of her sisters.

The anonymous woman in this story comes across at first and second glance as an uppity woman. She is depicted as interrupting Jesus' rest (Mark) and annoying the disciples (Matthew). She is shown pursuing her request for help from Jesus by a verbal sparring match worthy of the craftiest of teachers (a role explicitly denied to women in Jesus' society). She even wins the argument and is said in the short run to have obtained the healing of her daughter and in the long run to have opened the way for Jesus' (and the Church's) mission beyond the Jewish community.

The longer I spent with this story, coming to know and to befriend the woman in the context of the Church that continues to tell her story, the more perplexed I became. I found myself cheering the woman for her gutsiness, wit, and self-possession, and at the same time I was offended at the picture of Jesus that the story presents. I wanted to know where such a scandalous story came from, how it found its way into the Gospels, and what point it made for those who told and retold the story and for those who heard it in the Church.

The disciplines of biblical criticism have taught me to approach those questions by working backward through the stories as they are presented in the Gospels, much like peeling away the layers of an onion. The problem I met, however, was that working through the disciplines of source, form, and redaction criticism led to treating the text like an onion, whose bite and flavour is in the layers but which has no core. I learned from those layers, and from the process of examining them, how the Church has adapted the story to its ecclesiastical needs and, more generally, how we who are the insiders of the Church and the privileged of society work to domesticate the gospel to our point of view and to protect the Christ who is familiar and safe from the Christ who offends us. But the formal disciplines of biblical criticism left me on my own just when the only place to move was into the crucible of the story, where its power to confront and to transform could begin to work.

I invite you to journey with me, through the Church's struggle to find a place for this story in its gospel and across the bridge of those questions that traditional disciplines and Church interpretation leave unanswered. Finally, I invite you to enter with me into the woman's story, there to learn from her about the Christ and so also about God and about ourselves.

The evangelists' agenda: the critical task

Matthew and Mark set their similar versions of this story in or near the Gentile territory around Tyre and Sidon.[2] The two accounts differ in the point of view from which the story is told and in the relative emphasis given to the healing of the woman's daughter and to the dialogue between the woman and Jesus. In Mark a narrator sets the stage and tells us of the daughter's illness, the mother's request for Jesus to perform an exorcism, and the woman's witnessing of the successful cure. The sharp exchange between them ends in a blessing (of sorts) for the woman and in Jesus' recognition of the daughter's healing. In Matthew we are led into the event by an extended dialogue, instead of being informed about it by a narrator's report. Although Matthew uses both additions to and adaptations of the brief dialogue in Mark's account to develop his interpretation of the incident (such as by portraying the woman's reply to Jesus as less direct and perhaps more submissive),[3] the impression we get is that we are learning about the incident from the woman, the disciples, and Jesus directly. The result is that in Matthew there is less emphasis on the exorcism itself and more on the interaction of the characters.

Several details suggest that Matthew's account has been influenced by other portions of the gospel tradition and represents a reworking of the Markan story. First of all, this story and the story of the healing of the centurion's servant (Matt. 8.5–13; Luke 7.1–10) have several points in common. Both stories have to do with Gentiles, both depict Jesus at a distance from the person who is healed, and both mention the 'faith' of one of the characters. In both stories, Matthew's versions present more extended dialogues than are found in the parallel accounts, and in both cases the dialogues have to do with participation in the reign of God. Matthew's story of the healing of two blind men (Matt. 20.29–34), which parallels the story of Bartimaeus in Mark 10.46–52, may also have influenced Matthew's version of the story of the Gentile woman, since both stories tell of a rebuke of the petitioners by onlookers, and in both the petitioners address Jesus as *kyrios* (which carries the double meaning of a polite 'sir' and the confessional title 'the Lord' or 'Sovereign') and as 'Son of David'.

Figuring out the form of the story, and consequently the role it played in the Church before being incorporated into the Gospel, presents several difficulties. On the surface it appears to be a story of an exorcism, expanded by a controversy dialogue. Thus, following Mark's account, we are told of the severity of the child's illness (v. 25a) and of the earnestness of the mother's efforts to obtain help for her (vs. 25b, 26b) and the fact that the exorcism has indeed taken place (v. 30). The dialogue between Jesus and the mother comes at the place where we expect the means of healing to be disclosed. The absence of that detail (which Matthew supplies in v. 28b of his account), plus the coherence of the Markan story as a dramatic setting for the exchange between Jesus and the woman,[4] lead some scholars to suggest that this is therefore primarily a 'pronouncement story' and specifically (with Bultmann) a 'controversy dialogue', built around the sayings in verses 27–28.[5] However, that suggestion too presents a problem, because the exchange between Jesus and the woman reverses the pattern usually found in such stories. Usually a situation or event provokes a hostile question from some onlooker to Jesus, to which Jesus responds with a correcting or reproving question and then drives home his point by a concluding statement which the opponent would be hard put to deny. In this story, however, it is Jesus who provides the hostile saying and the woman whose retort trips him up and corrects him. It is hard to imagine why the Church at any stage of its development would want to present the Christ it confesses in such a light!

Many scholars rely on Mark's editorial placement of this story in the Gospel, supported by the fact that there is indeed evidence that in Jewish tradition Gentiles were called 'dogs',[6] to account for the existence of this story in the Church's lore about Jesus and even to legitimate the portrait of Jesus it presents. These scholars suggest that the story is to be understood in the context of the early Church's struggle to comprehend the Gentile mission and subsequent relationship between Jews and Gentiles in the Church and in God's agenda of salvation. This story would address such an ecclesiastical situation by grounding the solution to these problems in the remembered ministry of Jesus. Indeed, the place where

Mark has incorporated this story into the Gospel does suggest that he intended it to address the expansion of the limits of the community of faith. The episodes in Mark 6.45—8.26 portray Jesus not only in and around Gentile territory and enountering Gentile people, but also dealing with the principal issue in Jewish–Gentile relations: namely, the issue of defilement (Mark 7.1–23). These stories mirror many earlier episodes of Jesus' ministry reportedly carried out in Jewish territory.[7] Following the cycle of stories among the Gentiles is the story of the incident at Caesarea Philippi, which appears to seal Jesus' fate and to propel the Gospel to its inevitable conclusion in Jerusalem. In this context, the story of the Gentile woman appears to be part of the authentication by Jesus of the Gentile mission which took place later in the Church. As the woman's perception of Jesus contrasts with the exclusive concerns of those closest to Jesus (with whom Mark's community would doubtless identify), Mark seems to be addressing both what may have been his Church's claim to have an inside track on faithfulness and what may have been lingering concerns in that community about how to understand the Gentile presence.

Without the larger gospel context and the saying in verse 27, however, the Jewish–Gentile reference *within* Mark's version of this story is not clear. The picture underlying the exchange between Jesus and the woman is a simple one of a poor Palestinian household, in which family and pets shared the single room. In fact, the word translated 'dogs' might better be translated as 'puppies' or 'house dogs'. Thus one might hear Jesus' observation to mean, 'Scarce bread needed for the children is not given to the family's pets.' 'But what the chldren drop,' responds the woman, 'the dogs will take.' The logic is primarily that of the household and only secondary that of salvation history.[8]

To recognize that this story was elaborated in a way that brings into focus questions of Jewish–Gentile relations in the early Church is still not to suggest that the story was composed by the Church in order to address those concerns. To begin with, the earliest discernible form of the story need not be read as addressing Jewish–Gentile relations at all. Second, even if the saying in Mark's verse 27 is understood to be a proverb, and even if it was a metaphorical way of referring to the fact that the petitioner in this case is a Gentile, that saying addressed to the woman is offensive in the extreme. Metaphor or not, Jesus is depicted as comparing the woman and her daughter to dogs! No churchly or scholarly gymnastics are able to get around that problem. To note that the

Greek word is a diminutive, meaning 'puppies' or 'little dogs', does not soften the saying, for, as Burkill points out, 'As in English, so in other languages, to call a woman "a little bitch" is no less abusive that to call her 'a bitch' without qualification.

Jesus' flippant, even cruel, response to the woman defies justification. Try as we might, we really cannot see in this story a cosy domestic scene with family and pets happily coexisting under one roof and under the leadership of a benevolent householder (who becomes the stand-in for the Sovereign Christ in an inclusive Church). We also do not find Jesus simply testing the woman's faith by an initially contrived and only apparent rejection.[10] Equally hard to recognize here is Taylor's claim to find in this story a glimpse of an incident in Jesus' life, but even more a glimpse into Jesus' psyche, showing that at this point in his life there was 'tension in the mind of Jesus concerning the scope of his ministry.' 'He is speaking to Himself as well as to the woman,' Taylor concludes (wishfully, I think). 'Her reply shows that she is quick to perceive this.'[11] Apparently (though Taylor does not draw this conclusion), it would then have been her tolerance of Jesus' indecision that allowed her to swallow the insult.

The shocking quality of the portrait of Jesus, plus the indications of internal development in the story, suggest to me that instead of composing this story to address contemporary church problems, the early Church – at least from Mark's day on – made the best of a bizarre tradition about Jesus which it received. The very strangeness and the offensiveness of the story's portrayal of Jesus may suggest that the core of the story was indeed remembered as an incident in Jesus' life when even he was caught with his compassion down. I would suggest further that the story was originally remembered and retold in the community not for its ecclesiastical significance but primarily because of its Christological significance. It tells us something about Jesus as the Christ, and only consequently something about us as the Church.

In order to explore the Christological significance of this story, and perhaps to hear afresh a word through the text to our own day, we will need to consider the account by itself, outside the framework that Mark provides. We will need to hear it as a story, a story-within-a-larger-story, drawing us into itself through its characters and their interaction. Obviously the leading character in the larger Gospel story is Jesus, but in this particular episode the protagonist is the Gentile woman.

On gifts and ministries: the woman's story

We know at once very little and a lot about her. She is a resident of the Gentile region including the cities of Tyre and Sidon. She was thus a foreigner to Jesus in an ethnic sense; she was a woman, and in fact a woman alone.[12] She may have been a widow, or divorced, or never married. In any event, she appears to be totally isolated from family support, for if there had been any male relative in her family (or among her in-laws if she had been married), he would have had the responsibility of caring for her and her daughter and of interceding on their behalf. Perhaps these family members, if there were any, lived at a great distance. Or perhaps for some reason they chose no longer to acknowledge the woman as part of their circle. She may have had sons somewhere, but if she were widowed or divorced they would probably have been taken over by her in-laws.

When we meet her, she is left with a daughter. In her society's terms that is a further liability, for daughters were not greatly valued. Sons were the focus of one's hopes and one's longing. Daughters usually cost money (at least for a dowry) and were often regarded as troublesome pieces of property weighing on their families until they could be safely married off to a suitable husband. In addition, we know that according to the customs of first-century Palestinian society, this woman should have been invisible. No Jewish man, especially one with a religious task or vocation, expected to be approached by a woman (Jew or Gentile), except perhaps by one of the many lone women reduced to prostitution to support themselves.

But we know some other things about the particular woman in this story. Apparently she did not accept the low esteem in which her society held her daughter, or its restrictions on her own behaviour. She did not hesitate to approach Jesus, and even actively to importune him. And she valued her daughter, this one fundamentally like her who was still with her, who was suffering, and whose life was precious enough to demand healing and transformation, liberation from the alien forces that appeared to have taken her over. For the sake of her daughter, the woman broke custom, went after what she needed, and stood up to this visiting rabbi and miracle worker of whom so many stories had doubtless been told. And she bested him in an argument. Finally, she got what she wanted: her daughter was healed.

In so far as this is a story about a ministry, it is traditionally seen as an account of Jesus' healing ministry to this woman and her daughter. Hearing the story with ears tuned to women's experience, we might also point to the woman's intercessory ministry on behalf of her daughter. But there are two other dimensions of ministry suggested in both the Markan and Matthean accounts. First, there is the woman's ministry in a general sense as a witness to Jesus. In Mark her witness is primarily to him as miracle worker, but also to him as one whose attention and help could be won by persistence. Matthew helps us to recognize this witnessing ministry of the woman most clearly by the way he tells the story. We are led into the incident by the woman herself; we see it from her point of view. We are with her at the edge of the company around Jesus. We hear her words, and we hear and feel the response she gets. This greater use of direct discourse underlines the fact that this woman belongs in the company of others who by their active importuning (which is called by Matthew 'faith', here and elsewhere) proclaim who Jesus is.

The second additional dimension of ministry present in the story is the woman's ministry *to* Jesus by her 'faith' – a faith that is no doctrinal confession of his messianic identify, and no flattery of his apparently miraculous powers, but rather an act of trust, of engagement, risking everything. That act has the effect, as the story is told of enabling Jesus to see the situation in a different way. That new persective appears to free Jesus to respond, to heal, to become again the channel of God's redeeming presence in that situation. Whatever provoked the initial response attributed to Jesus (whether we should conclude that he was tired, or in a bad mood, or even that he appears to have participated in the racism and sexism that characterized his society), it is the Gentile woman who is said to have called his bluff. In so doing, she seems to have enabled him to act in a way apparently blocked to him before. Her wit, her sharp retort, was indeed her gift to Jesus – a gift that enabled his gift of healing in turn, her ministry that opened up the possibility of his. Her gift was not the submission or obedience seen as appropriate for women in her society, but rather the gift of sharp insight – the particular insight of the poor and outcast who can see through a situation because they have few illusions to defend. Her gift was also the gift of courage – the courage of those who have little more to lose and therefore can act in commitment and from faith on behalf of others, for the sake of life, wholeness, and liberation. Indeed, these highly political and encouraging words describe the quality of Jesus' ministry to this woman and to her daughter.

Thus, behind whatever ecclesiastical significance the Church has found in this story, there appears to be a Christological point: it sets forth who Jesus is as the Christ of God. The hallmarks of that identity, here as elsewhere in the gospel tradition, are qualities and actions of life and freedom, made known in painful human interaction. Elsewhere those who see themselves as the privileged people in social or religious terms are shown struggling to comprehend this Christ who so often offends them, while the 'poor' – the economically poor and socially outcast, the sick, the oppressed, the rejected – respond joyfully to the good news of God's reign. Here Jesus himself must learn about being that sort of Christ from one of the poorest of the poor and most despised of the outcast – a Gentile woman on her own before God and humankind. Her gifts and her ministry become the vehicle of the gospel to Jesus and to us. And we who hear and tell her story say, 'So be it.'

6 ELISABETH SCHÜSSLER FIORENZA
Missionaries, Apostles, Co-workers: Romans 16 and the Reconstruction of Women's Early Christian History

One can approach a text like Romans 16 with different questions and presuppositions. If one focuses attention on the theological teaching of Paul, this chapter is seen as a mere appendix to Paul's theological testament in Romans. If he is interested, however, in the social realities of early Christian communities and the cultural and religious world in which they lived, much can be learned from this chapter. Although the indirect information conveyed by the list of greetings is very scanty, it nevertheless allows us to learn something about the social status and missionary activity of early Christians.

Exegetes usually discuss the last chapter of Romans in terms of its original position in the Pauline letter collection. While they do not question that the chapter is written by Paul, they are divided on whether it was originally connected with the Epistle to the Romans or whether it was an independent letter of recommendation addressed to the church in Ephesus.[1] In the following I will presuppose that Romans 16 is best understood as an integral part of Paul's letter to the church in Rome rather than as an independent letter to the church of Ephesus. Instead of entering into the 'Romans 16 debate' directly, I will attempt to interpret the chapter as a source for the reconstruction of women's early Christian history. Before it is possible to analyse the text, however, two methodological issues must be considered.

First, in order to be able to perceive the significance of the information found in Romans 16 for our understanding of early Christian beginnings and women's role in it, we must place it in the overall context of the social and religious institutions and conventions of the time. Moreover, we have to become conscious of our overall understanding or framework for the reconstruction of early Christian beginnings into which we place the information gleaned from texts such as Romans 16. The works on the social world of the early Christian missionary movement, for example, have provided 'love-patriarchalism' as much as a social–sociological model for the historical reconstruction of the Christian missionary movement in the Greco-Roman world. Gerd Theissen has argued that the early Christian missionary movement in the Greco-Roman cities was well integrated into its societal structures because it adopted the patriarchal structures of the Greco-Roman household but softened it with Christian agape love.[2]

Not only the reconstructions of early Christianity, however, but historiography on the whole works with theoretical models and theological frameworks. In order to give a coherent historical interpretation scholars have to make inferences based in part upon their sources and based in part upon their general understanding of human behaviour and society. We not only interpret our historical sources in order to present a 'coherent' historical society, but also ascribe 'historical significance' to so-called 'data' in accordance with our theroretical model or perspective that orders our information and evidence. Just as a quilt brings together patchwork pieces into an artistic over-all design, so also the writing of history does not provide a ready-made mirror of past events, but a 'stitching' together of historical information into a coherent over-all design or interpretative model.[3]

The standard Western intellectual and scientific paradigm[4] is androcentric, that is, male centred and patriarchal. It generates and perpetuates scholarship that takes Euro-American man as the paradigmatic human being and thereby makes women and other races or cultures invisible or peripheral in what we know about the world, human life, and cultural or religious history. Far from being objective or descriptive, androcentric texts and knowledge produce the historical silence and invisibility of women. Although women are neglected in the writing of history, the effects of our lives and actions are a reality in history. While androcentric scholarship defines women as the 'other' or as the 'object' of male scholarship, feminist studies insist on the reconceptualization of our language as well as of our intellectual frameworks in such a way that women as well as men become the subjects of human culture and scholarly discourse. In the past decade, feminist historians have therefore tried to articulate the theoretical problem of how to move from androcentric text to historical context or of how to write women back into history. They have succinctly stated that the dual goal of women's history is both: 'to restore women to history and to restore history to women'.[5]

Women's leadership and contributions to early Christianity can only become historically visible when we abandon our outdated patriarchal–androcentric model of early Christian beginnings. Even when the New Testament source texts suggest a different meaning, such androcentric models can understand early Christian women only as marginal figures or see them in subordinate 'feminine' roles which are derived from our own contemporary experience and understandings of reality. Rather than to project our own cultural–historical assumptions on the New Testament text, we must replace them with a historical model that makes it possible to conceive of the early Christian movement as a movement of women and men.[6] Such a model allows us to do justice to these New Testament texts that suggest women's leadership and contributions were central to the early Christian missionary movement as well as to those texts that seek to prescribe women's role in terms of Greco-Roman patriarchal culture.

Second a historical–critical interpretation of early Christian texts can no longer take at face value grammatically masculine language that functions as so-called 'inclusive' language in a patriarchal culture. Instead, it must utilize this insight into the functioning of generic androcentric language for the reading of historical sources. Such grammatically masculine generic language mentions women only when we are explicitly addressed, when our presence has become in a way a problem, or when we are exceptional. However, it does not mention women explicitly in so-called 'normal' situations, but subsumes us under 'man' and 'he'. Before the ramifications of such androcentric inclusive language had become conscious, even women writers referred to themselves with grammatically masculine pronouns and expressions. Such so-called masculine 'inclusive' language functions in the same way in biblical texts as in modern Western languages.

Historians and theologians of early Christianity interpret such androcentric language in a twofold way: as generic and as gender-specific language. They presuppose that women as well as men were members of the early Christian communities and do not assume that the early Christian movement was a male cult like the Mithras cult. While grammatically masculine language with respect to the community is understood in an inclusive way, the same grammatically masculine language is understood in a gender-specific way when referring to leadership functions, such as apostles, missionaries, ministers, overseers or elders. If a recon-struction of early Christian history can no longer take androcentric texts as face value, it must develop a 'hermeneutics of suspicion' in order to read what they say and what they do not say about historical events and persons. Such a 'hermeneutics of suspicion' must be applied not only to scrutinize our own presuppositions and interpretations, but also to the New Testament texts them-selves.[7]   While the books and essays on 'women in the Bible' take androcentric language at face value I would submit that an historically adequate reading of our New Testament sources must take into account the functions of so-called generic grammatically masculine language. The passages that directly mention women are not descriptive or comprehensive, but indicative of the 'sub-merged' information conveyed in so-called inclusive androcentric texts. Those passages that directly mention women cannot be taken as providing all the information *about women* in early Christianity. The letter of recommendation concluding now Paul's Epistle to the Romans mentions women's early Christian leadershp only in passing, but still mentions it. Its references to early Christian women therefore should be read as 'the tip of an iceberg', indicating what is submerged in grammatically masculine language and how much historical information is lost to us for ever. These references, however, must not be fitted into an androcentric model of historical reconstruction, but must be appropriated with an understanding of early Christian beginnings that allows for the leadership not only of men but also for that of women.

1 Romans 16: a letter of recommendation for Phoebe of Cenchreae

Romans 16 begins with a recommendation that was written in order to introduce a woman by the name of Phoebe to the Christian community in Rome. As is the case with most of the women in the Christian missionary movement, we know of her only because Paul mentions her here. Like the other early Christian women leaders who are greeted in Romans 16, she would have been totally shrouded in historical silence if hers and Paul's ways had not crossed, or if she had belonged to Paul's 'opponents' in Corinth. Although Phoebe is given a recommendation by letter in the same manner as Timothy is (1 Cor. 16.10–11), her significance for the early Christian missionary movement is far from being acknowledged. In one of the few articles written on Phoebe, Edgar Goodspeed, for instance, suggests that Phoebe needed such a letter of introduction because 'the Roman world was a bad and brutal world, and inns were notoriously likely to be no places for a decent woman, particularly a Christian woman, to put up in'. Therefore he argues that Romans 16 must have been originally an independent letter to the church in Ephesus where Paul knew family circles who could make Phoebe feel 'safe and comfortable'. He says that the reason why so many women and their family circles are mentioned in Romans 16 is that they 'might lead to Phoebe's entertainment in more than one of them'.[8] In such a way, Goodspeed conjures subtly the image of a respectable lady to be entertained by other refined ladies, an image that has nothing to do with the realities of early Christian mission and women's role in it.

In antiquity, letters of recommendation were not restricted to women or primarily written for them. Numerous examples are found in the papyri or letter collections. They generally mention the person introduced, give a brief statement of her or his identity and relationship to the writer, and then request a favour for the person. The request is usually stated in a quite generalized form, just as is the case in Romans 16.2. Personal letters of recommendation are frequently found at the end of larger epistles. They served to introduce friends, business partners, or slaves of the writer to a circle of friends and acquaintances in a foreign city.[9] Travelling Christian missionaries and church leaders used such letters of recommendation in order to receive access and hospitality in communities to whom they were not known personally. Phoebe's example testifies that early Christian women leaders officially represented early Christian communities and that their travels served the communicaton between them. It is likely – but not explicitly stated – that she was the carrier of the letter to the Romans and thus the personal envoy of Paul.

Who was this woman Phoebe? 'Phoebe' is a mythological name

and could indicate that she was a freedwoman. Although in antiquity, just as today, women were characterized by their relationship to men, that is, by their family status as daughters, wives or widows, Phoebe is not defined by her gender role and patriarchal status, but by her ecclesial functions. Her position in the early Christian missionary movement is characterized with three titles: She is 'our sister', the minister or leader of the church at Cenchreae, a seaport of Corinth, and benefactor or *patrona* of many and even of Paul himself.

It is interesting to note that the Greek terms *diakonos* and *prostatis* are often translated with the verb form, for example, 'she serves' the community of Cenchreae and 'she has assisted' or 'helped many'. If *diakonos* is understood as a title it is translated with 'servant, helper, or deaconess', and interpreted in terms of the later deaconess institution.[10] Phoebe is understood as one of the first pastoral assistants helping Paul in his missionary work. Many scholars understand the office of Phoebe by analogy to the later institution of deaconesses, which in comparison to that of the male diaconate had only very limited functions. For instance, Phoebe is then seen as 'an apparently well-to-do and charitable lady who because of her feminine virtues worked in the service of the poor and of the sick as well as assisted at the baptism of women'.[11] Already Origen had promoted this interpretation of Phoebe as an assistant and helper of Paul. From this he concluded that women who do good works can be appointed as deaconesses.

Similarly, the Greek term *prostatis* is translated not with 'leading officer', 'president', or 'benefactor'[12] but with 'helper' or 'assistant', since many exegetes are unable to conceive of the idea that Paul could be supported or outranked by a woman. After reviewing again all the arguments for and against understanding Phoebe in terms of Greco-Roman patronage, a recent commentator of Romans concludes:

> There is no reference then to a 'patroness' . . . Women could not take on legal functions, and accordinging to Revelation only in heretical circles do prophetesses seem to have had official eccclesiastical powers of leadership . . . The idea is that of personal care which Paul and others have received at the hand of the deaconess.[13]

The reference to the Book of Revelation, which reflects a situation at the end of the first century in Asia Minor, is telling because it breaches all rules of historical–exegetical method. It is obvious that an androcentric perspective on early Christian history has to explain away the literal meaning of both words, because it does not allow for women in church leadership, or it can accord them only 'feminine' assisting functions. Since this traditional interpretive model takes it for granted that the leadership of the early Church was in the hands of men, it assumes that the women mentioned in the Pauline letters were the helpers and assistants of the male apostles and missionaries, especially of Paul. Such an androcentric model of historical reconstruction cannot imagine or conceptualize that women such as Phoebe could have leadership equal to and sometimes even superior to men in early Christian beginnings. The much invoked objectivity of historical–critical scholarship has a difficult time to prevail when the text speaks about a woman in a way that does not fit into traditional or contemporary androcentric models of historical reconstruction.

What can we say about Phoebe when we do not attempt to fit our information about her into an androcentric model, but seek to place it into a feminist model of historical reconstruction? The early Christian missionary movement was spread by travelling missionaries and organized in local churches similar to other private associations and religious cults. Whereas a woman such as Prisca engaged in missionary travels and founded house churches wherever she went, a woman such as Phoebe was the leader of a local community. Her 'ministry' or 'office' was not as that of the later deaconesses limited to women, but she was the *diakonos* of the whole Church in Cenchreae.[14]

Paul uses the same Greek expression when he characterizes his own ministry or that of the charismatic missionary Apollos, whose teacher had been Prisca. The word cluster *diakonos, diakonia, diakonein* is found most often in 2 Corinthians and it characterizes the so-called pseudo-apostles who were charismatic missionaries, eloquent preachers, visionary prophets, and Spirit-filled apostles.[15] Paul seems to have been criticized in Corinth because he did not make an impressive figure and was not an eloquent preacher and miracle worker, as well as because he did not have support of the community or 'letters of recommendation'. Such an understanding of the title in terms of preaching and teaching is justified, since it is used also in extrabiblical sources to refer to preachers and teachers.

Phoebe has the same title as these charismatic preachers in Corinth. Yet she is not one of the opponents of Paul but has a friendly relationship with him. She was acknowledged as a charismatic preacher and leader of the community in Cenchreae, the seaport of Corinth, who, like the members of the house of

Stephanas, had dedicated herself 'to the *diakonia* of the saints' (cf. 1 Cor. 16.15). Just as the closest co-worker of Paul, Timothy, is called 'our brother' and God's *diakonos* (1 Thess. 3.2) so Phoebe is not only introduced as *diakonos* but also as 'our sister', a title characterizing her as co-worker of Paul. In a similar way, the author of Colossians recommends a man by the name of Tychicus as 'our beloved brother' and 'faithful *diakonos*' (4.7).[16]

The significance of Phoebe's leadership is also underlined by the third title (after 'sister' and *diakonos*), *prostatis*, a word found only here in the New Testament. The usual meaning of this expression is 'leader', 'president', superintendent', or 'patron', a translation that is supported by the verb form which is found in 1 Thessalonians 5.12 and 1 Timothy 3.4–5 and 5.17. It refers in 1 Thessalonians to the leadership of the community and in 1 Timothy to the leadership functions of bishop, deacons and elders. Such an understanding of the words in terms of leadership does not rule out its understanding in terms of the patronage system of antiquity, since patrons and benefactors also could take over leadership in the associations and cultic groups supported by them.

Although we have little evidence for all-women associations, we have sufficient evidence that women joined clubs and became founders and patrons of socially mixed associations and cults. They endowed them with funds for specific, defined purposes and expected honour and recognition in return for their benefactions. The well-to-do converts to Christianity must have expected to exercise the influence of a patron in the early Christian community. Christians such as Phoebe acted as benefactors for individual Christians and the whole Church. In dealings with the government or the courts they represented the whole community. With their network of connections, friendships with well-placed persons and public influence, such benefactors eased the social life of other Christians in Greco-Roman society.

The motif of reciprocity stressed by Paul speaks for an understanding of *prostatis* in the technical–legal sense of the Greco-Roman patronage system.[17] Phoebe's patronage was not limited to the community of Cenchreae, but included many others, even Paul himself, who stood with her in a patron–client relationship. Therefore Paul asks the community in Rome to repay Phoebe according to the 'exchange law' of Greco-Roman patronage, the assistance and favours that Paul and other Christians owed her as her clients. Those who joined the Christian community joined it as an association of equals in which, according to the pre-Pauline baptismal formula of Galatians 3.28,[18] societal status stratifications in terms of the patriarchal family were abolished. This is the main reason why the early Christian movement seems to have been especially attractive to those who had little stake in the rewards of religion based on either class stratification or on male dominance. It is obvious why women were among its leading converts.

2 Paul's appeal to leading women in the Roman church

It is often observed than an unusually high number of women are found among those who are greeted in Romans 16.3–16. Of the twenty-six persons mentioned by name, roughly one-third are women. While seven women are explicitly mentioned by name, two are characterized by their family relationship: the mother of Rufus and the 'sister' of Nereus. Although it is difficult to know what Paul means when he claims that the mother of Rufus was also his own, it is generally assumed that she is not Paul's natural mother. Meeks suggests that she might have extended her patronage to him.[19] More difficult to resolve is the question whether 'the sister of Nereus' is the natural sister, the Christian wife, or the Christian co-missionary of Nereus, since the word can be used in these three ways.

In light of our discussion of androcentric language we must, however, insist that this is not all the information we have on women. If grammatically masculine language functions as inclusive language, then it is safe to assume that among those who belong to the house of Aristobulus and Narcissus are also women. Similarly, the 'brethren' and 'saints' who are with those groups of persons mentioned in 16.14–15 must have included 'sisters'. Finally, it is unlikely that the house church of Prisca and Aquila consisted only of men and not of women. In short, the women explicitly greeted in Romans 16 are not the only women in the Roman community and its leadership. However, their mention allows the exegete to read grammatically masculine language as inclusive, unless a case can be made to the contrary.

This list of greetings is further interesting in terms of the social compositions of the Roman church in so far as it contains not only Jewish, Greek and Latin names, but also those of free, freed, slaves – women and men. Since it is difficult to make a clear distinction betwen slaves and freed persons on the basis of names, it is no longer possible to say something about the actual economic situation and social mobility of those who are greeted. Those of the houses of Aristobulus and Narcissus are probably slaves, while

Junia, Ampliatus, Stachys, Herodion, Tryphosa, Persis, Rufus, Asyncritus, Hermes, Patrobas, Philologus, Julia, Nereus and his sister, and Olympas either could still be slaves or could be former slaves, since all freed persons carried with their name a certain stigma of their service origin. While freed slaves were still bound legally to their former masters and could not have public office or marry members of the senatorial aristocracy, the children born to them after they were set free enjoyed complete legal and social freedom. Children born into slavery, however, were the property of their mother's master, because slave women – even when married to other slaves or freedmen – were the sexual and economic property of their masters.[20]

The list of those greeted is clearly structured – not in terms of social status but in terms of ecclesial standing. It begins with the most important persons of the community – Prisca and Aquila – and ends with greetings to whole groups and to 'all saints' belongng to them (16.15).[21] The greetings to Prisca, Aquila, Ephaenetus, Mary, Andronicus, Junia, Ampliatus, Urbanus, Stachys, Persis, as well as Rufus and his mother, presuppose personal acquaintance. Paul's greetings to several house churches (16.10–11) and other individuals are more general, and do not indicate that Paul knew these persons personally. Since he had not yet visited the church in Rome, Paul – I would suggest – underlines his close ties with leading persons in the community in order to document that he was not a complete stranger to the Roman churches. While it would not have been necessary to explain, for example, that Ephaenetus was the first Gentile convert in western Asia Minor or to elaborate that Prisca and Aquila were his trusted co-workers in a letter to Ephesus, it makes sense for him to do so in a letter to the Roman church in order to claim them as his close friends and associates in Rome.

Prisca and Aquila have a place of prominence at the beginning of the list of greetings. They are called Paul's 'co-workers', to whom not only Paul himself but all the Gentile churches owe a debt of gratitude. When Paul was in danger (probably in Ephesus), they risked their lives for him. Not only they but also 'the church in their house' receive greetings. Exegetes have long recognized that it is unusual that in four out of six New Testament texts Prisca is mentioned before Aquila. The reason for Prisca's prominence in the Pauline letters and Acts might be either her higher social status or her prominence in the early Christian missionary movement or both.

Since Luke concentrates in the second part of Acts in the greatness of Paul, the apostle to the Gentiles, he refers to Prisca and Aquila only in passing. Acts 18 also indicates that Luke probably had more information about them than he transmits to us. Nevertheless, Luke's brief remarks illuminate the historical significance of this missionary pair. Acts 18 tells us that Aquila was a Jew from Pontus. Priscilla – Luke always uses the diminutive of Prisca – is identified as his wife, but it is not clear whether she also was Jewish. Her name is found in good old Roman families, and it is connected with the cemetery of the *gens* Acilia in Rome. However, her name does not necessarily prove that she is of noble birth, and therefore more prominent than Aquila. It could simply indicate that she was a freedwoman of the *gens* Acilia. That both she as well as Aquila are said to be tent-makers or leather-workers by trade (Acts 18.4) speaks for the latter. Meeks sums up the couple's social status as follows:

> Wealth: relatively high. They have been able to move from place to place, and in three cities to establish a sizable household; they have acted as patrons for Paul and for Christian congregations. Occupation: low, but not at the bottom. They are artisans, but independent, and by ancient standards they operate on a fairly large scale. Extraction: middling to low. They are eastern provincials and Jews besides, but assimilated to Greco-Roman culture.[22]

However, we must keep in mind that the last characterization might apply only to Aquila.

According to Acts 18, the couple was expelled from Rome when Claudius decreed that all Jews should leave the city (49 CE). They had already set up business in Corinth when Paul arrived there, and he stayed with them. Exegetes debate whether or not they had become Christians before they met Paul. Since it is customary for the writer of Acts to mention the conversion and baptism of prominent persons in the narrative, his failure to do so here speaks for the assumption that the couple had been members of the Christian community before their expulsion from Rome.[23] When Paul left Corinth, they moved with him to Ephesus where they estabished a house church (1 Cor. 16.19). Since Acts 18.19 does not mention this, but places Paul in the centre of the narrative, it is safe to assume that the same is true for Luke's account of Paul's stay in Corinth. This assumption is supported by the fact that in Ephesus the couple took in Apollos, one of the most erudite and eloquent missionaries of the early Christian movement. Priscilla became his teacher who instructed him in 'the way of God more accurately' (18.26). Might we assume that the Sophia and Spirit theology of Apollos was influenced by her catechesis? Priscilla certainly was also among the 'brothers' who wrote a 'letter of recommendation' for Apollos to the church in Corinth (Acts 18.27).

Prisca and Aquila were travelling missionaries who, like Paul and Barnabas, supported other missionary work with their own labour. Like Timothy or Titus they are Paul's co-workers, but unlike them they are not dependent on him or subject to his instructions. The opposite is true according to Romans 16. More-over, they also had other co-workers.[24] At Romans 16.9 Paul greets Urbanus as their and his own fellow worker who, together with Ephaenetus, might have moved to Rome with the couple. How-ever, Prisca was not the only woman missionary co-worker in Rome. Another expression for missionary co-workers is 'those who toil'. In 1 Corinthians 16.16–18 Paul admonishes the Corinthian Christians 'to subordinate themselves to every co-worker and labourer', and in 1 Thessalonians 5.12 he exhorts the community in Thessalonica to 'respect those who labour among you, and are over you in the Lord, and admonish you'. It is therefore significant that in Romans 16.6, Paul commends four women – Mary, Tryphaena, Tryphosa and Persis – for having 'laboured hard' in the Lord. These women are thereby characterized as leaders of the commu-nity who, like Prisca, deserve respect and recognition for their tireless evangelizing and community-building ministry.

While Prisca and Aquila do not receive Paul's favourite title 'apostle', another missionary pair does so. In Romans 16.7 Paul greets Andronicus and Junia(s), his co-patriots who have been in prison with him. Unlike in Prisca's and Aquila's case, the text is clear that they had become Christians before Paul and that they are renowned among the apostles. Exegetes have usually argued that the accusative form *Junian* must connote a male name, because no women can be counted among the apostles. In recent years, however, it is more and more recognized that this androcentric theological assumption cannot be maintained exegetically, since we have no evidence whatever for a male name Junias, but plenty of evidence for the occurrence of the female name Junia in anti-quity.[25] The name Junia indicates that this pre-Pauline Jewish Christian woman was either a noble lady of the *gens* Iunius, which is not very likely, or that she was a slave or freedwoman of a man Iunius or a descendant of former slaves of the noble house of Iunius.[26]

Like Prisca and Aquila, Andronicus and Junia are missionary partners. They might be Jewish Christians from Syro-Phoenicia, or they might have even come from Tarsus. Since they had become Christians before Paul, it can be conjectured not only that they had worked together with Paul and Barnabas in Antioch, but also that they belonged to the circle of apostles in Jerusalem who together with James and the twelve received a vision of the Resurrected One (1 Cor. 15.7) Moreover, since they are now in Rome, they seem to have been engaged in missionary activity. In the discussion with his rivals in Corinth and Galatia, Paul stresses that he is a true apostle because he has received a resurrection appearance and has proven himself to be an outstanding missionary to the Gentiles.[27] For Paul, however, the mark of true apostleship does not consist in mighty speech and pneumatic exhibition, but in the conscious acceptance and endurance of the labours and sufferings connected with missionary work. Andronicus and Junia fulfil Paul's criteria for apostleship: they were outstanding in the circle of the apostles and like Paul had suffered prison in pursuit of their missionary activity.

However, in one signal aspect these two missionary couples are different from Paul, who seems to have worked mostly in tandem with male co-workers like Barnabas, Silvanus or Timothy. The practice of partnership–mission appears to have been the rule in the Christian missionary movement, which allowed for the equal participation of women with men in missionary work. Moreover, it is likely that such missionary partners were at first couples. In 1 Corinthians 9.5 Paul maintains that he, like the other apostles, has the right to financial support by the community, as well as the right to be accompanied by a female co-missionary, because the other apostles, the brothers of the Lord and Cephas, were entitled to take with them on their missionary journeys 'sisters' as 'women or wives'. The difficult double accusative object 'sister, woman' is best explained, when 'sister' like 'brother' is understood as a missionary co-worker.[28] Thus the missionary pairs Prisca–Aquila and Andronicus–Junia were not exceptions in the early Christian movement. When Paul stresses celibacy as the best condition for missionary work (1 Cor. 7.24–40), he expresses his own opinion, which was not generally accepted. However, it must be noted that Paul characterizes neither Prisca nor Junia as 'wives'. Their patriarchal status in the household is of no significance. Rather, he greets both women because of their commitment and accomplishments in the work of the gospel.

Although co-workers of Paul, Prisca and Aquila seem to have

adopted a different missionary method and practice. While Paul can write eloquently about 'the building up of the community' as primary task for ministry, he himself seems to have moved from missionary centre to missionary centre using the hospitality of local churches. By contrast, Prisca and Aquila founded and supported 'a church in their house' wherever they moved. In so far as like 'the other apostles' they worked and travelled as 'a missionary pair', and gathered converts in house churches, they did not divide the apostolic *diakonia* into the service of the word that aims at conversion of individuals and that of Eucharistic table sharing that establishes community.

The house church[29] was the beginning and centre of the Christian mission in a certain city or district. It provided space for the preaching of the gospel and for worship gatherings, as well as for social and Eucharistic table-sharing. The existence of house churches presupposes that some Christians must have had the means to provide a place, as well as economic resources for the community. Prisca and Aquila appear to have been among such well-to-do Christians. However, Paul's greetings to those of the house of Aristobulus and of the house of Narcissus 'to the extent that they belong to the Lord' (Rom. 16.10–11) also indicate that slaves and family members did assemble in households whose masters were not Christians. As the movement spread, several house churches developed in a city like Corinth or Rome. Many dissensions and disagreements that are usually interpreted as having theological roots might have developed because of diverse house churches in a city.

In distinction to Acts, the Pauline letters do not assume that whole households were converted to Christianity. It is not the household of Prisca and Aquila but the church in their house that, like other house churches in Rome, receives greetings from Paul. Basic for the organizational structure of house churches, therefore, seems not to have been the structure of the patriarchal household, but a combination of organizational forms found in private or cultic associations and Jewish communal structures. While some of the religious clubs and associations admitted members of the lower classes, and women indiscriminately, others were reserved to persons of high social status, common nationality, or shared profession as well as to slaves, women or men exclusively. As Romans 16 indicates, the house church as well as the whole church in a city counted women as well as men, persons with high or low social status, and persons of different nationalities among its membership and leadership. Those who joined the early Christian missionary movement joined it as an association of equals. Membership and leadership in the early Christian missionary movement, therefore, was bound to come in tension with traditional patriarchal household and societal structures which still defined the life of those Christian freeborn women and slaves still living in pagan households.

4 Conclusion

Romans 16 gives us a glimpse of the rich social mix of early Christian communities, as well as of women's contribution to early Christian life and mission. The sgnificance of women's leadership in the early Christian missionary movement that emerges from a careful reading of Romans 16, however, is downplayed when exegetes argue that the leadership of women like Phoebe, Prisca, or Junia was 'unofficial' because it was not exercised in public but restricted to the private sphere of the house. This distinction is not only anachronistic but also overlooks that in the house church the 'private and public' spheres of the Church overlap. Moreover, there is no indication whatever that women's missionary work was restricted solely to women. Finally, the well-worn argument of Scripture scholars that women's early Christian missionary activity was possible because women, but not male, missionaries had access to the women's quarters has no basis in fact. Unlike their Athenian counterparts, Roman matrons were not sequestered in the house. Women worked in trades, dined with their husbands, attended shows, games, parties, and even political gatherings, and were notorious for receiving preachers of strange cults into their homes.[30]

The contributions of our early Christian foresisters to early Christian faith, community, and mission can only become historically visible when we are willing to abandon our outdated androcentric models of historical reconstruction. By highlighting the often unconscious bias of established so-called objective scholarship as well as the obfuscating functions of androcentric language of biblical sources, a hermeneutics of suspicion is able to recover glimpses of the discipleship of equals in the beginnings of Christianity as a heritage and vision for all of us.

7 ANGELA WEST
Sex and Salvation: A Christian Feminist Bible Study on I Corinthians 6.12—7.39

St Paul, to put it mildly, doesn't have a great deal of street credibility with feminists. He is seen as one of the great patriarchal figures of Christianity who was very authoritarian about everything, especially sex and women. Recently, I've come to the conclusion that, for the sake of the liberation that feminists believe in, and for the sake of all those women and men who have suffered under patriarchy's misreading of Paul, we must be prepared to revise that old stereotype that we so fondly love to hate.

Paul was a Jew, passionately concerned with his faith, who had persecuted Christians because he believed that they were subverting the basis of Jewish identity and salvation – the law (Torah). But after his dramatic encounter with Christ on the road to Damascus, Paul was accepted into the fellowship of that body which he had persecuted, and understood that in this body there was 'no Jew nor Gentile, slave nor free, male and female' – all the distinctions that had meant most to a Jew like Paul. And from then on, he began to preach that salvation was not to be found in these distinctions, however important they were, but in belonging to the body of the crucified Jew. And for Paul that meant that Jews must no longer impose on Gentile converts within the new body the mark of Jewish identity – and religious superiority – that is, circumcision. But for many Jewish Christians this relativizing of the Law was going too far. So, from the early days, Paul's authority was always being questioned. Other Christian preachers took a different line and opposed him, and his position was a desperately exposed one. For if it turned out that he had been wrong on the matter of circumcision, he had betrayed his own people, ruined his life and founded whole communities on the basis of a ghastly mistake. All this helps to explain why the deep internal strife that affected the newly founded Gentile Christian community at Corinth was so distressing to Paul. He needed them to prove by their unity that he had been right.

But unfortunately, unity was not the order of the day at Corinth. Different factions had formed who violently disagreed with each other. And sex was one of the things they disagreed about. The difficulty for Paul in responding to their disagreements is that he was dealing with people who sincerely believed that they were applying what he had taught them. If we look at the text, we can see him trying to grapple with this problem. 'All things are lawful for me' (1 Cor. 6.12) he writes, quoting the letter from the group who seem to be setting the tone at Corinth, probably an articulate minority which included many of the better-off members. But they in turn were referring to the justification Paul himself had used when he set aside the Jewish food rules. His permissive remark about the nature of Christian freedom, uttered in another context, had apparently boomeranged on him. One of the groups at Corinth – who were highly 'spiritual' people – had extended the logic of it and applied it to sex. The gratification of sexual desire, they imply, is like satisfying hunger – a bodily function without spiritual significance (6.13). So what is to stop someone gratifying this desire through prostitution (porneia)? Paul, if one can paraphrase him, is forced into the position of saying, 'Yes, but . . . yes, I did say that all things are permissible, but you have to realize that not everything you can do is helpful or liberating (6.12b). It is not because it's against the moral law that that sort of sex is wrong, but because it will enslave you. It's a fundamental denial of the spiritual freedom we are claiming. Yes, it is true that food is for the stomach and both are perishable and mortal and do not have any bearing on eternal life (6.13). But sex is not the same as consuming food. The body is more than just a stomach with its appetites and needs. Sex involves the whole body in its social and spiritual dimensions'. As he puts it, 'The body is not made for prostitution but for the Lord and the Lord for the body', that is, our bodies are not simply destined like the food we eat to be flushed down the loo, they are destined to be 'raised up' and transformed in the final future. Therefore it does matter what we do with our bodies – and sexual union with a prostitute is a fundamental contradiction of the union made with the community that is the body of Christ.

I find Paul's comparison of a man's sexual union with a prostitute to the union of a Christian with the body of Christ very fascinating. I get the impression that when most exegetes and theologians come across this verse they inwardly blush and stutter or pass it over in awkward silence, thinking to themselves, 'He's really going too far . . .' But I think what he says here paradoxically affirms the indivisible reality of sex, a bodily-social-spiritual reality which in many ways is the nearest analogy Paul can find for talking about our union with the body of Christ. And because it comes in the context of talking about prostitution, it is quite clear that it is sexual union itself he is talking about, and not the institution of marriage. According to Paul, our union in the body of Christ is real in the way sexual relationships are real, and this is a fundamental contradiction of the false spirituality of the 'super-spirituals' at Corinth – so much of which we have inherited.

It is interesting that Paul has to argue here not that prostitution is 'against the moral law' (he has already said, 'all things are lawful for me'), but he condemns it as being not helpful for freedom, a return to slavery. The Greek word that is translated by immorality/prostitution' is *'porneia'*, which has the same root as the word 'pornography'. In her book *Pornography and Silence*,[1] Susan Griffin shows how closely the ascetic or 'super-spiritual' mentality is related to the pornographic mentality. They are normally assumed to be completely opposite, but she shows convincingly how one is the flip-side of the other. The use of a woman's body made object for the purpose of fantasy, as in pornography and prostitution, serves to protect a man from real knowledge of his own body. Precisely because it is in the form of fantasy, he can distance himself from it and remain in control. This is the function of pornography, and also the reason why it becomes an obsession – the obsessive assertion of mind over matter. For the body has a reality that cannot be so easily denied. It represents itself again and again, and when it is refused recognition, it functions to subvert 'male' rational freedom. This obsession that Susan Griffin identifies is, I think, essentially the same as the 'slavery' that Paul warns the male Corinthians to avoid. Feminist analysis, starting from an entirely different point of view from Paul, has also concluded that a system where men have the power to rent women's bodies for sexual purposes is indeed a form of slavery for women. But the perpetrators are also involved in the degradation they impose on the victims: 'The immoral man sins against his own body' says Paul (6.18b). If we combine Paul's insight with feminist understanding, we could say: to humiliate women's bodies is to humiliate the one flesh of humanity.

In this letter, you can see Paul fighting with his back aganst the wall to preserve what he understood to be Christian freedom. It is important to realize that, historically speaking, he lost. It was the heirs of the super-spirituals, the Church fathers, who won – and who brought in the new morality with a vengeance. And it is very revealing to see how they have coped with Paul, how he has been 'made safe' for use in the morality of the patriarchal Church. By looking at a particularly notorious section of the next chapter, we can observe the process of how the good news of freedom became the basis of a new bondage.

'It is well for a man not to touch a woman'. So it is written in 7.1b – and most people think that this is what Paul *really* thought about sex. This quote was most beloved by the Church fathers. Tertullian drew the conclusion, 'It follows that it is evil to have contact with a woman: for nothing is contrary to good except evil.' Jerome heartily endorsed this opinion, and added plenty more of his own in the same vein. Augustine of Hippo honoured 7.1b as 'the very word of God, a voice from the clouds'. Nothing was said about it being Paul's words rather than God's direct – and not even exactly his, as we shall see. On the basis of this exegesis, Augustine, the most influential bishop in church history, declared that marital intercourse for the sake of mutual enjoyment is a 'venial sin'. Not all scholars followed Augustine in thinking that it was the Almighty speaking direct in this verse, but most of them, right up to the twentieth century, have assumed that Paul was expressing his own negative feelings about sex – as something that draws man away from God (it being assumed that woman is nowhere near God in the first place). Scholars of the history of sexuality regard 1 Corinthians 7.1b as the headwater in Christianity for repressive views on sex that have flowed through all branches of the Church. In Christian history, all those who have glorified sexual austerity have pinned their doctrines on it. So it comes as a shock to realize that, in this remark, Paul is not giving his own opinion directly – he is almost certainly quoting the opinion of his correspondent whose sexual ideals and practice he does not endorse. Although some translators as far back as Origen did realize that the verse was a quote, it is only recently that it has been widely recognized that Paul does not endorse the position he quotes. It is a thesis to argue against rather than his own position. As in other passages – for instance, 'All things are lawful for me' (6.12) – he cites what he finds objectionable or in need of qualification. Thus, a better translation would be something like this: 'now concerning the matters you mention in your letter. You say: it is good for a man not to have intercourse with woman. I say: that each man should have his own wife and each woman her own husband because of the dangers of prostitution.'[2]

The translation fits much better with what has gone before and with what follows, and with the whole context of the letter. It is quite sobering to realize how vastly influential this misinterpretation has been in our tradition. Virtually all non-biblical scholars presume that this remark represents Paul's position. Wiesen,[3] a Latin scholar, says that in writing this, Paul 'sowed the fateful seeds of Christian antifeminism' and Susan Griffin bases much of her thesis on just this presumption. But when we realize that he is quoting here, a completely different picture of what is going on in the community begins to emerge. We find that Paul is actually arguing for couples to get back to sex rather than get away from it (cf.7.5).

Some of the super-spiritual group, it seems, were using Paul's own preferred celibacy to endorse an ideology of ascetic celibacy. Those who were now living a new life in the Spirit, found freedom and excitement in the charismatic ecstasy of the 'tongues', and began to regard sexual activity as a mark of life in the flesh, which they had abandoned along with the rest of their unliberated past. It seems there may have been moral pressure on couples to adopt a celibate lifestyle, and give up sex as a token of their new spirituality (rather like when some feminists gave up heterosexual relations for lesbian ones for the sake of sisterhood). This might have been fine if both partners had been able to agree about it. But clearly, the enthusiasm for married celibacy wasn't universal – so there was going to be a lot of frustrated marital partners around. If this was indeed the case, then many of Paul's remarks in this chapter begin to fall into place and make sense: for example, his worry about the (possible) resort to prostitution, and his stress on the *mutuality* of any arrangements about giving up sex between a husband and a wife. Other writings of the time that give advice about marriage are addressed exclusively to men, and concerned with the problem from their point of view.[4] There is also his concern about the distracting effects of sexual desire (7.5 and 7.9). Paul considers sexual desire a force to be reckoned with, not one that can be simply suppressed in the interest of a spiritually or ideologically desirable lifestyle. He seems to be well aware of the futility of using up energy in the attempt to repress desire, when that energy is needed for the vital work of 'building up the body' of Christ, which was always his priority. He is concerned about the effects of the super-spiritual ideology on marriages – the imposition of an ideal of sexual continence which caused break-ups where one partner could not or didn't want to accept it. This seems to be the situation that lies behind Paul's advice in verses 10–11. Jerome Murphy O'Connor has examined the language of this section in its context and suggests the following scenario:[5] one of the husbands has been strongly influenced by the ideology of the super-spirituals and wants to renounce the sexual side of his marriage. His wife is not exactly delighted with the arrangement, so she is thinking in terms of divorce and remarriage. Paul, in line with what he has received of Christ's teaching, advises her not to accept a divorce, and the husband not to divorce her. He hopes the husband will return to his senses, and they can work out some sort of mutual conjugal contract such as he has been advocating (7.10–11, 3–5).

Contrary to our expectations, perhaps, Paul does not take a hard line on the matter of divorce. In the next section (vs. 12–16) he goes on to talk about the problem of mixed marriages – between believers and non-believers. The more separatist members of the community may have wanted to repudiate such marriages as a matter of principle. Paul, however, thinks that where the unbelieving partner is willing to carry on the marriage, the Christian partner should agree to this because it shows a willingness on the part of the unbelieving spouse to be incorporated in some sense into the life of the redeemed community, the community in which salvation is to be found. The existence of the sexual bond (the one flesh) makes this a possibility. But where the unbelieving partner wants to separate – and perhaps Paul had experienced this himself – he thinks this should not be opposed. He considers that divorce is possible in such circumstances. For, as he says, 'God has called us to peace' – not an unending state of marital warfare.

The patriarchal Church, in line with its sex-repressive ideology, has presented Paul as embodying its ideal of apostolic virginity. But, in fact, it is extremely unlikely that he had never been married. The Jewish attitude to marriage was based in the Torah of Genesis, 'It is not good for a man to be alone'. So it was part of his religious and social duty for a Jewish man to marry. The chances are that Paul was either a widower, or had separated from his wife, who as the wife – and possibly the daughter – of a Pharisee would have found his new allegiance scandalous and unacceptable. So when Paul writes, 'To the unmarried and widows I say that it is well for them to remain single as I do' (7.8), the translation here is misleading. The word used for 'unmarried' in fact means either someone who has separated after marriage, or a widower – for which there is no alternative term used in the New Testament. So when he goes on to discuss the problems of Christians married to non-Christians, it is by no means impossible that he is speaking from his own experience – out of which, perhaps, his own celibacy had been painfully born.[6]

Thus, members of the Corinthian community were faced with

issues to do with separation. In what ways were they to be separate
from the rest of society by their new allegiance? How did this affect
relations between marriage partners and members of the same
family? In the women's movement, similar questions have arisen.
And hardline ideology – like hardline morality – doesn't really
supply the answers; or, to put it another way, it doesn't mediate the
love of God in these situations. It merely produces guilt and a sense
of inadequacy for those involved. The inadequacy of the 'pure'
separatist solution is pointed up by Paul when he raises the
question of children (v. 14b). He suggests that if all believers are to
be considered 'unclean', then the children of mixed unions will
have to be deemed 'unclean' too. This is similar to the issue that
lesbian separatists have to face. If all men are to be considered
unclean, are their own male children also to be rejected? This
question, I think, helps to take us to the heart of Paul's understanding of the nature of our union in the body of Christ. For
wherever we are face to face with living human bodies whom we
love, and who are part of us as lovers or sisters, spouses or parents
or children, then all the rules about our religious or ideological
identity are never quite enough to deal with the reality of our one
flesh. Paul had passionately loved the Jewish law that gave Jews
their separate religious identity. In the same way, there are many
important reasons why feminist separatism has come into being,
and why it must still be defended in many situations. But if we
absolutize our separation, make it into a new law with codes of
purity and uncleanness, we may end up contradicting the vision of
wholeness that first called our new identity into being. For the
community of salvation is a living body which we belong to with
our living bodies: and all the clean lines of ideology we draw to
describe our identity are never quite adequate to encompass the
messy reality of our humanity as one flesh. This I think was part of
the meaning for Paul of belonging to the body of Christ.

At Corinth, Paul is faced with a group of ardent imitators who
want to make his own option for celibacy into the basis for a new
sexual and spiritual ideal for the whole community. But for Paul
this is similar to the mentality of those who would impose
circumcision on all the others. It leads to exactly the same
hierarchies of worth, the same tension and dividedness. He
explains that his own passion is not for spiritual freedom through
sexual abstinence, but for the body of Christ. He is attempting to
show that salvation cannot in the last analysis be equated with
gaining social or sexual freedom – with a shift in status from being

married to not married, uncircumcised to circumcised, from being sexual to being celibate – even from being legally a slave to being free. For however necessary it is to seek our freedom – and it *is* the heart of our Christian calling 'not to become slaves of men (and certainly our feminist one too) – yet that freedom cannot in the last analysis *depend* on the social or sexual freedom we have achieved. For this would mean that all those who had failed to achieve this freedom, for whatever reason, were necessarily excluded from any hope of being saved. Hence, for Paul, the paradox of our faith is that in choosing freedom by belonging to the body of Christ, we become slaves – those who have 'been bought with a price'.

Paul's commitment to the body of Christ is not to an idea or an ideal, but to the reality of living, struggling human beings faced with painful human dilemmas. The freedom and salvation he announces is a share in this suffering reality of Christ. But for some people, then as now, this is not what they had in mind as salvation. They were seaching for moral security in the authoritative pronoucements of spiritual leaders, and their wisdom enshrined in a set of principles. It is a very natural human desire, and corresponds to our deep need to know that our parents are wise and loving and do everything for our good. In some cases they are wise and loving and other times they are not, but in the helplessness of childhood we cannot do without parents to care for us. This is the freedom and safety available to us under the Law, the pedagogue who leads us to Christ, as Paul saw it. But the vision of salvation he had received and preached was for those who were seeking to become spiritually mature. Much of Paul's argument with the super-spirituals in Corinth concerns the subject of spiritual wisdom. They are convinced that they have it – after all, he had told them that it was the gift of the Spirit they had been given at baptism. But he sees their spiritual and sexual idealism as the opposite of mature spirituality – rather it is an ideology, a new morality that keeps them 'babes in Christ, not yet ready for solid food'. As he understands it, the Spirit's gift of wisdom is what enables us to deal with – and not deny – the difficult dilemmas that arise from the contradictions of morality and ideology.

For many of us these contradictions have to do with sex. In our own lives, and the lives of those close to us, we discover sex as the eternal transgressor of boundaries set by the moral and ideological structures with which we comprehend and contain our situation. And it is for this reason, I suggest, that sexual union is one of the primary metaphors in this letter for Paul's understanding of what it means to belong to the body of Christ. And I do mean sexual union, and by implication sexual passion, not simply sex for the procreation of children. For it is sexual passion that often leads us to cross or contemplate crossing moral, racial or ideological barriers. It frequently exposes us to vulnerability, pain and loss, and to the realization of the mortality of our bodies; and perhaps also to the knowledge that our common mortality confirms that we are one flesh with all humanity. These experiences had been Paul's too, as a result of his passion for the body of Christ. And our passions too may be what prepares us to understand what it means to share in the passion of Christ. But through our union with that body, we are taken beyond the fact of our common mortality that we share with our lovers and loved ones, because Christ was raised from the dead and we who, in Paul's phrase, 'have died with him, shall also be raised with him to share eternal life'.

My own agenda in this Bible study has been to show why, as a feminist, I remain deeply committed to Christian tradition; and how as a Christian, engaging with Paul's 'good news' in 1 Corinthians enables me to look with critical understanding both at that same Christian tradition, as well as at my recent experiences in the women's liberation movement. Through it I have understood that our calling is not to the institution of marriage, nor celibacy, nor even to political lesbianism if we are feminists. It is not to defend or uphold any particular institution of social or sexual status, but to preach the love of Christ in and through all the circumstances of our lives. And it is part of that good news that we do not preach this gospel as solitary individuals but as members and partners in Christ. Our partners may be our sisters, our lovers, our spouses or even our children. Through them we are enabled by the Spirit to know our one flesh with all humanity, and so to complete the building up of the body of Christ, which is the work of our salvation.

PART TWO
Christian History and Tradition

☐ Many distinguished women have by now contributed to the discussion of theology, but the present phase of specifically feminist theology may be dated from Valerie Saiving's important article, 'The Human Situation: A Feminine View', *Journal of Religion*, 40 (1960) pp. 100–12, which asked for a reconsideration of the categories of sin and redemption. She wanted this reconsideration to take notice of women's negation of self, learned in societies where women's realization of full self-identity was likely to be characterized as sin or temptation to sin. Some twenty years later, Judith Plaskow published her Yale dissertation on *Sex, Sin and Grace: Women's Experience and the Theologies of Reinhold Niebuhr and Paul Tillich* (Washington, University Press of America, 1980), which argued that in the work of these two theologians, certain aspects of human experience are highlighted and developed while others are regarded as secondary or ignored. This by itself hardly sounds revolutionary, but Judith Plaskow's point was that those human experiences that are developed, judged and transformed by the work of God in Christ were more likely to be associated with men, and women's experiences were more likely to be regarded as secondary, or reinforced by the Christian message in the worst possible way. What was thought to be inclusively human experience was in fact merely male experience, so theology was impoverished, and led to support for prevailing definitions of women. This led precisely to the problem identified by Valerie Saiving – the failure of women to take responsibility for their own self-actualization.[1]

Judith Plaskow's other concern was with the idea that women are 'closer to nature' than men, and the effect of this element of gender construction on their lives. She was not saying that the human experiences about which Tillich and Niebuhr wrote were not important, or that they were never shared by women, but was criticising the universality of their claims, as if males are the norm of humanity.[2] Quite apart from the details of Judith Plaskow's critique of the theologians, but arising from it, there is an important section on 'self-sacrifice', which repays attention. For self-sacrifice is a norm addressed to a self constantly tempted to sinful self-assertion. Women may have little 'self' to sacrifice, and theology may thus reinforce their servitude. 'It becomes another voice in the chorus of external expectation defining and confining the way women ought to live.' Women's selves need replenishment through the mutuality of their relationships, or they may give and give until they are depleted. Women rather need to hear of a 'grace' which has a dimension which 'corresponds to the sin of failing to live up to the potentialities of the structures of finite freedom'.

In the twenty-year period between the article and the book, feminist theology began to establish itself in the USA, not least because women gained acccess to divinity schools and seminaries, in the aftermath of the Second Vatican Council. It had become possible as early as 1943 for women to participate in a graduate programme in Roman Catholic theology at St Mary's College, Notre Dame, Indiana. The 1960s were deeply influenced by the event of the Second Vatican Council, and by the publication of its documents, very revealing for what they do and do not say about women. I will return to them in introducing the work of Mary Daly in Part Three, but would like to record here that it was one of the 'fathers' of that council (who was aged 90 in 1985), Marie-Dominique Chenu OP, who wrote in 1952, 'They say men make history . . . but in every case, it is men who write it and not women. Thus the whole history of civilization should be rewritten, for until now it has given little place to women in the evolution of social, cultural and even family life.'[3]

It was in response to the Council that one of the most

important books in feminist theology appeared. This was Mary Daly's *The Church and the Second Sex* (picking up Simone de Beauvoir's *The Second Sex*). Mary Daly's book is nowadays published together with her autobiographical preface to the 1975 edition, a feminist post-Christian introduction, and 'new archaic afterwords' (Boston, Beacon Press, 1985).[4] She and Rosemary Radford Ruether were crucial in forming the women's caucus in the American Academy of Religion, at which both delivered papers in 1971. Rosemary Radford Ruether's was to appear as 'Misogynism and Virginal Feminism in the Fathers of the Church', now available in *Religion and Sexism: Images of Woman in the Jewish and Christian Traditions* (New York, Simon & Schuster, 1974), which she edited.[5] Later in this *Reader* we can look at selections of work by both of these theologians. Here we need to familiarize ourselves with some of the work that has been done to help us rediscover some of the women of the period just after the apostles. The work of Elaine Pagels is immensely illuminating on this early period,[6] but my choice links us to both Paul and the post-apostolic period. It is a discussion of 'The Acts of Paul and Thecla', of which Karen Armstrong has given such an entertaining reading in her book, *The Gospel According to Woman: Christianity's Creation of the Sex War in the West* and which she connects with later tradition.

8 KAREN ARMSTRONG
The Acts of Paul and Thecla

One of the first of the virgin saints to act as an important role model for women was Thecla, the legendary disciple of St Paul. Her life was recorded in the second-century Encratist text *The Acts of Paul* which, despite its heretical assertions that only by celibacy and virginity could a Christian be saved, enjoyed great popularity in the early Church even among the Orthodox. We find Christians of unimpeachable orthodoxy, like St Ambrose, quoting Thecla's story in a sermon as though it were well known to every Christian. For a long time *The Acts of Paul* enjoyed the status of the Gospels and Epistles of the New Testament. Until the fourth century, Thecla was one of the most important of the holy women of Christianity.

We find St Methodius, in his *Symposium*, celebrating the glory of virginity, ranking Thecla as the most illustrious virgin of the Church. Later she would lose this position to the Virgin Mary. Her story celebrates the early Church's attitude to virginity, putting the theories of the theologians into a mythical form that the uneducated layman could easily understand. It demonstrates how virginity could bring a woman liberation as well as showing her some of the dangers the virgin would encounter in her pursuit of this difficult ideal. So perfectly did Thecla's story express the virginity myth that we find exactly the same elements being used when the lives of other virgins are written up, centuries later. Her story is still being told today. The Acts of Thecla are strongly reminiscent of novels describing how a woman frees herself of the shackles of her sex and becomes a liberated feminist. It might seem that novels by Marilyn French or Lisa Alther have nothing in common with a second-century Christian text, but in fact the modern feminist is simply translating into a secular idiom a myth that has always exerted a strong pull on the Western imagination: the myth of the liberated independent woman. The fact that she was once called a virgin and is now called a feminist is only of minor importance. Like the feminist, the virgin is a woman who has learned to do without men. Like the feminist, the virgin claims equality with the male world and insists that privileges (like apostleship and ministry) that were once only for men can easily be assumed by women. Like the modern feminist, the virgin of old had to make a painful transition from dependency and acceptance of sexism to liberation, and she often makes use of the same comforts as virgins like Thecla once did.

One of the first Gentile churches founded by St Paul was in Iconium in modern Turkey, and it was there, *The Acts of Paul* tells us, that Thecla saw him for the first time. For Thecla it was love at first sight. She sat enraptured, listening to him telling his hearers that celibacy was the only means of being saved and that Christianity meant renouncing 'filthy coitus'. Thecla was instantly converted to Christianity, although her conversion proved to be very dangerous to her. She was engaged at the time to a young man called Thamyris, but she renounced him on the spot and embraced a life of Christian virginity. Thus she not only enraged Thamyris but also her parents, who wanted her to make this fashionable match. They tried to force her to change her mind, and when nothing would dissuade her she was brought before the tribunal and sentenced to be burnt alive.

Despite this heroism in rejecting and defying the male world, Thecla still has a long way to go. She is still the typical passive woman of all feminist tales before their heroines are converted to feminism. She is hormonally and emotionally dependent upon her man, the extremely reluctant St Paul. Despite the veil of pious language, it is clear that she has fallen in love with him, although he gives her no encouragement and is positively embarrassed and unpleasant about her dogged pursuit of him. For three days Thecla listens to Paul's preaching, shaken by 'a strange eagerness and an awful emotion'. When Thamyris gets Paul thrown into gaol for inciting Thecla to rebel, Thecla visits him in prison and spends the whole night 'kissing his bonds'. When Paul is let out the next morning, Thecla is discovered 'enchained by affection . . . wallowing (!) on the place where Paul had sat in prison'. During the first part of her story she hardly speaks a word, but remains in a passive trance. Even when she herself appears before the tribunal she is utterly silent and has nothing to say in her own defence – no fiery and courageous proclamation of the truth of the Gospels, which is the sort of behaviour we will later come to expect of Christian martyrs. Thecla simply stands there mooning over her man; 'she stood looking only for Paul'. Paul by this time shows so little concern for Thecla that after being released himself, he callously leaves town, so that Thecla is still looking in vain for Paul, when she is led out to be burnt at the stake. It is clear that Jesus is a very secondary feature in Thecla's conversion. While she stands in the arena looking desperately for Paul, Jesus has to stand in for him, appearing to her 'in the likeness of Paul'. Thecla may be a virgin, but she still hasn't understood the most important freedom that virginity brings with it, which is a freedom from the male world. However, she does discover some of the other benefits of virginity. When they try to light the pyre to burn her to death, her naked virginal body is enveloped modestly by a nimbus from heaven, just as during another of her ordeals in the stadium her body is concealed by the clouds of perfume that the admiring spectators have hurled into the arena. The virginal body remains inviolable, impenetrable to the lascivious gaze of men and male hostility, so that Thecla cannot die. She is released by the bewildered Roman governor.

However, Thecla is still unliberated and instantly sets out in pursuit of Paul, who behaves like a real male chauvinist. Whenever Thecla really needs him he is conspicuously and callously absent. When she catches up with him at Daphne and begs for baptism, he refuses to baptize her because he fears that she could become 'mad after men', an attitude that we have now seen to be typical of the Christian and Western male. Even when she is publicly assaulted by one lustful Alexander at Antioch, Paul continues to disown Thecla: 'I know not the woman . . . nor is she mine.' He then abandons her and goes on his way, even though Thecla, because of the spite and machinations of Alexander, is to be thrown yet again into the arena, this time to face ordeal by wild beasts.

It is at this point that Thecla finds support in other women and so shakes off her humiliating dependence on unworthy men. A woman, Tryphema, takes Thecla into her house and is converted by her. When Thecla arrives in the arena it is the women who take up the cudgels for her against their menfolk in the audience, crying 'Evil Judgement! Impious Judgement!' and indeed it is a lioness who defends Thecla against the male wild beasts in the arena, tragically dying while striking a mortal blow to the most dangerous lion. It is here, as all true feminists would expect, that once she has experienced the sisterhood, Thecla discovers her own female dignity. She lays aside her besotted passivity and in one of the most absurd scenes in the story she baptizes herself – she is no longer dependent upon Paul's ministrations. She flings herself into a trough of man-eating seals that conveniently stands near her in the arena, crying aloud the words, 'I baptize *myself* in the name of the Lord Jesus!' Needless to say, Thecla is saved from the seals by divine intervention, is released, and sets off to find Paul at Myra, dressed, as befits the liberated woman, in a man's cloak. She coolly informs Paul that she is now his equal: 'He who wrought along with thee for the gospel, has wrought in me also for baptism.' Paul, 'greatly wondering', is forced to agree, confirms her in her mission and Thecla goes off to preach in Paul's stead in Iconium, her home town.

In some manuscripts Thecla's story of acceptance by the male world has a rather instructive epilogue. She spends some seventy years living as a hermit in a cave in the deserts of Seleucia. However, she is still much sought after for advice and also for her healing powers, for she has a miraculous gift. Her success infuriates the male physicians of the locality, because she is taking away their trade, so they come to her cave in a body to rape the ninety-year-old virgin, convinced that if she loses her technical virginity she will also lose her miraculous powers. Thecla's position seems hopeless, but with God's help she remains *intacta* to the end. The men find (not surprisingly) that they cannot rape her, so they rush forward to kill her. God miraculously opens up the rock in front of which Thecla is standing and she disappears into it. Her invulnerable virginal body doesn't even have to die and she remains superior to the male world and proof against its hostility to the end.

Advocate of sexual equality in the Church certainly used the story of Thecla to further their cause, for we find Tertullian writing very angrily against those who quote the case of Thecla in support of the ordination of women. The virgin may have been honoured in the Church from the beginning, but she was not allowed to fulfil any male tasks. She was not allowed to preach or to baptize. In the Eastern Church women became deaconesses with pastoral power, but this arose from the social conditions in the Eastern Empire, where women were traditionally segregated from men. Deaconesses could visit women and minister to them more easily than the male priests. In the West, however, where there had never been such seclusion, the virgins had no chance of becoming deaconesses. However, even though the Church would not allow her to do male jobs, the theologians were clear that the virgin became an honorary man. Thus Jerome:

> As long as woman is for birth and children, she is different from man as body is from soul. But when she wishes to serve Christ more than the world, then she will cease to be a woman and will be called man (*vir*). (*Commentary on the Epistle to the Ephesians*, III,5.)

It is interesting that Jerome should compare women with the body. We have seen how he regarded his body as an enemy which had to be starved and brutally put to death, so that the spirit could be free. The body was responsible for the disgusting lust which bubbled forth and produced lewd hallucinations. If a woman could free herself from her sexuality, she became spiritual and masculine. Ambrose is just as clear that in order to be saved a woman has to become a male:

> . . . she who does not believe is a woman and should be designated by the name of her sex, whereas she who believes progresses to perfect manhood, to the measure of the adulthood of Christ. She then dispenses with the name of her sex, the seductiveness of youth, the garrulousnesss of old age. (*Exposition of the Gospel of St Luke*, lib.X, n.161.)

For Ambrose, salvation for a woman means shedding her femaleness and becoming fully human and fully adult, that is becoming male. Leander of Seville makes the real point very clearly:

> . . . a virgin remains a woman and yet knows nothing of the drives and compulsions of her sex. Forgetful of her feminine weakness, she lives in masculine strength; nor has she any need to become a slave to her body which by natural law should be subservient to a man. Happy the virgin who takes her body from Eve but not her punishment. (*Regula Episcopi*, Preface.)

Much modern feminism is equally scornful about 'femininity' and urges a masculine style of dress and behaviour on women. Yet to enforce 'masculinity' (whatever that really means) on women is as artificial as the 'femininity' that the feminists and the early Fathers denounce. It can also be a dangerous solution: Thecla found that her virginity was deeply threatening and constantly resulted in her getting thrown into the arena. Eventually, her mastery of male skills caused the physicians to attempt rape and murder.

The legends of the women virgins frequently show that Christendom admired a mannish woman. We have seen how fascinated Christians were by the classical legend of the Amazons. Certain women saints, like St Martha and St Margaret of Antioch, are envisaged as female versions of St George, slayers of dragons. St Margaret's dragon was Satan himself. She was dedicated to virginity, but unfortunately Olybrius, the Roman prefect, lusted after her and had her thrown into prison when she refused him. There she encountered a much worse foe, because she was tempted by the Devil to abandon her virginity. In the twelfth-century English version of her life in which Satan attacks her first in the form of a horrible dragon and then as a frightening Ethiopian, the ferocity of this saintly virago is gleefully dwelt upon:

> That mild (!) maiden grasped that grisly thing which frightened her in no way and firmly took him by the hideous hair of his head, and hove him up and dusted him adown right to the ground, and set her right foot on his rough neck and began thus to speak, 'Lay off now wicked plague, at least now that you, O deceitful dark devil, afflict me no more, as my virginity has been of little help to thee!'

Certainly virginity could give a woman a truly masculine strength, and even though Olybrius finally had Margaret executed she remains triumphant over the male world in moral strength.

☐ Also now available to us is material to do with the desert *mothers* and other 'holy women'.[7] And when we move away from this early, post-apostolic period, we have to come to terms with a whole series of notable Latin-speaking Christians, such as Tertullian and Augustine, particularly the influence the latter has had at least within the Western Christian tradition. As it happens, the Christian world has recently celebrated the sixteenth centenary of Augustine's conversion and baptism (386–387). Conferences and colloquia have explored his theology yet again and, given the influence of feminism on the present climate of opinion, there have been some perceptive and constructive examinations of his views about women.[8]

Apart from that, Kari Elisabeth Børresen has published a distinguished study entitled *Subordination and Equivalence: The Nature and Role of Women in Augustine and Thomas Aquinas*, trans. C.H. Talbot (Washington, University Press of America, 1981), which connects us through into the study of another great 'master' of the Latin West. Thomas Aquinas was a thirteenth-century Dominican whose intellectual courage enabled him critically to appreciate the newly discovered work of Aristotle as this became available in the West, via the mediation of Arab Muslim philosophers and theologians. The effect of this so far as women were concerned was less than fortunate, it seems.

The following extract is by Genevieve Lloyd, who is engaged in a feminist critique of the entire Western philosophical tradition.[9] One of her basic observations is that our ideals of reason have historically incorporated an exclusion of the feminine, and that femininity itself has been partly constituted through such processes of exclusion. The symbolic antithesis of femaleness and the activity of knowledge was brought into play with Judeo-Christian theology, especially in relation to the interpretation of Genesis 2. Here is at least one reason for the fresh look at that chapter by Phyllis Trible in her *God and the Rhetoric of Sexuality* – to try to read the text without Greek philosophical clutter. As with theology, so philosophy – both contain within them resources for critical reflection. Neither Augustine nor Aquinas are exempt from such reflection, any more than the thinkers of the Enlightenment period, or those of our own day. These two sections from Genevieve Lloyd's critique are, in the case of Augustine, on the theme of spiritual equality and natural subordination, and in the case of Aquinas, on the theme of 'the principle of the human race' and his 'helpmate'.[10]

9 GENEVIEVE LLOYD
Augustine and Aquinas

Augustine

The use of male–female symbolism to express subordination relations between elements of a divided human nature continued in the Christian tradition of biblical exegesis. By the fourth century, Augustine was able to locate his own explication of the Genesis story against the background of a prolific tradition of allegorical interpretations relating to gender difference; his version of the exercise is important and interesting.[1] Earlier synthesis of Genesis with Greek philosophical concepts had, following Philo, tended to associate woman's inferior origins and subordination with her lesser rationality. Augustine strongly opposed such interpretations, seeing them as inconsistent with Christian commitment to spiritual equality, which he provided with content in terms of Greek ideals of Reason. Augustine also opposed any interpretation of the separate creation of woman which would detract from God's serious purpose in creating sexual difference, as if woman's very existence symbolized the Fall. His own interpretation of the sexual symbolism of Genesis is clearly supposed to defend woman against what he perceived as the misogynism of earlier exegesis. But despite this conscious upgrading of female nature, his own interpretations still put women in an ambivalent position with respect to Reason.

Although the existence of the female sex is no corruption, but natural, male–female relations can none the less, Augustine thought, be appropriately taken as symbolizing relations of proper subordination and dominance within human nature; he devotes much attention to finding a content for woman's subordinate position and helpmate role which does not locate her outside sovereign Reason. There is more at stake here than a quaint preoccupation with getting the right interpretation of Genesis.

Within the traditional framework of synthesis of biblical texts and Greek philosophical concepts, Augustine attempted to articulate sexual equality with respect to Reason, while yet finding interpretative content for the Genesis subordination of woman to man. What woman *is* as a rational spirit must, he insists, be distinguished from what she symbolizes in her bodily difference from man. It is this bodily difference that must bear the symbolic weight; and its symbolic role must be articulated without detriment to woman's equality to man in respect of Reason. In the *Confessions*, Augustine tries to meet the challenge by saying that rational man, made in the image and likeness of God, rules over the irrational animals. And just as in man's soul there are two forces – one which 'rules by virtue of the act of deliberation', and another which is 'made subject so that it may obey' – so, also, corporeally, woman was made for man. She had:

> a nature equal in mental capacity of rational intelligence, but made subject, by virtue of the sex of her body, to the male sex in the same way that the appetite for action is made subject, in order to conceive by the rational mind the skill of acting rightly.[2]

In respect of her rational intelligence, woman, like man, is subject to God alone. But her bodily difference from man, and the physical subjection that Augustine seems to see as inseparable from it, symbolically represent a subordination relation between two aspects of Reason. Augustine gives a fuller account of their difference in the *De Trinitate*. Woman's physical subordination to man symbolizes the rightful subordination of the mind's practical functions – its control over temporal things, managing the affairs of life – to its higher function in contemplating eternal things. The Genesis story of a helper for man having to be 'taken from himself and formed into his consort' symbolizes the diversion of Reason into practical affairs.

> Just as in man and woman there is one flesh of two, so the one nature of the mind embraces our intellect and action, or our council and execution, or our reason and reasonable appetite, or whatever more significant terms there may be for expressing them, so that as it was said of these: 'Two in one mind'.[3]

This symbolic association with the lesser, practical function of mind is not at all supposed to mean that woman does not possess that higher contemplative function of Reason in virtue of which human beings are made in the image of God. According to Genesis, 'human nature itself, which is complete in both sexes, has been made in the image of God'. None the less, there is a dimension to this image which is sexually differentiated. Man 'by himself alone' is the image of God, just as fully and completely as when he and the woman are joined together into one. Whereas woman, in so far as she is assigned as a helpmate, can be said to be the image of God only together with her husband. This is Augustine's rendering of Paul's injunction (1 Cor. 11.7,5) that man, as the image and glory of God, ought not to cover his head; whereas the woman, as the glory of the man, ought to have her head covered.[4] It would be inaccurate here to represent Augustine as claiming that it is only in so far as she is considered in relation to man, whose helpmate she is, that woman can be said to be 'made in God's image', whereas man is thus made in his own right. Augustine's point is, rather, that it is only in so far as woman is considered in her 'helpmate' role that she is *not* in God's image. Woman is rightly said to be not made in the image of God, only in so far as she is the symbol of the mind's direction to practical affairs.

There is, again, much more at stake in all this than a zealous concern with the precise interpretation of a biblical injunction. In these passages, Augustine attempted to make a clear separation between claims about female nature and the role of woman as symbol; to combat any suggestion that women are excluded from the 'renewal in Christ', which is for him a reinforcement of that wherein human beings are made in God's image – Reason. This, he insisted, is located in the spirit or mind, 'where there is no sex'. And woman's role as symbol of mind's diversion into the temporal in no way means that she is incapable of the higher, contemplative form of Reason.

> But because she differs from man by her bodily sex, that part of the reason which is turned aside to regulate temporal things, could be properly symbolised by her corporeal veil; so that the image of God does not remain except in that part of the mind of man in which it clings to the contemplation and consideration of the eternal reasons, which, as is evident, not only men but also women possess.[5]

In all this, Augustine displayed much more sensitivity than Philo to the difference between allegory and the actual character traits of men and women. But, despite his good intentions, his own symbolism pulls against his explicit doctrine of sexual equality with respect to the possession of Reason. Against the background of earlier associations between femininity and inferior aspects of human nature, his symbolic relocation of the feminine can be seen as an upgrading. It is, he insists, only in respect of her bodily difference from man that woman is an appropriate symbol of lesser intellectual functioning; and this, in his philosophy, is a comparatively insignificant difference. What really matters is her status as rational mind, where she is equal to man. But from our perspective it can of course be pointed out that mere bodily difference surely makes the female no more appropriate than the male to the symbolic representation of 'lesser' intellectual functions. What is operating here, again, is the conceptual alignment of maleness with superiority, femaleness with inferiority. Despite his professed commitment to spiritual equality, Augustine's symbolism leaves femininity precariously placed in relation to Reason – close to the sensory entanglements with which Reason must contend in its diversion from superior contemplation. And he elaborates this aspect of the symbols in terms of the corruption of the will through its dealing with sense, thus reinforcing older associations between femaleness and weak-mindedness.

For Augustine rational mind by right controls external things; but it can instead be drawn into them in excessive love. This was his version of the Fall; and it remained symbolically associated with woman, although it was now presented as a malfunctioning of Reason itself, rather than the subjection of Reason to an alien, intruding sense-perception. The mind's dealings with temporal things can lead it to 'slip ahead too far' in an 'uncontrolled progress':

> and if its head gives its consent, that is, if that which presides as the masculine part in the watch tower of counsel, does not check and restrain it, then it grows old among its enemies, namely the devils with the prince of devils, who are envious of virtue; and that vision of eternal things is likewise withdrawn from the head itself, which in company with its spouse eats what is forbidden, so that the light of its eyes is not with it.[6]

It is true that the mind's practical diversion, symbolized by woman, is not for Augustine a descent into a realm which is alien to Reason. But this application of Reason has 'appetite' very near to it, and is hence vulnerable to corruption. The capacity to form images of material things is essential to the mind's functioning in the material world. And it can readily bind itself excessively to these with the 'glue of love'.[7] Augustine saw this defiling 'fornication of the phantasy' as a defect of the will. And the surrender of the will in such entanglements remained for him symbolically associated with woman. This is an aspect of a wider symbolic association between women and passion – with the 'carnalization of

the mind' which is the consequence of the will's loss of control. For
Augustine, it is this loss of control which makes bodily lust so
disturbing; for it is out of keeping with the body's rightful
subjection to mind. Such 'contention, fight and altercation' of lust
and will is the consequence of man's original sin of disobedience.
Without it, the 'organ of generation' would have obeyed the will, as
do other bodily organs, sowing seed in 'the field of birth' as the
hand sows seed in the 'field of earth'.[8] Woman, as the object of
male lust, is associated with this distressing subjection of mind to
body.

Augustine replaced the older sexual symbolism in deference to
spiritual equality, but structurally the situation is much the same as
before. It is by resisting being dragged down into the will's
entanglements with 'fornications of phantasy', still associated with
woman, that the soul pursues the life of Reason and virtue. Woman
remains associated with bodily perturbation, in opposition to
Reason. And her 'natural' subordination to man represents rational
control the subjection of flesh to spirit in the right ordering of
things.[9] The life of Reason, Augustine insisted, is open to woman
as the spiritual equal of man. But it remained the case that the
male, in pursuing the life of Reason, need deny only those aspects
of human nature which are already external to his symbolic being.
Woman, despite her status as co-heir of grace, must pursue that
same path burdened by the symbolic force of her subordination to
man, which Augustine saw as natural.

Aquinas

Augustine's utilization of Greek thought drew mainly on Plato. In
the thirteenth century, his own thought – with the Platonic
overtones somewhat played down – occurred, alongside that of
Aristotle, as an 'authority' in the most famous of all the attempted
syntheses of Greek and Christian thought – the *Summa Theologica*
of St Thomas Aquinas. From Aristotle, Aquinas derived a more
integrated view of human nature than was typical of the more
Platonic spirit of Augustine. Augustine had stressed the soul's
unity amidst the diversity of its operations. But an array of
Aristotelian distinctions between 'actualities' and 'potentialities',
'powers' and 'functions', 'subjects' and 'principles', allowed Aquinas a much more precise articulation of this theme. The soul is a
unity, despite its different powers; and the power which is the
mind is a unity, despite its different functions.

Another dimension of the soul's unity in Aquinas's philosophy came from his development of the Aristotelian notion of substantial form as the intelligible principle of a body. The intellectual soul is the form of a living human body. This soul has intellect as one of its powers; but it is also the principle of the lesser, non-intellectual processes involved in being human. In non-rational animals, these sensitive or vegetative processes have as their principle inferior, non-intellectual souls. But the intellectual soul contains 'virtually' within it the less perfect forms, to which are ascribed the less noble, non-intellectual functions of human nature.[10] Being but one thing, the living human being has but one substantial form – the intellectual soul – but that soul is the principle not just of intellect, but also of the lesser functions. This does not mean, however, that it is in all cases their 'subject'. The intellectual soul is the principle of sense, as well as of understanding and will. But only understanding and will are properly said to be *in* it as their subject. Sensation is present not in the soul, but rather in the human composite of soul and body; although it is *by* the intellectual soul that the composite has the power of sense.

With this comparatively sophisticated apparatus for handling the theme of the soul's unity amidst diversity, it is not surprising that Aquinas should have found no use for male–female symbolism as an expression of a division between parts or elements of the soul, or of the intrusions of sense into mind. None the less, his account of human nature yields yet another rendering of the Genesis story of male–female relations.

Aquinas's interpretation of the Genesis story makes use of the concept of *principle* as that from which operations flow – that in which they have their intelligible rationale: 'as God is the principle of the whole universe, so the first man, in likeness to God, was the principle of the whole human race'.[11] And this provides a sense in which man, but not woman, is made in the image of God. Citing Augustine as authority, Aquinas insists that intellectual nature – the image of God in its principal signification – is found in both men and women; it is in the mind, 'wherein there is no sexual distinction.' But in a secondary sense it is found in man, but not in woman, 'for man is the beginning and end of woman; as God is the beginning and end of every creature'. Man was not created for woman, but woman for man.[12]

This secondary sense, in which woman, not being the principle of the race, is not made in God's image, is spelled out by Aquinas in terms of a distinction between human 'vital functioning' as against 'generation'. There is among all animals a vital operation – nobler than generation – to which their life is principally directed. And in the case of man this vital function which provides the direction of life involves something still nobler – intellectual operation. Because human vital functioning, unlike that of the animals, includes this noble intellectual aspect, there is in this case, he thinks, a greater reason for the distinction between vital functioning and generation. For Aquinas, it is this distinction that is symbolized by the Genesis story of the separate creation of woman. The first man symbolizes human vital functioning, including Reason; he is the principle of the race, that in which its nature can be identified. Woman, separately created, symbolizes generation – the perpetuation of that nature summed up in man. It is her role in generation, Aquinas suggests, that makes her man's helpmate. In areas of life other than generation 'man can be more efficiently helped by another man'.[13]

For Aquinas, then, woman does not symbolize an inferior form or lesser presence of rationality. But her meaning is bound up with the reproduction of human nature, in distinction from those operations – including noble intellectual functioning – which define what human nature *is*. Despite Aquinas's insistence that she is 'made in God's image' in respect of the 'rational principle', she is symbolically located outside the actual manifestations of Reason within human life. And despite his insistence that the subordination of woman in Genesis should not be taken as symbolizing her lesser rationality, there are many indications in the *Summa Theologica* that this is not because he believed that women were as rational as men. The inferior and subordinate being of woman does not, as some of Aquinas's opponents would have it, mean that her very existence is to be attributed to the corrupting effects of the Fall, rather than to the original state of creation. But, like Augustine, Aquinas is committed not only to the naturalness of woman's existence, but also to that of her subordination; and he sees it as grounded in the predominance of Reason in the male: 'good order would have been wanting in the human family if some were not governed by others wiser than themselves. So by such a kind of subjection woman is naturally subject to man, because in man, the discretion of reason predominates.'[14]

Aquinas, in a later section of the *Summa Theologica*, cites with approval Aristotle's assertion that women are not properly describable as 'continent', because they are 'vacillating' through being unstable of reason, and are easily led, so that they follow their passions readily.[15] And he groups women with children and imbeciles as unable to give reliable evidence on grounds of a 'defect in reason'.[16] His acceptance of the Aristotelian doctrine of generation means, too, that even in reproduction, of which she is the appropriate symbol, woman plays only an ancillary passive role, and her own generation is defective. The active force in the male seed, he says, echoing Aristotle:

> tends to the production of a perfect likeness in the masculine sex; while the production of woman comes from defect in the active force or from some material indisposition, or even from some external influence; such as that of a south wind, which is moist, as the Philosopher observes.[17]

Aquinas repudiated interpretations of Genesis which treated woman as a symbol of lesser possession or lesser forms of Reason. But her new symbolic location, associated merely with the reproduction of a human nature outside her, serves to reinforce her symbolic exclusion from the actual manifestations of Reason. And the influence of Aristotle in Aquinas's thought gives new strength to the idea of the actual inferiority of female Reason.

These early versions of woman's relations to Reason presented her, in some manner or other, as derivative in relation to a male paradigm of rational excellence – as an addition to and, despite her helpmate role, often as an encumbrance to an essentially male humanity. It should by now be clear that more is at stake in all this than the niceties of biblical exegesis; and more, too, than a succession of surface misogynist attitudes within philosophical thought. The 'male bias', if we can call it that, of past philosophical thought about Reason goes deeper than that. It is not a question simply of the applicability to women of neutrally specified ideals of rationality, but rather of the genderization of the ideals themselves. An exclusion or transcending of the feminine is built into past ideals of Reason as the sovereign human character trait. And correlatively, the content of femininity has been partly formed by such processes of exclusion.

☐ Anyone who wants to pursue different views of women's identity as *women* understood it can now read the work of women from the medieval period too. There are more women whose writing has survived than Dame Julian of Norwich and the much misunderstood Margery Kempe. Caroline Walker Bynum[11] has introduced us to the nuns of

Helfta, and Barbara Newman has published *Sister of Wisdom: St Hildegard's Theology of the Feminine* (Berkeley, University of California, 1987). And with particular reference to the influence of Aristotle on the concept of woman, Prudence Allen RSM has made a critical comparison of Hildegard and Thomas Aquinas's views of women's identity, which establishes the radical differenes between the two within approximately one hundred years.[12] In summary, Thomas argued 'for a two-level theory of sex-identity which can be summarized as sex polarity on the level of nature and sex complementarity on the level of grace. Hildegard, on the other hand, argued fairly consistently for a theory of sex complementarity throughout.' The differences between them can be accounted for by reference to two factors. Hildegard wrote prior to the translations of newly discovered Aristotelian texts. Thomas modifies Aristotelian sex polarity by accepting 'the Christian orientation towards a sex complementarity on the level of grace, that is in the belief in resurrection, and the equal access of women and men to infused wisdom and theological virtue'. The second factor was the radically divergent context in which each lived and wrote. Hildegard lived in the double monastery at Disibode, continually in contact with men, not the least important of whom to her was her secretary, Volmar. She had extensive personal experience of a variety of women through her work as nurse-physician in the hospice associated with the monastery. Aquinas lived and studied only with men, whether in the houses of the Dominican order of which he was a member, or in the University of Paris – from which women were of course excluded – so there was no opportunity to test the texts against the living reality. Prudence Allen concludes, 'The challenge for contemporary philosophy and theology within with Christian context is to work out the dynamic ways in which sex complementarity can flourish.' Something of the sort may be discerned in the medieval period in Eleanor McLaughlin's essay, 'Women, Power and the Pursuit of Holiness in Medieval Christianity', which may point us to new evaluations of the medieval context in which some women flourished.[13]

10 ELEANOR McLAUGHLIN
Women, Power and the Pursuit of Holiness in Medieval Christianity

Recent shifts in the feminist movement and in American religious sensibilities have made attractive a search for models of wholeness and empowerment for women in the vast storehouse of traditional spirituality. We read that some of the many American women who are 'turning East' do so in hope of recovering the woman in themselves and finding theories and disciplines for society.[1] Many are attracted to the mystical as well as the exotic corners of Eastern or heterodox spiritualities, ranging from Zen to witchcraft. One may search for religious meaning in the inner recesses of wild nature, as in Margaret Atwood's *Surfacing*, or choose the cooler quest of God the verb, but it seems intolerably remote to look for meaning and viable models in the lives of the medieval saints with their sturdy piety of obedience and order lived out as virgin brides of Christ. It would appear difficult for contemporary Christian women to find vital models in a culture so alien to our own. Peter Laslett, the demographer, terms that world before modernity, 'The Age We Have Lost'.

An abbess may well have exercised the juridical powers of a bishop, but what woman today usefully aspires to the authority of the feudal *domina* over manors and serfs?[2] If anything, this is the kind of power that the women's movement has gracefully and prophetically criticized. So often medieval women exercised power out of the blood rights of family, clan or queenship which, in their premodern familial and hierarchical contexts, are interesting and admirable but hardly relevant to a post-industrial democracy.[3]

Perhaps even more difficult, because more subtle and fundamental for Christian women, are the ambiguities raised by the apparent characteristics of Christian spirituality implied in the lives of the saints. What does one do today with obedience, passivity, contemplative enclosure as a flight from the world, and the apparent loss of self in the pilgrimage towards dependence on God? There seems little in this traditional Christian view of human nature and God to attract contemporary women or men in search of meaning and personal authenticity.

Then, finally, even if the equivalence of women and men in the vocation to saintliness as pursued especially within the monastic life is granted, there is a suspicion among twentieth-century Christians that the female holy ones were not quite as equal as their brothers.[4] Was not the Queen of Sciences, theology, dominated by the lives and works of Saint Augustine, Saint Gregory I, Saint Anselm, Saint Bernard, Saint Dominic, Saint Bonaventura, Saint Thomas? It would seem that just as medieval businesswomen in the textile trade specialized in embroidery and small cloths,[5] so the female saints exemplified a piety extravagant or sentimental, marred by erotic, amorous imagery,[6] removed from the normative rigour and clarity of the scholastic luminaries. If women today need to recover a history that is instructive beyond the legitimate delight of discovering 'how it was then', must one not look to the corners, the fringes of medieval society, to meet with witches, heretics and the wise old women of the fairy tales? Is this so?

I would like to suggest that the foregoing is at best misleading; that historiography has often badly served the Christian woman who is also a feminist. Hints of an alternative interpretation are already abroad, and Francine du Plessix Gray, in her provocative review of Atwood's *Surfacing*, points in our direction with her title, 'Nature as the Nunnery'. She comments on the 'demise of that monastic ideal that had prevailed in Europe until the Reformation, and had suggested that women's first allegiance is to a divine order, rather than to any patriarchal rule'.[7] I wish to explore here how that empowering prior obedience to God needs to be seen in a context broader and deeper than the historical institution of monasticism with its real, although sometimes ambiguous, space for women. The focus here will be the pursuit of holiness, which was the reason for the existence of those monastic institutions, of anchorholds and Beguinages. I hope to show how the spirituality of the women who were called holy by their friends, their neighbours and the Church was a source of wholeness, meaning, power and authority. The effectiveness of these women was rooted in their holiness. Power out of holiness.

A second theme suggested by the lives and work of some medieval saints, both men and women, is the possibility that the ideal of human nature they exemplified – or their biographers set forth – represents a range of human possibility, a richness of human expression, that has been particularly hospitable to women and to whatever is meant today by the 'feminine'. Dangerous though this suggestion be in its implication of stereotypes, I want to explore the notion that these holy women exemplified a human nature and a vision of divine nature that gave more weight to affectivity, love and the integration of love and intellect, than has been the usual, acceptable or mainstream idea of 'human nature',

as we perceive it, since the seventeenth century. This more
'feminized' human nature was *not* seen as 'feminine' by men and
women of the pre-Reformation Church, but rather as Christian,
typical and in the image of God, who was Mother as well as Father,
love more than intellect. Holiness called forth a Christian theology
and an anthropology radically *less* androcentric than that which
dominates Christian piety today.

Such far-reaching assertions can at this stage be only a tentative
beginning in the exploration of human meaning and possibility as
recorded in the history of our own culture. The living context, local
and political, economic and legal, must eventually be fully
explored. Here we will approach these questions through lives and
stories, limiting our attention to holiness – what it meant, and how
the pursuit of holiness seemed to empower. Is this approach elitist
historiography, even hopelessly romantic? Christians must say no
to the first, for all are called to the wholeness of sainthood. One
thinks of Mary Magdalene, who was a favourite medieval saint, a
model for all Christians: repentant sinner, faithful disciple, joyful
lover of God. A more serious objection is the instinctive sense that
medieval religion, however attractive, speaks a mythic language
and carries a dualist, hierarchical, magical world-view that simply
cannot work for twentieth-century people in any dialogue with
contemporary reality.[8] All of this carries some weight. Yet,
students of language, and of epistemology and religion, are suggesting today that our cultural, psychic and perhaps even physical
salvation requires that we move to that 'second naïveté' which can
be nourished by the wisdom of mythic language and insight in a
world near burned out by the historical/critical method and its
scientific/technological counterparts.[9] In a culture starved by the
language of the machine, image and vision, symbol and sacrament
may once again enlighten and feed. Let us suspend our disbelief,
and listen to the lives of the saints.

Saint Lioba was an Anglo-Saxon nun of good Wessex family, a
scholar, an abbess, a missionary in the wilds of Germany. She
became the spiritual friend and confidente of Saint Boniface,
bishop and Anglo-Saxon missionary to the Germans, who called
her and a number of other women from the abbey at Wimborne to
minister among the heathen of Saxony.[10] Lioba's *Life*, written half
a century after her death in 779, was intended to edify, like all
hagiography, but we can glean from its pages a sense of the
strength and influence available to a woman within the eighth-
century ideal of holiness.

In addition, unintended evidence of the grounds of her effectiveness can be read between the lines of the story itself. Both the ideal and the story, then, are sources for our understanding of how and why a holy woman functioned with power in the forests of eighth-century Germany. The basis of her esteem and power in that primitive, still virtually tribal society was twofold: learning and holiness. The importance of learning for holiness should be noted. The practical, almost administrative character of the sense of obedience and order that permeated the holiness may also be surprising to us, but both characteristics, learning and order, were central to the Benedictine monastic piety she represented.

Rudolf's *Life of Saint Leoba* begins with childhood. We see her mother sending the child, a miraculous birth of her old age, to be trained as a religious at Wimborne, where under Mother Tetta she was taught the sacred sciences. The translator records 'she [Lioba's mother] gave her her freedom'[11] – that is to live for God alone as a nun was to be freed of family under whom all women of that day lived as in bondage, to father, brother or uncle. The way in which the religious life transcended biological bonds is also symbolized by the observation that it was Lioba's wide reputation for learning and holiness that caused Boniface to summon her to work with him in Germany, not his blood relationship to her mother.[12] There is a self-conscious opposition between the bonds of sanctity and family which we will see repeated in later Christian literature. Also explicit is the wholly female context of Lioba's education. Mother Tetta was her intellectual and spiritual mentor, and Tetta herself, we are told, possessed the gift of prophecy as well as scholarship. Lioba also learned from her community of sisters:

> She learned from all and obeyed them all, and by imitating the good qualitities of each one she modeled herself on the continence of one, the cheerfulness of another, copying here a sister's mildness, there a sister's patience. One she tried to equal in attention to prayer, another in devotion to reading.[13]

Spiritual direction emerged out of community life as well as from the gifts of the abbess – and all was at the hands of women.

Boniface placed Lioba as abbess over the women, giving another English religious, Sturm, direction of the men. What Lioba did amid the wilderness, violence and moral chaos of eighth-century Europe is inextricably entangled with who she was – her doing cannot be separated from her being. The reasons for her call to Germany, learning and holiness, were elaborated in that new context, and these virtues were the source and the fruit of her effectiveness. Lioba, we are told, was a skilled classicist.[14] She sent Latin verses to Boniface.[15] She was never without a book to read, excepting only during times of sleep and prayer. She was learned not only in Holy Scripture, but in the works of the Church Fathers, in canon law and in the decisions of all the councils.[16] In the world of the eighth century, such erudition gave her an almost magical authority, and in addition afforded practical power in the vast administrative task of bringing order to the raw new Church of Germany. Learning was no mere decoration, it was what made Lioba an abbess-founder, whose disciples and daughter houses spread like good seed over new-ploughed fields. Her learning, then, was an aspect of her holiness, for it was the very stuff of that good order, that rootedness in faith and tradition, that the biographer finds so worthy in her monastic foundations. This good order was a 'space' for Christian living and prayer, which was at once revolutionary in its resistance to cultural (including male) pressures and in its effectiveness as a missionary strategy in the spreading and deepening of the Christian life among the newly converted Germans. We might say, from our twentieth-century perspective, the calm and order of the cloister was a space for women. We read that Mother Tetta (the sister of a king) was so powerful in her ability to lead her community that no man dared enter her monastery; even bishops were forbidden.[17] Cloister in the eighth-century context meant freedom, not constraint. From a historical perspective, Lioba's ability to create ordered, disciplined communities was perceived as the very core of her sanctity, and as guarantee of the powerfulness of her prayers. In the midst of a terrible destructive storm, the still half-pagan mob rushed to Lioba, an obvious Christ figure, to arouse her from prayer and seek her protection:

> '. . . arise, then, and pray to the Mother of God, your mistress, for us . . .' At these words Lioba rose up from prayer and, as if challenged to a contest, flung off the cloak which she was wearing and boldly opened the doors of the church . . . she made a sign of the cross, opposing to the fury of the storm the name of the High God. . . . Suddenly God came to their aid. The sound of thunder died away, the winds changed direction and dispersed the heavy clouds, the darkness rolled back and the sun shone, bringing calm and peace. Thus did the divine power make manifest the merits of His handmaid. Unexpected peace came to His people and fear was banished.[18]

The miracles attributed to Lioba were often like this one – evidences of her power, her control, her calm equanimity. The holiness to which the miracles gave witness encompassed her learning, her constancy in prayer, her utter confidence in the power of prayer, the discipline and order of her life, her convents, her disciples. This holiness bore fruit in healing, as well as in calming storms, and in producing many vocations to the religious life. She visited the numerous convents, the abbesses whom she had trained, and stimulated the novices to vie with each other in pursuit of that life of perfection she so exemplified. She was venerated by all. 'The princes loved her, the nobles received her, the bishops welcomed her with joy.'[19] She was especially honoured, we are told, by the great Emperor Charlemagne – an honour symbolic for the hagiographer of her leadership and competence as well as her piety. Her advice was sought by the powerful and, 'because of her wide knowledge of Scriptures and her prudence in counsel they often discussed spiritual matters and ecclesiastical discipline with her'. Lioba embodied an ideal of sainthood that included the tools of worldly authority.

Finally, we see in Boniface's esteem witness to Lioba's power and authority. Boniface gave her permission to pray at his monastery at Fulda, 'a privilege never granted to any woman either before or since'[20] – a reminder that holiness and power were as charisms granted to individual women which relieved them, as it were, of the disabilities of their sex. More impressive is the fact that Boniface so respected his co-worker that he wished after his death that she be buried beside him, 'so that they who had served God during this lifetime with equal sincerity and zeal should await together the day of resurrection'.[21] This is nicely symbolic of the equality between men and women that existed among the saints – that is, those moving towards freedom from worldly categories of the socially acceptable, because they belonged to God. The simple monks of Fulda, more bound by social convention than their master, failed to carry out Boniface's instructions, and Lioba was buried at Fulda apart from her colleague. Despite this resistance to Lioba and Boniface's experience of each other as sister and brother, one in Christ, it is significant that the hagiographer left to posterity an image of a woman whose holiness, whose claim to Christian perfection, was set forth in terms quite beyond sexual distinction. We hear of Lioba that 'her deepest concern was the *work* she had set on foot.'[22] Her work was grounded in an amalgam of prayer, rock-like faith, learning, instinct for order and discipline, and energetic dissemination of the monastic vision of radical Christian detachment which was purely and simply the Benedictine ideal. It was a sanctity neither male nor female. It was a sanctity powerful, public, practical, even administrative, and it was a power and holiness to which women were called coequally with men. The society was vaguely aware of the anomaly between the authority accorded Lioba and the usual 'place' for women, but the ideal and expected living embodiment of holiness in their midst provided a place for women beside men (in life as in the tomb) beyond the conventions of social custom. There are, of course, complex sociological reasons why Anglo-Saxon family, political and ecclesiastical structures afforded a place for powerful women,[23] but we are choosing to focus here on the ways in which ideals of sanctity contributed to that space. We turn now to another time and a later date in English history to explore this issue – holiness and power – in the life of another Christian woman.

The *Life of Christina of Markyate* is again a work of edification, written in the latter part of the twelfth century by an anonymous monk of St Albans who must have known Christina well. [24] The *Life* reads with the directness and immediacy of autobiography and is singularly free of the numerous miracles that twentieth-century individuals sometimes find difficult to accept. Christina's story is so powerful, the miraculous seems unnecessary. Her life gives evidence of three ways in which sanctity was empowering for a twelfth-century woman: it enabled her to defy family and social expectations, to challenge the Church and enjoy churchmen's warm support, and to follow with success and esteem a life she chose for herself through which she shaped and affected the lives of the small and the great. As with Lioba, we will be interested to explore the character of that sanctity that seemed so empowering for Christina.

Her story can be briefly told, although losing in condensation the delight and emotional impact of rich detail and sometimes hilarious dialogue. Christina, baptized Theodora about 1096–98, was the daughter of an influential Anglo-Saxon noble family in Huntingdonshire. At age thirteen or so, while visiting St Albans Abbey with her family, she made a vow to be the spouse of Christ and of no other. Firm in her resolution to remain a virgin and live for God only, Christina resisted the intention of her family to see her married, fending off all suitors, especially the young and persistent Burthred. She successfully defied the bishop who was bribed by her father to reverse his initial support and was pressuring Christina to relent. Finally, after some adventurous confrontations with Burthred and his friends, Christina escaped the family to take up hiding first with an anchoress, then more permanently with Roger, a hermit. Though Roger served initially as her spiritual director, the two of them grew into a maturity of spiritual friendship where each furthered the other in that pilgrimage towards God which was their common calling. Christina's fame as a holy woman and director of souls spread beyond England to the Continent. She became the particular spiritual friend and director of Geoffrey, abbot of St Albans. The final years of her life were peaceful, combining a personal intimacy with God with a public ministry as director of souls and shaper of Christian life and practice far beyond the confines of the still point of her anchorhold.

Three aspects of this story throw special light on the relationship between holiness and power: Christina's resistance to family, society and Church out of her sense of commitment to Christ; Christina's relationship with men in the context of her chosen vocation; and the character of that holiness that afforded her strength.

First, we need to appreciate the obvious and conscious rebellion against family and society supported by Christina's decision to belong to Jesus Christ alone. How symbolic is the fact that one of Christina's first acts after her decision was to discard her baptism/family-bestowed name, to call herself Christina, belonging to Christ.[25] She named herself and chose her own vocation in the teeth of fierce resistance. Her family put her under virtual house arrest when she refused to consummate the marriage she had been forced into through unrelenting pressures. She was isolated from any 'religious God-fearing man' and forbidden access to the chapel.[26] Her parents let Burthred into her bedroom to take her while asleep, but by 'providential intervention' she was found dressed and awake, and she engaged the young man in a long theological discussion of the chaste marriage of Cecilia and Valerian.[27] When again her room was invaded by Burthred and his drunken friends, she was emboldened in prayer to escape ingeniously by hanging from her fingertips between the wall and the bed curtains. At stake was the boy Burthred's virility '. . . they joined together in calling him a spineless and useless fellow, . . . warned him not to lose his manliness . . . all he had to mind was to act the man.'[28] She resisted also the argument of her family's honour and her father's and mother's power and fury. At the onset of the campaign, in a conversation between the family and the prior of St Mary's Huntingdon, these issues were made clear as her father complained:

> . . . let her marry in the Lord and take away our reproach. Why must she depart from tradition? Why should she bring this dishonour on her

father? Her life of poverty will bring the whole of the nobility into disrepute. Let her do now what we wish and she can have all that we possess.[29]

The prior Fredebert supported her father with traditional defences of Christian marriage and assurances that mothers as well as virgins are saved, quoting heavily from Scripture in favour of the family and society's will for Christina. Encouraged, the father, Autti, and his noble friends went to the Bishop of Lincoln, expecting that he 'would immediately order the betrothed woman to submit to the authority of her husband'.[30] Autti was furious when the Bishop recognized both the priority of her vow to Christ and the unacceptability of the forced nature of the betrothal. The Church insisted in canon law that a marriage was invalid unless the free consent of both parties was obtained. Again, the father angrily announced the real issues in his outburst:

> Well, we have peace today, you are even made mistress over me: the bishop has praised you to the skies and declared that you are freer than ever. So come and go as I do, and have your own life as you please. But don't expect any comfort or help from me.[31]

The Bishop, bribed by Autti's money and threatened by his family's wide influence in the country then turned against Christina and tried with abundant Scripture quotes to force her submission. Christina, certain of her vocation and her vow, defeated the Bishop in the ensuing contest of prooftexting. Nor did the Church abandon her entirely; it was with the help of the priest Sueno, who was persuaded by her visions, that Christina made a dramatic escape from her family's house. The angry determination of her family to treat their daughter as nothing more than marriageable property is brutally apparent in the mother's reported sentiments: 'In the end she swore that she would not care who deflowered her daughter provided that some way of deflowering her could be found.'[32]

Supported by prayer and her total obedience to Christ, whom she loved as a spouse through all this, Christina finally fled, disguised as a boy. She is reported to have told herself to 'put on manly courage and mount the horse like a man'.[33] She found refuge in a safe though miserably uncomfortably hermitage, first with the anchoress Alfwen and then with the hermit Roger, with whom she remained until his death. She then took his place in the hermitage, having been absolved from her marriage, and made her vows as a religious to the abbot of St Albans and before the Bishop of Lincoln.

If the first part of Christina's life is a story of ultimately successful resistance against great odds to familial and male authority of father, betrothed and bishop, what of this new stage in her vocation as a spouse of Christ? Did she merely exchange her father and husband for submission to Roger and to the abbot of St Albans? I think it possible to say such was not the case. To an extraordinary degree, Christina's relationship with Roger, her spiritual director and mentor, became one of mutuality in a common pilgrimage:

> Furthermore, through their dwelling together and encouraging each other to strive after higher things their holy affections grew day by day like a large flame springing from two brands joined together. The more fervently they yearned to contemplate the beauty of the creator the more happily they reign with Him in supreme glory. And so their great progress induced them to dwell together.[34]

Their common 'Holy Desire' for Christ bound them together in a mutuality of spiritual friendship which witnessed to an equality, a oneness in Christ, in which there was neither male nor female. Such a spiritual friendship was described by another twelfth-century English religious, the Cistercian Aelred of Rievaulx, as that bond which exists between two equals in the presence of and commitment to a third, Jesus.[35] I believe it possible to say that Christina and Roger could have been the personae of Aelred's Christian Ciceronian dialogue on friendship as well as the two male religious of whom he wrote so gracefully.

Even more persuasive of this interpretation is the record of Christina's friendship with Abbot Geoffrey of St Albans, an intimacy that the hagiographer reports occasioned some malicious gossip during their lifetime. Christina here was the dominant figure, for the abbot, a worldly, powerful feudal ecclesiastic, was converted under her influence. Geoffrey grew under her tutelage into a serious Christian. We read he 'became so changed a man from what he once was'.[36] The account of his gradually deepened piety is so free of the supernatural, so human and straightforward in the telling, the reader is hard pressed to throw it out as hagiographical exaggeration. Geoffrey came to admire and love Christina. 'He had deep respect for the maiden and saw in her something divine and extraordinary.'[37] In fact, the mutuality of this spiritual friendship sometimes moved the newly converted abbot to an open dependence on Christina, whom he consulted in every act or political decision of importance. She was under obedience to his office as abbot, he was under obedience to her grace as a spiritual friend, powerful in prayer, clairvoyant in insight. 'And he had to admit that the virgin's pure heart had more power with God than the factious and shrewd cunning of the great ones of this world.'[38]

The mutuality of their love was sealed in the prayer by which Christina expressed her care for Geoffrey, whom she called her 'beloved', confident that Jesus held them both.

> . . . she was rapt in ectasy and saw herself in the presence of her savior; and she saw him whom she loved above all others, encircled with her arms and held closely to her breast. And whilst she feared that since a man is stronger than a woman, he would free himself from her grasp, she saw Jesus, the helper of the saved, closing her hands with his own loving hand, not by intertwining her fingers with His, but by joining them one over the other; so that by joining her hands no less than by the power of her arms she should feel greater strength in holding her friend back. She gave effusive thanks with joy both because she knew that her friend was relieved of trouble and also because she was aware of the presence of her spouse and Lord.[39]

This vision sets forth in great clarity the basis of Christina's power. Her spirituality was rooted in an affective experience of belonging to Christ, a radical belonging and desiring symbolized by the nuptial imagery – she was the spouse of Christ. Against this bond the gates of hell, her father, Autti, and Burthred and the bishop could not prevail.

Christina's holiness was grounded first in this unsparing obedience to the vision of her life in Christ. Her vocation, her vow to Christ, prevailed over every man, obstacle, misery or doubt. 'My one desire, as thou knowest, is to please thee alone and to be united to thee for all time without End.'[40] The erotic imagery, spouse of Christ, perfectly expressed the 'Holy Desire', the love that lay at the centre of her piety and kept her safe. God speaks: 'the key of your heart is in my safekeeping and I keep guard over your mind and the rest of your body. No one can enter except by my permission.'[41] The freedom Christina enjoyed to name herself, to resist father, husband, bishop, flowed out of an obedience to God which was a *love affair*. She abandoned the world for this love affair with God, and was in return girded against anything the world could inflict. Intimately involved in her life with Christ was a ready acceptance of the way of the cross; suffering was expected, and it was not simply transcended but was used to enable her to become the more loving person that being a spouse of Christ implied. 'All who wish to travel to Jerusalem must carry this cross.'[42] The external difficulties were met by Christina with constant prayer, a placing of herself in the loving presence of God. In that mode of prayerfulness, Christina was visited and encouraged and directed constantly by a 'Presence of Love' in visions or dreams, some of which have been cited here.[43] It is interesting to note that the most frequent mediator of God to Christina was the Virgin Mother. Christina was comforted and instructed by the divine in female form far more often than by a direct encounter with her spouse, Jesus. And at a crucial time of sexual temptation Jesus came to her and was held by her, not as a male lover, but as a child taken to the breast of its mother – in this case Christina.[44] I would like to suggest that the spousal imagery, the prominence of the Virgin Mary in Christina's visions, and the virginity that freed her from male control make a unity with the great importance given to human spiritual friendship in Christina's troubled but ultimately triumphant realization of her vocation. The unity was love – and her strength was love. To be a virgin and spouse of Christ symbolized the enhancing, freeing, empowering love and touch of God in her life which gave her strength to stand victoriously against all who opposed her. It was a love, a friendship with God, full of affective, even erotic power in which she moved beyond all self-doubt or fear or internalized sense of female incapacity to name herself, to be herself, and to be recognized as a person of authority and power in the world beyond her cell.

The life of Saint Catherine of Siena (1347–80) presents to us a story very different from those of Lioba and Christina, but the three share important similarities in their consciousness of a common source of strength. Catherine also exemplified a particular kind of vocation to holiness that is especially attractive today. In her self-conscious combination of the active and contemplative life, she found God's will in action. Though the stillness of prayer, ascetical discipline, and contemplation were ever the starting point, a vigorous reform politics was the way in which the life of prayer shaped her will. I will outline in the briefest way her life and work and then ask again how the special character of her holiness issued forth in power and effectiveness for herself and her world.

Born Catherine Benincasa, the youngest of twenty-five children of a Sienese dyer, she was reported to have experienced visions of Christ at an early age, vowed herself to a life of virginity at seven, and thereafter resisted the pressure of her family to marry.[45] Catherine finally prevailed, and for the first three years of her formal religious vocation she lived as a Dominican Tertiary, a recluse or anchoress, in her own room, within that home with its numerous brothers and sisters. External peace was never Catherine's lot. After this period of seclusion and contemplation, she experienced a mystical marriage with Christ and was called back to a life of service and ministration within her own household and to the needy and sick of the city. Her gradual emergence into a life of intense reform activity, was associated wth a growing reputation for mystical gifts, ecstasies and visions. Catherine was surrounded by a group of disciples, her *famiglia*, as her reputation for sanctity and ecstatic prayer spread. In the mid 1370s she embarked on a public effort to return Pope Gregory XI from the Avignonese exile to Rome, seeing this effort as a necessity for the larger task of the reform of the Church. At the same time she became heavily involved in diplomatic negotiations between the city of Florence and its implacable enemy the Pope, believing that the universal Christian brotherhood of all people could be effected only through obedience to the Church and its head. We cannot follow here the details of Catherine's work as ambassador, negotiator, reformer, gadfly, all of which she carried on with great personal presence and through a voluminous correspondence which is fortunately preserved. The letters are wondrously revealing of her wit and sarcasm, the depth and practical wisdom of her life with God and her great ability to discern and speak to the particular strengths and weaknesses of her correspondents. The letters are a welcome addition to her confessor's *Life*, which was written primarily as an instrument for her beatification.[46]

Catherine's influence was a crucial factor in Gregory's return to Rome, but the victory was short-lived. Following Gregory's death and the confusing, disputed election of Urban VI, the Church was confronted with the chaotic claims of two popes, as the French cardinals, offended by Urban's immoderate or impolitic efforts towards reform, elected as pope a Frenchman, Clement VII, and declared Urban's election invalid. The last years of Catherine's life were spent in hapless attempts to rally support for the weak and often unworthy Urban. Through letters and personal persuasion, she attempted to realize her vision of a united humanity bound together by Christian love and justice under the leadership of the Church. Externally these efforts failed as the schism deepened its political ties. Catherine understood the source of this chaos to be sin, and, taking this sin upon herself, she died following a paralytic stroke. In that last turbulent year, she wrote her *Dialogue* on the spiritual life and successfully quelled a Roman revolt against Urban. During her final days she experienced a vision of the ship of the Church, its burden descending on her shoulders. She died, surrounded by her disciples, on 30 April 1380, giving herself in expiation for the sins of the Church.[47]

Catherine was a powerful and effective woman by anyone's standards. She dominated Pope Gregory and, to a lesser extent, Urban VI. She was held in highest regard in Florence and was widely recognized as a saint during her lifetime. The people of Rome witnessed her hours of ecstatic prayer in St Peter's. She shared their poverty; they knew of her role in bringing the head of the Church back to Rome. We read that as her body lay in state at Santa Maria Sopra Minerva, there were those among the vast crowds who found themselves cured of their ills.[48]

What was the foundation of this energy and power in Catherine's life? The historian must say something other than the hagiographer who points to God met in prayer. Catherine seems first of all to have been a personality of charismatic force; her presence was irresistible. The Florentine businessmen who did not share her enthusiastic trust of Gregory could not say no to her peace proposals in her presence. They had to avoid her and treat by letter. This personal power can be explored from the perspective of her spirituality. Catherine was truly selfless in her capacity to identify in genuine humility with the sinner. She persuaded the Pope to share in her sense of sin by walking to the Vatican through the streets of Rome barefoot, an act of papal penitence never done before or repeated since. She was at the same time inflamed by a passionate vision of goodness, of the Church reformed, of the righteousness of God's will, an irresistible passion for the salvation of those persons she addressed. Her hatred for sin was combined with a love for the sinner which apparently moved many to seek their better selves and act accordingly. 'If you are what you ought to be, you will set all Italy on fire,' she wrote to a religious confraternity to move them to the support of Urban VI.[49]

Suffering and awareness of sin were part of this persuasiveness. She gave great importance to an identification with the suffering of Christ and was drawn to a Christ-like vocation to take the sins of the world or those of the person before her on to her own shoulders. This embracing of the cross of suffering is a clue to the power of her persuasion. She shared all with those she urged on.

> Fear and serve God, with no regard to thyself, and then do not care for what people may say, except to have compassion on them . . . if it shall

be for His honor and thy salvation, He will send thee means and the way when thou art thinking nothing about it, in a way that thou wouldst never have imagined. Let Him alone, and lose thyself; and beware that thou lose thee nowhere but on the Cross, and there thou shalt find thyself most perfectly.[50]

Her ideal, her vision of holiness, her holy desire for God was a gift of contemplation which forced her and all who heard her into action for love of neighbour and reform of the Church. To a group of hermits whom she sought to bring to Rome to encourage Urban towards reform, she wrote:

Cursed are ye, the lukewarm! Would you had at least been ice-cold! This lukewarmness proceeds from ingratitude, which comes from a faint light that does not let us see the agonizing and utter love of Christ crucified, and the infinite benefits received from Him. For in truth, did we see them, our heart would burn with the flame of love, and we should be *famished for time*, using it with great zeal for the honor of God and the salvation of souls. To this zeal I summon thee, dear son, that now we begin to work anew.[51]

This movement from the love of God, stirred up by contemplation of God's love for humanity in the crucified Christ, into that zeal of being 'famished for time' to honour God and save souls is a key to Catherine's activism, as it is also to the Puritan's zeal of three centuries later!

Inseparable from the love that issued in action, the love that embraced the cross, was obedience. Catherine's obedience was like that of Lioba and Christina – a radical, world-ignoring attachment to Jesus and God's will for her. Out of that obedience was forged a reformer of unshakeable purpose. She spoke of obedience to vocation to one of her young followers: 'Resist no longer the Holy Spirit that is calling thee – for it will be hard for thee to kick against Him. Do not let thyself be withheld by thine own lukewarm heart, or by a womanish tenderness for thyself, but be a man, and enter the battlefield manfully.'[52]

Obedience was often associated with this militant sense of doing God's battle which she knew herself called to take up. She was a general, urging forth armies. Catherine's obedience was also very concrete. The very visible and sinful Church and its priests and popes were the symbols for her of God's presence in the world. She was obedient to the Church. But she insisted that pope and Church be worthy of obedience, and by the very stubborn loyalty of her attachment called churchmen from the inside, as it were, to be the pastors their office signified.

> Alas, alas, sweetest 'Babbo' mine, pardon my presumption in what I have said to you and am saying; I am constrained by the Sweet Primal Truth to say it. His will, father, is this, and thus demands of you. It demands that you execute justice on the abundance of many iniquities committed by those who are fed and pastured in the garden of Holy Church; declaring that brutes should not be fed with the food of men. Since He has given you authority and you have assumed it, you should use your virtue and power; and if you are not willing to use it, it would be better for you to resign what you have assumed; more honor to God and health to your soul would it be.[53]

Her obedience to Urban VI enabled her to insist that he exercise his authority as one who feeds, and who sees to it that the Church becomes the Mother she is called to be rather than a rapacious robber. Catherine's obedience to the Church seemed to be bound up with her image of the Church as mother and nurturer. The Fathers of the Church are to be mothers whose principal role is to feed the faithful.[54] Hers was no servile obedience to hierarchy, but rather an obedience to the presence of God in the world in the sacramentality of the Church. And if Gregory XI was unwilling to fill out that office of good shepherd, resign or be damned, wrote Catherine. Such an obedience was a powerful instrument for change.

Another source of Catherine's strength was that peculiarly medieval marriage of passion and reason, mysticism and scholasticism that she so pre-eminently lived out: 'Love follows the intellect, and the more it knows, the more can it love. Thus the one feeds the other, and, with this light, they both arrive at the Eternal vision of Me, when they see and taste Me.' [55] The effectiveness of her political fervour was greatly enhanced by the strength and relentlessness of her mind. She brooked no nonsense.

> The second and last way is that we ought to recognize the truth about our neighbor, whether he be great or humble, subject or lord. That is, when we see that men are doing some deed in which we might invite our neighbor to join, we ought to perceive whether it is grounded in truth or not, and what foundation he has who is impelled to do this deed. He who does not do this acts as one mad and blind, who follows a blind guide, grounded in falsehood, and shows that he has no truth in himself, and therefore seeks not the truth.[56]

The love and the anger and the often violent urging were never disconnected from analysis.

Finally, as between love and reason, medieval spirituality chose the way of Holy Desire, and in this passion lies the bond between holiness and power. Constantly on her lips was the wonder at God's love shown to humankind in the passion of Christ, which image in turn aroused in those who beheld it a love of God and neighbour which could move the world. 'I beg you by that love of that precious Blood shed with such fiery love for you, that you give refreshment to my soul, which seeks your salvation,' Catherine wrote to a recalcitrant queen, and she expected a positive action in response to her letter.[57] Catherine loved in a god-like way, with a powerful desire which bound and carried sin and pain: 'But I wish to bind myself to bear you before God with tears and continual prayer, and to bear with you your penitence.'[58] Her love therefore continually created relationships – it fed, nourished, forgave, and in this was maternal. It was also violent, militant, relentless. One of her favourite words of action was 'manfully', *virilemente*. Catherine's love that moved cities and popes was expressed in metaphors both male and female. It was nurturing and judging: 'I tenderly love your salvation . . . wait not for this rod; for it will be hard for you to kick against divine justice.'[59]

Desire was her power, for God, for God's will on earth, for the salvation of individual souls, for the purifying of the Church. Everywhere the relationships that were formed out of this holy desire cemented the human basis for political authority. The love caught in mystical ecstasy was transformed into springs for action in every arena of life. And so she understood her power to lie in that meeting with God in prayer when, says Christ, in the *Dialogue* of souls, 'they are another myself, inasmuch as they have lost and denied their own will, and are clothed with Mine and are united to Mine, are conformed to Mine.'[60]

Catherine of Siena is a singular example of the mystic reformer theologian who moved with power through medieval society by virtue of her sainthood. She referred to feminine weakness and identified virility with goodly and godly action, yet did not seem to perceive herself as suffering from the disability of 'feminine vacillation' or softness. It appears that Catherine could use the theological and social stereotypes of female weakness without being personally touched, for she was among those whom 'the Highest God Eternal . . . has placed in the battlefield as knights, to fight for His Bride (the Church) with the shield of holiest faith'.[61] Yet this is the same woman who writes of humility as 'the foster mother and nurse of charity, and with the same milk she feeds the virtue of obedience'.[62] She wrote also of Christ as 'man's foster mother enduring, with the greatness and strength of the Deity united with your nature, the bitter medicine of the painful death of the Cross to give life to you little ones debilitated by guilt'.[63] The very mixture of the images for God and human nature point to a consciousness which embraced a fullness of possibility beyond the limitations of social or linguistic stereotype. Catherine's relationship to her womanhood was transformed by that loss of ego-self which was the prerequisite of the wholeness that was holiness. It is difficult, if not impossible, for us to judge the wholeness, especially in view of the violent ascetical assaults on her body that were part of her early religious practice – although never advised for others! Yet we can see in the vigorous activity of her life, as in that of Lioba and Christina, evidence of the personal integration and effectiveness that made all these women powerful and public figures.

The stories stand for themseves, their message is in the telling. Yet we can make some generalizations about the stories and their context which may permit that power and that holiness to be more readily appropriated today.

A first observation is that God's lovers, the saints, of the pre-modern Church exhibitied a high degree of personal integration or wholeness in areas of human experience which in every age all too easily fall into conflict. Not every model of medieval sainthood illustrates this integrity, but many do, and our three women reveal that wholeness. They demonstrated an ideal of Christian perfection which united contemplation and action, learning and piety, preserved individual gifts in the context of obedience to community, embraced common sinfulness in the joy of experienced forgiveness, and held together the realities of a God transcendent and immanent, all-might and all-love, father and mother. This mystery of contained paradox resisted even the deeply held opposites of body and soul, for that metaphysical dualism was tempered in a sacramental understanding of self and cosmos, microcosm and macrocosm. The material universe of the world before modern science was never merely body stuff, but rather mysteriously a vehicle for participation in the holy. Sainthood or holiness was a pilgrimage towards God which supported a human nature of paradoxical and mysterious wholeness, paradoxical for us especially because it was an integration sought within the confines of celibacy. Christian women like Lioba, Christina and Catherine through this ideal of sanctity moved beyond the limitations of biology and social convention, especially as these touched their womanhood, to an uncommon integration of act and vision, reason and love, obedience and self-affirmation. Their wholeness as human beings burns through every page of the record in the power and effectiveness of their personal and public lives.

If love was the driving force of holiness for these women, discipline and obedience were the forms in which that love was trained. In each of these lives we see a conjunction of highly personal experiences of God and the saints in dream, vision, in vow and contemplative prayer, with *obedience*, a disciplined following after that experience or vision. The obedience to God and the mediators of God's will, often female – Mary or other female saints – was the firm rock on which they stood for personal vocation against every familial and social, even ecclesiastical pressure to conform. Obedience was the form of holiness and power for these women. It was an obedience and a listening, self-imposed, which gave an inner sureness of direction and supplied an intellectual and moral clarity so charactistic of the Benedictine spirit that shaped much of medieval piety.

This obedience was also very concrete and incarnational, for their listening was to God whose body was the Church. Christina's or Catherine's obedience to God through the Church was a powerful and personal support which, when necessary, could be turned against churchmen as well as family. Bishop Grossetest of Canterbury witnessed to this paradox of the revolutionary power of obedience when he wrote in the thirteenth century to Pope Innocent IV condemning a shameful appointment: 'Because of the obedience by which I am bound to the Holy See, as to my parents, and out of my love of my union with the Holy See in the body of Christ . . . as an obedient son, I disobey, I contradict, I rebel.'[64] This obedience carried a powerful potential for reform and was the opposite of passive submission. Catherine set before churchmen an ideal of Christ's body, pure and holy, a vision that judged the historical reality. Her obedience to that vision of what office ought to be was a powerful fulcrum for change and a bulwark of personal integrity and autonomy over against Church and world.

It is important for Christian women today to observe the power of obedience to which churchwomen witnessed in contrast to the fate of women who found their place within the medieval heresies. The historical evidence is overwhelming that Waldensian and Albigensian women played some leadeship roles in those groups, teaching and preaching in the early years. After a century or so of the groups' existence, women disappeared almost wholly from the leadership as these 'sectarian' groups developed a clerical hierarchy which mirrored the male clerical order of the Church and of feudalism. Unlike the Church, the 'sects' retained no special vocation of holiness, sainthood or monastic community within their groupings to which women and men could be called equally. The *perfectae* disappeared as the *perfecti* became more like bishops than religious.[65] Before the sixteenth century, it was in the Church, not in sects, that women found the most enduring and powerful roles. Rebellion in the context of obedience, the vocation of the saint, provided more space for women than did sectarian protest.

Finally, I must hazard to suggest that the powerfulness of sanctity in women's lives had something to do with the peculiarly medieval apprehension of the holy. Medieval people wrote of their encounter with the holy in varieties of symbols reflecting a broader range of human experience than is the case within the mainstream of Christian expression today. Their language of prayer was less androcentric, more balanced between 'male' and 'female' metaphor and symbol for God and the holy, than is the case in the West since the seventeenth century. The realm of the holy in medieval spirituality was populated with female figures: the saints; the Queen of Saints, Mary; and even God himself was 'as really our Mother as He is our Father'.[66] There is not space here to document the great importance of female saints in the pre-Reformation Church beyond the mention of the obvious and not yet fully understood role of the Virgin Mother,[67] or, for example, the popularity among all Christians of devotion to that model of Christian penitence, love and ecstatic vision, Mary Magdalene.[68] My purpose in alluding here to this aspect of medieval piety (not forgetting the contrasting androcentrism, even misogyny, of the theological tradition) is to suggest strongly that the historical phenomenon of powerful and effective women is related to this context of worship and popular devotion. Jesus was experienced and sometimes addressed as a nurturing, caring mother and mediated his will most frequently through his mother; Christians were saved in the womb of God's body, the Church, nourished at her breasts, fed and led by bishops and abbots whom Saint John Chrysostom and Saint Bernard bade to be mothers as well as fathers.[69] The scholars can with legitimacy point out that the mother-namings of Jesus or the bishops were not 'mainstream', yet the existence of this current of female metaphor and naming was part of a total realm of the sacral which was heavily coloured by an affective spirituality which twentieth-century Christians often apprehend as female or feminine. Obedience was balanced by nurturance, imagery of battle was accompanied by imagery of birth, labour and growth, and God's transcendence was contained within the immanence of sacramentality and the mystical union.

This affective spirituality was not, at least until the later Middle Ages, perceived as especially a woman's piety.[70] The sense of the motherhood of God and the Church seems to have patristic roots, and it became more prominent in the emergence of devotion ot the human, suffering Jesus at the hand of the medieval 'Fathers', Saint Anselm, Saint Bernard and other Cisterican authors of the twelfth century. The flowering of Marian devotion and the widely popular cults of Saint Mary Magdalene, Saint Margaret, and Saint Brigid of Sweden served and were cultivated by men and women with like fervour. It is too early to be able to demonstrate with the rigour of modern historical method and canons of causality the relationship between the empowerment of medieval holy women and this affective piety and its associated peopling of heaven, including the Godhead, with female figures and metaphors. This is a thesis that requires our most serious attention, especially in view of the general loss of the affective and female God-language in Christian spirituality since the seventeenth century and the Enlightenment.

The dominance of love over reason, love rather than *sola fides*, in medieval piety was accompanied by a world view which was deeply sacramental, incarnational and even materialistic in character. This religious world view hallowed rather than overcame nature, was associated with a strongly immanent or mystical experience of God which expressed itself in images of growth, nurture and feeding, and love, erotic and filial. Such a piety seems to have fostered the existence of powerful and stubbornly obedient women who served as models of human excellence and divine will. Theirs was, to use Catherine's words, a religion of holy desire. The integration of mind and affect implied in this piety was opposed by theological and ascetical dualism, but never so defeated as has been the case since faith overshadowed love, and reason broke away from desire, in the centuries since the seventeenth. Of course family histories and economic, ecclesiastical and social structures play significant, even determining roles in the privatization of women and the loss of female sacral power. Yet it may still be possible for us today, seeking to discover meaning at the centre of the self and the cosmos, to quicken the imagination and enrich our symbolic vocabulary by listening once more to the stories and the vision which lie readily at hand within the Western Christian tradition shaped by powerful, holy women such as Dame Julian of Norwich, who wrote:

> . . . and the Second Person of the Trinity is Mother of this basic nature, providing the substance in which we are rooted and grounded.

But he is our Mother also in mercy, since he has taken our sensual nature upon himself. Thus 'our Mother' describes the different ways in which he works, ways which are separate to us, but held together in him. In our Mother, Christ, we grow; and develop; in his mercy he reforms and restores us; through his passion, death, and resurrection, he has united us to his being. So does our Mother work in mercy for all his children who respond to him and obey him.[71]

☐ I hope that the material so far included in Part Two has pointed up some of the good and the bad in the developing tradition, and shows us how very problematic it is simply to appeal to the past for authority in an uncritical way, to provide warrant for present-day practices and beliefs. Equally, it seems mistaken to suppose that we have nothing to learn from Christian experience very different from our own, despite the problems the past can cause us unless we learn the skills of evaluating it and acting appropriately for our own time. We now need to shift to the Reformation and post-Reformation period, leading up to an important essay by Rosemary Radford Ruether, which will pull a lot of threads together from Part One, on the biblical tradition, as well as the other essays so far. At least some aspects of what went on in the Reformation period could well be described as having to do with the re-exploration of the sex complementarity mentioned above.

Some of the best introductions to the importance of Luther for the discussion of the relationship between Christianity and feminism are produced by Jean Bethke Elshtain.[14] In one of her essays, 'Luther *Sic* – Luther *Non!*', she writes constructively on Luther on the family and the 'woman in the home'. In Luther, she says:

We find a powerful insistence on conjugal equality, though man and wife have different authoritative status since men were heads of households. Men and women are bound by the same set of moral rules and each has available a life of simple piety, each can know 'the freedom of the Christian'. The social relations of everyday life gained a new sanctity, no longer construed as second best to lives of the ecclesiastical orders. The 'natural desire of sex' is compatible with mutual respect and is granted new legitimacy.

Elsewhere she quotes Luther's defence of the goodness of sexual desire, which led him to comment on Crotus who:

> wrote blasphemously about the marriage of priests, declaring that the most holy bishop of Mainz was irritated by no annoyance more than by the stinking, putrid, private parts of women. That godless knave, forgetful of his mother and sister, dares to blaspheme God's creature through whom he was himself born. It would be tolerable if he were to find fault with the behaviour of women, but to defile their creation and nature is most godless. As if I were to ridicule a man's face on account of his nose! For the nose is the latrine of man's head and stands above his mouth.[15]

Hardly the most helpful analogy – but the general point stands. Jean Bethke Elshtain also writes that an enrichment in intimate life, 'including more open expression of familial love and devotion, is attributable in part to the revolution in sensibility Luther helped to inaugurate'. As a political philosopher she is paying special attention to Luther's understanding of authority, and of course, the institution he aimed to strip of all authority was, as she says, construed in gendered terms as female, specifically as a mother, *mater ecclesia*, and so, 'This is the institutional moment of Luther's masculinization of theology.' Despite his (and other Reformers') devotion to Mary the mother of Jesus, he explicitly diminishes the symbolism associated with her, which had at least existed, although in tension, with the symbolism of women as responsible for mankind's downfall. Unfortunately, the 'masculinization' of theology did not free women from limiting ideals, but 'invited the loss of a female-linked transcendent moment', the fading of 'the female-as-metaphor', as politically charged symbol and emotional repository of human hopes.

I have therefore included here an essay that illustrates this last point cited from Jean Bethke Elshtain, and also the devastating consequences of belittling the Mary, sister of Martha, who chose to devote herself to learning Christ's teaching. Before reading the essay it is perhaps worth recalling the incident from Luke 10.38–42. It follows on from the parable of the good Samaritan, the man who proved neighbour to the man who fell among robbers. The evangelist tells us how Jesus had set his face towards Jerusalem, and gives us an account of this curious and difficult encounter between Jesus, Martha and Mary. Jesus travels with his disciples, and Luke has him provided with a good back-up team – very necessary if he and his disciples are not to go around half-starved, scavenging raw grain from the edges of fields. Luke gives us the names of some of that team – Mary of Magdala, and Joanna, wife of one of Herod's stewards. They, with others, follow Jesus, look after him, learn from him, and are to stay as close as they dare when he ends up in the Roman equivalent of death row. They stay near during the horror of his crucifixion, and finally, they take care of his dead and mutilated body. All this is still on the horizon, but in the incident recounted by Luke, some women are acting fairly unconventionally, in not merely supporting him, but actually travelling with him. Martha and Mary are one pair of friends who do not travel, but provide care and rest for him and the others, as and when they can. Luke does not tell us where the house was, but it was probably Bethany, about two miles outside Jerusalem.

A householder like Martha goes out of her way to make such travellers comfortable, and can manifestly cope perfectly well, though perhaps sometimes feels unappreciated, as at this point. She is upset in any case because her sister Mary is behaving in an 'unfeminine' way. The description of Mary sounds harmless enough, but the phrase 'to sit at someone's feet' means that Mary was learning from Jesus, listening to him, even asking him questions, the way a disciple learns from a rabbi. It was not completely unknown for a woman to learn from a rabbi, but it was very unusual, and no doubt Martha will not let it happen in her house if she can help it. Obviously, it was no good talking to Mary about it, so Martha bursts in on the conversation, hoping to get Jesus on her side, and so put a stop to it. Jesus, however, is part of her problem.

Jesus could be said to be thoroughly appreciative of what Martha and women like her do for him; in fact, Martha is the sort of woman he would tell parables about, for instance, in the parable of the woman who turns her house inside out to find her lost coin. And in Proverbs 31.27 there is a perfect description of a Martha, praising her: 'She looks well to the ways of her household/And does not eat the bread of idleness.' Just before *that* praise are found the words, 'She opens her mouth with wisdom/And the teaching of kindness is on her tongue.' Martha and Mary need to learn from someone prepared to talk to them about wisdom and kindness if they are to become the sort of people Psalm 119.32 represented as saying, 'I will run the way of thy commandments when thou hast set my heart at liberty.' Mary has seen the point, one could say, and Martha may have done so too, and here is the main reason for her anxiety. She may know already that when Jesus finds people like Mary who are eager to listen, that he puts before them the claims of the divine reign, putting those claims even above those of his own family. Luke tells us that Jesus blesses first those who hear the word of God and keep it. Martha may well be right to be anxious, if Mary is likely to turn into the kind of person who wants to extract herself from home, and care about beaten-up strangers left half dead by the roadside.

Merry Wiesner's essay is about the Martha/Mary contrast.[16]

‖ MERRY WIESNER
Luther and Women:
The Death of Two Marys

God has created men with broad chests and shoulders, not broad hips, so that men can men understand wisdom. But the place where the filth flows out is small. With women it's the other way around. That's why they have lots of filth and little wisdom.[1]

Women are created for no other purpose than to serve men and be their helpers. If women grow weary or even die while bearing children, that doesn't harm anything. Let them bear children to death; they are created for that.[2]

There is nothing better on earth than a woman's love.[3]

Oh how passionately I yearned for my family as I lay at death's door in Schmalkald. I thought I would never see my wife and little children again. How much pain that distance and separation caused me! Since by God's grace I have recovered, I now love my dear wife and children all the more.[4]

From just these four statements, one can easily understand the tremendous variation in assessments of Luther's opinion of women. His champions, from the sixteenth century to the present, have seen his attack on celibacy and stress on the positive side of marriage as rescuing women from the depths of scholastic misogyny and denigration.[5] In the words of William Lazareth:

> The union of Martin and Katie was not cursed with the birth of the Anti-Christ. Instead it was blessed by God with the birth of the Protestant parsonage and the rebirth of a genuinely Christian ethos in home and community. Luther's marriage remains to this day the central evangelical symbol of the Reformation's liberation and transformation of Christian daily life.[6]

Elizabeth Ahme agrees:

> Luther's appraisal of women was basically determined through the realization that she was also created by God and saved through Christ. With this Luther overcame all obstacles that stood in the way of fulfillment as a woman, and opened the way for a happy acceptance and affirmation of the role which God had given her.[7]

Luther's acceptance of male dominance and belittling of female ability is seen as simply a continuation of classical, biblical, patristic, scholastic, and humanist misogyny, a tradition that even Luther couldn't break.

Those who emphasize Luther's negative views also range over centuries, from Counter-Reformation biographers to contemporary feminist observers. Sigmund Baronowski in 1913 cautiously noted:

> His judgment of women is not exactly as ideal as some would have us believe . . . We hear nothing from Luther about the personal worth and dignity of women . . . The brutal openness with which he thrusts women into the natural 'law' of sexual life, the shocking ruthlessness with which he portrays the burning and sinful lusts of consecrated virgins, not out of his own experience but with alleged Biblical proof – all of this degraded female honor and dignity much more than simple vulgar satires did.[8]

Martha Behrens, sixty years later, was much more harsh:

> His remarks indicate a basic, almost pagan and mythological fear of woman and her power . . . Idealized by Luther, marriage was a masculine institution calling for complete self-abnegation by woman either as mother, wife or daughter. Rather than freeing her from the medieval ideal of celibacy, this idea chained her to a restrictive ideal of servitude. Moreover, Luther's teaching that God was pleased by this servitude served to spiritualize or hallow these biological roles, causing resistance against development in other areas.[9]

As usual with any area of Reformation scholarship, there are also those who take a middle view, pointing out the continuity between Luther's ideas and those of his predecessors, both humanist and scholastic. John Yost notes:

> The Renaissance humanists, civic and Christian alike, emphasized marriage and family life as the best means for all social relations . . . God had established marriage and family life as the best means for providing spiritual and moral discipline in this world . . . In this way, civic and Christian humanists enable us to see more clearly the larger context for the revolutionary change in domestic life brought about by the Protestant reformers.[10]

Kathleen Davies also finds more continuity than change in pre- and post-Reformation attitudes towards married life as reflected in English sermons, pamphlets and conduct books.[11]

Thus the range of opinions on Luther's ideas about the position of women, and the impact of those ideas, is very broad. There is ammmunition enough in his writings to support any position. Rather than simply adding my own interpretation of *what* Luther said, I want instead to retreat from that battlefield somewhat and explore *how* he said what he did. In other words, what kind of language, images and metaphors did he use when speaking to and about women? How does he use the female and the feminine?

One of the most important contributions of feminism to all disciplines has been to make us aware of just this point – that *how* we say things, the implicit and sub- or unconscious message which comes through our choice of words, may be as or even more important than what we are actually saying. There is no such thing as 'just semantics'. Language is power. Language is both a reification of power relationships in any society, and a way of exerting power over others. It rises out of social, political and intellectual structures, and then in turn affects those structures. And no one recognized this more clearly than Luther. He chose his words, images and illusions carefully, because they would evoke a certain response.

Though the two are related, I think it will be useful if we make a distinction between the female and the feminine in Luther's writings. By female, I mean his descriptions and discussions of actual women or 'woman' in the abstract. By feminine I mean his use of imagery, particularly when referring to God or Christ or the Church, which stresses qualities which were then, and are still, felt to be more 'feminine' than 'masculine' – gentleness, nurturing, undemanding love, submissiveness and so on.

The female image that occurs most often in Luther's writings is his ideal, the wife and mother:

> What better and more useful thing can be taught in the church than the example of a godly mother of the household who prays, sighs, cries out, gives thanks, rules the house, performs the functions of sex and desires offspring with the greatest chastity, grace and godliness: What more should she do?[12]

The word that Luther uses again and again in his descriptions of this ideal woman is *natural*. It is natural for people to want to marry and have children, it is natural for women to be subject to the authority of men, it is natural for women to experience pain and even death in childbirth, and so on. What is 'natural' for Luther comes both from what he views basic human nature to be, and from the order he feels God imposed on the world. Women's subjection to men is inherent in their very being and was present from creation – in this Luther essentially agrees with Aristotle and the classical tradition:

> The man has been given so much dominion over the woman, that she must name herself according to him. For that reason, a woman adopts her husband's names and not vice versa. This has happened because of God's gracious will so that she stays under her husband's rule, because she is too weak to rule herself.[13]

This subjection was made more brutal and harsh, however, because of Eve's responsibility for the Fall – in this Luther agrees with patristic tradition,[14] though he repeatedly admonishes husbands to rule their wives reasonably and gently: 'The woman is a weak vessel and tool, and must be used carefully as you use other tools.'[15] Wives were to accept this rule unquestioningly no matter how severe, even from husbands who were not Christians.[16] Luther realized this might be difficult or unpleasant. 'Women are generally disinclined to put up with this burden and they naturally seek to gain what they have lost through sin.'[17] Challenging this was a sin, however:

> But if a woman forsakes her office and assumes authority over her husband, she is no longer doing her own work, for which she was created, but a work that comes from her own fault and from evil. For God did not create this sex for ruling, and therefore they never rule successfully.[18]

Obedience had replaced chastity as women's prime virtue:

> It is the highest, most valuable treasure that a woman can have to be subject to a man and certain that her works are pleasing to him. What

could be happier for her? Therefore if she wants to be a Christian wife, she should think: I won't mind what kind of husband I have, whether he is a heathen or a Jew, pious or evil. I will think instead that God has put me in marriage and I will be subject and obedient to my husband. For all of her works are golden when she is obedient.[19]

Marriage and motherhood, instead of virginity, was now a woman's highest calling, as Luther repeats over and over again. God has established marriage in the Garden of Eden, which made marriage the only institution present before the Fall, the 'order' on which all other 'orders' – the economic, the political, etc. – were based.[20] While Luther acknowledges that some women, because of physical ailments or a shortage of men, might be forced to act 'unnaturally', and not marry, in no case should a woman choose to do so.[21] Men choosing to remain celibate were going against their natural sexual drive, but Luther does allow that the ability to remain truly celibate, though rare, could be a gift from God. Women choosing to remain celibate, however, were not only fighting their natural sex drive, which Luther and everyone else in the sixteenth century felt to be much stronger than men's, but also the divinely imposed order which made woman subject to man. For Luther it was inconceivable that a woman would choose not to marry. He says at one point, when advising people how to console women in childbirth: 'Say, yes, dear lady, if you were not a wife, you would certainly wish to become one, so that you could do God's will by suffering and perhaps dying through these delicious pains.'[22] Marriage and motherhood was the only way for women to fulfil their God-given function.

Even a woman as prominent and respected as Margaretha Blarer, the sister of Ambrosius, was suspect because of her decision not to marry. Martin Bucer accused her of being 'masterless', to which she answered, 'Those who have Christ for a master are not masterless.' Her brother defended her decision by pointing out that she was very close to his family, and took care of the poor and plague victims; he compliments her by calling her 'Archdeaconess of our church'. Even Ambrosius limited his sister's role somewhat, however, for when Bucer encouraged her to learn Greek, he answered, 'I ask you not to encourage her, for she already pays too much attention to Latin. You know the ingenuity of women. They need to be reined in more than spurred on, so that they don't throw themselves into learning and neglect their more appropriate and worthy tasks.'[23] Even a woman who chose to remain unmarried was to be limited to appropriate, 'natural' female activities.[24]

Luther's supporters point to his idealization of the wife and mother as the best evidence for his positive view of women. The wife and mother was finally awarded her due place, and her labours in support of her husband and children appreciated. If we look more closely at some of the metaphors Luther uses to describe her, however, the view is not such a positive one:

> The woman is like a nail, driven into the wall . . . She sits at home. The pagans have depicted Venus as seated on a seashell for just as the snail carries its house with it, so the wife should stay at home and look after the affairs of the household.[25]

> She enjoys staying home, enjoys being in the kitchen . . . does not enjoy going out . . . does not enjoy speaking to others.[26]

How was she to best serve God? Yes, certainly by faith and prayer, but primarily by obedience to her husband and carrying out her normal household tasks without complaint:

> When a woman is in the kitchen or when she is making a straw bed, this is an everyday thing. This does not bother the Holy Spirit. . . . A wife is appointed for things that are very ordinary in the judgment of the flesh but nevertheless extremely precious in the eyes of God.[27]

For Luther, the ideal woman in the home is Martha, seeing to the preparation of food and overseeing the servants, not Mary, trying to understand Christ's teachings better. He belittles his own wife's efforts to understand or learn: 'There is no dress that suits a woman as badly as trying to become wise.'[28]

This ideal bothered at least one woman. Katherina Zell, the wife of Matthias Zell and a tireless worker for the Reformation in Strasbourg, worried that she was too caught up 'with the cares and service of Martha'. Luckily for Katherina, 'My dear husband has given me place and time, and always encourages me to read, listen, pray or study, allowed this day or night, yes, it gave him great joy, even when it led to neglect of his needs or harm to his household.'[29] Luther could perhaps have learned something from Zell on this point.

Women other than the ideal wife and mother appear occasionally in Luther's writings, but are usually depicted in a negative or belittling manner. Eve, of course, is given the harshest treatment:

> The rule by women has brought about nothing good from the beginning of the world. When God set Adam up as Lord over all creatures, everything was good and right, and everything ruled for the best. But the woman came and also wanted to have her hand in things

and be wise; then everything collapsed and became a complete disorder. We've got you women to thank for that.[30]

Women have inherited from Eve their tendency to believe lies and nonsense.[31]

This is certainly nothing new, for many writers since Jerome had laid the responsibility for the Fall on Eve alone, but Luther's de-emphasis of the role of Mary weakened one side of the standard best woman/worst woman dichotomy, and thus stressed the negative side of all women's 'nature'.

The female saints and martyrs also receive somewhat ambiguous treatment. Luther felt that celibacy was so difficult to maintain, that only their early deaths had sent them to heaven still virgins:

> God has not allowed many virgins to live long, but hurried them out of this world, as with Cecilia, Hagne, Lucia, Agatha and so on. He knows how precious their treasure (virginity) is and how difficult it is to maintain very long.[32]

Luther's opinion of the character and piety of most nuns and sisters is even harsher, as his scathing depictions of life in the convent point out.

Other than female religious and biblical characters, prostitutes are the only kind of unmarried women that Luther refers to frequently. Most German cities, including Wittenberg, tolerated – and even licensed and taxed – some prostitution, provided women were discrete and lived either in city brothels or in certain quarters of the city. Luther saw prostitution as an abomination, and preached and spoke fervently against it, not because it was degrading and harmful to the women involved – though there are occasional cases of women in the sixteenth century even sold into prostitution to pay back their father's debts – but because the women corrupted and enticed his students. He describes them regularly as 'Stinking, syphilitic, scabby, seedy and nasty. Such a whore can poison 10, 20, 30, 100 children of good people, and is therefore to be considered a murderer, worse than a poisoner.'[33] They were the tools of the Devil, who had sent them to Wittenberg to bewitch his students. The power to bewitch men was not only held by prostitutes, however:

> All women know the art to catch and hold a man by crying, lying and persuasion, turning his head and perverting him . . . it is often more difficult for him to withstand such enticements than to resist his own lust.[34]

All women, therefore, share the qualities of a prostitute to some degree.

Luther also uses the image of the whore symbolically. As Donald Kelly notes, 'Feminine epithets (next to scatology) were among the commonest forms of abuse. The equation of simony with prostitution made Rome a "whore" to Luther and the Sorbonne the "Pope's whoring chamber".'[35] 'The devil's whore' is Luther's favourite epithet for human reason:

> Usury, drunkenness, adultery and murder can all be detected and understood by the world as sinful. But when the devil's bride, reason, the petty prostitute, enters into the picture and wishes to be clever, what she says is accepted at once as if she were the voice of the Holy Ghost . . . She is surely the Devil's chief whore.[36]

By extension, all women who attempt to act reasonably may also be seen as whores of the Devil.

Unmarried women in the abstract are almost never considered in his writings. When they are, it is as a problem to be dealt with, and Luther's solution is that which many cities adopted in the sixteenth-century – requiring them to live with a family, forbidding them to live on their own or with each other. They would thus fall under the 'natural' control of a male head of household.

This emphasis on marriage not only as the only ideal for women, but as their only natural vocation may have contributed to feelings of hostility towards unmarried women. This came at a time when the sex ratio in Europe was changing in favour of women, which meant fewer women could find a mate with whom to carry out their 'natural' inclinations even if they wanted to. How much this contributed to witchcraft accusations, which were usually first directed at just such women, is difficult to say, but it certainly is a factor to be considered, as Erik Midelfort has pointed out.[37] Ian MacLean also noted recently, 'The prosecution of widows or single women as witches may be due to an unspoken fear of abandoning the traditional view of woman as a person married or destined for marriage.'[38]

Gerald Strauss has stressed the class bias in Luther's message, that it was 'pitched to the solid burger'. I would also emphasize its sexual bias. As Strauss comments, it did not appeal to the 'great multitude of men and *women*' (my emphasis).[39] Unmarried women certainly found little in Luther's message which was directed to them, and may have stayed with or gone back to their old, less formal beliefs and practices in which they did have a place, such as soothsaying and witchcraft.

Thus the image of the female which emerges from Luther's works is an ambiguous one. Yes, she was created by God, and yes she could be saved through faith. Marriage was an order blessed by God, and a proper theatre for exhibiting Christian virtues. But as we have seen, the words used to describe even the woman who lived up to the ideal are hardly complimentary ones – a weak vessel, a nail, a tortoise – and those used to describe women who do not follow the ideal even harsher – burning with lust, stinking, tools of the Devil, and so on. These are no harsher than those used by medieval theologians, but in Luther they are not balanced by praise of the Virgin. As has been often pointed out, the cult of Mary may have been detrimental to women's actual position, as it set up an ideal to which no normal woman could hope to attain, but it did describe at least one woman in totally positive terms. Luther does refer to Mary occasionally when defending women against satirists and vulgar writers – as in his answer to the author of 'The Stinking and Putrid Female Bodily Parts' – but even in this he weakens his praise by going on to say, 'One should just as easily accuse and hate the nose, as it is the latrine of the head.'[40]

Mary was a symbol of women's chief reason for being – motherhood – 'Even Christ himself wanted to be called the seed of a woman, not the seed of a man', but this, too, was qualified:

> Yet how great would the pride of the men have been if God had willed that Christ should be brought forth by a man. But this glory has been completely taken from the men and assigned to the women (who are nevertheless subject to the rule of the men) so that the men should not become vainglorious but be humble.[41]

Even the best woman was simply God's tool to teach men a lesson.

Along with a transformation and lessening in the role of Mary and a reduction of the female ideal from heavenly to housebound, one also finds a de-emphasis on what might be termed the feminine qualities of God the Christ.

Luther does use some maternal and nurturing images to describe Christ, particularly that of the brood-hen and her chicks: 'Look at the hen and her chickens and you will see Christ and yourself painted and depicted better than any painter could picture them.'[42] He also uses some emotional and ecstatic images to describe the believer's experience of faith, especially in the Magnificat: 'All the senses floating in God's love . . . saturated by divine sweetness.'[43]

The overwhelming image of both God and the believer in Luther's writings is a masculine one, however. True faith is energetic, active, steadfast, mighty, industrious, powerful – all archetypally masculine qualities in the sixteenth (or the twentieth) century.[44] God is Father, Son, Sovereign, King, Lord, Victor, Begetter, 'the slayer of sin and devourer of death' – all aggressive, martial and totally male images.[45] With the home now the centre of women's religious vocation, even the imagery of the Church becomes masculine, or at least paternal and fraternal. Instead of 'The Bride of Christ', we now have a brotherhood of believers, honouring divine paternity with the Lord's Supper. It was a supper, an *Abendmahl*, a domestic image, but no mother served the meal, not even 'Holy Mother Church'.

The late medieval period had been one rich in feminine images of God – Jesus our Mother who bears, comforts, revives, consoles, feeds and nurtures us. Not only Mary, but God as well offered unquestioning, accepting, 'feminine' love. St Anselm of Canterbury, Marguerite of Oingt, Julian of Norwich and numerous others use phrases like 'our tender Mother Jesus (who) feeds us with his blessed breast', or 'You on the bed of the Cross . . . gave birth in a single day to the whole world', or 'By your gentleness the badly frightened are comforted'.[46]

As Caroline Bynum has recently pointed out, these feminine images of God not only made the Divine appear to feel more personal and imminent, but also allowed women to feel more Christ-like.[47] Female mystics, anchoresses, nuns or other holy women exemplified affectivity and love, that is, the 'feminized' parts of God, and could gain authority and power through this. Their mystical union with or direct experience of 'Jesus our Mother', 'which was sometimes expressed in visions of themselves as priests, enabled them to serve as counsellors, mediators, and channels to the sacraments – roles which the 13th century Church in some ways increasingly denied to women and the laity'.[48] 'The God of medieval piety was a Mother/Father, Sister/Brother, Lover/Child, a God of demanding *and* accepting love, a God who is born within each one of us and who bears us into life as a travailing mother.'[49] Women could thus not only identify with and emulate Mary, but could directly identify with the feminine side of God.

For Luther and most other Protestant theologians, this was impossible. God and Christ were male and transcendent, not androgynous and immanent. As Caroline Bynum notes:

> I would say that we can see Luther, and much of Calvin and some of Catholic Reformation theology as an attempt to recover the sense of God's glory that was characteristic of the early Middle Ages, i.e., as a reaction against the emotional piety of the late Middle Ages that made

God human and comforting and accessible to those in all walks of life, but thereby undercut in some sense man's ability to believe that salvation was done for him by a power infinitely other than himself.[50]

It was through that emotional piety, however, that some late medieval women had forged a link to God which gave them authority and power as acceptable as that provided by the priestly office. 'Their spirituality sometimes even suggests that the combination of mystical authorization and a peculiarly female freedom from the power of office is a superior role (to the priestly role that theologians denied them).'[51]

Protestants also denied women a priestly role, and by stressing God's glory and power, archetypally male qualities, rather than God's accessibility and nurturing, made it more difficult for women to identify with God. 'One woman's proclamation that she was a female "Christ" was denounced as a "horrible thing" by the Protestants as much for its sexual impropriety as for its theological presumption.'[52] Christ was no longer 'Our Mother', so women could not be Christs for sexual as well as spiritual reasons.

Thus Luther established Martha, the obedient wife serving God through daily household tasks, as the ideal woman, belittling both Mary her sister who chose to devote herself to learning Christ's teaching, and Mary the Virgin Mother of Christ, who had almost become a female God in much late medieval Marian piety. By downplaying the feminine qualities of God and using paternal or fraternal imagery in describing the Church, he also placed religion clearly within the male sphere. The domestic, female realm was private, affective, immanent; the worldly, male realm, which included not only politics and education, but also religion, was public, rational and transcendent.

Luther was, of course, not the first or only one to differentiate sharply between male and female realms, to feel that woman's subjection to man was 'natural'. The Renaissance humanists had clearly felt this.[53] As Joan Kelley points out, women could never hope to achieve the Renaissance ideal of 'man', whereas they could achieve the medieval ideal of sanctity.[54]

On the level of popular opinion the matter may perhaps be summed up by saying that in the private world women represented the positive virtues of adornment, service and moral strength; in the public world they posed at best a threat to order and at worst a deformation of nature. In most ways, then the key to sixteenth-century social, religious and political structure – and change – was the principle of male domination.[55]

Luther added his voice, then, to widely accepted notions of the proper role of women, but the strength of that voice and the power of his language gave contemporaries and followers new ammunition. His metaphors and imagery were repeated for centuries; his words became Protestant dogma on the subject. Women themselves have made various attempts to combat this, to reclaim the 'nurturing values in their religious heritage', from seventeenth-century pietists to the nineteenth-century women Ann Douglas describes in *The Feminization of American Culture*, to twentieth-century feminist theologians trying to go 'Beyond God the Father'.[56] So far, however, Luther's language has prevailed. Woman has become wife, the two Marys have been replaced by Martha. Luther did sanctify marriage – in this one may agree with his defenders – but by that sanctification feminized and domesticated women.

As Ian MacLean concluded, 'Marriage is an immovable obstacle to any improvement in the theoretical or real status of women in law, in theology, in moral and political philosophy.'[57] A woman fulfils her only God-given and natural function through marriage, but always remains, in Karl Barth's words, 'B, and therefore behind and subordinate to man'.[58] Barth is, of course, simply putting Luther in twentieth-century terms. The image is the same.

☐ Those interested in pursuing the theme of the Reformers' discussion of women should read Jane Dempsey Douglass on 'Women and the Continental Reformation', in *Religion and Sexism*, and also her book *Women, Freedom and Calvin* (Philadelphia, Westminster, 1985), in which she concludes that 'Calvin's persistent teaching that the silence of women in church is a matter of time-bound apostolic advice rather than divine law for all time is an example of his openness to major change in the future' (p.121). Karl Barth's struggle with the tradition is also worth reading.[17] As Clifford Green assesses it, the sequence male-female, initiative-following, simply will not do, no matter how many qualifications Barth (or any other theologian or bishop offers):

How can one possibly say that in all matters affecting the relationship of, say, a husband and wife – sexual life, careers and professional activity, faith and church life, physical and psychological health, social life, family economics, child rearing, concern for parents, education, artistic sensibility, political responsibility – *he* is to lead and *she* is to follow? Initiatives and responses should come from *both* partners, depending on their particular gifts, temperaments, previous experience, and sensitivities.[18]

Like others, Barth compromises Christian freedom by assigning 'leading' and 'following' along sexual lines.

Since I have now referred to one element of a twentieth-century theologian's struggle to evaluate the Christian tradition, we need to move to an essay by Rosemary Radford Ruether which, as I said some pages ago, should help us to pull some threads together from Parts One and Two. Before reading this essay, I think it is important to acknowledge the exceptionally important place Rosemary Radford Ruether occupies in the whole movement of feminist theology.

I said of her earlier that she read an important paper at the same time as did Mary Daly at the American Academy of Religion in 1971. She has now been responsible for the production of some twenty-two books, which she has either single or co-authored or edited, and at least 500 articles. Of all the most notable feminist theologians, she has addressed herself to the widest range of 'areas of contradiction', to employ the terminology of Mary Tardiff OP who is studying her theological method.[19] Rosemary Radford Ruether has written on the question of Christian credibility, with particular attention to ecclesiology and its engagement with Church–world conflicts; on Jewish–Christian relations ('anti-Semitism is the left hand of Christology'); on politics and religion in America; as well as in feminism and feminist theology. Feminist issues are integral to all areas of her work, however, and 'sample' essays on each area may, as it were, be found in her *To Change the World: Christology and Cultural Criticism* (London, SCM, 1981) with the essay, 'Christology and Feminism: Can a Male Saviour Save Women?' developed in Chapter 5 of *Sexism and God-Talk: Towards Feminist Theology* (London, SCM, 1983).

A reading of *In Memory of Her* reveals the differences between her and Elisabeth Schüssler Fiorenza, but they have in common that both are prepared to struggle for the future of the Christian tradition. Rosemary Radford Ruether explicitly advocates as a norm 'both self and other-identified men and women in a mutual discipleship of equals', using liberating historical prototypes translated out of and recontextualized in the present and the future. For her, Jesus proclaims an iconoclastic reversal of the system of religious status: 'The last shall be first and the first last', that is, the *kenosis* of patriarchy, discarding hierachical caste privilege. The redeemer is one who can be encountered even in 'the form of our sister', as, for instance, in the case of those who saw the martyrdom of Blandina, but without the violence to one another that image of the imitation of Christ has helped to perpetuate, and believing that 'Divine Grace keeps faith with us when we have broken faith with her.' There are ways of making women's speech and presence normative, as we can learn from the history of radical Protestant women, especially those of the Quaker tradition. Christine Trevett has now edited a collection of writings by Quakers beginning with the 1666 pamphlet by Margaret Fell which gives the collection its title, *Women's Speaking Justified: and Other Seventeenth-Century Quaker Writings about Women* (London, Quaker Home Service, 1989).[20]

Rosemary Radford Ruether's *Women-Church: Theology and Practice of Feminist Liturgical Communities* (San Francisco, Harper & Row, 1985) includes not only possible liturgies for women responding to the failure of Christian institutions to meet their needs, but two valuable introductory sections that summarize her enterprise as a feminist theologian.[21] She is reaching forward to a symbolic universe which can 'heal the splits between "masculine and feminine", between mind and body, between males and females as gender groups, between society and nature, and between races and classes' (p. 3). She works, one could say, to do something about the intolerable disjunction between talk of redemptive community and actual lived experience. One aspect of 'church' for today is women-church, which means the particular historical movement and organization today which is sensitive to one such disjunction, not fogetting the 'idea and reality of the *ecclesia* of women throughout history indicated by the term women-church' (p. 293, n. 4). Her language is that of 'liberation Christianity', which is not peculiar to Roman Catholicism, but which seeks active, committed believers in a covenanted community, dissolving the clerical/lay distinction, and the dualism of sacred/secular. It works from a creation-based theology, trusting that this is rooted in and renewed in authentic relation to God and others.

She is thoroughly and splendidly subversive. To begin with, she flatly denies that institutional churches have a monopoly on truth, salvation and grace. So, on the one hand, women have an ambivalent relation to existing institutions, symbols, texts and traditions, such that 'attendance at their founts poisons our souls'. On the other hand, women need communities of nurture – hence her collection of the work of others supplying those communities. The institution, *any* institution, is simply the occasion and context in which grace and spirit may be dispensed, as to the whole human community. Baptism, then, has to do not with the rejection of one's natural life but with redemptive human relationality. The Eucharist is about mutual empowerment; rites of penance and forgiveness are concerned with admitting fault and becoming reconciled, and need thorough disentangling from control of human sexuality. What is at stake here is to recover the sense of 'original blessing', the recognition of our true selves, 'something with which we are already gifted, not something we have to strive to achieve' (p. 87). She writes with great perception about authentic leadership functions and skills to enable others, pointing out, too, that liturgical roles are the easiest to rotate, needing no special skills, and stripped of pretensions that the liturgical president possesses a special power to create redemptive life and mediate it to others.

Her essay on 'The Liberation of Christology from Patriarchy'[22] must therefore be central to her position, and has been deliberately chosen to focus attention on the sort of theological shift we need to make.

12 ROSEMARY RADFORD RUETHER
The Liberation of Christology from Patriarchy

The doctrine of Christ should be the most comprehensive way that Christians express their belief in redemption from all sin and evil in human life, the doctrine that embraces the authentic humanity and fulfilled hopes of all persons. The theological categories adopted by early Christianity to define the doctrine of Christ – early Christology, in other words – would seem to be inclusive of women. And yet, of all Christian doctrine, it has been the doctrine of Christ that has been most frequently used to exclude women from full participation in the Christian Church. How is this possible?

Early Christianity used the word 'logos' to define that presence of God which has become incarnate in Jesus Christ. This term drew on a long tradition of religious philosophy. In Greek and Hellenistic Jewish philosophy, the divine Logos was the means by which the transcendent God came forth in the beginning to create the world. The Logos was simultaneously the immanence of God and the ground of creation. Through the Logos God created the world, guided it, was revealed to it and reconciled the world to God.

The Logos was particularly related to the rational principle in each human soul. By linking the term Christ, the Messiah, through which God redeemed the world, to the Logos, early Christianity prevented a split between creation and redemption threatened by early gnosticism. The God revealed in Christ was the same God who created the world in the beginning, the authentic ground of creation manifest in fulfilled form over against the alienation of creation from its true being. The term Logos as the divine identity for Christ should have been a term that pointed all humans to the foundations of their true humanity.[1]

Yet the Greek and Hellenistic Jewish tradition was shaped in a patriarchal culture which gave the terms Logos and Christ an androcentric bias. Since rationality was presumed by these patriarchal cultures to be normatively male, all the theological reference points for defining Christ were defined androcentrically. Essential humanity, the image of God in humanity and the Logos of God were interrelated in androcentric definitions. These definitions re-enforced the assumption that God was male and that Christ must therefore be male in order to reveal the male God.

Although Christianity has never said that God was literally a male, it has assumed that God represents pre-eminently the qualities of rationality and sovereignty. Since men are presumed to have these qualities and women not to have them, the male metaphor has been seen as appropriate for God, while female metaphors have been regarded as inappropriate. The Logos or Word which reveals the 'Father' therefore also has been presumed to be properly imaged as a male. The title 'Son of God', an inadequate metaphor for divine immanence, imagined as something like a parent begetting an offspring, has also been taken literally and seen as further indication that the Logos is male. These notions of the maleness of God, in turn, affected the Christian interpretaton of the *imago dei*.

Genesis 1.27–28 says, 'So God created man in his own image; in the image of God he created him; male and female he created them.' This passage leaves open the possibility that the term man (Adam) is to be understood generically and that Genesis 1.27b teaches that this image of God is possessed equally by both sexes (which would also mean that women share in the sovereignty of 'man' over the earth referred to in Genesis 1.26).[2] But practically the whole patristic and medieval tradition rejected the possibility that women were equally theomorphic. It split the concept of *imago dei* from gender difference. This might also suggest that the *imago dei* was asexual or spiritual and therefore was neither male nor female. Gregory of Nyssa reads the text this way.[3] But most of the Church Fathers concluded that it was the male who possessed the image of God normatively, whereas women in themselves did not possess the image of God, but rather were the image of the body, or the lower creation, which man was given to rule over.[4]

This view is found in Augustine's treatise on the Trinity where he says:

> How then did the apostle tell us that the man is the image of God and therefore he is forbidden to cover his head, but that the woman is not so, and therefore she is commanded to cover hers? Unless forsooth according to that which I have said already, when I was treating of the nature of the human mind, that the woman, together with her own husband, is the image of God, so that the whole substance may be one image, but when she is referred to separately in her quality as a helpmeet, which regards the woman alone, then she is not the image of God, but as regards the man alone, he is the image of God as fully and completely as when the woman too is joined with him in one.[5]

Augustine and other Church Fathers never denied that women had a redeemable soul. But, neverthelesss, they believed that the female in her specific femaleness, psychic and bodily, was the opposite of the divine. So they concluded that the woman was not theomorphic; in other words, she could not image God. This idea was carried further in the scholastic appropriation of Aristotelian biology. This biology (which we know today to be false) asserted that the male alone provided the seed or genetic form of the child, while the female provided only the material substratum which was formed. Since the seed from the father is male, a fully formed offspring would also be male. Females are the result of a defect in gestation by which the maternal matter is not fully formed, and so a female, or 'defective' male, is produced who is inferior in body, intelligence and in moral self-control.[6]

The female is defined by medieval theologians (such as Thomas Aquinas) who use this Aristotelian tradition, as a non-normative human who does not possess human nature fully. The male is the 'perfect' or normative expression of the human species. Aquinas concluded from this anthropology that the maleness of Christ was an ontological necessity and not just a historical accident. In order for Christ to represent generic humanity, he must be male, because only the male has the fullness of human nature. The female cannot represent the human species either for herself or generically.[7]

These notions of the maleness of God, the Logos, the *imago dei* and of Christ threaten to undermine the basic Christian faith that Christ indeed possesses a humanity which includes the humanity of women and that women are included in the incarnation and redemption of Christ. The Church Fathers assumed that she was included in redemption while, at the same time, being non-normative and non-theomorphic. This assumption was based on the partriarchal ideology that women lack equally human capacities for intelligence and leadership and that female humanity is included within the lower part of male humanity, ruled over by male rationality. As these assumptions are refuted by the actual incorporation of women into higher education and public leadership today, and Aristotelian biology is shown to be false, all the androcentric biases of this theological construct are thrown into question. Today a Christology which elevates Jesus' maleness to ontologically necessary significance suggests that Jesus' humanity does not represent women at all. Incarnation solely into the male sex does not include women and so women are not redeemed. That is to say, if women cannot represent Christ, then Christ does not represent women. Or, as the women's ordination movement has put it, 'either ordain women or stop baptizing them'. Some women believe that women should leave Christianity and seek another religion which genuinely includes their humanity in its theology of the divine–human relationship.[8]

In order to reassess the relationship of the doctrine of Christ and gender, we need to examine alternative possibilities within the Jewish tradition that shaped early Christianity. Jewish tradition thinks of God as beyond gender. God is thought of in terms of sovereignty and power. This power is expressed in wrathful and judgmental ways and also in compassionate and long-suffering ways. Male social roles predominate in the image of God. But, when speaking of God's compassion and long-suffering, Jewish thought sometimes uses female images, especially that of a mother.[9] No images for God are to be taken literally, a taboo that includes the spoken names of God as well as pictorial images. From this tradition it should be clear that the female can be taken as imaging God, while no gender images for God can be taken as literal or exclusive.

Most notably, in the Wisdom tradition of Hebrew Scripture, the immanence of God in creation, revelation and redemption is imaged in the female personification of God's Wisdom.[10] This concept of divine Wisdom is the same theological idea that is expressed in the Christian tradition by the Logos or Word of God. At times, the two words are used interchangeably. Thus the idea that the immanence of God is 'like' a male offspring in relation to a male parent cannot be taken literally, either in the sense that God's immanence is a 'second God', or in androcentric descriptions of this immanence as a 'son'. The Logos-Sophia of God is neither male nor female, and was imaged in the major Jewish tradition that lies behind Christian Trinitarian thought in female personification.[11]

The Jewish tradition thought of the Messiah as a future king of Israel. In a patriarchal society this was presumed to be a male, although the key idea here is an elect human person who exercises God's sovereignty. Jesus preferred as his title for the coming One (whom he did not identify with himself) the term 'Son of Man'. But this term, drawn from the Book of Daniel and other apocalyptic literature, makes the Messiah a collective expression of Israel, in turn representing generic humanity. (Since generic humanity cannot today be seen as normatively male, the Inclusive Language Lectionary, presently being prepared by the National Council of Churches in the United States, has chosen to translate this messianic title used by Jesus as 'the Human One'.)[12] Moreover, it is important to recognize in the teachings and practice of the historical Jesus (as interpreted by early Christianity) a prophetic vision that stands in judgement on social and religious systems that exclude subordinated and marginated people from divine favour. Jesus sees his divine mission as one which is to bring 'good news' to these despised people who are regarded by the priestly and clerical classes of his day as unworthy of redemptive hope. Central to the Jesus story is a prophetic practice that stands in judgement on these priestly and clerical classes for their pretences of special privilege with God and their exclusion of the unlearned and 'unclean'. It is often women among the despised groups who become the example of those who are able to hear God's new prophetic word and be converted, while the religious elites not only close their hearts against it, but plot to destroy God's Messenger.

Precisely because women were at the bottom of those systems of privilege that Jesus decries in the Gospel stories, they often become the representatives of the 'last who will be first in the Kingdom of God'. Thus Luke in the Magnificat makes Jesus' mother, Mary, the representative of the new or Messianic Israel as servant of God who will be lifted up as the mighty are put down from their thrones.[13] All four Gospels tell the Jesus story as a drama of mounting conflict in which the messianic prophet is rejected first by his family and hometown folks, then by the religious leadership, then by the crowds, then by his own male disciples, in the upper room.[14] Much has been made in modern (male) scholarship of the secondary and unhistorical character of the 'empty tomb' story,[15] but this begs the question. Why do all four Gospel traditions tell the story of Jesus in this way, if not to make the point, in ultimate dramatic form, that those who are last in the present social order are the faithful ones who will be the first in the Kingdom, the first to witness the resurrection and bear the good news to others? Luke further stresses the inclusion of women in his account of Pentecost, where he uses the text of the prophet Joel to say that the spirit of prophecy, restored to the messianic community of the last days, is given to the 'menservants and maidservants', and 'your sons and your daughters shall prophesy'.[16] Women were included in the prophetic office in Hebrew Scripture, as well as early Christianity.[17] We know from the Church order, the Didache, that there were still Christians in the late second century who thought that the prophet was the normative leader of the local Christian community.[18]

If the praxis of Jesus mediated in the vision of early Christianity was one that saw itself as overturning established hierarchies and as including women as first among the believers, why did this inclusiveness seem to vanish so quickly? To answer this question we must realize that the early Christianity that interpreted the Jesus story in this prophetic and gender-inclusive way also understood this message in the context of a world-view that was inherently unstable and could not endure historically in that form. Seeing itself as the messianic community of the last days of world history, it has no basis for its own historical institutionalization. Its concept of the Lordship of Christ was that of an alternative foundation of being, transcendent to the present systems of society and 'this world', upon which those powerless within this world could stand. Moreover, since it assumed that the patriarchal hierarchy of family, religion and state was inherent in 'this world', early Christians could only imagine a new humanity in which women were included as equals as one where the reproductive role of women was abolished. Already in St Paul those who belong to the messianic community of the redeemed are believed to be no longer under that divine mandate to marry and reproduce, which belongs to the order of nature and the historical perpetuation of the human species.[19]

Thus, by the end of the first century, we find Christianity splitting into two contrary interpretations. One branch of Christianity incorporated its social structure back into the patriarchal family and interpreted its normative leadership as that of the male who is a proven *paterfamilias*.[20] This patriarchial Christianity was engaged in a polemic with an alternative Christianity which enjoined its members not to marry and also promoted the participation of women in public teaching. To combat this alternative Christianity, the texts of Genesis 2 and 3 were evoked to declare that woman's place is both second in nature and under punishment due to sin. Therefore, she is to keep silence and will be saved by childbearing (1 Tim. 2.12–15).

The alternative Christianity is represented by the *Acts of Paul and Thecla*, where Paul's authority is claimed for precisely the opposite view. Here the conversion of a woman is expressed in her embrace of chastity and her renunciation of marriage, a choice that is rewarded, after a series of adventures, when Paul commissions Thecla to preach and to return to her home town as an evangelist.[21] This alternative Christianity was expressed in the second century in both millennialist and spiritualist groups, who affirmed the inclusion of women, but did so by interpreting the Church as the messianic community of the redeemed who has transcended the reproductive order of sexuality and childbearing.[22] Such eschatological sects could only survive historically by either converting new adults in every generation, or drawing upon a population of married Christians who they then drew into what was seen as the higher and more authentic Christianity of the celibate.

What we find is that, by the fourth century, those sects that demanded that all Christians be celibate have been declared heretical,[23] while the patriarchal Church and a modified version of eschatological Christianity are merging into a new synthesis. In this synthesis, married people are regarded as the lower order of the Church, while a celibate elite is regarded as its higher and fuller expression. But since this church also assumes that ordained leadership follows the patriarchal order of creation, celibate women are deprived of pastoral ministry and marginalized into convents, while celibacy, drawn from the monastic (and, originally, non-clerical) tradition is imposed on married priests and bishops.[24] This synthesis of patriarchal and eschatological Christianity is passed on to the Middle Ages as normative Christianity.

The Reformation represents a revolt against the eschatological counter-culture institutionalized in monasticism. It abolished monasteries for either men or women and also clerical celibacy. But this meant that it rooted itself all the more exclusively in the patriarchal type of Christianity. The patriarchal family is now stressed as the nucleus of the Church, to be modelled by the married pastor and his obedient wife and children. However, this reform did not abolish the eschatological counter-culture from Christianity. It only meant that it popped up again as separate mystical and millennialist sects that declared the Church to be the messianic community living in the last age of world history. They anticipated the Kingdom by withdrawing from the evil social structures of this world. For some of these mystical and millennialist sects, this also led to the further conclusion that the redeemed had transcended the procreative order of history. Thus freed from gender roles, they were equal in the new order of redemption. Some combinations of ideas about the androgyny of God, the inclusion of women in teaching and church administration and the adoption of the celibacy of all the redeemed is found in many of these sects.[25]

These two different lines of Christianity lend themselves to two alternative Christologies, although most Christologies have contained elements of both traditions. On the one hand, patriarchal Christianity moved towards a total integration of the Lordship of

Christ into the lordships of worldly hierarchies. Christ as the divine Logos is seen as the apex of a hierarchical social order baptized as Christendom. Coming forth from the Father, Christ reigns over the cosmos. He, in turn, is the font of both the ecclesiastical and political hierarchies of Christendom and is imaged on the more personal level by the headship of male over female in the family and the rule of reason over the body in the human (male) microcosm. Women as subjects, as laity, as wives and as the image of the body, represent that which is to be ruled over by the male Christological principle in all these systems of dominance and submission.[26]

In the mystic and millennialistic Christologies, by contrast, Christ represents a transcendent ground of being for the redeemed who have departed from this present world and its social systems and are awaiting and anticipating the redeemed order beyond history. Christ is either beyond gender (i.e. is asexual) or encompasses both genders on a level transcendent to the split into separate genders and reproductive roles (i.e. is spiritually androgynous). The redeemed participate in this eschatological life of Christ by transcending sexuality and reproduction (becoming celibate, in other words), thereby also recovering their spiritually androgynous humanity that existed prior to the fall into sin and death, and the consequent need for sex and reproduction. All sex hierarchy is thereby overcome, and women may participate equally with men in the leadership of the community of the redeemed.[27]

Although these two views appear opposite, they are both based on a common presupposition; namely that patriarchy is the order of creation. So, on order to transcend gender hierarchy, one must also transcend the order of creation which is the order of the reproduction of the species. A definition of redemption that transcended patriarchy, without abolishing one's relation to reproduction, was inconceivable until this presupposition was overcome. One had to be able to imagine an original order of nature that was egalitarian, rather than patriarchal, an original order of nature regarded as our natural embodied state, and not some spiritual existence prior to embodiment. In relation to this egalitarian order of nature, patriarchy would then be able to be named as a distortion of nature. The vindication of equality between the sexes could then be seen as a restoration of authentic humanity through historical reforms of culture and institutions, rather than as an a-historical departure from history and embodied existence.

The basis for this new anthropology was laid between the seventeenth and nineteenth centuries in Europe and America. On the one hand, the patriarchal types of Christianity, of established Christendom, were increasingly repudiated as representative of unjust moribund social orders, rather than bearers of a redemptive future. On the other hand, the radical millennialist wing of Christianity began to naturalize itself into movements, such as the Levellers and Diggers in the English Puritan Revolution, that saw the egalitarian future as a new historical future, rather than as an eschatological future beyond history.[28] This led to further secularization of millennialist Christianity in the Enlightenment and the liberal and socialist movements of the nineteenth century.[29]

These movements rejected the hierarchies of Church and society of the *ancien régime* as contrary to true humanity. Instead, they declared them to be unjust departures from an original egalitarian order of nature. They set about creating new societies that would give equal citizenship to all 'men' (i.e. white propertied males). This would restore that 'order of nature' where all 'men' were 'created equal'. These liberal movements originally only sought to abolish the social hierarchy that divided the feudal classes of nobility from the merchants. But the universalist language they used lent itself to more radical efforts at inclusion of others in this promised future, such as workers (socialism), slaves (abolitionism), and women (feminism). Thus feminism expresses the explicit application of the new egalitarian theology of creation to gender, and hence a judgement on patriarchy as unjust and evil, rather than as the order of nature and the will of God.

We are now in a position to ask what effect it would have on Christology if this egalitarian anthropology was applied to all aspects of our understanding of the God–human relationship. First of all, it would mean a dismantling of that anthropology (with its false biological underpinnings) which regarded women as less complete expressions of human nature than men. This would further mean that we would have to affirm that women are equally theomorphic. They share equally in the image of God and the joint responsibility of humans for rule over creation (or, more correctly, care of creation). They do not symbolize that which is to be ruled over as body, or non-human nature. If women are equally theomorphic, this also means that God is to be imaged equally as male and female. God, as transcendent source of being, and God's manifestation as Logos-Sophia, can be imaged in metaphors drawn from maleness and femaleness, without any subordination of the female symbols to the male symbols.

Thus we must say that the maleness of the historical Jesus has nothing to do with manifesting a male 'Son' who, in turn, images a male 'Father'. The divine 'Father' is equally mother. The 'Son' is equally daughter. Perhaps the parental language for transcendence and immanence itself should be relativized by some metaphor other than parent and child to better state this relationship between God transcendent and God manifest in creation and history.

Turning to the historical Jesus, as the particular and paradigmatic expression of God's Logos-Sophia for the Christian Church, what is necessary is not a further evacuation of his particularity. Rather, we need a fuller ability to accept his particularity, without confusing one aspect of that particularity, his maleness, with the essence of Christ as God's Word incarnate. What we find in most Christology is an effort to dissolve most aspects of Jesus' particularity (his Jewishness, as a first-century messianic Galilean) in order to make him the symbol of universal humanity; yet an insistence that the historical particularity of his maleness is essential to his ongoing representation. This idea, as we have seen, has been based on the assumption that maleness could indeed represent universal generic humanity, an androcentric anthropology which must now be rejected. How then should we understand the relationship of Jesus as a historical individual in all his particularity, not only as male, but as first-century messianic Galilean Jew, and yet also make these particularities no longer limits on his representation as the embodiment of God's universal new Word?

We should do that, not by emphasizing biological particularities, but rather by emphasizing his message as expressed in his ministry. This message was the revolutionary word of good news to the poor. Good news to the poor means that favour with God and hope of redemption is not based on social status in the hierarchies of unjust society, but is a free grace available to all who respond to it by repenting of their hardness of heart and being open to each other as brothers and sisters. In this perspective we see that the emphasis on Jesus' maleness as essential to his ongoing representation not only is not compatible but is contradictory to the essence of his message as good news to the marginalized *qua* women.

This means that we, the Church, who know Christ no longer after the flesh but after the Spirit, carry on his presence in our midst, not by imitating any of his particularities of race or gender, but rather by preaching his word and living it in our lives. We must live as those who preach good news to the poor and repent of our false privileges of gender, race, class or culture. When we open our hearts to all persons as bearers of God's image, we also must be prepared to incur the hostility of those of this world, including those who call themselves 'Church', committed to the opposite view. This means we can and must be able to encounter Christ, as one early Christian martyr text puts it, 'in the form of our sister'.[30]

□ To conclude this section, we can move to consider what must be the next important agenda for feminist theology – though perhaps, if we put it first, some of the problems we have with Christology would fall into place. The language that we use for God is obviously at the core not only of formal doctrine, but of our spirituality and liturgical life. Recent work by Sarah Coakley, Anne E. Carr, Denise Lardner Carmody and Sallie McFague,[23] as well as Rosemary Radford Ruether's *Sexism and God-Talk*, represent some of the options within the Christian tradition, and some of the difficulties. From the British development in feminist theology I have selected first an essay by Sara Maitland. Well known as an exciting and distinguished novelist, another essay of hers that is important to follow up is 'A Case History of Structural Oppression', in *All Are Called: Towards a Theology of the Laity* (London, Church House, 1986) pp. 18–21, a topic largely ignored except implicitly, since so much effort and attention goes into the discussion of women's ministry and ordination. To introduce the topic of God quite directly in the final part of this section of the *Reader*, then, is Sara Maitland's 'Ways of Relating'.

13   SARA MAITLAND
Ways of Relating

GOSSIP sb. (GOD + sibb – skin, related).

1. One who has contracted a spiritual affinity with another by acting as sponsor at a baptism. 2. A familial acquaintance, friend, or chum. Formerly applied to both sexes, now only to women: and *esp.* applied to a woman's female friends invited to be present at a childbirth. 3. A person, mostly a woman, of light and trifling character, *esp.* one who

delights in idle talk, a newsmonger, a tattler. 4. The conversaton of
such a person, idle talk, trifling or groundless rumour; tittle-tattle.
GOSSIP vb. To talk idly, mostly about other people's affairs; to go about
tattling.

Oxford English Dictionary

(I was twenty-seven hours in labour with my first child. The
people, not all of them women as it happened, who talked me and
held me through that laborious time were not of 'light and trifling
character', thank God, but they and I contracted there a spiritual
affinity which I will not see debased.)

I did not choose the title of this essay; it was a pure gift. 'Relating'
has two meanings: it signifies both 'connecting' and 'telling'. This
is not just a dictionary game. It is important to be as aware as
possible that the intricacies of language open and close doors,
throw coloured balls sparkling in the air, juggle, trick, manipulate
and create reality. ('God *said*. "Let there be light"; and there was
light'.) The language we have determines quite profoundly what
we can think, imagine, create, and even feel. We are dependent,
when it comes to relating (even to and about the eternal), on these
socially constructed, delusive ephemera – words, sentences, gestures, all dense with history, with ideologies of dominance, with
confusion, with aloneness and with structured responses. The
Word became flesh and dwelt among us; more fool God.

Right now I had better make clear that I am neither a theologian
nor a linguist. I am a writer and a Christian. However, this does
mean that I have to look, quite often, at the theory that underpins
and describes both these activities – linguistics and theology. In
both I am, in the literal sense of the word, an amateur – a lover. As
lover I cannot help wanting both theology and linguistics to relate
to me more closely, to be more sensual, more responsive, more
open, more ready to be wooed and played with. This essay is an
open attempt to seduce them both, though it may well end up as
flirting.

I am also a feminist: to all questions whatsoever I bring my sense
of myself as a woman – which is not primarily a biological
definition, but a social and historical one, constructed through
relating. Gender is a powerful social and psychological determi-
nant, so I might as well know it. I am white and middle class and
educationally privileged, and European and female. I have to work
hard on not deluding myself that these are either neutral or

universal. They are my perspectives and consciously or uncon-
sciously they mediate all my ways of relating. It is only by bringing
them into consciousness, however, that I can hope to explore the
whole question of relating with anything like the joy and hope that
are appropriate.

Alla Bozarth Campbell, who is perhaps as near as the Christian
feminist movement gets to a traditional mystic of our own,
describes this shared realization thus:

> As I came to own and accept my own womanhood as a gift from God,
> bringing my own new value for the female side of life into prayer, I
> experienced a kind of inward leaping which was ecstatically physical as
> well as spiritual; an inward bodily leaping that made me feel God in my
> nerves and blood and deep down in my bone marrow as in my emotions
> and my intellect.
>
> I was not able to approach God with this kind of engagement until I
> began to open up my prayer life to the feminine aspects of God, and to
> celebrate my own femaleness in that aspect. And I didn't suspect the
> wholeness I missed until I began to experience it. . . . I don't suggest
> that this process is possible only for women. I only know that I came to
> it self-consciously as a woman, open to deeper discovery of my own
> nature through closer contact with the nature of God. . . . Now I know
> with my whole being that I am connected with God . . . and that the
> realization of this connection is the reason for which I was born.[1]

What is not named does not exist – conceptually: limits on
language really are limits on thought, and on the capacity to act. An
amazing, magical thing happens to small children when they first
learn to speak, which proves the point that I am trying to make. It
is not just that they learn to communicate, though that is exciting
enough. There is something more: an explosion of mind which is
geometric rather than arithmetic. They can, with the power of
words, conceptualize and project and memorize and manipulate
and co-operate in an entirely new way.

Christianity has always acknowledged this central truth, drawn
from our Jewish roots. God is veiled from sight and known in and
by words, by god-speaking. 'In the beginning was the Word and
the Word was God'. Our faith is in the 'the Word incarnate', that
which came from the mouth of God and took flesh. God and
god-speaking are co-eternal and inseparable. The Word is our
primary and fundamental way of relating to God. Sacramentalists
of all persuasions believe that for validity you need the right rite –
the rights words – as well as the right intention and the right
matter. Protestantism, in stressing the authority of the Bible and
the centrality of preaching, is saying the same thing. It is not just

that words have some intrinsic magical power, because precision of meaning has always been stressed in the Christian tradition – mumbo-jumbo, 'vain repetition', incantation have always been frowned upon. Paul, for instance, insists that no one should speak in tongues unless there is an interpreter available. When we are accused of 'playing word games' (from condemning Arianism down to 'non-sexist liturgy'), we should stand up proudly and delight in it; playing with the Word is a primary obligation.

Whilst talking about word games I think it is worth mentioning one of the rules: people seem to have an extraordinary amount of difficulty with symbolic language. ('It's only a symbol', they say. What more in heaven's name should or could it be?) All the language we use for God is metaphorical (even the word God): God, we know from common sense as well as the tradition, is 'without qualities' (physical, mental or material attributes of any kind whatsoever) – you cannot say anything concrete about God because 'qualities' cannot exist except in the concrete realm of time and space. But since we need (and yearn and long) to speak of the unspeakable, we use metaphors, images, symbolic terms. So far so good, but language is sneaky; if the image is a strong one it always demonstrates a tendency to 'drift' into 'reality'. And this is marked in Christianity because we do have a faith grounded in the materiality of time and space; a weakness for the word as well as a strength in relating to it. It is vital, as the words are juggled about, to keep a grip on the fact that there are no universal metaphors – that stretch through all time, all people, all social modes, that transcend the social reality that generated them.

Changes in social reality change the meaning of images. The current scientific model, for example, affects the content of Christian imagery. When Aquinas spoke of God as Father/Creator, he was basing his metaphor not just in the social dominance of maleness, but also on a specific biology *in which we no longer believe:* that male sperm contained the complete and perfect living child and the woman's body provided nothing but a growing place for it. God as male, impregnating nature as female made good – no, beautiful – image sense, but it does not any more. If we look at the God/nature, male/female imagery in any depth at all, it is patently rubbish and moreover creates all sorts of heretical complications in the light of *our* scientific model. Changed gender-roles, the discovery of the non-geocentric universe, the 'invention' of the psyche by the post-Enlightenment nineteenth-century, evolutionary theory – all change the implicit meaning of symbols. Even the fact that shepherds now drive their sheep from behind and use dogs instead of leading them from the front means that the image of Jesus as the good shepherd has a different emotional content. This is true of *all* the ways we relate to or about God. They are all metaphors and have therefore no abstracted eternal verity.

The women's movement (possibly because of its middle-class and intellectual bias) has taken up the issue of language more seriously and directly than most other liberation movements. (As the longest and oldest liberation movement still present in the West, Christianity ought to be slightly ashamed about this.) What we have come up with is a series of exposures, some of which are worth illustrating.

(a) The exposure of *exclusion*, or absence – women's experiences have been excluded from language and therefore are not known to exist.

(b) The exposure of *denigration* – where women's experiences are named they are not valued. 'Gossip' is a good example of this, but there are a thousand others, most easily seen in words that are grammatically equivalent but affectually not: master and mistress; sissy and tom-boy; bachelor and spinster.

(c) The exposure of *ambiguity*. (This is especially noticeable in English.) The obvious example is the word 'man', which is supposed to carry two *inherently contradictory* meanings, both 'any member of the human species' and 'any member of the human species who is not female'.

(d) But the most important exposure is the exposure of *effect*. Language is not neutral, it informs and creates concepts and actions, it is 'owned' by the dominant ideology of its time. All language is value-laden; and access to changing it and controlling its values is in the hands of certain social groups. The word 'man', for example, does not just make one more likely to think of a male person than a female person; it does not merely subsume the female to the point of disappearance. It also comes with an affectual sub-text, a hidden agenda of meaning. In 1972 two American sociologists did a tidy little piece of research: they asked 300 students to create collages from magazine pictures to illustrate certain themes. Half were assigned the theme using the word 'man': Industrial Man, Political Man, and so on, and half were given the same themes differently expressed: Industrial Life, Political Behaviour, Society. Not only did the group with the word 'man' in their titles show fewer pictures of women and children;

they also showed that the word 'man' induced images of power and dominance. For example:

> Social Man was portrayed as a sophisticated, white, party-going male (half to two-thirds of the pictures included the consumption of alcohol) . . . while Society involved scenes of social disruption and protest with a sub-theme of co-operation among people.[2]

If we relate to God and each other through exclusively male images, we must remember that we are naming holiness as a 'sophisticated white party-goer'.

The point about all this is that when women say there are other ways of relating to or about God, they are not merely talking about making themselves feel better, or claiming their own holiness (though both these things seem highly desirable to me); we are primarily trying to wrest the 'ownership' of God away from a discourse of dominance and on to the side of 'co-operation among people'. Rosemary Ruether suggests that: 'It is not just that God is imaged as male, but as male warrior élite. God is not imaged as black male garbage collector either. It is important to keep a hold on this connection.'[3]

In the light of this let me look for a moment at some of the ways we do relate God in the tradition and what this may mean.

There are the names of God that are based on the images of personal relationship. God as father, as brother, as husband (not always to the woman as bride/wife; sometimes to a man's soul, sometimes to the whole Church). Father is perhaps the most important images here, because it is so central to the whole Christian tradition and was recorded as an instruction of Jesus – 'When you pray, say Father'. There are a lot of ways you can relate to this naming. Firstly, you can criticize it. It is biologically and specifically masculinist. It is also not very close to present-day experience if what we are trying to express is the tender and nurturing qualities of God; the constant, and constantly loving carefulness. Very few children growing up in Britain today have much experience of their fathers in this role. I think it is interesting that the concept of the first person of the Trinity as increasingly distant, judgmental and punitive, with a newer focus on Mary as mother and Jesus as friend and brother, grew up in Europe at almost exactly the same time as the educated writing and thinking people were becoming urbanized – that is, their father's work and family life were being separated; the image changed content.[4] Now these ideas about God's nurturance and fondness might be better related to the image 'mother'. The danger here is that this might suggest that tender nurturing was somehow a female characteristic, and that it was less incumbent on men to develop it. If we wish men to grow up into decent nurturing human beings we should be careful.

The really positive content of mother imagery, it seems to me, is in fact rather more basic. 'Mother' in our society really does express 'the person with whom the buck stops'. Now that is something we really do want to say about God – and of course in our desire to claim our autonomy from our mothers we also want to say that God, like a good mother, is one who hands the buck back again to the people who try to pass it on. Another use of 'mother' is, of course, about giving birth; and this is one that has something particular to say to Christians. Birthing is the creating of new life through hard work (labour) and blood. Of course men do create life, just as much as women do, and must be held to their responsibility for this (I have no wish to swap a thomistic myth for a 'separatist feminist' myth); but they do it differently – in joy and delight. 'God said "Let their be light" and there was light', seems a lovely image of ejaculatory creation. But God also brought new life, gospel life to birth, stretched out for hours on the cross, autonomy removed by aggressive experts, the eternal Word reduced to wordless cries, bleeding down into the dark, overwhelmed by the sense of desolation, the doubt as to how much more you can put up with. And afterwards the joy, the new life, the sense of mystery and distance. It seems that the creative birthing of God as expressed in Christ's passion (and reiterated in the rituals of baptism) can be given a deeper relating if we can learn to hear as holy the bodily experiences of women and trust the metaphor of God as mother.

Moreover, if we liberate our relating with God to a rather desperate attempt to wring tenderness out of stone, we close our eyes to an image of 'father' which cannot in our society (because of the oppression of women, and their subjugation within the home) be properly carried by the name 'mother'. Fatherhood is, partly and importantly, that which frees one from childhood and the private, and unites one with the social and the historical. We all have to forge our identities over against the mother and her loving; the good father is one who enables this process (ideally by taking on the weight of her caring, and thus liberating both child and mother from the burden of it).

I am trying to suggest that because of the social relationship of word and meaning there is a deep complexity in the use of mother/father imagery that cannot be put right while we hold that God is primarily one or the other, eternally and outside of a social understanding of how the two relate to each other and to their children within the real material context.

While I am at this point I would like to mention very briefly that it is curious how little the image of God as child is allowed to surface. There is the child who will *play* for ever with us. ('Then I was at God's side each day, God's darling and delight; playing in the presence continually, playing on the earth when it was made',[5] says *Sophia* who is the wisdom of God, who is God.) However, equally there is the one who wakes us in the night with demands for attention when we would rather be asleep, forever reminding us of the disciplined necessities of love; and also of the great divine yearning and need to be loved. Again, I suspect the fullness of this image has not flowered among us precisely because child-care and children themselves have been given such a low status compared with the glorious work of abstracting and rationalizing. Adoptionism, however, has been named as a heresy: the neo-natal child at Bethlehem is where 'the fullness fo God is pleased to dwell' just as much as in the miracle-working teacher.

Space requires me to pass swiftly through the non-personal images for God and how they can bring us into better ways of relating. It is an androcentric as well as a sexist culture which has named God in its own image. Women have had their noses so rubbed in the dust of nature that we often feel like popping up to point out that Jesus frequently chose non-personal namings for himself – the Way, the Truth, the Resurrection, the Vine. The created order and its processes are as much created of God as we are, and we might be brought into a more just relationship by remembering to image as rock and as growth, as order in the seasons and as chaos in the atom.

But I want to speak a little about the well-known feminist claim that God cannot be imaged at all satisfactorily in the essentialist, noun-based way that has usually been employed. There is also a whole, and perfectly traditional, language of God as movement; God as verb. For people in power, an eternal substantive, an eternal noun and eternal object has a clear purpose, because an eternal object – however constructed – obviously stands over against transformation and radical change. Women, with other oppressed groups, need to relate to God as verb, as process, as act because we see the need for that transformation – we have felt it in our own experience. The God of the Hebrews is not only 'the Lord of Armies' but also 'I AM', a pure verb of being-ness. We want to go further than this, finding ways of relating God not just as the verb of being, but as *active* verb too. Bernard of Clairvaux put this more clearly than I can when he described the Holy Spirit as the passionate kiss between the Father and the Son. Although you construe 'kiss' as a noun, it is really a verb, because the kiss only exists in the act of kissing. There is a tension – I mean that as a healthy thing – always between God transcendent and God imma-nent. Those two points are filled, joined, spilling over with God as mediator, God is the mediator of God, and God is also the mediation. Likewise, when we talk of the God of history we do not just mean that God controls history from *outside*, but also that God is the process of history, and we are therefore liberated to engage with that process in the knowledge that we are made in God's image. Or, as Yeats so precisely asks, 'How can you tell the dancer from the dance?'

It always seems to me interesting that, in the biblical tradition, whenever you find God described as verb, as movement or process, you intend to get grammatically feminine forms allowing personi-fication. Both *Ruach* (the spirit of God in creation) and *Sophia* (the wisdom of God in action) are feminine. And women from the women's movement can tell that sisterhood is a process, not a substance: and that the verb of sisterhood is a way of relating that is holy.

I do not believe, finally, that women have ontological skills, knowledge or anything else that makes them essentially different from men. To believe that is to fly in the face of known facts (women can be as war-like as any men when they get the chance; men can be as tender and nurturing as any women if they have to be), and to question our redemption through the incarnation (for if God could not assume the whole of humanity in Christ, then we are not saved). I do believe that women, through the mediation of language and beyond it, have a different experience of the world, different ways of relating to it, and the immensity of God requires all experience to be brought to bear on the task of living out and mediating God's love and justice. I have a profound sense that at some deep level it ought to be right for women to describe immanence in terms of themselves and transcendence in terms of the other, the beloved other, in terms of male metaphors. For men it would work the other way round. God can be imaged as rich and as poor, as black and as white, as verb and as noun, as female and as male, according only to what the individual speaker is trying to relate about the relationship at that moment in time. But this cannot happen while either side of the polarities is socially known or experienced as 'better', superior to, holier than or conveying power to, more that the other. The language we use describes and recreates the social relationships we experience. Thus in the end, language and relating are political as well as theological issues; striving to name God demands, in the process of the enterprise, political action for justice so that we are able both to connect with and to tell aloud the living God, the life in God and the God of the living, freely and ever more fully.

I want to end by reiterating one thing: believing all that I have written, I do not want to take over all the old models and simply brand them with female transpositions. I want the process freed for ever. What I perceive as important, what may actually be important at this point in the process of history, may not remain so. There are other true namings, real relationships, than female ones. I do not actually believe that God will be hurt by any honest attempts at expanding and correcting the ways we relate, but since I started with Alla Bozarth Campbell I would like to end with another story of hers which gives me hope and joy and, with a bit of luck, humility. It is a story about her guardian angel:

> I had long had a verbal communication with my angel, but never any visual image, so I invited my talky angel to put in an appearance. Despite initial reluctance which annoyed me, I finally gained consent. . . . I looked and could not believe what I saw! A stereotyped creature with golden hair, long white robes and wings, no less! I said, 'O come on!' and the angel roared with laughter. The joke was on me. Angel said, kindly but still laughing at me, 'Remember you too are a product of your culture'.[6]

☐ My second reading is from the work of Janet Morley, whose psalms, litanies, collects and eucharistic prayers have been collected together in *All Desires Known* (London, Women in Theology, 1988).[24] This essay reflects on why and how she has developed the art of writing prayers which employ feminine language and images to describe and address God.

14 JANET MORLEY
I Desire Her with My Whole Heart

I am asked, why write psalms and prayers that call God 'She'? A simple answer is that I currently find it a devotional necessity. I grew up with a strong, traditional Christian faith: and when it was put to me, in the context of the women's movement, that God might be as appropriately called 'Mother' as 'Father', I found the idea initially startling, even shocking. On reflection, though, I became interested in my gut reaction. Intellectually, I could see that the idea was much more reasonable than my feelings would allow. My literary training had made me aware of the enormous power of imagery in language to shape perception; it was not as if I could brush off the question of what particular words may or may not be used as trivial or irrelevant. Theologically, I could see how inappropriate it was to *identify* God with actual maleness – so why did it feel not just unconventional but wrong to refer to God in feminine terms? Especially since, as feminist scholars were discovering, there is a significant strand of feminine imagery in the Bible.

Exploring further my ambivalent reaction, along with other women, I began to realize how interlinked were my perceptions of God, through the masculine language taught me in prayers, hymns, and sermons, and my relationship to women and men. There was a felt coherence between the greater authority and value I was encouraged to give to men than to women (including myself), and the authority I gave to God. And there was a similar coherence between my experience of being a woman in society, and therefore an example of 'the feminine point of view' (rather than the human norm), and my experience of feeling creaturely and 'other' in relation to God. Some of us began to campaign for more inclusive language in the liturgy: to include women as well as men in reference to worshippers, and to minimize the use of the male pronoun for God. I found that as a matter of course I was leaving out pronouns altogether when speaking of God, to avoid referring to 'him'. But the problem is, of course, that however much it is inaccurate to attribute a gender to God, it is also undesirable to lose a sense of God as deeply personal. And since we have no experience of persons who are ungendered, it is virtually impossible (and probably equally undesirable) to envisage one. I began to feel that it would be a good idea, even if I didn't actually do it yet, to think of God in the feminine as well as in the masculine.

In the end, it was a growing appreciation of how important were the women friends in my life, how much I loved them, and how significantly they mediated God's love to me, that made a difference to the language of my prayer. Finally to let myself adore 'her' was like the opening of a floodgate, an overwhelming and rather terrifying new act of surrender. It was rather like my experience of giving birth to a daughter after two sons: having implicitly accustomed myself to the idea that my body for some reason had the capacity only to bring forth males, it was a surprising discovery to find that I could do the other thing too. So with my prayer. This new language and imagery did not now feel like something strange or exceptional grafted on to a traditional spirituality: rather, it was a releasing of something that I had long prevented myself from knowing. My writing, then, is in part a continuing attempt to understand what it is about God that unrelievedly male language has allowed me to avoid.

This brief description of my own journey may give some pointers to the importance of the imagery we use in prayer. In particular, I believe it is worth noting that the capacity of language to offer definition (in the end a hopeless quest when what we are trying to define is God) is less crucial than its capacity to have certain effects: on our perceptions, on how we construe the world and our own humanity, and on our worship. So, in relation to the activity of prayer, and in the context of my own writing practice, I want to explore: what does feminine imagery *do*?

As I have suggested, it is often the conscious introduction of a feminine image, pronoun or motif that first indicates how extensively the feminine has been omitted from traditional religious language. Its power to shock is a measure of its previous exclusion from the discourse; and we realize that it does not just happen that our tradition largely fails to draw on female experience as a source of imaging God. Somehow, it has come about that our religious discourse is constructed *over against* the feminine; only this could explain our immediate feeling that feminine imagery simply should not be there. I think what has happened is that our culture's notion of 'the feminine' has collected a great many more associations than simply a reference to the female of the species: and these associations carry negative value, and hence are not felt to be appropriately evoked in speaking of God. They include weakness (God is almost inevitably addressed as Almighty), sexuality (it is rare these days to invoke God as Lover), and, as it were, the 'dark' side of human nature, with its chaotic and mysterious emotions (God is always presented as a God of light, order and stability). These are qualities that we as a culture, heavily valuing what have been seen as masculine characteristics, would much prefer not to know about.

It has been my experience, working in the context of women's groups who are seeking to worship together in a new way, that to address the exclusion of the feminine is to become aware of what else has been left out. In devising an Advent service on the theme of light and darkness, and seeking words to praise God for the darkness of waiting, hoping and taking risks, I drew a blank among existing worship resources, and had to write my own prayer. The resulting 'Darkness' litany has been used in a variety of contexts, and seems to have the effect of putting people (espcially men) in touch with areas of vulnerability and uncertainty in themselves that are not easy to bring to worship. Similarly, imagery drawn from the language of sexual passion is not commonly found in worship (though mystics of previous ages, like John of the Cross, used it freely). A psalm of mine that addresses God as Beloved, and has much of the atmosphere of a love poem, has a powerful effect when read to lecture audiences. I have not used it in a worship context, but in groups it certainly gives rise to discussion, which is both excited and vulnerable, about the place of sexuality within sp
ituality. So it seems that a great deal more is at stake than a simple matter of male or female pronouns; and to use unfamiliar imagery, especially imagery that on a conventional reading has a negative feel, can be productive of new insight and openness in worship.

Some years ago, I was at a conference that was exploring this issue, and one of the speakers described movingly how her relationship with her husband had made the biblical image of God as Husband alive and important to her. In later discussion I asked the men in the audience whether they could similarly relate to God in the image of Wife, and a strange sort of shudder shook their ranks. One of the results of not using feminine imagery of God is precisely an incapacity to recognize and honour how experience and behaviour that is inherently female can mediate God to us. Many women have found the experience of pregnancy, breastfeeding, and nurturing children to be powerful images of the all-embracing tenderness of God towards us. Many people can recognize in relationship with our own mother or sister a complex combination of fierce loyalty and hardly articulable anger which may well be a rather illuminating metaphor of our relation to God. Many have found in our women friends a source of inexhaustible patience, supportiveness and discernment, that mirrors what we often seek in prayer. Many have found in our solidarity with other women (whom we may not always like) the experience of a God who speaks for the oppressed and requires human justice. But unless the words exist which will link our prayer and our experience of women and as women, we may diminish that experience, and deny ourselves fresh discovery in prayer. The psalm that is printed along with this article was written for a women's workshop entitled 'Mothering and God', and it seeks to combine the aspects of tenderness and challenge which 'mothering' (an activity not confined to biological mothers) implies. I was fascinated by one woman's reaction: 'That sounds just like my therapist!' This was an image that I had not consciously had in mind, but her response illustrates how unusual imagery can engender a new series of connections between prayer and life-experience.

One of the effects of the traditional use of the word 'he' to designate either a male person, or a representative human being, is to encourage the belief that men are normative in a way that women are not. Thus, just as important in changing perceptions is the use of the term 'she', not to highlight distinctively feminine attributes, but as a neutral way of referring to a person or indeed to God. One of the frustrations experienced by 'token' women in professional situations or on committees is that they find themselves expected only to exemplify the feminine point of view. It is as if women can only represent or 'stand for' other women, and not the human race generally. So it would be unfortunate, I think, if the practice of calling God 'She' only developed alongside imagery drawn from exclusively female roles. There is no reason, in my view, why 'She' should not 'stand for' all of what we mean by the word 'God', just as adequately (and as inadequately) as the word 'He'. Thus, in one of my liturgical prayers, modelled on the *Benedicite*, or Song of Creation, while using no particularly feminine images, I have repeated the refrain: '. . . bless your creator: praise her and glorify her for ever'.

It is particularly important to use female language when dealing with problematic aspects of God's nature. Recently, witnessing shocking pain endured by a friend who was dying of cancer, I found myself raging at God. How could he allow or inflict such meaningless suffering? I caught myself out in the realization that the God I opposed and wrestled with was still definitely 'him'.

Somehow it was easier to fight a God I could associate with the forces of patriarchy; how much more disturbing to confront 'her'. But it really will not do for me to call God 'she' only when I mean what is tender and unproblematic; this is a new kind of dualism. If I do this, I am identifying God's difficult 'otherness' with the otherness that I experience in relation to masculinity. This identification, of course, is what traditionally male language has always allowed women to do, but it is a false parallel. It is the wrong kind of 'otherness'.

Job, in his agony, longs for an opportunity to dispute with God as a man does with his neighbour, face to face; but he realizes that the complete inequality of power and perspective will make the contest impossible, 'for He is not a man, as I am'. Only when I am deeply accustomed to using feminine language of God, recognizing that it points to what is distant and alien and incomprehensible, as well as what is warm, attractive and motherly, can I acknowledge that she is not a woman, as I am (and not because she is 'really' male instead). Women need feminine imagery in prayer, then, not only to affirm our identity, but to pose in an intimate and costly way some of the classic dilemmas of religious belief – to give us no distancing escape route from the struggle.

One deeply felt objection to the use of feminine language for God is that it appears to be *contradicting* language that is distinctively and traditionally Christian, and indeed, specifically taught by Jesus. Isn't feminine language re-introducing paganism and goddess worship? I believe that to approach religious language in this way is to mistake its nature. First, there is a real problem about literalism. If it is argued that female metaphors for God necessarily imply belief in a sexually female deity (a 'goddess'), then male terms would imply a sexually male deity (a 'god'). Both of these were prominent in the pagan thought-world, and the Judeo-Christian tradition has repeatedly opposed either conception. So it ought to be as shocking to us that many modern Christians unreflectively envisage God as male, as it would be to think of confining God within a female mould. Again, there is no doubt that Jesus' teaching about God emphasizes the term 'Father' or 'Abba'. But I find it difficult to believe that a Jew, trained to treat the sacred name of God as essentially unsayable (hence the custom of using a circumlocution instead of vocalizing the four letters YHWH), was likely to be inculcating a dogmatic, literal title for God, which was totally adequate. Further, there is the problem that words and images do not operate in a social vacuum: they have

concrete effects on users and hearers. If, as seems possible, Jesus'
use of 'Father' was intended to lead people to greater intimacy with
God, then to insist on the continued, exclusive use of the term,
even where it effectively prevents intimacy, or indeed is used
actively to oppress women, is itself contradictory.

Actually, I believe that feminine terminology is currently very
illuminating in the debate about how we may speak of God,
precisely because it clearly draws attention to its own inadequacy.
If there is a sense of 'tripping' on this language, then that is quite
appropriate. Much more subtly dangerous, and potentially idolatrous, is familiar male language which *feels* transparent and literal.
For religious language cannot but be metaphorical in character;
that is, pointing in an imaginative way to a reality that is, in the
end, unsayable. The problem is that many people regard metaphor
as somehow *less* than literal statement, or at best a good illustration
of what is 'really' meant. In fact, as any creative writer will
acknowledge, poetic or metaphorical language can carry considera-
bly more depth, density, and associative possibility than 'plain'
statement. And what makes metaphor a peculiarly appropriate
vehicle of religious truth is that it works in two ways at once. First,
it offers a vivid, illuminating comparison. There is a sort of
imaginative explosion, brought about by putting together two ideas
unexpectedly; but simultaneously, the reader is denied the chance
to identify the two things together. So it is powerful and helpful to
call God a 'rock', both because God is like a rock in important
ways, and because it would hardly be possible to *confuse* God with a
rock. The image can be used, and then let go, which is how we
should treat all religious language. I believe my position to be
completely traditional here; it is no coincidence that the great
mystics of the past, whose insights into spirituality are of continuing value, tend to combine a preference for silence, and a distrust
of *any* particular conceptual formulations, with a writing style that
is luminous with unusual and striking imagery – including the
feminine. Those who sit light to the adequacy of language to render
God, can in fact employ words with considerable vigour, originality
and love.

A Psalm

God is my strong rock in whom I trust,
and all my confidence I rest in her.

Deep in my mother's womb, she knew me;
before my limbs were formed, she yearned for me.
Each of my movements she remembers with compassion,
and while I was still unseen, she did imagine me.

Her strength brought me forth into the light;
it was she who delivered me.
Hers were the hands that held me safe;
she cherished me upon my mother's breast.

When I stammer, she forms the words in my mouth,
and when I am silent, she has understood my thought.
If I shout and rage, she hears my plea and my uncertainty.

When I am afraid, she stays close to me,
and when I am full of terror, she does not hide her face.
If I struggle against her, she will contain me,
and when I resist her, she will match my strength.

But if I am complacent, she confronts me;
when I cling to falsehood, she undermines my pride;
for she is jealous for my integrity,
and her longing is for nothing less than truth.

To all who are weak she shows compassion,
and those who are downtrodden she causes to rise.
But she will confound the arrogant at the height of their power,
and the oppressor she will throw to the ground;
the strategies of the hard-hearted she will utterly confute.

God pities the fallen, and I will love her:
she challenges the mighty, and I desire her with my whole heart.
God is the rock in whom I put my trust,
and all my meaning is contained in her;
for without God there is no security,
and apart from her there is no place of safety.

☐ From the USA I have chosen two selections from a Lutheran scholar of liturgy, Gail Ramshaw[25], a past President of The Liturgical Conference. Her *Letters for God's Name* (Minneapolis, Seabury, 1984) quotes in its introduction Catherine of Siena writing, 'And what shall I say? I will stutter "A-A," because there is nothing else I know how to say.' From her 'primer of praise' it is good to read Q and W.

15 i   GAIL RAMSHAW
Letters for God's Name – Q and W

Q

What if our God were Queen of heaven?

If our God were Queen of heaven, we could burn incense to her and bake cakes for her, and our adoration would be acceptable.

If our God were Queen of heaven, her crown would rest on hair long and curly and rainbowed, and we could grab on to that hair as we nursed and so be saved from falling. Her shining face, smooth and clear as light, would enliven the universe. And when we were poor, the Queen would take from her necklace flowing with pearls and opals and every coloured gem perhaps an amber to fill our needs. The resplendent gold of her majestic robe would be what we call the sun, and the sheen of her nightdress the moon. Her rule would reach to the deepest corners of the darkness; her beauty would rout the devils and her wisdom rear the world. Her royal blood would give us divinity. Our being born again in God would be a nativity from the divine womb. God's labour an agony of necessity: for we know it is the essence of the reign of our Queen to love with mercy. Our death would be, as with all babies, a going home to mother. Our life would be, as with heirs apparent, following in the train of the Queen.

Hebrew poetry and Christian metaphor have made our divine Sovereign only a king. But a king, say the fairy tales, requires a queen. The universe must be balanced. So the court was filled: The Queen is Mary, bearing the king's son and wedded to Christ the King. She was the first to enter God's reign, from the moment of her birth and since the moment of her death accepting God's crown of grace. Like Queen Esther, she takes our petitions to the throne. And again, the Queen is the Church, which is sometimes a virgin, sometimes a whore, always the desired, the divine lover, married to God and reigning with God over all of creation. The rabbis too played word games, and God reigned as king with the divine spirit, Ruah, or with law, Torah, or with wisdom, Hokmah, or with the holy space of divine presence, Shekinah – these feminine nouns a kind of queen attending the royal throne.

But it could have been another set of images as well. The Sovereign of heaven and earth is also a womb of mercy, a majesty of grace and beauty, one who creates the royal children out of herself: 'In the beauty of holiness have I begotton you, like dew from the womb of the morning' (Ps. 110).

The people of God could be a symbolic man, perhaps the Human One of Daniel's vision, who serves the divine monarch by accompanying her pangs of life-giving. Or the Sovereign could be the Queen and we all be Mary, divine generation, dynasty of Amazons, sharing in the world's labour: the first birth, like creation, a birth unto death; and the rebirth, like the resurrection, a birth into life.

The beauty of the Sovereign has terrified the world. She has borne us in pain and nursed us with care; and we, like Jewish children, carry her blood and are royal from rebirth in her. For our God is Queen of all the earth, and adoration of her splendour is our life:

> To you I lift up my eyes,
>   to you enthroned in the heavens.
> As the eyes of servants look to the hand of their masters,
>   and the eyes of a maid to the hand of her mistress,
> So our eyes look to the LORD our God,
>   until the LORD show us mercy (Ps. 123).

But it is all so many words, noises grunting out adoration, a cat purring affection, babble ill-informed and misdirected, and alphabet shouted out into the abyss, preceded by a prayer that the angels will shape it into a canticle of praise.

W

The scribes wrote, 'In the beginning God created . . .' At first it was enough to give God's title, just 'God', the God who is God, and to declare that God created the world. But language moves towards specificity: What we believe to be significant we distinguish linguistically from neighbours near and far. So the simple noun God was soon found to be meagre, insufficient.

So to the question seeking discrimination, 'But how did God create the world?' the ancient Hebrews sang a clarification: 'God who by wisdom made the heavens, whose mercy endures for ever' (Ps. 136).

What is it about God that created the world? Wisdom. What did God use to create the world? Divine wisdom alone. Now we have a handle on this untouchable God: Wisdom. Why, we know about wisdom! – the workings of mind meshed with compassion. We can understand a little bit, at least, of God: wisdom.

So much did divine wisdom occupy Hebrew imaginations that a figure is born, a mighty woman springing fully armed from the Hebrew poet's head: Lady Wisdom herself, whom God created first in the primeval time of creating. Lady Wisdom was God's companion, God's help, meet for creating the universe. The Hebrew writers prize her judgement, her stature, her beauty. This first-begotten of God stands by life's pathways and points us the way to her home in God. Later, Jews speaking Greek called her Sophia, the Wise Woman, a feminine personification of that essential attribute of omniscient God. In some poems she lives so triumphantly that she is imagined as the divine consort, the very woman of God.

But imaginations ran also in a second direction. To that original question, With what did God create the world?, came a second answer: 'By the word of the LORD were the heavens made' (Ps. 33).

God spoke in Genesis: Let there be, and there was. Not God's sight, no divine agent, but the spoken word creates. And so there develops also a tradition about the divine word, the powerful word that calls into being that which it names, the word which creates reality by bringing order out of chaos. Throughout the Hebrew Scriptures God is said to be speaking. God's word saves, condemns, blesses, destroys. It is God's word that the prophets speak, a burning coal on the lips, a sweet scroll to swallow.

In the last of the Old Testament books, the Book of Wisdom, Jews writing in Greek wed these two together: Sophia and Logos, wisdom and word, are interchangeably invoked as the names of God. God's wisdom, God's word – that is what we praise. The God who is wisdom and word is the God who knows us and by whom we are named. The way is set, the vocabulary prepared, the conceptual systems merged, so that two centuries later John's prologue can be written: In the beginning – the same story told again, anew – was the Word, the personified creation of God who created the world with God, Sophia become Christ, the powerful Hebrew speech

made into Jesus. All things were made through him, John says of
the Word.

Wisdom, Word: potholders for the sacred tripod. Wisdom,
Word: God is personified by human attributes which are our pride
– we, alone in the creation, like God, having wisdom, speaking
words. Yet Paul writes that the wisdom of God is the opposite of
ours: folly, foolishness, absurdity. And Mark suggests that the
Word spoke most powerfully when he endured his passion in
silence.

□ One of Gail Ramshaw's essays from 1982 has recently
been republished as the penultimate contribution in her own
collection *Worship: Searching for Language*, and it provides us
with an account of what a liturgist thinks she is doing in
reflection on the language Christians use. It concludes Part
Two of the *Reader*.

15 ii   GAIL RAMSHAW
The Gender of God

How does human language name God? Which revealed words has
the tradition canonized, and how do the faithful verbally express
and interpret their relationship with God? 'You shall not make
yourself a graven image,' it was said. Yet more solid than stone,
more resistant to icononclasm than bronze, are the images cast in
theological language and so engraved on our minds and throughout
our prayers. We must always be inquiring whether the tendency of
theological language towards immutability is wholly a healthy one.
It is to that theological language which names God as 'he' that this
inquiry is addressed.

With the phrase *de divinis nominibus*, on the divine names, we
recall both Dionysius and Thomas Aquinas.[1] It is with both that
we must converse, the elaborate metaphors of Christian imagery
and the reasoned discourses of systematic theologians. We know
that Christian poets and mystics have a rare ability to talk to and of
God in unique ways. But by definition their vision is a private one,
and while we admire Dionysius' *via negativa* or Julian of Norwich's
praise of Jesus as Mother, we do not employ their writings in

public prayer. Offshoots of Christianity more intrigued by metaphor than by dogma enjoy a release from canonized language, but
the Gnostics were anathematized, the Shakers have died out, and
Jung was hardly a worshipping church member. Heinrich Ott's
recent theological study of God as person notes correctly that
problems in naming God arise in conversation *about* God. Hence he
urges conversation *to* God.[2] Yet he writes about the safety of direct
address in language which is unquotably sexist. We are responsible
at least for the language we engrave on the minds and prayers of
others. While like the Cistercians we realize the inadequacy of
language, we must also like the Cistercians choose some language
with which to pray faithfully.

Conversations about the naming of God as Father are becoming
increasingly common,[3] and recently publications have pointed to
the difficulty in calling God 'he'.[4] But serious investigation into the
gender of God has not proceeded very far. About God's gender it is
far easier to hold an impassioned opinion than to articulate a
reasoned argument or a reasonable solution. This study will
address the 'God-he' problem with the following questions: How
does language talk of God? How has the Judeo-Christian tradition
named God's gender, and why? How does gender function in
modern American English? What are the alternatives to calling
God he? If we agree that refusing to examine our engraved speech
leads to an idolatry more sophisticated but no less culpable than
that with the golden calf, we have at least begun at the same place.

'All I have written seems to me like so much straw compared
with what I have seen and what has been revealed to me.' With
these words Thomas Aquinas admitted the inadequacy of words to
describe God, and he ceased work on the *Summa Theologiae*. While
some may suggest that we need no words to address God in the
interior of our heart, human beings do require words at least to talk
together to and of God. In searching for the best words to use, we
turn first to Thomas's discussion of theological language. For
despite his final disclaimer of language, and despite his sexism
much derided by shocked moderns, he investigates the naming of
God with a clarity which has undergirded all subsequent inquiry.
For critical historical study has shown that a thinker can be entirely
brilliant on one subject – say, linguistic philosophy – while being
completely wrongheaded on another – say, women.

How does language talk of God? In the linguistic philosophy of
the ancient Near East, a thing had no reality prior to its naming.
This theory has been adapted in modern philosophy as the theory

of the interrelationship between language and reality. That is, we know as we name. But God, Genesis claims, is prior to language. The divine is beyond the human, outside our categories. In some religions, the sacred is held so far beyond the secular that a wholly separate language is employed for worship and theology. But the self-revelation of our God in history and the incarnation of Christ Jesus encourages Christians to talk of God in their finest vernacular speech.

One recent study of God's gender suggests that modern Christianity can talk directly of God and so need not use anthropomorphisms in worship and theology.[5] Besides sounding naively optimistic about human maturity, this suggestion has not deeply understood language. Human language cannot express the essence of God, nor its power effect communication with God, any more than the human mind can grasp at divinity. Different languages and genres use various techniques to varying degrees in their worship and theology. Aquinas begins his discussion of theological language by describing metaphoric use of language, and we shall begin with him there.

'Holy Scripture delivers spiritual things to us beneath metaphors taken from bodily things.'[6] We talk of divine truth as though human categories applied; thus we are talking of two quite different things – the human and the divine – simultaneously. Theological language is to great degree metaphoric talk: language that is open to associations, which encourages insight and facilitates disclosure by its linking of disparate things.[7] 'God is said to have no name, or to be beyond naming, because his essence is beyond what we understand of him and the meaning of the names we use.'[8] We speak the metaphors with utter humility, believing in the God beyond the words and concluding our metaphoric speech to be so much straw.

Metaphors can be anthropomorphic. That is, we can talk of God as though God were a woman or a man or a child or a people. We ascribe to God breasts or a strong arm or a shining countenance. We use personification when we ascribe to God personal characteristics: anger, delight, speech, age. Non-human metaphors are common in the Judeo-Christian tradition. Interestingly, we speak of God as an animal or a natural phenomenon more easily than as a woman: God has wings. God belches fire. The Psalms were bold in objectifying divinity. 'Rock' recurs often in the Psalms as a metaphor for God.

Aquinas offers metaphoric language the test of contradictability.

'It is part of the meaning of "rock" that it has its being in a merely material way. Such words can be used of God only metaphorically.'[9] God is a rock: but of course God is *not* a rock. Nor has God a shining countenance or milk-filled breasts. The power of metaphor can tease us into believing the reality of our human language, and the East has employed more than the West the *via negativa*, the God-is-not speech. But even if we say God is not light, the technique of objectification is present despite the disclaimer.

Literature professors teach the proper interpretation of metaphoric language. The reader must be honest to the metaphor and not press it beyond its intent. 'We are the hollow men / We are the stuffed men / Leaning together / Headpiece filled with straw'[10] does not imply that we are literally scarecrows. Nor does metaphoric talk of God as mother mean that in any essential way God is half female or acts in some stereotypically feminine manner. We must be careful of anecdotes about God's sitting up in the sky on his throne or pictures of God as two men and an amorphous third. Metaphoric language must always be contradicted. God is like a father, but a father who wills his son to die. God is like a castle: but as my two-year-old retorted, 'God is not a castle. God is God.'

In some contexts, naming God 'he' is metaphoric. Sustained metaphors which liken God to a king might use 'he' in the same metaphoric fashion (although 'sovereign' sounds more noble and as a nonsex-specified noun would not require a 'he'). Our recognizing the metaphoric nature of God-he language would be facilitated if we used God-she in similar constructions. It is God as she who calls us into the ways of wisdom. But the possibilities of this metaphoric language are limited. Too easily most human occupations – shepherd, judge, teacher – are assigned male pronouns, and objectifications are often assigned male pronouns, as in 'Refuge, he'. If only images of motherhood are granted female pronouns, we remain impoverished.[11] But even when the metaphoric use of pronouns is employed most creatively, there is still the contradictability: God is not he. God is not she.

Yet we must be bolder in our use of metaphors for God. In the disclosure of surprising metaphors we meet God anew. The startling language invites us to conversion. Reviving biblical metaphors ought not to be as controversial or risky as it apparently is. To ascribe to God a full range of human activity and emotions; to balance in God the strength of God who reigns with the weakness of God who suffers; to objectify God; and finally to negate these images, pleading God-is-not: opening up God language will combat the incipient idolatry in one's traditional speech.

A second way that language talks of God is analogical. By analogy Aquinas means those verbal expressions by which we are trying to say what we mean. Of these statements one does not postulate the opposite. 'Words like "good" and "wise" when used of God do signify something God really is, but they signify it imperfectly because creatures represent God imperfectly.'[12] Our saying 'God is good' is not countered by our saying 'God is not good.' Although our category 'good' is inadequate to attach to God, we use such analogical language because through it we try to speak what we mean. Aquinas insists that in analogy the Christian revelation establishes the definition, and not the other way around. That is, we look to the Scriptures for a description of God as good, from which we arrive at our definition of good. This adaptation of Platonic idealism acts to corect our natural error of imagining a God in our own image and within our own language.

We are to be humble about language even in its most careful, credal usage. God is called Father not, as a prominent fundamentalist preacher recently announced, because otherwise the American family structure will further erode. Rather, God is named Father because in the revealed tradition Jesus called God Abba, and to that extraordinary religious event we struggle to attach human words. In the inaccurate translation of Abba into Father we see that human words are a far cry from the divine reality revealed in the seminal stories of the faith.

Trinitarian language is analogous language. The naming of the three persons of the Trinity, the calling of relationships within God, uses language that tries to say God's self-naming. All relational language concerning God is analogous. When we say that God relates not only within God's self but also with humankind, we use analogous language. Some usages of God-he language are similarly analogous. The revelation says that the Judeo-Christian God is a relational being, a God known as who, not which. The tradition has tried to say this by rejecting the pronoun 'it' and using instead 'he', always in this analogous usage recognized as a nonsex-specific but personal pronoun. While we can appreciate the historic intent of this language, it remains to be seen whether it is any longer possible.

Only when analogy, as Wolfhart Pannenberg says, opens up to mystery, only when our language of God leads to awed doxology, are we recognizing the limits of human language in its speech of God.[13] When in a homily an anecdote about a father–child relationship or about the birth process affirms a basic similarity with God, the simile has shrunk our God. Always in analogy what is unlike is more than what is like. Theological sensitivity in explicating analogical language frees us from distortions and helps point to the glory of God. If we would grant often in our speech that 'he' is wholly inadequate as a personal pronoun in referring to God, much of our difficulty would be lessened. Instead, we hear vociferous defence of this masculine designation, as if it were in some way true.

Edward Schillebeeckx talks of the kerygma breaking the human models.[14] He sees that human language has developed God talk, but that Christianity breaks apart that language even while being required to use it. With Jesus, he writes, we use the models of Messiah or of Wisdom: yet the models are admittedly inadequate, and even in some cases inappropriate, to the reality made known in Christ. So with all God talk: the models provided by human speech are recast by the proclamation of our God. It is not only, as Ian Ramsey notes, that paradox exists within the parts of the divine title, that 'God' and 'Father' are opposite to one another and standing creative tension.[15] It is even, Schillebeeckx would say, that the meanings of the individual words are shattered, that 'God' and 'Father' are broken by the reality of the cross. It is time that we examine the model of God-he for its undoing by the cross.

Several recent studies provide thorough discussions of how God's gender was expressed throughout the Judeo-Christian tradition. Leonard Swidler offers a concise treatment of the relationship between the worship of Yahweh and of Asherah and then lists biblical, extrabiblical, rabbinic, and historic Christian references to the 'feminine' aspect of God.[16] Other scholars have tried to account for the pattern of masculine language for God.[17] While this essay cannot be the place for a detailed historical study, we can review the most important aspects of the history of the naming of God's gender.

All the languages formative in the Judeo-Christian tradition had grammatical gender. That is, all nouns and pronouns were assigned, either naturally, logically, or arbitrarily, to grammatical categories called gender. Sometimes a noun's grammatical gender was elaborated upon for poetic purposes, and sometimes we can guess why a certain inanimate object was assigned its specific gender. But in languages with grammatical gender there is no actual significance in gender designation. That a table is feminine does not mean that the table has female sexuality or that it is necessarily related to a characteristically feminine realm. Hebrew, Aramaic, Greek and Latin all have grammatical gender. In polytheistic cultures, the assigning of masculine gender to the word god is evident from the word goddess, which, as in poet–poetess, is a diminutive form. Perhaps the cultural pattern of male domination in religious matters was a, or the, significant cause. But it remains that the assignment of masculine grammatical gender does not prove anything about a supposed sexuality of the Judeo-Christian God. Hebrew and Christian theologians insisted that their God was not of one or both sexes but was beyond sexuality. Gregory of Nazianzus addresses specifically the question of masculine gender of God and ridicules those who would draw from the gender designation a notion of actual sexuality within God.[18] Aquinas, also, in defending the expression 'He who is' as the most appropriate name for God, states that the term 'does not signify any particular form, but rather existence itself'.[19] Aquinas assumes here that the pronoun 'he' does not suggest the form of the human male.

A second important aspect of the historic situation is that in the ancient world, the Judeo-Christian God stands counter to polytheism, in which there was a powerful supply of female gods. In both the Old and New Testaments, Yahweh God, the Father of Jesus Christ, opposes a significant cult of the female god, and the biblical proclamation includes polemic against the sexual rituals offered before the female god. We are now studying the effects of this situation on the proclamation. Furthermore, the written documents and the cultural patterns within which Judaism and Christianity developed indicate a deeply engrained sexism, and we are only beginning to estimate to what degree and in what ways this cultural sexism influenced theological thought and expression.

Recent studies are showing us the openness of this sexist tradition to feminine gender for God. There are the oft-cited biblical references to God as woman. Jewish tradition, in its reluctance to speak directly of God, relied increasingly in its speech on feminine personifications of God. Law is hypostatized as Torah. God's presence as *shekinah*, wisdom as *hokmah*, and spirit as *ruah*. We do not know, however, how much the female personifications of these words affected theology and proclamation. It is not clear how this tradition can be imported into modern English, in which these words are not in any respect 'feminine'. The pattern remained, even in this tradtion, that a masculine god possessed feminine characteristics. Finally, while it is illuminating and potentially corrective to read about deviant traditions, like the Gnostics, the Jewish mystics, and the Shakers, in which radical measures were tried in the naming of God's gender, the idiosyncrasies of those traditions make any appropriation of their attempts unrealistic.

Recent use of the word person in association with God has unfortunately tightened the tie between God and male sexuality. In the classic Christian formulations, the word person was a technical term which meant something like mode of being. God has three persons: that is, God has three ways of being within the one being of God. There are relationships within God. Language of Father and Son had to do with relations within the being of God, not with relationships between God and the faithful.

But in the last century theology has spoken of God as personal, and even of God as person. At the start this reflected relationships between God and humankind. But increasingly talk of God as person is influenced by modern definitions of person as a self-conscious being, and different theologians can stress quite different things when referring to God as person. Ott refers to God's mutuality with humankind.[20] Pannenberg defines God's personhood as God's non-manipulability (a highly rationalistic definition of person, I might add).[21] But language of God as person can lead to images of God as a superperson, and then all too easily to God as a supermale. Finally, the word person is linked in modern American English to human personality, and we find ourselves open to anthropomorphism of the cheapest sort.

In recent debates concerning the ordination of women a dangerous example of this erroneous use of person surfaced. The priest's likeness to Christ spilled over into talk of the priest as a symbol of God, and thus male sexuality is linked not only to Christ, but in some essential way also to God.[22] But Richard Norris outlines the credal understanding of unity in the Godhead and demonstrates that even the sexuality of the man Jesus has no essential significance in the being of God.[23] It would seem as if agreement on this is possible: that while some languages assign the word God a gender, there is no sexuality – male, female, or both – inherent in the Judeo-Christian God; that any metaphoric statements which suggest such sexuality must be qualified; and that all analogical statements must be explicated in light of the theological assertion that God is beyond sexuality.

What of gender in modern American English? Anglo-Saxon, the linguistic family spoken in the British Isles in the year 1000, was an inflected language with grammatical gender like its Germanic antecedents. Into Anglo-Saxon came the Christian God, talked of in masculine gender, so translated from the Christian parent languages. Through the centuries English has become a less and less inflected language. We have now only vestiges of the old system of declining nouns and pronouns and conjugating verbs. One grammatical variable which has been almost completely abandoned is gender. Nouns no longer are arbitrarily assigned to categories called gender which influence pronoun selection and verb endings through rules of agreement. Modern American English functions almost totally with what grammarians call natural gender. That is, an animate female is 'she', an animate male is 'he', and all singular else is 'it'.

Language guidelines of publishing houses, especially those houses that produce children's books and texts, indicate the state of the language with regard to gender. Of course such thorough-going alterations of the gender system are not already commonplace in America. But we see a movement, legislated in some significant places, further to remove gender consideration in American English. The guidelines of publishers like Macmillan and McGraw-Hill make the following policies: [24] 'man' and its compounds are no longer acceptable as generic terms; words like ship and country are 'it', not 'she'; occupations are not to be typecast by sex; occupational titles must not be sex-specific (except for sperm-donor and wet-nurse!); human emotions and manners of behaviour are not to be stereotyped by sex; female gender word forms (poetess) are to be abandoned. These guidelines say of the 'generic he' that it is no longer acceptable; the sentence can be reworded or cast into the plural; 'he' can be replaced by 'one' or 'he or she' (as in 'one or the other'); 'he' might alternate with 'she'. An indication of the force of these moves is the 1977 statement by the National Council of Teachers of English that, except in the most strictly formal usage, 'their' is preferable to 'his' as a singular possessive pronoun.[25]

Perhaps the insularity of the Church has allowed this development to catch us unprepared. Are the clergy who preach about 'man's salvation' aware that the children no longer define 'man' to mean 'human being'? Both simple and radical alterations of our speech are being called for. For example, since God is not a male being, there is no need for the word goddess. Furthermore, 'masculine' and 'feminine' are difficult terms, being among the most sexually stereotyped words in the language. To say that nurturing is a feminine attribute is appropriate in a discussion of

Jungian archetypes, but such sexual stereotyping is not freeing to either men or women; it deepens the cultural division between women and men; and certain respectable publishing houses would find it unfit for children.

It is time to break the model of God-he. The abandonment of grammatical gender in modern American English forces religious language to alter its terminology – a move to which the Church remains lamentably resistant. If increasingly in American English 'he' denotes male sexuality, it becomes a simple matter of idolatry to refer to God as 'he', and this is a more seminal issue than the desire to balance male with female imagery or to ascribe to God a full range of human characteristics. English-speaking linguists have long proposed options of nonsex-specific pronouns, from Charles Converse's coinage 'thon' of 1859 to the contemporary suggestion of 'tey-ter-tem' for subjective, possessive, and objective cases.[26] But such a pronoun change, although attractive, is unlikely in the near future, and theologians and church people are seldom in a position to effect such a change. Even granting such a change, as in the dropping of thou-thy-thee, we need a plan for the present. Let us review the options, which unfortunately are few.

The Judeo-Christian tradition of God's not being 'it' is focal, and while Dionysius called the Godhead 'it' with moving awe, we do not propose to refer to God as 'it'. 'It' is used for human persons only for infants and dead bodies, and nothing suggests that 'it' will be used as a nonsex-specific personal pronoun in the future.

The third singular pronoun is 'she'. Some people are urging that 'she', which includes the word 'he', be used as the generic pronoun. (It is painfully clear that the sexual connotation of any generic pronoun is of high significance, when one hears how readily this suggestion is dismissed out of hand.) If 'she' were to become a generic pronoun, God would be named 'she'. But this is highly unlikely.

From various corners comes the suggestion that especially God the Spirit be called 'she'.[27] In Hebrew, spirit, *ruah*, is feminine, and some see in the Spirit's nature stereotypically feminine characteristics. But any use of 'she' for God ought not be saved exclusively for God the Spirit. Assigning 'he' to two persons of the Trinity and 'she' to the third only further entrenches the notion of God as a sexual being. God the Spirit as 'she' is unacceptable not because our God ends up only one-third female, but because we must speak of God with the highest accuracy possible, and God is neither, as modern American English knows them, he or she.

Yet there are occasions when 'she' can be used metaphorically in the naming of God. Use of 'she' immediately indicates the inadequacy of 'he'. Such metaphors occur most easily in the images of hymnody or in the extended conceits of a homily. God the Spirit might be 'she' more often than God the Son, although our tradition offers examples of the Son as Lady Wisdom and Mother Church. The appositives are already in use; we need only to extend the image to include the pronoun. Furthermore, faithfulness to God as Jesus' Abba, recital of the trinitarian creeds, and reverence to Mary as Mother of God do not imply that the first person of the Trinity is not also the mother of the faithful and the mother of creation (two very different things). However, alternate use of 'he' and 'she' for God in metaphoric constructions is only a partial solution, and such language always requires the Aquinas test of contradictability; God is not he, God is not she. Formal theological writing would be obscured further than it already is by an arbitrary alternation of pronouns. After all, a pronoun is meant to be a silent, unseen shorthand. Only recognition of our sexist pronoun structure forces us to focus on pronouns at all.

About the pronoun 'they': contemporary grammarians realize that 'they' is used regularly in spoken language as a singular generic pronoun. Some predict, even advocate, that 'they' receive official singular sanction.[28] However, even if such a linguistic change would occur, 'they' would not be an acceptable pronoun for God. Granting that in the Hebrew tradition one name for God. Elohim, is plural, that plural name was assigned singular meaning. The historic stress in the Judeo-Christian tradition on monotheism forces us to reject any pronoun that connotes God as plural.

Dismissing 'it' and 'they', awaiting 'tey', and alternating 'he' with 'she', is hardly a happy solution. It is incumbent upon us to eliminate altogether in American English the expository use of pronouns referring to God. A growing number of Christians for whom this is a matter of conscience regularly write and speak of God without ever using masculine pronouns. Their lectures are not clumsy nor their writings awkward. They testify that it does not take long to learn to speak and write of God without such pronoun references and that the audience remains unaware of the change. As with any translation, one cannot merely substitute one word for another. Sentences must be recast. The adjective 'divine' is helpful in possessive constructions. 'Godself' works well as a reflexive.[29] Its initial strangeness only adds a healthy awe in speaking of God and a refusal to picture God as a superperson.

The issue is not whether one can speak and write with ease and clarity without calling God 'he'. There is ample and eloquent proof that such is possible. Rather, far too many theologians and church people refuse to take the matter seriously and make no attempt whatsoever to alter their speech. One would not mind occasional slips and would welcome a metaphoric use of 'he' and 'she' if there was evidence that the church was working against imaging God as male. As a result of the Black Power movement, educated Americans removed from their active vocabularies the word 'Negro'. Such alterations are quite possible if the motivation is present.

What is required is not only the will to change one's vocabulary, but a renewed perception of God. If we continue to think of human occupations as stereotypically male or female, then we must fight against our inclination to call a mailman 'he' and a nurse 'she'. But when we think of human occupations as nonsex-specific, then mailcarriers and nurses are released from the categories of sex. If we again meet the God of the burning bush, the God of the parting waters and the raining manna, the God of the wings – the mother eagle teaching her young to fly, the mother hen protecting her chicks – the God of the cross, we might be so overwhelmed by God that we laugh at the inadequacy of 'he' and resolve to be more articulate in our speech. Change of speech is a willing task if it follows a conversion of mind.

The matter of translating the Bible and theological works is more difficult than the renewal of one's own speech. Of course, biblical translations must be accurate translations of the original language. But the implications of 'translation' are not self-evident. How much the original concepts require translation, especially for lectionary reading, is a highly complex questions. Concepts like outdated measurements – a league, a span – are usually granted contemporary substitutions without objection, but on more sensitive issues we cannot agree as to what all constitutes translation. During the next decades as some consensus in this matter is being reached, at least we can all be responsible for our own speech, and so testify both to our intent and to our understanding of how language in America functions. Meanwhile, sympathetic linguists ought to proceed with the massive task of retranslating the classic library of Christian theology. Contemporarily accurate translation of theological works will rid the study of Christianity of much of its overwhelming male overtone.

Fortunately one genre is remarkably free from the difficulty of God-he, and that is the genre of public prayer. Liturgy, since it is in the main direct address to God, has few of the third person pronouns that cause us concern. The archiac thou-thy-thee has been to a great extent replaced by you-your-you, and so at least direct address to God now speaks in modern American English. So let this be our comfort: that if we are tongue-tied in preaching, speaking, and writing, we need not be so tongue-tied in praying. But our search for a new way to speak and write makes more and more attractive the Hebraic circumlocutions for the name of God. Perhaps in the end we all will agree to write in the place of God's name only four dots and to speak for the name of God only the monk's silence.

1 Anthropomorphism, to the extent that it is used in the description of and naming of God, should be recognized as metaphor and must be explicated with poetic sensitivity. We should balance male with female imagery, as well as use objectification and recall the *via negativa*.

2 Human relationship terms, to the extent that they are used in the description of and naming of God, should be recognized as analogical language and must be explicated with theological sensitivity in which the revelation establishes the definition.

3 The naming of the Christian God requires a paradoxical use of human language. Human models are broken by the kerygma of the cross.

4 Masculine or feminine language used in the description of and naming of God must never imply or defend male or female sexuality in the being of God. Use of 'person', as in the three persons or in God as person, must never imply inherent sexuality.

5 Modern American English is moving towards a total replacement of grammatical gender with natural gender. This is, increasingly, gender equals sexuality. To the extent that this is true, expository prose cannot refer to God as he.

PART THREE

Practical Consequences

☐ Some of the most powerful re-evaluations of the Christian tradition have come from those who have stayed within the Roman Catholic Church, or in association with it, as well as with Women-Church in the USA. At this point in the *Reader*, lest anyone should feel too comfortable with the possibilities on offer and not find the energy to take the issues seriously enough to work for change, I think we should try to appreciate why Mary Daly, the writer of the 1968 *The Church and the Second Sex*, is now at odds with those women who have stayed inside the Christian tradition. Mary Daly has become the most formidable and uncompromising critic of all, precipitating herself out of Christianity with writing *Beyond God the Father* of 1973, now re-issued (1986) with an original re-introduction, and published in the UK by the Women's Press, as are *Gyn/Ecology* of 1978 and *Pure Lust* of 1984. These are books on a feminism sprung from Christianity but which has left it behind, and are very widely read by, and influential upon, women. Mary Daly's work shapes their perceptions of the tradition in a way little else will do, and sharpens and deepens the divide between those who still hope to find resources from within Christianity as sufficient reason for staying within it, hoping and working for change, and those who have discovered, or simply assume, that no such resources are there to be found.

Anthropologist Gwen Kennedy has written about the religious socialization of women in the subcultures of the USA, whether at the verbal, rational level, or at the invisible, behavioural and private level. Of the kinds of religious cultures to be found, torn from European environments and reinstated in North America, she comments on 'Mediterranean culture' as characterized by a highly ordered and hierarchical universe, with an institution run by all male prelates, stressing honour of family and lineage, reverence for motherhood, idealization of women, associated with buildings designed to keep arrows out and women in.[1] And Beverly Wildung Harrison has noted that the Roman Catholic Church is one in which orders and ordination are still principally understood in terms of public sacramental mediation. 'In these churches, the patterns of sexism are legitimated at a symbolic level so potent that women struggling in them need to be forearmed with a special understanding of the emotional load their demands for change carry . . . where *patriarchy* and the *public* mediation of grace are deeply intertwined, there are very special problems.'[2]

Marjorie Reiley Maguire has recently written on 'Catholic Women and the Theological Enclave', in *Christian Century*, 3–10 February 1982, pp. 109–11. Here she describes how renewed interest in theology after Vatican II led to women seeking entry to seminaries (seed-beds!), women who in time became candidates for teaching posts as peers of those who had equipped them to do so. They brought different questions with them, about liturgy, about the value of affective knowledge, about the recognition of ministry for women other than that of the religious education of women and children, about their exclusion from 'spiritual formation activities'. This whole area is only just beginning to be faced by the Roman Catholic Church in the UK, where open access to non-denominational institutions of tertiary education with their departments of religious studies and theology has mitigated some of the problems. So, of course, has been being able to apply for jobs in non-Roman Catholic theological colleges!

It is worth noticing paragraph 22 of *Ministry and Mission: Proposals for a National Policy for Lifelong Priestly Formation* (published as *Briefing* 87 in 1987 by the Bishops' Conference of England and Wales). This acknowledged the fact that a significant proportion of full-time lay ministers are women, reflecting the way in which the place of women in society and Church has changed, though women are still expected to play a limited role. The writer (a Roman Catholic layman and philosopher) continued:

> This is very much to be regretted and attitudes and practices need to change further so that they can contribute fully to the mission of the Church. Women must be welcomed into the work of priestly formation. They have gifts, skills and knowledge to share and their participation is essential if future priests are to develop in human maturity and avoid insensitive assumptions of male dominance.

This certainly does not go nearly far enough so far as those who seek for the full ordination of women are concerned, but the North American versions of these points helped to precipitate the kind of situation addressed by Marjorie Reiley Maguire. This is not just a problem for the laity in the way we unthinkingly use the word – and with which writers as different at Letty Russell[3] and Sara Maitland are preoccupied. The North American Roman Catholic Church has to cope also with its formidably well-educated and articulate women 'religious', all irretrievably 'lay' simply by virtue of their sex. Irene Woodward of the Sisters of the Holy Names of Jesus and Mary[4] writes of women growing up in a Church situated in a society trying to live the American dream, a pragmatic society that told them that anything was possible; that there were always new frontiers to conquer in a society that valued free enterprise and the expression of personal opinion; and that they had a right to participate in democratic processes and determine the direction of the policies under which they lived. Ten years *prior* to Vatican II, there had been much development in the professional education of 'religious', and they had since 1943 been able to read for postgraduate degrees in Roman Catholic theology at St Mary's College, closely associated with the University of Notre Dame, Indiana. By contrast, women were admitted to Harvard Divinity School only in 1975, and by 1973 only seventy-nine women had degrees, Letty Russell being one of the first three to graduate in 1958 and be ordained by the United Presbyterian Church.

By the time of Mary Daly's article, 'The Forgotten Sex: a

Built in Bias', in *Commonweal*, 15 January 1965, pp. 508–11, which led to the invitation to write *The Church and the Second Sex*, some 67 per cent of women religious had at least one university-level degree and 28 per cent had master's degrees. They had become one of the best-educated groups of women in the country, well equipped to assess the documents of Vatican II. The point of attending to these here is both to illustrate the predicament of women like Mary Daly, familiar with such examples of 'sisterhood', and also, to remind us of the Christian gender constructions of which I wrote in my Introduction. These are, as I have made sufficiently clear, by no means peculiar to the Roman Catholic tradition, which happens, in my view, to perform a regular service for the whole Christian community in the way it puts the issues 'out front'.

There are many things that have been said about the Vatican council documents (relying here on the Abbott edition), but we could notice especially, perhaps, the sentence adding during the final drafting to paragraph 9 of the document on the laity, in the section on 'the various fields of the apostolate'. This points out the importance of women's participation in the various fields of the Church's apostolate. Readers are no doubt meant to be reassured by the footnote that draws attention to the point that this is one of the few places in all the council documents where special attention is given to the contribution of women to the mission of the Church, though it was clearly (to whom?) the mind of the Council 'and eminently so', whenever the general role of the laity was discussed. The note adds that by the time the Council ended, twelve lay and ten religious women were present as 'auditrices', though, of course, it does not also add that no woman was permitted to read a paper to the Council (presumably in accordance with 1 Tim. 2.12) and that, as Anne Carr records (p. 30 of *Transforming Grace*), an attempt was made to bar women journalists from attending council Masses during its meetings.

Real exasperation was provoked by the closing messages of the Council, messages to men (males) regarded in terms of their diversified contributions to society, with women having a message addressed to them alone, as is usual in Christianity, with reference to their sexual states. Women are addressed as girls, wives, mothers and widows, consecrated virgins and women living alone, though with the acknowledgement that they constitute half of the immense human family, and with the problematical and even paradoxical claim that the Church has 'glorified and liberated them'. Women are associated with 'the protection of the home', with cradles and deaths (the power of the nativity[5] and crucifixion stories?); mothers are exhorted to 'pass on to your sons and daughters the traditions of your fathers'. (Mothers presumably not having any?). Women are invited to reconcile men with life, to guard purity (of course), unselfishness and piety, to aid men to retain courage in *their* great undertakings, with women's own concerns to be particularly with the peace of the world (Greenham Common was not yet a symbol of that concern). They are clearly excluded from the address to 'workers' – 'very loved sons' (as though women did not and do not work, despite the production of probably three-quarters of the so-called 'Third World's' food) with its sense of unease, mistrust and lack of understanding between Church and workers.

The post-Council renewal of religious orders was not of course without its problems, with the loss from the US Roman Catholic Church of one-third of its women religious. But they gained other strengths, by responding in 1961 to the call by a papal representative visiting the University of Notre Dame, for religious communities to contribute 10 per cent of their membership to work in Latin America. If feminism in the nineteenth century was forged and sharpened in the anti-slavery campaigns and the fight for the vote, the second half of the twentieth century has seen women involved in the search for justice in poor communities, honing the edge of their commitment. This has helped to overcome any residual antagonism between the sisters and other lay women. Irene Woodward writes that the sisters, removed from family tensions, with opportunities for leadership and self-development, saw for themselves the abuse, helplessness and meaninglessness of many women's lives. They found that all alike wanted realization of gospel values for themselves, inside structures that formally legitimated the religious orders, but which now deemed to be debilitating to men and women alike. And no one could ignore the problem for the

Church of women who were too disaffected to transmit their faith within their families.

Readers of Mary Daly will soon become alert to her political criticism – the unholy trinity of rape, genocide and war, run by godfather Reagan, Pentagon and company. The connections she draws between politics and patriarchy-given-religious-legitimacy, indicate major reasons why reform for her could not be an option for long. Rosemary Radford Ruether's *Women-Church* also exhibits strong political criticism too, focused in her case on the conflict between 'base-Christian communities' and the Nicaraguan Roman Catholic hierarchy. North American Roman Catholics are now a potentially very promising counter force to American intervention in popular revolutions in Central America. (We could now also recall the recent North American Bishops' critique of nuclear war in *The Challenge of Peace* and of the conduct of the economy.) For criticism of foreign policy is mediated back to the Church by members of religious orders whose boundaries are transnational.[6]

In her *Commonweal* article of 1965, Mary Daly made points that her readers needed to assimilate – that props offered by social conditions in the past, by false biological and philosophical theories (see the material on Augustine and Aquinas in this *Reader*) and anti-feminist legislation, had all melted away, as had women's 'natural' timidity and ineptitude. No one was going to deny 'difference'; the problem concerned the meaning and application of the word. There was no such thing as a static, immutable conception of female nature which would survive scrutiny of the actual possibilities and permutations. She wanted people freed from *a priori* stereotypes, with polarity between groups of human characteristics fostering egoism, getting from the 'other' what 'I' lack.

By the time Mary Daly came to preach in Harvard on 14 November 1971 (the first time a woman had preached at a Sunday sermon in Harvard's 336-year history, to a congregation that included women training for ministry), she proclaimed her irritation with the repetition of the line quoted by would-be pacifiers of women, of which, as she rightly said, *even if* in Christ there is no male and female (that used to shut them up) everywhere else there damn well is.

The quotation can function as a refusal to look at specific oppressive facts, rather than, as Elisabeth Schüssler Fiorenza was to argue in *In Memory of Her*, the requirement that to be a member of the early Christian community, privileges of race, social status and sex have to be abandoned. And given that the Christ-image is male, one has still to ask what meaning-content the passage can possibly have. And if Jesus was a feminist, 'Fine, wonderful. But even if he wasn't, *I am*.' In other words, why try to get back to the alleged 'purity' of the original revelation, giving the past prior claims over present experience, as if recourse to the past is necessary to validate experience now? And it is a very big assumption to make that there *are* adequate models to be extracted from the past. Women have the option of giving priority to their own experience, without looking to the past for some kind of justification. The Harvard sermon was, then, the occasion for an 'acted parable' of 'exodus', expressing her conviction that 'women whose consciousness has been raised are spiritual exiles whose sense of transcendence is seeking alternative expression to those available in institutional religion'. Hence her image of the women's movement as an 'exodus' community, and her invitation to the other women present to follow her out.

In another article in 1971, 'After the Death of God the Father', in *Commonweal*, 12 March, pp. 7–11, she gave an account of the way in which she believed the images and values of a given society are projected into a realm of beliefs, which in turn then seem to justify the social infrastructure. The belief system becomes hardened and objectified, seeming to have an unchangeable and independent existence and validity of its own. It resists those social changes that rob it of its plausibility. But change does occur, and ideologies die, even if they die hard. So, 'Religious symbols die when the cultural system that supported them ceases to give them plausibility. This should pose no problem ʹo authentic faith, which accepts the relativity of all symbols, and recognises that fixation upon any of them as absolute in itself is idolatrous.'[7] As she was to urge in *Pure Lust* (p. 272), 'a creative Prude not only acts within a context of given circumstances. She changes circumstances and spins new ones.'

Her articles and *Beyond God the Father* helped to put 'patriarchy' into currency,[8] connecting together the political, personal, conscious and unconscious, material and spiritual together in the worship of masculine identity. It functions as a unifying term indicating oppression, linking together consciousness of superior values, methods of control, power struggle and physical coercion. And Eugene Bianchi was to identify the core dogma of our patriarchal era as 'psychic celibacy', keeping women mentally and emotionally at arm's length. 'Women can be exalted as wife, virgin, mother or deprecated (and enjoyed) as temptress, playmate, whore. In whatever way this male projection works, woman is object, non-equal, manipulated, distanced.[9]

Mary Daly's attack on patriarchy was to be without quarter. Of the two crucial papers delivered at the American Academy of Religion in 1971 – hers and Rosemary Radford Ruether's – hers had the more menacing title: 'Theology after the Demise of God the Father; a Call for the Castration of Sexist Religion',[10] which was hardly likely to secure the ready sympathy of ecclesiastical power-brokers, unless she thought by that time that all hope for changing social structures was to be vested in new sisterhoods. But she wrote of castrating language and images, in the sense of 'cutting away the phallus-centred value system imposed by patriarchy', asserting too that the value system that has been thrust upon women has amounted to 'a kind of gang rape of minds and bodies'.

It is a form of retaliation to the label of 'castrating female' to retort that it is *women* who have been deprived of power, potency, creativity, ability to communicate, and that sexist religion has also done damage to black males, poor males, non-competitive males, third world males, all of whom however could still look down on women. An alternative to the metaphor of castration seems to be a kind of exorcism to be performed by women on themselves, to dislodge the images that reflect and reinforce prevailing social arrangements. If women can dislodge themselves from the role of the 'other', and dislodge the problem of evil from its peculiar association with women, they can also dislodge the need for a male saviour. Inviting men to lay claim to their own complete identity has nothing to do with easy reconciliation, with cheap grace, but takes the form of a very positive refusal of co-optation.

Beyond God the Father develops this material particularly in its closing pages, in which she reworks a metaphor taken from Virginia Woolf's *A Room of One's Own*, first written for university women in 1929. Virginia Woolf asks at one point why men become so angry with (feminist) women, and she comes up with the suggestion that they were protesting against some infringement of their power to believe in themselves. She decided that women had served all these centuries as looking glasses capable of reflecting the figure of man at twice its natural size. So here to read are the closing pages of *Beyond God the Father*.

16 MARY DALY
The Looking Glass Society

Our planet is inhabited by half-crazed creatures, but there is a consistency in the madness. Virginia Woolf, who died of being both brilliant and female, wrote that women are condemned by society to function as mirrors, reflecting men at twice their actual size. When this basic principle is understood, we can understand something about the dynamics of the Looking Glass society. Let us examine once again the creatures' speech.

That language for millennia has affirmed the fact that Eve was born from Adam, the first among history's unmarried pregnant males who courageously chose childbirth under sedation rather than abortion, consequently obtaining a child-bride. Careful study of the documents recording such achievements of Adam and his sons prepared the way for the arrival of the highest of the higher religions, whose priests took Adam as teacher and model. They devised a sacramental system that functioned magnificently within the sacred House of Mirrors. Graciously, they lifted from women the onerous power of childbirth, christening it 'baptism'. Thus they brought the lowly material function of birth, incompetently and even grudgingly performed by females, to a higher and more spiritual level. Recognizing the ineptitude of females in performing even the humble 'feminine' tasks assigned to them by the Divine

Plan, the Looking Glass priests raised these functions to the supernatural level in which they alone had competence. Feeding was elevated to become Holy Communion. Washing achieved dignity in Baptism and Penance. Strengthening became known as Confirmation, and the function of consolation, which the unstable nature of females caused them to perform so inadequately, was raised to a spiritual level and called Extreme Unction. In order to stress the obvious fact that all females are innately disqualified from joining the Sacred Men's Club, the Looking Glass priests made it a rule that their members should wear skirts. To make the point clearer, they reserved special occasions when additional Men's Club attire should be worn. These necessary accoutrements included delicate white lace tops and millinery of prescribed shapes and colours. The leaders were required to wear silk hose, pointed hats, crimson dresses and ermine capes, thereby stressing detachment from lowly material things and dedication to the exercise of spiritual talent. They thus became revered models of spiritual transsexualism.

These annointed Male Mothers, who naturally are called Fathers, felt maternal concern for the women entrusted to their pastoral care. Although females obviously are by nature incompetent and prone to mental and emotional confusion, they are required by the Divine Plan as vessels to contain the seeds of men so that men can be born and then supernaturally (correctly) reborn as citizens of the Heavenly Kingdom. Therefore in charity the priests encouraged women to throw themselves gratefully into their unique role as containers for the sons of the sons of the Son of God. Sincerely moved by the fervour of their own words, the priests educated women to accept this privilege with awestruck humility.

Since the Protestant Reformation, spiritual Looking Glass education has been modernized in some rooms of the House of Mirrors. Reformed Male Mothers gradually came to feel that maleness was overstressed by wearing dresses all the time and even decided to include a suitable proportion of females (up to one-half of 1 per cent) among their membership, thereby stressing that the time for male snobbism was over and the time for democracy had come. They also came to realize that they could be just as supernatural without being hemmed in by a stiff sacramental system. They could give birth spiritually, heal and console, and give maternal advice. They therefore continued the Looking Glass tradition of Mother Adam while at the same time making a smooth transition to the Modern Age.

Thus, Western culture was gracefully prepared by its Supernatural Mothers called Fathers to see all things supernaturally, that is, to perceive the world backwards clearly. In fact, so excellent had been our education that this kind of thinking has become like second nature for almost everybody. No longer in need of spiritual guidance, our culture has come of age. This fact is evident to anyone who will listen to it when it talks. Its statesmen clearheadedly affirm the fact that this is 'the Free World'. Its newscasters accurately report that there has been fighting in the demilitarized zone, that several people were killed in a non-violent demonstration, that 'our nation' is fighting to bring peace to South-East Asia. Its psychiatrists proclaim that the entire society is in fact a mental institution and applaud this fact as a promising omen of increasing health for their profession.

In the Looking Glass society females, that is, Magnifying Mirrors, play a crucial role. But males have realized that it would serve no good purpose if this were to become known by females, who might then stop looking into the toy mirrors they have been taught to use incessantly. They might then begin looking inside or backwards or forwards. Instead of settling for the vanity of parakeets they might fall into the sin of pride and refuse to be Magnifying Mirrors any longer.

The females, in the terrifying, exhilarating experience of becoming rather than reflecting, would discover that they too have been infected by the dynamics of the Mirror World. Having learned only to mirror, they would find in themselves reflections of the sickness in their masters. They would find themselves doing the same things, fighting the same way. Looking inside for something there, they would be confused by what at first would appear to be an endless Hall of Mirrors. What to copy? What model to imitate? Where to look? What is a mere mirror to do? But wait – How could a mere mirror even frame such a question? The question itself is the beginning of an answer that keeps unfolding itself. The question-answer is a verb, and when one begins to move in the current of the verb, of the Verb, she knows that she is not a mirror. Once she knows this she knows it so deeply that she cannot completely forget. She knows it so deeply that she has to say it to her sisters. What if more and more of her sisters should begin to hear and to see and to speak?

This would be a disaster. It would throw the whole society backward into the future. Without Magnifying Mirrors all around, men would have to look inside and outside. They would start to look inside, wondering what was wrong with them. They would have to look outside because without the mirrors they would begin to receive impressions from real Things out there. They would even have to look at women, instead of reflections. This would be confusing and they would be forced to look inside again, only to have the harrowing experience of finding *there* the Eternal Woman, the Perfect Parakeet. Desperately looking outside again, they would find that the Parakeet is no longer *out there*. Dashing back inside, males would find other horrors: All of the other Others – the whole crowd – would be in there: the lazy niggers, the dirty Chicanos, the greedy Jews, faggots and dykes, plus the entire crowd of Communists and the backward population of the Third World. Looking outward again, mirrorless males would be forece to see – people. Where to go? Paroxysm towards the Omega Point? But without the Magnifying Mirror even that last refuge is gone. What to do for relief? Send more bombing missions? But no. It is pointless to be killing The Enemy after you find out The Enemy is yourself.

But the Looking Glass society is still there, bent on killing itself off. It is still ruled by God the Father who, gazing at his magnified reflections, believes in his superior size. I say 'believes', because the reflection now occasionally seems to be diminished and so he has to make a renewed act of faith in Himself.

We have been locked in this Eden of his far too long. If we stay much longer, life *will* depart from this planet. The freedom to fall out of Eden will cost a mirror-shattering experience. The freedom-becoming-survival of our species will require a continual, communal striving in be-ing. This means forging the great chain of be-ing in sisterhood that can surround non-being, forcing it to shrink back into itself. The cost of failure is Nothing.

Is this the war to end wars? The power of sisterhood is not war-power. There have been and will be conflicts, but the Final Cause causes not by conflict but by attraction. Not by the attraction of a Magnet that is All There, but by the creative drawing power of the Good Who is self-communicating Be-ing. Who is the Verb from whom, in whom, and with whom all true movements move.

☐ Other clear attacks on Christianity's core symbolism can be found in Mary Daly's subsequent books. For instance, in *Gyn/Ecology* (p. 38) she writes of the Trinity, excluding female mythic presence from the divine being, denying female reality in the cosmos, the original love story performed by the Supreme All Male Cast, 'sublime' (and therefore disguised) erotic male homosexual mythos, 'the mold for all varieties of male monogender mating'. And to 'the timid objections voiced by Christian women, the classic answer has been: "You're included under the Holy Spirit. He's feminine."' As she rightly retorts, 'The point is, of course, that male made-up femininity has nothing to do with women. Drag queens, whether divine or human, belong to the Men's Association.' Not the least of the problems she identifies is that we can hardly do justice to the feminine in ourselves, let alone in the divine, because we can hardly know what it is to be female and feminine in a patriarchal society.

And on Paul's proposals about our adoption as sons (Gal. 4.3f.) she says in *Pure Lust* (p. 9), 'We do not wish to be redeemed by a god, to be adopted as sons, or to have the spirit of a god's son artificially injected into our hearts, crying "father".' If the symbolism associated with Mary the mother of Jesus is deemed to be core symbolism, her critique of it also repays detailed attention. She comes to think that there are no possible resources in a biblically-related religion to aid the journey, to find out where we should be heading. Tucked away in a footnote of *Beyond God the Father* (p. 205) is her assessment of Phyllis Trible's tactics: 'It might be interesting to speculate upon the probable length of a "depatriarchalized Bible". Perhaps there would be enough salvageable material to comprise an interesting pamphlet.'

Daly is a leading example of one of those who can be charged in sexist terms with being 'not feminine', as Beverly Wildung Harrison puts it. Such a woman will have 'said something she should not have said, aspired to do or have done something which she should not have done. In short, she has crossed that invisible but powerful boundary out of her territory. The charge of being "not feminine", I submit, is aimed at thwarting Initiative. Its message is: "Go back".'[11]

Beverly Wildung Harrison is a specialist in Christian social ethics, and, fortunately for her readers, a collection of her essays, edited by Carol S. Robb, is now available, under the title *Making the Connections: Essays in Feminist Social Ethics*

(Boston, Beacon Press, 1985). Taking some clues from Mary Daly's work, she is especially concerned with a critique of *dis*-embodied, *dis*-interested 'love', destroying the power of relation, rather than acknowledging and discovering our power to celebrate the gift of life. Especially significant to women who have suffocated themselves in the name of 'sacrifice' she acknowledges the importance of feeling, loving and life-giving in relationships and mutuality. Next, then, is 'The Power of Anger in the Work of Love: Christian Ethics for Women and Other Strangers', the first essay in *Making the Connections*, and an example of someone who can take clues from Mary Daly, but still work within the tradition in the hope of changing it.[12]

17 BEVERLY WILDUNG HARRISON
The Power of Anger in the Work of Love
Christian Ethics for Women and Other Strangers

This essay is an expansion of my inaugural lecture as Professor of Christian Ethics at Union Theological Seminary in New York. Those who heard it in its original form in 1980 also witnessed an academic procession. On that occasion, however, the academic procession was planned to ritualize – that is, to express in embodied form – what I believe the work of radical love involves. It would be possible, in retrospect, to describe that procession in a way that would emphasize its similarity to other such academic processions. It could be reported merely that participating were faculty colleagues as well as representatives of the Board of Directors, distinguished clergy and lay leaders from a number of denominations and scholars from other seminaries and academic departments of religious studies. Yet those present, seeing and hearing my lecture, also saw a procession radically unlike most others of its genre because 70 per cent of the marchers were women and most were arrayed in garb of breath-taking colour. This essay is a slightly amended version of one that appeared in the *Union Seminary Quarterly Review*, vol. 36 Supplementary, 1981.

Undoing patriarchal processions

Readers who are knowledgeable in feminist theology and who have had sufficient intellectual energy to read and appropriate Mary Daly's powerful, angry book *Gyn/Ecology: The Metaethics of Radical Feminism*, may already understand why it was important then, as now, to begin a discussion of feminist ethics by focusing on the issue of academic processions. Processions, Daly argues, exemplify all that is wrong with the patriarchal world; they are the essence of 'the deception of the fathers'.[1] Daly believes that this 'deception of the fathers' – the way we were all taught to view the world through rigidly compartmentalized, static categories and academic disciplines – is killing us all. This fixation with processions, she contends, has its origins in Christianity, beginning with the procession of the trinitarian god. The god of Christian orthodoxy – with its threefold, exclusively male manifestation – is, she suggests, expressive of the male homosexual fixation that underlies the dominant spirituality of our culture, whether in an ecclesiastical or an academic expression. In either academic or ecclesiastical contexts, processions mark out clearly, and protect, male privilege and control. Daly stresses that this sacralizing and deification of male functions in our world will be ended only if women who understand the idolatry involved give up participation in processions altogether. In fact, she is so serious in this claim that the power of procession sustains the patriarchal oppression of women that she designates 'procession' as the *first* (the very first) of the eight deadly sins of Phallocracy.[2] These eight deadly sins represent Daly's alternative way of viewing human evil; they replace the traditional seven deadly sins of Christian teaching. It should not be lost on any of us that on the traditional list of deadly sins the 'sin' of anger was usually given conspicuous emphasis. Happily, no feminist analysis could perpetuate the notion that anger, *per se*, is evil, and Daly's analysis surely does not do so.

I acknowledge that Mary Daly would not exempt even an academic procession numerically dominated by females from her unequivocal indictment of processions as instruments of patriarchy. She is adamant that processions can be only a 'frozen mirror image' of 'Spinning', which is her metaphor for the wholistic, spontaneous, intellectually imaginative modes of knowing, being, and doing of which women – when not dependent on patriarchy for self-definition – are capable. There can be no doubt that the mere presence of a *few* women in traditional processions serves, first and foremost, to disguise the devastation that dominant institutions wreak upon women and others who do not 'fit in' – for example, males of colour or males whose ideological viewpoint or sexual orientation does not reinforce the dominant cultural mode. Even so, my theory of social change obviously diverges from hers or I would not have organized a procession at all.

I agree with Daly that a chief evidence of patriarchal control in our world is women's subtle conditioning that reinforces our reluctance to develop a sense of our own power to identify, name, and characterize our world. For all of the methodological differences that separate my position from Daly's, [3] it is no part of my argument with her to deny the depth of the problem of misogyny in human history or in the dominant forms of historical Christianity. Among the many debts we owe Mary Daly is this: She has described the problem in an uncompromising way and has made it impossible for any intellectually honest person to deny the necessity of a feminist critique of Christianity. I have long argued this point in light of Daly's analysis – that it should never be the business of any feminist who remains within the Christian community to mitigate the painful encounter that the Christian Church must have, and has yet to have, with the full force of a feminist critique. We have very far to go before Christianity acknowledges adequately its complicity in breeding and perpetuating the hatred and fear of the real, full, lived-world power of female persons! Misogyny, as Daly claims, is hydra-headed, having as many forms as there are cultures, languages, and social systems. She is right to insist that what is feared is not 'femininity', that clever nineteenth-century invention, but the spooking, sparking power of *real* women, who do not need to stand around waiting for male approval. Misogyny's real force arises only when women assert oursleves and own our power. Mark this point well: It is never the mere presence of a woman, nor the image of women, nor fear of 'femininity', that is the heart of misogyny. The core of misogyny, which has yet to be broken or even touched, is the reaction that occurs when women's concrete power is manifest, when we women live and act as full and adequate persons in our own right. Even when Daly's specific historical portrayal of misogyny is carelessly done,[4] she still has a firm sense of the depth of what must be undone in human life if the culturally diverse patterns of woman-hating are to end. It would be a form of deep intellectual dishonesty not to acknowledge that only Mary Daly's profound rage has produced a feminist critique strong enough to assure that some minimal attention must be given it within ecclesiastical and academic circles.

At times I wish I believed, with Daly, that the power of patriarchy could be overthrown if only we women would absent ourselves from patriarchal processions altogether. If only the *withholding* of power were adequate to bring about social change in our world, undoing oppression would not be difficult. However, we women should be the last to allow ourselves to be trapped in a 'spiritualizing' notion that real change in our flesh and blood world ever comes from absenting ourselves from what is going on in that world. Only a few women are in a position even to fantasize such options of withdrawal. Hardly any of our foresisters had such an option.

Even if many contemporary women were to choose the option of nonparticipation, we may be sure that processions would continue precisely because they are such powerful human actions, which is to say that they express energy, movement, and festivity. If men have enjoyed them, why should women not enjoy them too? Like all powerful public rituals, all dramatic human activity, processions shape our sense of who we are as actors, or what in the language of ethics we call 'moral agents'. They shape not only what we call our 'personal moral sense' or sense of identity and self-worth but also our sense of destiny and community – what we call our 'moral ethos'. They always have and they always will. Processions cannot be abandoned because we *all* live by a sense of plausibility and legitimacy that we gain from them. Be assured that whatever passes in our common life as sacred truth or profound wisdom has been and will always be shaped and celebrated through such occasions. So those excluded from processions in our flesh and blood world suffer very palpable loss, real injuries to dignity, real assaults on self-respect and sense of worth.

This is why I cannot concur with Daly's call to women to abandon processions and join the 'Journey to the Otherworld' of segregated feminism. The joyful world of Womanspace, which she commends to us as a permanent habitat, can be at best only an occasional sanctuary for the feminist *for whom life itself, and the embodied world of flesh and blood*, are the true gifts of God. For this reason the turn in Mary Daly's writing, marked by a new emphasis on the language of otherworldliness, disturbs me. In contrast to Daly, my basic ethical thesis is that women, and other marginated people, are *less* cut off from the real, material conditions of life than are those who enjoy the privileges of patriarchy and that, as a result, an otherworldly spirituality is far removed from the life experience of women. Even if Daly were clear, as I hope she is, that her use of the language of otherworldliness is metaphorical, her imagery still seems misguided. Our need is for a moral theology shaped and informed by women's actual historical struggle. Women's experience, I submit, could not possibly yield an 'other-worldly' ethic. Nor can feminists ignore the growing but morally dubious fascination with forms of world-denying spirituality in our culture. In light of a massive trend toward escapist religiosity, Daly's imagery, even if it stems from poetic license, is dangerous. It gives aid and comfort to those who have very strong political and economic reasons to encourage a spirituality that does not focus on injustice and the personal suffering it generates. Feminists, whose commitments must be to deep and profound change, should have no part in supporting a world-denying spirituality or in encouraging ways of speaking about the world that may invite withdrawal from struggle.

'Otherworldliness' in religion has two very different sources in our social world of knowledge. One sort of otherworldly religion appears among the poor and downtrodden, reflecting a double dynamic in their experience: It reflects a hopelessness about this world that is engendered by living daily with the evil of oppression, but it also fuels and encourages an ongoing struggle against the present order by conjuring a better time and a better place, beyond the oppressive here and now. However, an entirely different form of otherworldliness appears amongst those of us who have never been marginated, who have lived well above the daily struggle to survive, when our privileges are threatened. This form of other-worldliness is merely escapist, and its political consequences are entirely reactionary. Its result is to encourage denial of responsi-bility for the limited power that we do have, and it always results in reinforcing the status quo.

Daly's metaphorical leap into Otherworldly Womanspace may well come from the real agony and pain she has experienced in the face of misogyny.[5] The inexhaustibility of her rage suggests that this is so. However, a feminist metaethics must not fail to affirm and generate our power to affect the existing world. We must wrest this power of action from our very rightful anger at what has been done to us and to our sisters and to brothers who do not meet patriarchy's expectations. The deepest danger to our cause is that our anger will turn inward and lead us to portray ourselves and other women chiefly as victims rather than those who have struggled for the gift of life against incredible odds. The creative power of anger is shaped by owning this great strength of women and of others who have struggled for the full gift of life against structures of oppression.

We need not minimize the radicality of women's oppression in varied cultures and communities nor minimize Christianity's continuing involvement in that oppression, but we must not let that recognition confirm us in a posture of victimization. Let us note and celebrate the fact that 'woman-spirit rising' is a *global* phenomenon in our time. Everywhere women are on the move. Coming into view now, for the first time, on a worldwide scale, is the incredible *collective* power of women so that anyone who has eyes to see can glimpse the power and strength of women's full humanity. We dare not forget, in spite of the varied forms of women's historical bondage, that we have also been, *always*, bearers of many of the most precious and special arts of human survival. The Chinese revolutionary slogan 'Women hold up half the sky' is not mere hyperbole. In spite of a literary historical tradition that has ignored the fact, women always have held up half, or more than half, of the sky. This astonishing cross-cultural phenomenon of women's rising consciousness going on all around us could not have happened if this deep human power of women were not already grounded reality. I submit that even the present widespread cultural and political backlash against feminism is strong testimony to this fact. To be sure, the full world historical project that feminism envisages remains a distant dream – that is, that every female child in *each* and *every* community and culture will be born to share a full horizon of human possibility, that she will have the same range of life options as every male child. This is, and remains, 'the longest revolution'. But this revolution, for which we have every right to yearn, will come sooner if we celebrate the strength that shines forth in women's lives. This strength and power must stand at the center of the moral theology that feminism generates.

What I propose to do in the space remaining is to identify several positive dimensions of women's historical experience that I believe are most urgent to the reshaping of traditional Christian theological ethics to bring that ethics closer to a moral norm inclusive of all humanity. I also invite you to consider what difference it would make to our undertanding of 'the great commandment' – our love of God and our love of neighbour – if these basepoints drawn from women's experience received their due. It is out of such a process that we can begin to develop an adequate feminist moral theology.[6]

My basic thesis that a Christian moral theology must be answerable to what women have learned by struggling to lay hold of the gift of life, to receive it, to live deeply into it, to pass it on, cannot be fully defended here. My theological method is consonant with those other liberation theologies that contend that what is authentic in the history of faith arises only out of the crucible of human struggle.[7] This I take to be *the* central, albeit controversial, methodological claim of all emergent liberation theologies. That the locus of divine revelation is in the concrete struggles of groups and communities to lay hold of the gift of life and to unloose what denies life has astonishing implications for ethics. It means, among other things, that we must learn what we are to know of love from immersion in the struggle for justice. I believe that women have always been immersed in the struggle to create a flesh and blood community of love and justice and that we know much more of the radical work of love than does the dominant, otherworldly spirituality of Christianity. A feminist ethic, I submit, is deeply and profoundly worldly, a spirituality of sensuality.[8]

Basepoints for a Feminist Moral Theology

Activity as the mode of love

The first point at which women's experience challenges the dominant moral theology is difficult to see historically because of the smoke screen created by a successful nineteenth-century male counter-attack on the first women's liberation movement. Because of this counter-attack, most educated, middle-strata women have internalized an ideology about ourselves that contradicts our actual history. Historically, I believe, women have always exemplified the power of activity over passivity, of experimentation over routinization, of creativity and risk-taking over conventionality. Yet since the nineteenth century we have been taught to believe that women are, by nature, more passive and reactive than men. *If* women throughout human history have behaved as cautiously and as conventionally as the 'good women' invented by late bourgeois spirituality, *if* women had acquiesced to 'the cult of true womanhood', and *if* the social powerlessness of women that is the 'ideal' among the European and American 'leisure classes' had prevailed, the gift of human life would long since have faced extinction.

This very modern invitation to us women to perceive ourselves under the images of effete gentility, passivity, and weakness blocks our capacity to develop a realistic sense of women's historical past.

The fact is that while there are few constants in women's experience cross-culturally, the biological reality of childbearing and
nursing (never to be confused with the cultural power of nurturance) usually gave women priority in, and responsibility for, those
day-to-day activities that make for human survival in most societies. For example, women – not men – are the breadwinners and
traders in many precapitalist societies. If we modern women
acquiesce in the seductive invitation to think of ourselves primarily
as onlookers, as contemplators, as those who stand aside while men
get on with the serious business of running the (public) world, we
should at least recognize what a modern 'number' we are doing on
ourselves! The important point here, however, is that a theology
that overvalues static and passive qualities as 'holy', that equates
spirituality with noninvolvement and contemplation, that views the
activity of sustaining daily life as mundane and unimportant
religiously, such a theology *could not have been formulated by
women*. In contrast, Sojourner Truth spoke authentically, out of
the real lived-world experience of women, when she defined her
womanhood in this way:

> Nobody ever helped me into carriages, or over mud puddles, or gave
> me the best place. And ain't I a woman? Look at me! Look at my arm! I
> have ploughed and planted and gathered into barns, and no men could
> head me! And ain't I a woman? I can work as much and eat as much as
> any man when I can get it and bear the lash as well. And ain't I a
> woman? I have borne thirteen children and seen most of them sold off
> to slavery, and when I cried out with my mother's grief, none but Jesus
> heard me. And ain't I a woman?[9]

Women have been the doers of life-sustaining things, the 'copers,'
those who have understood that the reception of the gift of life is no
inert thing, that to receive this gift is to be engaged in its tending,
constantly. I believe we have a very long way to go before the
priority of activity over passivity is internalized in our theology and
even farther to go before love, in our ethics, is understood to be a
mode of action. In *Beyond God the Father*,[10] Mary Daly began the
necessary theological shift by insisting that a feminist theism has no
place for a God understood as stasis and fixity, that out of women's
experience the sacred is better imaged in terms of process and
movement. Her proposal that God be envisaged as Be-ing, as verb
rather than as noun, struck a deep chord in her readers, and not
merely in her women readers.

Even so, Daly's reformulation does not seem to me even to go far
enough. Susanne Langer has rightly noted that philosophies of

being – those philosophies that take the structures of nature as their starting point – have long since incorporated the notion that process is *the* basic structure of reality.[11] Process theologians rightly protest that Daly has not paid enough attention to, or given enough credit to, modern philosophy of religion for incorporating these new views of nature. However, not many process theologians – indeed, even Daly – recognize the further need to incorporate the full meaning of the human struggle for life into our understanding of God. It is necessary to open up the naturalistic metaphors for God to the power of human activity, to freedom not only as radical creativity but also as radical moral power. It is necessary to challenge the classic ontology of Be-ing even more deeply than Daly has done. Catholic natural law theologies, it has often been argued, fail to do justice to the fact that the power of nature passes through what Marx called 'the species-being' of human nature. Our world and our faith are transformed, for good or ill, through human activity. A feminist moral theology needs to root its analysis in this realm of radical moral creativity. Such freedom is often abused, but the power to create a world of moral relations is a fundamental aspect of human nature itself. In my opinion, the metaphor of Be-ing does not permit us to incorporate the radicality of human agency adequately. *Do-ing* must be as fundamental as *be-ing* in our theologies. Both do-ing and be-ing are, of course, only metaphors for conceptualizing our world. Both are only 'ways of seeing things'. However, we can never make sense of what is deepest, 'wholiest', most powerfully sacred in the lives of women if we identify women only with the more static metaphor of being, neglecting the centrality of praxis as basic to women's experience. We women have a special reason to appreciate the radical freedom of the power of real, concrete deeds.

To be sure, some male-articulated 'theologies of praxis' have given feminist theologians pause on this point. Men often envisage the power of human activity under images that suggest that domination and control are the central modes of human activity, as though political or military conquest were the noblest expressions of the human power to act. Because of this, some women have urged that feminist theologies eschew historical categories and operate exclusively from naturalistic metaphors. I believe that such a theological move would have disastrous consequences. We dare not minimize the very real historical power of women to be architects of what is most authentically human. We must not lose hold of the fact that we have been the chief builders of whatever human dignity and community has come to expression. *We* have the right to speak of *building* human dignity and community.

Just as do-ing must be central to a feminist theology, so too be-ing and do-ing must never be treated as polarities. Receiving community as gift and doing the work of community building are two ways to view the same activity. A feminist theology is not a theology of either/or.[12] Anyone who has lived in 'women's place' in human history has had to come to terms with the responsibility of being a reciprocal agent. Women's lives literally have been shaped by the power not only to bear human life at the biological level but to nurture life, which is a social and cultural power. Though our culture has come to disvalue women's role, and with it to disvalue nurturance, genuine nurturance is a formidable power.[13] Insofar as it has taken place in human history, it has been largely through women's action. For better or worse, women have had to face the reality that we have the power not only to create personal bonds between people but, more basically, to build up and deepen *personhood itself*. And to build up 'the person' is also to deepen relationship, that is, to bring forth community.

We do not yet have a moral theology that teaches us the awe-ful, awe-some truth that we have the power through acts of love or lovelessness literally to create one another. I believe that an adequate feminist moral theology must call the tradition of Christian ethics to accountability for minimizing the deep power of human action in the work of or the denial of love. Because we do not understand love as the power to act-each-other-into-well-being we also do not understand the depth of our power to thwart life and to maim each other. The fateful choice is ours, either to set free the power of God's love in the world or to deprive each other of the very basis of personhood and community. This power of human activity, so crucial to the divine-human drama, is *not* the power of world conquest or empire building, nor is it control of one person by another. We are *not* most godlike in our human power when we take the view from the top, the view of rulers, or of empires, or the view of patriarchs.

I believe that our world is on the verge of self-destruction and death because the society as a whole has so deeply neglected that which is most human and most valuable and the most basic of all the works of love – the work of human communication, of caring and nurturance, of tending the personal bonds of community. This activity has been seen as women's work and discounted as too mundane and undramatic, too distracting from the serious business

204 Practical Consequences

of world rule. Those who have been taught to imagine themselves as world builders have been too busy with master plans to see that love's work *is* the deepening and extension of human relations. This urgent work of love is subtle but powerful. Through acts of love – what Nelle Morton has called 'hearing each other to speech'[14] – we literally build up the power of personhood in one another. It is within the power of human love to build up dignity and self-respect in each other or to tear each other down. We are better at the latter than the former. However, literally through acts of love directed to us, we become self-respecting and other-regarding persons, and we cannot be one without the other. If we lack self-respect we also become the sorts of people who can neither see nor hear each other.

We may wish, like children, that we did not have such awesome power for good or evil. But the fact is that we do. The power to receive and give love, or to withhold it – that is, to withhold the gift of life – is less dramatic, but every bit as awesome, as our technological power. It is a tender power. And the exercise of that power begins, and is rooted in *our bodies, ourselves*, as women are never likely to forget.[15]

Our bodies, ourselves as the agents of love

A second basepoint for feminist moral theology derives from celebrating 'embodiment'.[16] A moral theology must not only be rooted in a worldly spirituality but must aim at overcoming the body/mind split in our intellectual and social life at every level. Feminist historical theologian Rosemary Ruether and, more recently, a number of male theologians have begun to identify the many connections between this body/mind dualism and our negative attitudes toward women.[17] Ironically, no dimension of our Western intellectual heritage has been so distorted by body/mind dualism as has our moral theology and moral philosophy, which is why a feminist moral theology is so needed. A number of male theologians – notably my colleague Tom Driver[18] – have begun to re-envisage a Christian theology that repudiates the mind/body split. However, fewer men in the field of Christian ethics have grasped the connection between body/mind dualism and the assumption many moral theologians make that we are most moral when most detached and disengaged from life-struggle.[19] Far too many Christian ethicists continue to imply that 'disinterestedness' and 'detachment' are basic preconditions for responsible moral action. And in the dominant ethical tradition, moral rationality too often is *disembodied* rationality.

If we begin, as feminists must, with 'our bodies, ourselves', we recognize that all our knowledge, including our moral knowledge, is body-mediated knowledge. All knowledge is rooted in our sensuality. We know and value the world, *if* we know and value it, through our ability to touch, to hear, to see. *Perception* is foundational to *conception*. Ideas are dependent on our sensuality. Feeling is the basic bodily ingredient that mediates our connectedness to the world. When we cannot feel, literally, we lose our connection to the world. All power, including intellectual power, is rooted in feeling. If feeling is damaged or cut off, our power to image the world and act into it is destroyed and our rationality is impaired. But it is not merely the power to conceive the world that is lost. Our power to value the world gives way as well. If we are not perceptive in discerning our feelings, or if we do not know what we feel, we cannot be effective moral agents. This is why psychotherapy has to be understood as a very basic form of moral education. In the absence of feeling there is no rational ability to evaluate what is happening. Failure to live deeply in 'our bodies, ourselves' destroys the possibility of moral relations between us.

These days there is much analysis of 'loss of moral values' in our society. A feminist moral theology enables us to recognize that a major source of rising moral insensitivity derives from being out-of-touch with our bodies. Many people live so much in their heads that they no longer feel their connectedness to other living things. It is tragic that when religious people fear the loss of moral standards, they become *more* repressive about sex and sensuality. As a result they lose moral sensitivity and do the very thing they fear – they discredit moral relations through moralism. That is why the so-called moral majority is so dangerous.

By contrast, a feminist moral theology, rooted in embodiment, places great emphasis on 'getting clear', on centering, on finding ways to enable us to stay connected to other people and to our natural environment.[20] Unless we value and respect feeling as the source of this mediation of the world, we lose this connection. To respect feeling is not, as some have suggested, to become subjecti*vistic*. To the contrary, subjecti*vism* is not the result of placing too much emphasis on the body and/or feeling. Subjecti*vism* and mora*lism* derive instead from evading feeling, from not integrating feeling deeply at the bodily level. This is not to suggest, however, that feelings are an end in themselves. We should never seek feelings, least of all loving feelings. Furthermore, the command to love is not now and never was an order to *feel a certain way*. Nor does the command to love create the power to *feel* love, and it was never intended to do so. Action does that. Feelings deserve our respect for what they are. There are no 'right' and 'wrong' feelings. Moral quality is a property of acts, not feelings, and our feelings arise in action. The moral question is not 'What do I feel?' but rather 'What do I do with what I feel?' Because this is not understood, contemporary Christianity is impaled between a subjectivist and sentimental piety that results from fear of strong feeling, especially strong negative feeling, and an objectivist, wooden piety that suppresses feeling under pretentious conceptual detachment. A feminist moral theology welcomes feeling for what it is – the basic ingredient in our relational transaction with the world.

The importance of all this becomes clear when we stop to consider the relation of our acts of love to our anger. It is my thesis that we Christians have come very close to killing love precisely because we have understood anger to be a deadly sin. Anger is not the opposite of love. It is better understood as a feeling-signal that all is not well in our relation to other persons or groups or to the world around us. Anger is a mode of connectedness to others and it is always a vivid form of caring. To put the point another way: anger is – and it always is – a sign of some resistance in ourselves to the moral quality of the social relations in which we are immersed. Extreme and intense anger signals a deep reaction to the action upon us or toward others to whom we are related.

To grasp this point – that anger signals something amiss in relationship – is a critical first step in understanding the power of anger in the work of love. Where anger rises, there the energy to act is present. In anger, one's body-self is engaged, and the signal comes that something is amiss in relation. To be sure, anger – no more than any other set of feelings – does not lead automatically to wise or humane action. (It is part of the deeper work of ethics to help us move through all our feelings to adequate strategies of moral action.) We must never lose touch with the fact that all serious human moral activity, especially action for social change, takes it bearings from the rising power of human anger. Such anger is a signal that change is called for, that transformation in relation is required.

Can anyone doubt that the avoidance of anger in popular Christian piety, reinforced by a long tradition of fear of deep feeling in our body-denying Christian tradition, is a chief reason why the Church is such a conservative, stodgy institution? I suggest, however, that while many of us actually hold out little hope for the moral renewal of the Christian Church in our time, we are reluctant to face the cause of moral escap*ism* in the Church – namely, the fear of feeling and, more specifically, fear of the power of anger. We need to recognize that where the evasion of feeling is widespread, anger does not go away or disappear. Rather, in interpersonal life it masks itself as boredom, ennui, low energy, or it expresses itself in passive-aggressive activity or in moralistic self-righteousness and blaming. Anger denied subverts community. Anger expressed directly is a mode of taking the other seriously, of caring. The important point is that where feeling is evaded, where anger is hidden or goes unattended, masking itself, there the power of love, the power to act, to deepen relation, atrophies and dies.

Martin Buber is right that direct hatred (and hatred is anger turned rigid, fixated, deadened) is closer to love than to the absence of feeling.[21] The group or person who confronts us in anger is demanding acknowledgment from us, asking for the recognition of their presence, their value. We have two basic options in such a situation. We can ignore, avoid, condemn, or blame. Or we can act to alter relationship toward reciprocity, beginning a real process of hearing and speaking to each other. A feminist moral theology, then, celebrates anger's rightful place within the work of love and recognizes its central place in divine and human life.

The centrality of relationship

The final and most important basepoint for a feminist moral theology is the centrality of relationship.

As a feminist moral theology celebrates the power of *our* human praxis as an intrinsic aspect of the work of *God's* love, as it celebrates the reality that our moral-selves are body-selves who touch and see and hear each other into life, recognizing sensuality as fundamental to the work and power of love, so above all else a feminist moral theology insists that relationality is at the heart of all things.

I am perfectly aware that our current preoccupation with 'human relations', with 'skills of relationship' is such that some have declared that our modern concern for relationship is merely trendy and faddish. It is true that, like everything else in late capitalism, 'relationship' becomes transformed into a commodity to be packaged and exchanged at a price. To speak of the primacy of relationship in feminist experience, and to speak of a theology of relation, however, is not to buy in on the latest capitalist fad. It is, above all, to insist on the deep, total sociality of all things. All things cohere in each other. Nothing living is self-contained; if there were such a thing as an unrelated individual, none of us would know it. The ecologists have recently reminded us of what nurturers always knew – that we are part of a web of life so intricate as to be beyond our comprehension.[22] Our life is part of a vast cosmic web, and no moral theology that fails to envisage reality in this way will be able to make sense of our lives or our actions today.

In a recent, powerful, and pioneering work that lays the groundwork for a feminist theology of relationship,[23] Carter Heyward has made clear how far traditional Christian theism has wandered from the central concern with relationality that characterized the faith of the Israelite community and that was so central to Jesus' ministry. She stresses that the basic images of God that emerged in patristic Christianity were devoid of relationship. By stressing that God is 'being itself' or is 'the wholly other', the Christian tradition implies that a lack of relatedness in God is the source of divine strength. And this image of divine nonrelatedness surely feeds images of self that lead us to value isolation and monadic autonomy. In our dominant theologies and intellectual traditions, do we not think of ourselves as most effective, most powerful as moral agents when we are most autonomous and most self-reliant, when we least need anyone else's help or support?

In a brilliant work entitled *About Possession: The Self as Private Property*,[24] philosopher John Wikse notes the connection of the metaphors of self we use with the property metaphors dominant in the socioeconomic order. To be a free person, to be a self in this society, now, means 'to possess oneself'. We actually think of real freedom as 'self-possession'. Self-reliance and freedom from dependence on others is everything. Wikse argues, most plausibly, that it is now difficult to tell the difference between the way this culture's 'ideal person' is supposed to behave and the way we have traditionally viewed the behaviour of those who are idiots or suffer madness. The idiot, we had always assumed, is one cut off from relationship, one who does not share common meaning. Now, however, we also see maturity as involving the same freedom from relatedness; *self*-relatedness is now so much the highest value that we speak as if 'being at one with oneself' were a condition for relationship to others rather than a consequence of it. The hope that we can control our identity from within fulfills a dream that we can live 'beyond vulnerability' to others.[25]

Not surprisingly, Wikse sees an intimate connection between these ideals and the way in which one 'grows up male' in this society. Learning this script of so-called 'authenticity as self-possession' means being a *real* man. He illustrates how he learned to 'take it like a man', how he got the hang of 'hold(ing) onto oneself':

> I was taught that a real man is a masked man; the Lone Ranger. If others could see beneath the mask of self-possession, if they could know you in your real needs, they might reject you; a real man should not have needs. As a heroic stranger, a man performs a mission of salvation; problems are their problems, needs are theirs, not one's own . . . I was . . . taught [in graduate school] that to succeed I must present a facade of invulnerability to other men, performing my work as a finished and perfect product, a performer immune to criticism and with no connection to the people with whom I work.[26]

I submit that a theological tradition that envisaged deity as autonomous and unrelated was bound over time to produce a humanism of the sort we have generated, with its vision of 'Promethean man', the individual who may, if he chooses, enter into relationship. Where our image of transcendence is represented to us as unrelatedness, as freedom from reciprocity and mutuality, the experience of God as living presence grows cold and unreal. But even after such a God is long dead, the vision of the human historical agent as one who may, or may not, choose relationship lingers with us.

Such notions of love as also linger in a world like this – whether they are images of divine or of Promethean human love – are images of heroic, grand gestures of self-possessed people. It is an image of patronizing love, the love of the strong for the weak, or conversely, the sniveling gratitude of the weak toward those stronger who grant 'favours'.

Never mind that none of us wants, or has ever wanted or needed, transactions with this sort of love. Never mind that we all know – unless our sense of self has already been twisted almost beyond human recognition by sadism and brutality – that the love we need and want is deeply mutual love, love that has both the quality of a gift received and the quality of a gift given. The rhythm of a real, healing, and empowering love is take and give, give and take, free of the cloying inequality of one partner active and one partner passive.

I shudder to think how many times during my years of theological study I came upon a warning from a writer of Christian ethics not to confuse real, Christian love with 'mere mutuality'.[27] One senses that persons who can think this way have yet to experience the power of love as the real pleasure of mutual vulnerability, the experience of truly being cared for or of actively caring for another. Mutual love, I submit, is love in its deepest radicality. It is so radical that many of us have not yet learned to bear it. To experience it, we must be open, we must be capable of giving and receiving. The tragedy is that a masculinist reified Christianity cannot help us learn to be such lovers.

To dig beneath this reified masculinist idolatry is also, I believe, to move toward a recovery of a New Testament ethos of faith. Can Jesus' active embodiment of love be illumined by this image of mutuality? I believe it can. Orthodox Christological interpretations imply that somehow the entire meaning of Jesus' life and work is to be found in his headlong race toward Golgotha, towards crucifixion – as if he sought suffering as an end in itself to complete the resolution of the divine human drama once and for all.[28] I believe that this way of viewing Jesus' work robs it of its – and his – moral radicality. Jesus was radical not in his lust for sacrifice but in his power of mutuality. Jesus' death on a cross, his sacrifice, was no abstract exercise in moral virtue. His death was the price he paid for refusing to abandon the radical activity of love – of expressing solidarity and reciprocity with the excluded ones in his community. Sacrifice, I submit, is not a central moral goal or virtue in the Christian life. Radical acts of love – expressing human solidarity and bringing mutual relationship to life – are the central virtues of the Christian moral life. That we have turned sacrifice into a moral virtue has deeply confused the Christian moral tradition.

Like Jesus, we are called to a radical activity of love, to a way of being in the world that deepens relation, embodies and extends community, passes on the gift of life. Like Jesus, we must live out this calling in a place and time where the distortions of loveless power stand in conflict with the power of love. We are called to confront, as Jesus did, that which thwarts the power of human personal and communal becoming, that which twists relationship, which denies human well-being, community, and human solidarity to so many in our world. To confront these things, and to stay on the path of confrontation, to break through the 'lies, secrets and silences'[29] that mask the prevailing distortions and manipulations in relationship and the power of relations is the vocation of those who are Jesus' followers.

It is one thing to live out a commitment to mutuality and reciprocity as the way to bear up God in the world and to be clear-eyed and realistic about what the consequences of that radical love may be. It is quite another to do what many Christians have done – that is, to rip the crucifixion of Jesus out of its lived-world context in his total life and historical project and turn sacrifice into an abstract norm for the Christian life. To be sure, Jesus was faithful unto death. He stayed with his cause and he died for it. He *accepted* sacrifice. But his sacrifice was *for* the cause of radical love, it was in order to make relationship and to sustain it, and, above all, to right wrong relationship, which is what we call 'doing justice'.

Needless to say, in the best of times and under the most propitious of circumstances, it is risky to live as if the common-wealth of the living God were present – that is, to live by radical mutuality and reciprocity. Radical love creates dangerous precedents and lofty expectations among human beings. Those in power believe such love to be 'unrealistic' because those touched by the power of such love tend to develop a reluctance to accept anything less than mutuality and self-respect, anything less than human dignity, anything less than authentic relatedness. It is for that reason that such persons become powerful threats to the status quo. As women have known, but also as men like Martin Luther King Jr and Archbishop Oscar Romero understood, as any must know who dare to act deeply and forcefully out of the power of love, radical love is a dangerous and serious business. Without blessed persistence, without the willingness to risk, even unto death, the power of radical love would not live on in our world. There are no ways around crucifixions, given the power of evil in the world. But as that poetic theologian of the gay liberation movement Sandra Browders has reminded us, the aim of love is not to perpetuate crucifixions, but to bring an end to them in a world where they go on and on and on! We do this through actions of mutuality and solidarity, not by aiming at an ethic of sacrifice.

Mark the point well: *We are not called to practise the virtue of sacrifice.* We are called to express, embody, share, celebrate the gift of life, and to pass it on! We are called to reach out, to deepen relationship, or to right wrong relations – those that deny, distort, or prevent human dignity from arising – as we recall each other into the power of personhood. We are called to journey this way, to stay in and with this radical power of love. When you do that for me, I am often overwhelmed by your generosity, and I may speak of the sacrifice you make for me. But we both need to be perfectly clear that you are not, thereby, practicing the virtue of sacrifice on me. You are merely passing on the power of love, gifting me as others have gifted you, into that power to *do* radical love.

Conclusion

There is much more to be said about the envisionment of the work of radical love within a feminist moral theology that takes its signals from what is deepest and best in women's historical struggle. Certainly, more also needs to be said about the depth of sin and evil in the world. It is important to remember that a feminist moral theology is utopian, as all good theology is, in that it *envisages* a society, a world, a cosmos, in which, as Jules Girardi puts it, there are 'no excluded ones'.[30] But feminist theology is also mightily realistic, in that it takes with complete seriousness the radical freedom we human beings have for doing good *or evil*. Since we acknowledge that we have, literally, the power to person-each-other into love – that is, into relationship – we can also acknow-ledge our power to obliterate dignity, respect, care and concern for humanity from our world. All of that is within our power.

Far more than we care to remember, though the evil that we do lives on, after us. The radicality of our vison of love gains its urgency from that very knowledge. The prophets of Israel were right to insist, long ago, that the sins of the fathers (and the mothers) live on in us, corroding and destroying the power of relation. This is why our human moral task sometimes seems overwhelming. We live in a time when massive and accumulated injustice, acted out over time, encounters answer in the rising anger of those whose dignity and life are being threatened by collective patterns of privilege that have to be undone. In a world such as this, actively pursuing the works of love will often mean doing all we can to stop the crucifixions, resisting the evil as best we can, or mitigating the suffering of those who are the victims of our humanly disordered relations. In the midst of such a world, it is still within the power of love, which is the good news of God, to keep us in the knowledge that none of us were born only to die, that we were meant to have the gift of life, to know the power of relation and to pass it on.

A chief evidence of the grace of God – which always comes to us in, with, and through each other – is this power to struggle and to experience indignation. We should not make light of our power to rage against the dying of the light. It is the root of the power of love. So may it never be said of any of us feminist theologians that we merely stood by, ladylike, when that power of love was called for or that we sought refuge in an Otherworld when we were needed here and now, in the line of march.

After Mary Daly lectures – on those somewhat rare occasions when men are invited to attend – it often happens that the first questioner is a man who inquires, in a befuddled way, 'What about men? What does this mean for us?' Since I do not share Mary Daly's reverse Thomism[31] – that is, since I believe that the major differences between men's and women's behaviour are rooted in culture and history rather than in a relatively fixed 'nature' – I trust that my male readers will not at this point be suffering any confusion about what this essay means for them. It is not that it is wrong for any of us to ask: 'What does all this mean for me?' That is a good question. But in a feminist moral theology, good questions are answered *by something we must do*. It is, I submit, urgent that men join women in doing feminist moral theology[32] – that is, acting to keep the power of relationship alive in our world – because men have more public power than women and because there is so much to be done.

But I do not wish to end on too sentimental a note about the relations of men and women in our world. Mary Daly had very good reasons for warning us women about the dangers of joining male-originated patriarchal processions. Since her diagnosis of the problem is so much on target, none of us must ever forget that, if we must join patriarchal processions in order to get on with the radical work of love, we had better be very sure that we invite a lot of our friends to come along.

☐ All too much has been written on the topic of women's ordination, but two of the very best essays are those by R.A. Norris Jr, 'The Ordination of Women and the "Maleness of the Christ"', to be found on pp. 71–85 of Monica Furlong's collection, *Feminine in the Church* (London, SPCK 1984); and a profoundly moving essay by Daniel C. Maguire, 'The Exclusion of Women from Orders: a Moral Evaluation', pp. 130–40 of his *The Moral Revolution* (San Francisco, Harper & Row, 1986). [13] A kind of preview of a book she published with SPCK in 1989, *The Case for Women's Ministry*, is Ruth B. Edwards's reply to her own question, 'What is the

Theology of Women's Ministry?' to be found in the *Scottish Journal of Theology* 40 (1987), pp. 421–36, a revised version of the Opening of Session Lecture given at Christ's College, Aberdeen, in 1985.

Just as the debate about ordination will continue in some denominations for some time, so will the debate about whether women can truly find themselves within the Christian Church. Someone who wants to integrate her religion with her ethics, her spirituality, and her experiencing of the world, but who has left the Christian Church is Daphne Hampson. She was one of the first to be involved in the late 1970s in producing theological work in connection with the attempt to get women ordained in the Anglican churches in Britain. She became first Co-ordinator for the Group for the Ministry of Women in the Scottish Episcopal Church, and became the first President of the new European Society of Women for Theological Research. A feminist theologian who can no longer be Christian, she was the British 'half' of a dialogue with Rosemary Radford Ruether held on 16 May 1986 at Westminster Cathedral Hall. The question they discussed was 'Is there a Place for Feminists in a Christian Church', first published in *New Blackfriars* 68: 801 (1987), and reprinted and sold through Women in Theology as a separate pamphlet. Her position fundamentally has two points of reference. One is that Chritianity cannot be true, and that Christology as we have known it can no longer be a vehicle that can carry our religious consciousness and love of God.[14] The other point is that Christianity is not moral, that is, it is irretrievably sexist because it is necessarily tied to a point in human history which is patriarchal. Her first book is *Theology and Feminism* (Oxford, Basil Blackwell, 1990). Her next book will be concerned with a re-writing of the concept of God which reflects feminist insights on the nature of the self and human relationships. The essay of hers published here, therefore, is a stage on the way to that second book. It arises out of her doctoral thesis in theology, which concerned the understanding of the self in relation to God in Luther as compared with Catholic thought. The essay connects with the agenda suggested by Valerie Saiving mentioned at the beginning of Part Two of this Reader.

18 DAPHNE HAMPSON
Luther on the Self: A Feminist Critique

It is imperative that feminists working in theology should pay
attention to the implications of feminist thought for the structure of
theology. In this essay I shall suggest that, while there can be no
incompatibility between feminism and being religious, feminism
comports ill with Christianity. This is particularly the case when
we consider Christianity in its Lutheran form. On the other hand, I
believe that Luther's understanding that, if one is to speak of God,
one must say that the self cannot be itself except as God is
fundamental to the constitution of that self, must be retained
within theology, and indeed can appropriately be developed by
feminists. (Luther would not have used the term 'self', and lacked
a post-Enlightenment conception of the 'self', but this is the best
word to use when translating his insight into a modern idiom.)

Luther's achievement lay in his reconceptualization of the
human relation to God. The medieval Catholic understanding of
the human relation to God, grounded as it was in the thought of the
ancient world, had supposed (as does modern Catholicism) that it is
God's work to transform the human. Luther denied this. For him
the revolution involved in being a Christian is that one is no longer
concerned about what one is in oneself, or what one could become
through God's grace. For the Christian lives by God's righteousness and not by his own.

Therefore to be a Christian means that one has a radically
different sense of oneself, a sense of oneself as being bound up with
God and what God is. As my teacher in Lutheran theology, Arthur
McGill, expressed it, one's understanding of the 'circumference' of
oneself is changed. The Christian, Luther said in his essay of 1520
in which he first fully grasped his breakthrough, lives 'not in
himself'.[1] Catholic scholars have often failed to understand the
import of Luther's thought here, saying that in the Lutheran
scheme justification consists solely in the non-imputation of sins,
whereas Catholicism allows that God should actually change the
person. But it is not that Luther would rather that God should give
him grace for himself, so transforming him. He has got away from
any such self-preoccupation. 'We know that our theology is

certain', says Luther 'because it sets us outside ourselves.'[2] The Christian lives *extra se*.

The word for this placing of oneself with God is faith. For faith is trust, and when I trust, my sense of who I am comes to lie with another. This novel sense that the Christian has of himself is well captured by Wolfhart Pannenberg:

> Luther not only added the notion of trust, but he wanted to emphasize that the personal center itself changes in the act of trust, because the trusting person surrenders to the one in whom such confidence is entrusted. The point was crucial in Luther's argument, but difficult to grasp. . . . Melanchthon did not grasp Luther's profound insight that faith by way of ecstasis participates in the reality of Christ himself. . . . Even Calvin did not realize that the very foundation of the traditional concept of a personal self was shaken by Luther's discovery concerning the nature of faith.[3]

The relation with God is not an interrelationship with one who is conceived as an other – a relationship of a type that would best be known as love, such as we have with our neighbour. The passage from which I quoted in *The Freedom of a Christian* reads at greater length:

> A Christian lives not in himself, but in Christ and in his neighbour. Otherwise he is not a Christian. He lives in Christ through faith, in his neighbour through love. By faith he is caught up beyond himself into God.

To have this new self-understanding is what it means to be Christian.

But it is not natural for humans so to base themselves on God. Thus central to the structure of Luther's thought is a dichotomy. Once and again we try to set ourselves up in apposition to God, to deal with God as with an other, attempting to be adequate of ourselves. This is sin. Once and again we must hear the gospel message that it is not for us to try to be adequate of ourselves, that God accepts us independently of our merits. Once and again we learn to trust in God, to live by 'extrinsic' righteousness, and not by our own 'intrinsic' righteousness. We are, says Luther, '*semper justus, semper peccator, semper reformans*'. Again he comments: 'Progress is nothing other than constantly beginning.' [4] It follows from this that there is no history of the development of the self; no movement within ourselves from being a sinner to being righteous. Rather, there are two ways in which we can live: in apposition to

God (sin), and from God (faith). Each moment we must live anew from God. Luther writes: 'When security comes, then God imputes it again for sin.'[5]

This structure to Luther's thought is found again in the thought of later Lutheran theologians. I take as examples one from the nineteenth century and one from the twentieth. For the nineteenth-century Danish thinker Søren Kierkegaard, it is not that God confirms the ethical man (the man who attempts by himself to be himself); it is not that the religious stage in life is built upon the ethical. Rather, a man must fall down before his own eyes, recognizing that he has failed, before he can have any reason to make recourse to God. Kierkegaard's ethical man who tries of himself to be adequate in the face of God (as Luther's man who would justify himself by good works) lands up in despair. It is only as we consent to dependence on God (faith) that we can be the person whom we should be. (Kierkegaard, however, also differs from Luther here, for he not only – in a parallel way to Luther – speaks of the self as being 'grounded transparently' in God (faith), but also of there being a reciprocal relation between the person and God (love).[6]

In the twentieth century Rudolf Bultmann's thought has such a structure. Only God can deliver one into authenticity; the attempt to become oneself by oneself will fail. We must, he says, live from the future, from God. This we must in each moment do again, not falling back on what we already are. Thus Bultmann: 'The new life of faith is not an assured possession or endowment. . . . Life in faith is not a possession at all. . . . In other words, the decision of faith is never final; it needs constant renewal in every fresh situation.'[7]

There is for Bultmann no self, which is indeed a self which has come to itself, which can be carried forward from one moment to the next. We must find ourselves each moment anew as we live from God. Of man's relation to his past, Bultmann can say: 'He may take it with him as that for which he has been forgiven.' Of the Christian proclamation, that it announces to man 'the possibility of becoming free from his past'.[8]

There is thus a dichotomy running through the centre of Lutheran thought, the dichotomy between trying to exist by myself (sin) in which I shall fail to be a self, and living from God (faith), whereupon I come to live as God intended that I should live. It should be noted that this dichotomy is the necessary corollary of saying that there is God, and also that it is not natural for man to depend on God. Since God is other than myself, I must transfer my centre of gravity to one who lies outside myself. God is integral to the self's being itself, such that God is conceived to be fundamental to the very constitution of the self in each moment. This could not be said to be the case were one to speak (as does Catholicism) of the person as existing through creation and then as having the capacity to choose to relate to God; or of God as completing in salvation what is given in creation. Luther contends that each moment I must anew base myself on God and so be the creature I was intended to be. To think that I could in some sense first possess myself, then relate to God as to another, would be to have an idol – one with whom I think I can deal.

What then of the person who tries to exist of himself in the face of God? (And unlike for Kierkegaard, for whom the ethical man can be in essential ignorance of God's existence, for Luther as a sixteenth-century man it is always in the face of God that one tries to maintain oneself.) The situation of the human *coram deo*, before God's face, is one of terror. Luther here was a student of the Hebrew Scriptures. Moreover, God's transcendence and the goodness that God demands were accentuated in the late Nominalism within which his sensibilities were formed. There is a sense of the human's aloneness, unable to support himself. (Was Luther the first modern man?)[9] Furthermore, for Luther such a person is caught up in himself, bent into himself: the human in sin is *incurvatus in se*. Thus the move from sin to faith is a move from an essential isolation to a connectedness to another who is God. Echoes of this are once again found in the later tradition. Notably, in Kierkegaard's writing the attempt to exist of oneself before God represents a situation of terror; the Jews, he says, were a wise people – they knew that to see God was to die.[10] Likewise for Kierkegaard the self as it comes to itself has an essential relationality. Martin Buber observes that when, in his youth, he had read Kierkegaard he had thought that Kierkegaard's man was 'man on the edge'. But in comparison with Heidegger there is a connectedness: 'Kierkegaard's Single One is an open system, even if open solely to God.'[11]

Within this tradition, then, there is no sense that the self, secure in itself, can freely exist, in easy intercourse with others. We cannot maintain ourselves; we are insecure. For Luther we are always bound, if not to God, then to the Devil. To be 'free', as his famous debate with Erasmus makes clear, is to be bound to God. The person who tries to maintain himself will, in his insecurity, see all else (even God, says Luther) in relation to himself. Such an analysis is markedly present at a later date in existentialism. Bultmann sees us as grasping at others, using them as tools which are *vorhanden*, available to us, in our attempt to shore ourselves up. Of this tradition as a whole we may – to use a phrase of Heidegger's – say that the human is 'not at home' in the world. It could not be said of humans as depicted by Luther, Kierkegaard or Bultmann that we are creatures contentedly. The later tradition has named this basic dis-ease *Angst*; that anxiety which, not arising from a specific situation, belongs rather to our basic constitution. Kierke-gaard it was who attributed this basic insecurity to the fact that humans are twofold, both body and spirit. Man in his imagination soars into the realms of possibility, yet knows that like other creatures he must die. It is this analysis that Reinhold Niebuhr – not himself a Lutheran – takes up in his well-known depiction of sin as a pride stemming from insecurity.[12] But Luther too knows of a dis-ease, often spoken of as *Anfechtung*, a terror before God, which should cause us to flee. It is to this situation that the gospel speaks. By putting our trust in God we are delivered from our insecurity.

The relation to God is thus held to be primary. It is in relation to God (and not through the world) that we come to ourselves. Constituted by God, however, we are turned to the world as the scene of our activity and services. (There is no mysticism present, as though we could simply 'be' in God: we are not speaking of loss of self in God, but of God being that through dependence upon which the self is constituted.) The good tree, says Luther, will bear good fruit. Theology (the relation to God) leads, as Gerhard Ebeling puts it, to ethics (the relation to the world). This structure is particularly apparent in Bultmann's Gifford lectures, delivered in Scotland to an audience which, after the Third Reich, might well have been tempted to believe of Lutheranism that, having no natural law ethic, it lacked any ethic. Faith (the relation to God), says Bultmann, leads to love (a serving of the neighbour).

Now feminists, in considering women, have conceived of the nature of the human person in a profoundly different way.

In the first place, feminists conceive differently how women naturally are. For they speak of women as having an essential connectedness with others, a relationality that is integral to the self. It is suggested that women tend to think in terms of (and to have as their ideal), a 'web'-like participatory structure of human relation-ships. It has been shown that to a marked degree in comparison with men, women in speaking of themselves make mention of significant others.[13]

A sense of anxiety resulting from an essential isolation may then be much less pronounced in women. Not having been in command, women have had to see themselves as being in relationship. Through the very tasks on which they have expended their daily lives, women have often experienced greater intimacy with others. They have been less divorced than have men from the very material needs of children, or indeed other adults for whom they care. The society of women has allowed for a greater interrelatedness and sanctioned the expression of feelings. Relationships between women have been less hierarchical than in the male world of work. The characterization of sin within masculinist theology as consisting in the domination of others, on the part of an isolated self, in a mistaken attempt to gain security, would as a result seem to be less accurate as a depiction of women.[14]

Furthermore, feminist women are unhappy about the disjunction, prevalent in masculinist thought, between 'mind' and 'body'. Of course it is the case that, in that we have self-consciousness, humans are not like other creatures. Having only too often been classed with 'nature' while men were seen as more 'spiritual', women should be the last to deny this. But does it follow that we have a disjunction between 'mind' and 'body', such that we are in the schizophrenic situation of reconciling the fact that we are more than the brute creation with the knowledge that we shall die? Can we not be creatures? Indeed, the obsession that masculinist thought manifests with the possibility of preserving an individuated self even after death may well be thought to be an extreme instance of the male's inability to see himself as bound up with the whole. Again, it must for feminists be highly questionable that we should think of ourselves as 'not-at-home' in the world. The feminist ethicist Eleanor Haney conceives that just the opposite should be the case. She writes of the ideal of 'being at-home-in-the-universe and of living freely – graciously, gracefully'. 'Grace' connotes for her 'the reality of being a host as well as a guest, a resident as well as a stranger and pilgrim'.[15]

Feminism, in both theory and praxis, has been concerned for women to come into their own. Only too often have women been unable to sufficiently value themselves. The reality of women's lives has been that they had to circle round other people. What plans they might have had gave way to what others determined should be, resulting in a sense of powerlessness, of lacking control even of their own lives. Meaning had to be found through the lives of others. Typically, the 'problems' that women have manifested have been those resulting from the lack of a sense of self-worth, leading to depression, anorexia, or suicidal tendencies. The feminist response of recent years has been 'consciousness–raising' groups, in which women were enabled to find voice, therapy that allowed a feminist analysis of the situation in which a woman was placed, and assertiveness training in which women learnt to hold their own. In a word, feminism has stood for empowerment.

In this situation, to advocate, as does the Lutheran tradition, that the self should be broken, that the person should learn to live from another who is God, must be judged highly detrimental. Women are not typically self-enclosed and in need of finding connectedness. Their problem has rather been a lack of centredness in self; their need, to come to themselves. The whole dynamic of being a self is very different from what Lutheranism has proposed. Thus its prescription must appear irrelevant, indeed, counter-productive.

Furthermore, it may well be thought to be the case that women naturally have a strong sense of continuity and growth. They wish to see their lives as an unfolding pattern. More women than men – and I count this statistic favourable to women – seek to understand themselves in therapy. Women are more thoughtfully introspective. Their conversations revert to the personal, or weave that dimension into a greater whole. They are interested in human lives, whether in their own person or the lives of others. Typically, women have written letters, biographies and novels. Often they have tended life. They have raised children and nursed the sick. (It is women who grow pot plants!) Women, in sum, are concerned for growth and becoming within a continuity of caring relationship.

To one who thinks in these terms, again the Lutheran system must be judged negatively. For it must be profoundly jarring to hear that she is only herself as she bases herself on one who lies outside herself; that she must constantly live from some future not yet given, or from another's sense of her – even though that other be God; that, indeed, a growth from within oneself and a concern with continuity of self is in essence 'sin'. There is some evidence that (to use the terms popularized by William James) women's religion is of the 'once-born' type, a religion in which life is seen to come forth from life. Men, by contrast, tend to find natural a religion that speaks of a discontinuity – a discontinuity that may reflect the break which the male experiences when he leaves behind the world of mother and sisters to join male society. Masculinist religions – Christianity here is no exception – may typically be religions of death and re-birth, crucifixion and resurrection, a breaking and reconstituting of the self.[16]

To advocate – within a feminist context – that persons should come into their own, is not once more to understand the self as the atomic entity of which feminists are so critical. For women conceive selfhood to be achieved in and through relationship. One may say that there needs to be a creative tension between autonomy (which has in the past been denied to women) and relationality. Nor are these two mutually exclusive. It has been the experience of many within the women's movement that one can come to clearer self-understanding and greater self-assurance when held within relationship. Conversely, it may be said that it is the person who has come to herself, who can truly be in relation. Such a person neither dominates others, nor attempts to lose herself in them. The love of others promotes a rightful love of self, while a secure self is self-forgetful in delight in others. Thus it is within the interplay of relationship and individuality that we become ourselves. Within such a context, 'salvation' may well be understood as becoming whole.

Women must will that men too should come to such a sense of the self in relation. This is not of course to say that the male analysis which is central to Lutheran theology is false! That men tend to have an isolated self and that, in its insecurity, the isolated self exploits others, is not a dynamic the truth of which women are likely to contend! Could men, however, but learn both to come 'to' themselves and to develop a relationality with others, a violent breaking of an egocentric self would be unnecessary. At present, the lack of a perspicacious knowledge of self, and an inability to relate in personal ways (particularly with other men but also with women) seem to many women to be only too characteristic of the male world. What women must long for is that men should come to be centred, yet relational, selves.

Has God, then, become superfluous? Should it be said that we acquire relationality in relation to other persons? The great advantage of this would seem to be that one can speak of growth from a centred self, rather than of having to break the self and be based on another (who is God). Feminists may well be more optimistic about our being able to learn relationality in relation to others than Lutheran thought has allowed. And they may, out of women's past experience, both negative and positive, wish to put more stress on developing a centredness and a continuity of self. (It could further be asked whether the acceptance that Luther believed God gives us, and which he found so life-transforming, cannot be given by others? Indeed, whether we should demand complete acceptance, or whether it is not important to learn also to stand on one's own in the face of a less than total acceptance? Luther's system, if it suggests that we can have no sense of our own integrity, could be said to work against becoming a centred self.)

The direction in which feminism pushes us here would seem to be in accord with much else. In a world in which it becomes increasingly apparent (as modern physics suggests) that all is interconnected, it is difficult to think in terms of a God who is separate from the world and humankind. Indeed, feminists may well contend that the postulation of God, conceived as exterior, other and in apposition to the self, is a striking instance of male thought-forms.[17] How, moreover, should we think of such a God 'intervening' in the world when we know history and nature to be closed causal nexuses? Last but not least, it may be asked whether it is moral to think in terms of such a God? Since the Enlightenment that has become increasingly doubtful. Feminists, who have wanted to get away from a heteronomous situation, in which the will of one other than themselves ruled them, will scarcely want to replace dominant males by such a God. (Indeed, one may note that much manifestation of human religiousness in recent years has started with the human person, as people – since the 1960s in particular – have developed techniques of meditation, contemplation and cultivated an intrinsic human spirituality.)

It becomes all the more imperative to develop Luther's insight that God must be seen as one who is fundamental to our being ourselves, not as some exterior other with whom we interrelate. In that respect his thought surely needs to be taken up. Protestantism, in at least one of its strands, has indeed done this. I am thinking in particular of the work of Friedrich Schleiermacher (who in fact saw himself as taking the Reformation to its logical conclusion). Schleiermacher was not a Lutheran, and the Lutheran dichotomy is not present in his work. But he does have the sense, perhaps much more than Luther, that God is that on which I base myself (my sense of being derived, he named it), and not one with whom I interact as with an other. Thus for Schleiermacher the relation with God and the relation with neighbour are quite distinct. God is one through whom I become myself, my neighbour one with whom I interrelate in a relationship of reciprocity.

Thus the response to be made to one inclined to say that relationality can be developed in relationship to other persons must surely be that, though up to a point this may be true, when one speaks of God one is conceiving of what is far more fundamental to being oneself than the relationship with another person (who must always in some sense remain an other) could ever be. Feminism may well be a context within which such understandings may be developed further, for feminists have thought much both about connectedness and about what it means to come into one's own. (I believe therefore that the direction which much Christian feminism has taken in recent years in speaking of God as 'mother', 'friend' or 'lover' is beside the point, for so conceived God remains one with whom I interrelate as with an other, and this may not be the function which God, but rather other people, should perform.)

What women may find unacceptable about the Lutheran system is the sense that one must be continually breaking oneself and basing oneself on one who is not oneself. (Yet this is integral to that system in that it has posited God as exterior to the self.) Rather, should one speak of continuity and growth from within oneself. This alone I think to be commensurate with feminism. One may in passing ask whether Catholicism would here be more acceptable? In one sense yes. For Catholicism sees God as working with an already given self, rather than as enabling us to have a new sense of ourselves. But God is still in large part postulated as an exterior other. Meanwhile, Catholicism lacks (other than through a doctrine of creation and preservation which is not at all the same thing) a sense that God is fundamental to the self's being itself in each moment.

If then we feel constrained as a religious person to speak to God, I think that we must conceive God to have an essential connectedness with all else that is. God then cannot become an other, one whose will to act in accord with which would be to act heteronomously. Nor shall we have to base ourselves on another in order to be based on God. The starting point for knowledge of God, becomes knowledge of ourselves. But this is not Christianity. For Christians of all varieties, in so far as they look to the Bible, see God to be in apposition to us. God is conceived to have existed before creation and to intervene in the world. Indeed, essential to the knowledge of God is revelation. Even Schleiermacher, who comes the closest to what I would want to say, having spoken of religious experience, must also – for he wishes to remain Christian – speak of revelation. For myself I would wish to have an explicitly theistic sense, developed through prayer, while seeing God as not disconnected from myself and the web of human relationships.

It will be clear, then, that there is nothing intrinsically incompatible between being a feminist and conceiving of oneself as a religious person. Indeed, feminism may well allow us to develop our conceptualization of God in helpful ways. There is, however, I believe, an incompatibility between being feminist and Christian. (This quite apart from the question of the truth of Christianity.) This clash is structural and relates to the nature of feminist and of Christian thought. It is extraordinarily important that feminists should think out these basic structural issues. Only so will their theology be commensurate with their ideals and their structuring of reality.

☐ From the position represented here by Daphne Hampson's work, for those who wish neither to be ordained nor to leave the institutional Churches, there are some fundamental questions about authority to be addressed. Here, these questions are represented by essays from the work of two women who teach feminist theology at Yale Divinity School: Letty M. Russell and Margaret Farley. Letty Russell's essay on 'Good Housekeeping' contributes to feminist ecclesiology, but it prepares the reader very effectively for the problem of how women are to make their voices heard with authority in respect of matters integral to women's lives in our time; it is this issue with which Margaret Farley deals. First, however, Letty Russell on 'Good Housekeeping'.

19 LETTY M. RUSSELL
Good Housekeeping

A discussion of good housekeeping seems appropriate for a book that develops 'household of freedom' as a metaphor for authority in partnership. Certainly there has been a great deal of talk of 'bad housekeeping' in the household of bondage. Yet the experience of the feminist touch, turning the questions of feminists into questions of authority, has warned us that the patriarchal paradigm of authority as domination controls the minds, hearts and institutions of Church and society. A great deal of housecleaning is in order if the Church is to live out its calling as an eschatological sign and instrument sign of God's household.[1]

Questions multiply from every direction as we try to picture ourselves in new relationships of authority. How can our families, congregations, trade unions, offices, political parties, schools, advocacy groups, and so on, look a little more like households of freedom? How would we recognize a household of freedom if we were lucky enough to stumble across its threshold? How would we care for such a household, and work to build it up as a sign of God's good housekeeping intentions for the world? What are the implications of a new paradigm of authority for reinterpreting biblical theology, ecclesiology, or ethics of family life?

It is a mistake to assume that the last chapter of a book on theology should end with 'the answers'. In the first place, there are no easy answers to such difficult questions. Households happen where mutual love, care and trust happen. They are not mass produced; there are no prefab households! There is only the possibility of checking out some of the clues about paradigms of authority, asking if they make sense in the lives of those who are struggling to create partnership in a world of division. In the second place, this is not the style of feminist/liberation theologies. They do not begin with theory and move to practice. Rather, they begin with the communities of faith and struggle who are acting in new ways, and then ask how this experience leads to new questions and ways of thinking.

Although I do not have any easy answers and examples, what I have been saying is founded in my experience and in the experience of many other women and men who are critical of the hierarchical structures in our churches and societies today. In fact, I have spent thirty-five years trying to find out how to subvert the Church into being the Church! Working in the East Harlem Protestant Parish, I helped design missionary structures of the congregation, and from the 1960s until now I have never stopped trying to find a way to make the Church into an 'open circle' of those gathered in Christ's name for service to and with others.

For a while I thought I had found the heart of the problem: the 'clergy line'. It seemed that every restructuring would always end in a pyramid if some had higher status than others in our congregations. But I have gradually come to see that the issue of authority underlies even that issue, because the meaning and function of ordination is determined by how we picture the authority conferred in ordination. At present I am serving on the Faith and Order commissions of the National Council of Churches and the World Council of Churches, studying 'The Unity of the Church and the Renewal of Human Community'.[2] This study is trying to find out how the experience of churches struggling for human renewal leads to new ecclesial self-understanding and new perspectives on unity. A still unresolved problem of the study is again what theological paradigm of authority will decide the methods and questions of the study.[3]

This book began with several years of action and reflection with sisters and brothers engaged in struggle against the patriarchal paradigm of domination and its legitimization of oppression. In it I am reflecting on what people are already doing to create new households of freedom. Their stories and accumulated wisdom make it possible to ask if indeed a new paradigm of authority would make better sense of their experiences. In 1981 I published *Growth in Partnership* in order to explore how relationships of mutuality are nurtured.[4] But examples of change do not create change without a shift in perspective. A change in paradigm happens for persons, disciplines, and entire societies as accumulated experiences of cognitive dissonance lead to conversion. People see and act differently when the old paradigm of domination no longer make sense and they are somehow forced to turn around and welcome the messengers of God's household!

In this final chapter the hints about good and bad housekeeping are not intended as answers to our questions, but as clues that might help us on our continuing journey. After a brief analysis of how authority of domination functions through forms of paternalism and autonomy, I will look for clues to building up households of freedom that may be found in partnering relationships. Finally, the signs of God's own partnership with the 'least of our brothers and sisters' become a continuing clue for our journey home. On this journey only the Spirit grants Good Housekeeping seals of approval, but our own limited perspective can give us a few hints about how to 'keep on keeping on' towards a household of freedom.

Paternalism and autonomy

When we turn to ask how this understanding of authority *in* community is expressed in Christian churches today, we find that the more usual model is that of authority *over* community. Without much effort we can discover that churches still carry with them a great deal of the baggage of the patriarchal understanding of authority that was shaped in the social world of the ancient Near East, rather than the partnering paradigm exhibited in Jesus' own critique of hierarchy and solidarity with the outcasts of society.

Relational bond

In his book *Authority*, Richard Sennett helps us to understand some of the social and psychological dynamics of relationships of authority as they have evolved in the history of the Church. He describes authority as a relational bond that leads persons to give assent without coercion or persuasion because they find needed security in the real or imagined strength of others.[5] His analysis helps us to see how patriarchy changes and yet continues in our churches and society in illegitimate forms of paternalism and autonomy that undercut more mature relationships of partnership. His analysis is also important for family relationships, where authority of domination continues to legitimize many kinds of psychological and physical brutality.[6]

According to Sennett's socio-historical description, 'patriarchy' refers to social relationships in which people are consciously related by blood ties to elder males, who claim obedience through these ties. Although this tradition of authority was called into question by Jesus' teaching about God's household and by some of the models of early Church life, it was reinforced by the culture of the Roman Empire as well as the theological traditions that portrayed God as the ruling patriarch.

In Western medieval society the evolving paradigm of authority was patrimonial. Control rested in the hands of the eldest males because property was handed down from one generation to the next through this male line. But the advent of modern industrial society has resulted in the gradual erosion of patrimony so that we now live in a Western world where two patterns of patriarchal authority predominate, paternalism and autonomy.[7]

Sennett describes *paternalism* as a form of male domination without a contract. Males still use the language of patriarchy, but they seldom have the property or power to provide security to those who consent to their control. He calls paternalism an authority of false love which claims to offer nurture and care but leads to dependence.

The other illegitimate form of modern patriarchal authority is *autonomy*. Male dominance in society is perpetuated by those who have rebelled against paternalism and sought to free the individual from dependence on anyone else. Such persons exert power through projecting an appearance of superiority through the claim to complete self-sufficiency. Such autonomy is what Sennett calls an authority without love.[8]

This analysis of the evolution of personal relationships of authority may help us understand more clearly how church congregations and their clergy preach a gospel of partnership and yet continue to function as households of domination and subordination. This may also help us to base the partnering relationships of good housekeeping on an authority of freedom that responds to people's need for solidarity and care by empowering them through a relationship of mutuality.

Authority in congregations

It seems to me that paternalism is a predominant pattern of authority in congregations. Paternalism can be an authority of false love that uses people's need for strength and assurance to dominate them through a relationship of dependence. It allows the clergy and other church leaders to continue to use the vocabulary and images of the patriarchal traditions, even though much of that basis for authority has disappeared. Even when persons exercise power as domination over others, they are able to use the language of fatherly caring to evoke feelings and responses of dependence. Thus church leaders can exercise the caring, nurturing, serving tasks of ministry without any threat to their leadership positions. They often are firmly in control of which groups meet and what curriculum they will use, even when there is no need for such care.

Persons need the kind of support that seeks to eliminate dependence, so that persons can care for themselves and others. They do not need care that continues to make them dependent, uncertain and needy. For instance, it would be paternalistic to use the authority of one's knowledge and expertise to keep people dependent by refusing to preach or teach in such a way that a congregation has the opportunity of understanding and acting out the biblical story. When they are only handed a message rather than encouraged to seek it out themselves through group story and action, they remain dependent on the messenger and do not learn to carry out the ministry of the word together with others. An extreme form of paternalistic authority would be offering to care for people as a father while carrying out many actions and policies that hurt them and keep them dependent.

The opposite extreme is autonomous authority, which projects an image of strength by appearing to be totally self-sufficient and invulnerable: needed by others but never needing others. This form of individualism is actually a valued and envied trait in white Western society. It is small wonder, therefore, that we seem to forget that all persons are interdependent. Growth in self-dependence is part of a maturing process that leads to full interdependence. Self-dependence is not an end in itself, either for those in ministry or for any other group of persons.[9]

In preaching or teaching, an autonomous relationship of authority with the listeners would most likely involve a display of the speaker's skills and knowledge in such a way that the person appears self-possessed and all-knowing. The bond of authority is formed through this image of superiority, in which everyone assumes the speaker is so powerful and full of wisdom that he or she cannot be challenged openly. This may reinforce a sense of inferiority and dependency among many of the listeners. They, in turn, withdraw from any attempt to develop a healthy independence of thought and action in the life of the community.

Although all persons need to develop self-dependence in their lives, subjection to autonomous behaviour by pastors, employers, or government officials is more likely to reinforce feelings of inferiority and dependence. Therefore, the exercise of autonomous authority is not a creative alternative for ministry because it leads persons to deny their co-responsibility with God for their neighbour and for the world. Nor is paternalism helpful to the life and growth of the Christian community. Paternalistic authority continues the use of patriarchal imagery to justify the need for laypersons, and especially women, to remain dependent. In my view an alternative paradigm of authority that would foster interdependence in a household of freedom is partnership.

Building up the household

Partnership is an authority of freedom that uses people's need for solidarity and care to empower them through a relationship of mutuality. This would not be the only alternative to forms of paternalistic and autonomous authority. Yet it seems to me that bonds of assent based on partnership would be more responsive to God's actions in freely becoming partner with humanity, as well as the actions of Jesus in reaching out to restore human wholeness and community. In my books on partnership I describe it as a new focus of relationship in Jesus Christ that sets us free for others.[10] Like faith, partnership – *koinōnia* – is a relationship of trust with

God and others that comes to us as a gift of Christ's love. Like faith it is 'caught, not taught'. *Koinōnia* is a word used frequently in the New Testament for sharing with someone in something, and it usually stresses a common bond in Jesus Christ that establishes mutual community. The emphasis is on a two-sided relationship of giving or receiving, participation or community (1 Cor. 10. 16–17).

Strengthening partnerships

In this new focus of relationship there is continuing commitment and common struggle in interaction with a wider community context. Such relationships happen as a gift; nevertheless, we know that commitment is more likely to grow where there is responsibility, vulnerability, equality, and trust among those who share diversity of gifts and resources. Because partnerships are living relationships that share the 'already/not yet' character of God's new household, they are always in process and never finished as they draw us together in common struggle and work, involving risk, continuing growth, and hopefulness in moving towards a goal or purpose transcending the group. By defintion, partnership involves growing interdependence in relation to God, persons and creation. Interaction with a wider community of persons, social structures, values and beliefs helps to provide support, correctives and negative feedback. There is never complete equality in such a dynamic relationship, but a pattern of equal regard and mutual acceptance of different gifts among partners is essential.

Authority in partnership grows in a community when people take time to be partners with one another. In preaching, this might mean that mutuality would be developed by group Bible study in preparation for the sermon. The sermon in turn would be a sharing of community action, insight and questioning. Rather than providing answers to what the congregation should believe and do, it would make use of the preacher's theological training and gifts to lift up the ongoing life of that congregation as part of God's continuing action. The stories of the participants could become the vehicles of biblical interpretation as the community discovers its mutual ministry of preaching.

Looking at these various alternative relational bonds of authority, we can see that paternalism is a pale imitation of the old patriarchal paradigm of authority *over* community. Yet in our society it has become a means of covering up alienation and loss of meaning with empty rhetoric and family clichés.[11] In the Church it is an invitation to the sin of dependence and immaturity in faith and action. Autonomy is also not helpful in building up households of freedom. As a rebellion against dependence by claiming egoistic authority *outside of* community, it has led to equally disastrous results for the health of technological society. In the Church it is also an invitation to the sin of pride and selfishness masked in the rhetoric of objectivity and excellence. Even though the glimpses of partnership as authority *in* community are few and far between, they are a genuine invitation to the freedom of Jesus Christ, whose love and acceptance sets us free to bear our own burdens and those of our neighbours in mutual housekeeping (Gal. 6.2).

Subverting structures

Many persons are concerned about how we can develop alternative structures of authority that move beyond those imaged in patriarchal forms of domination. While still living in these forms of relationship, we can, nevertheless, make use of the insights of the social sciences to help subvert these forms and to open up the possibility for more persons to find space in new households of freedom. To live in the present setting but to be constantly living out of an alternative future reality is to be *bi-cultural*.[12] This is a survival skill for anyone who wishes to participate in God's housekeeping chores. By knowing the social structures and psychological dynamics of the old house of bondage, we can work to subvert those structures and to limit their power in our lives and institutions. Subversion is most certainly one way of standing against the powers in this time before the full realization of God's eschatological household.

In the second part of his book, Richard Sennett is helpful in providing some psychosocial clues to the dynamics of authority. For instance, it is possible to increase democracy and participation in an organization even when the structures are paternalistic and hierarchical by *disrupting the links* in the top-down chain of command.[13] This type of action may appear to cause trouble or 'disorder', but it results in challenging and opening up organizational structures and attitudes so that people are better able to see the way things function and to understand what is going on. Authority as domination works through a chain of command from top to bottom. It works most effectively when the right to exercise power is unquestioned and the structures of the organization are assumed but not understood. If we are to avoid either anarchy or co-option into the system of domination, we need to develop strategies of disruption that reflect our bi-cultural vision.

Sennett suggests a few strategies that we might want to try.[14] In discussions with persons in authority it is important to require the 'active voice'. An order that is couched in terms of 'It has been decided', needs to be explained in terms of who and why, so the decision may be questioned. A second suggestion is that the 'assumed categories' or roles in which persons are placed need to be discussed. Perhaps there are other persons who need to be involved in a particular decision; perhaps there are other ways of carrying out decisions. In congregations there is certainly the possibility of doing this, rather than assuming that decency and order require unquestioned interpretation of the church order and traditions. Just because the church council has the authority to decide if the congregation will minister to women and children in crisis does not mean that they should make that decision without consulting those with experience of victimization or of intervention and counselling.

Two other important ways of disrupting the accustomed chain of command are that of 'role exchange' and of 'challenging paternalism'. Role exchange disrupts the order of things because those in charge take on 'subordinate tasks' through rotation and temporary inequality. I used to do this as a pastor in the East Harlem Protestant Parish. I would share in tasks of cleaning and typing so that the janitor and secretary could share in teaching, worship and calling. I learned more about what it really takes to keep a church running, and my partners learned more about their own gifts for ministry.

Challenging paternalism happens as persons question the assumption that a particular action is really helpful and nourishing. In the Church there are many promises of nurture and care that need to be challenged if they leave persons more dependent. For instance, the practice of giving out food and money without acting to change the situation that is causing the person's need for free food may need to be challenged. People prefer service or ministry that is empowering, that helps them gain the ability to care for themselves. Although direct aid is needed in emergency, it sometimes becomes a way of increasing dependence and subordination of the poor and of increasing false feelings of superiority among the rich. Reflecting critically on our own actions as well as those of others may help challenge many of our paternalistic assumptions about service and doing good.[15]

None of these are very dramatic ways of subverting the Church into being the Church, but they represent a beginning step in creating space for new household relationships to spring up. A household of freedom has no one structure or shape; it simply represents the two or three – or two or three thousand – gathered in Christ's name and seeking to participate in Christ's continuing housekeeping ministry for the world. Often these households are found within established congregations in the form of sanctuary churches, basic Christian communities, or shalom communities working for justice and peace. The ministry of such congregations is crucial in a society where religion is often a tool of 'political messianism'.[16]

But just as often, households of freedom can be glimpsed among those who form the *paroikia*: those outside the house of the Church who come together around the needs of the oppressed and God's good housekeeping agenda. Such groups do not consider themselves separate Churches, so they are not what would be called 'sects' in classical sociology. Nevertheless, they have the qualities of other such *paroikia* groups.[17] They have a distinct identity whose source is solidarity with the poor, the marginal, the dominated of society. Their internal coherence stems not from hierarchical structuring but from commitment to the task of struggle for change against the web of oppressions in which our world is engulfed. They make sense of the present situations of suffering and victimization by an appeal to a vision of a new household in which all persons will be treated as full human beings.

An example of this is the development of 'women-church' groups. These groups understand the early egalitarian Christian community as a prototype for their life together, but they take on as many shapes and varieties as there are men and women who take part in the gatherings. Elisabeth Fiorenza describes women-church as 'a feminist movement of self-identified women and women-identified men [which] transcends all traditional man-made denominational lines' and is committed to solidarity with the most despised women.[18]

These groups are particularly popular among Roman Catholic women because of their exclusion from ordination and decision-making in that Church.[19] But they provide a supportive community for women of all confessions who find that they are constantly ignored, put down, and excluded by the language and actions of their own congregations. Some have developed *Womanguides* for more inclusive readings, as well as a book of liturgy for *Women-Church*, both edited by Rosemary Ruether.[20] These groups are attempting to build up the household of freedom by focusing on those who constituted the bottom of the old house of bondage.

Authority from the bottom

This is the major clue to finding our way into a new metaphor for relationships of authority in community. The clue is not some form of strict mathematical equality, for relationships of authority and power are constantly changing as they are lived out in human interactions. Rather, it is the foundation of authority that is built up from the bottom rather than established from the top down. In a speech delivered to a Hispanic audience in 1984, Jesse Jackson expressed it this way: 'When the black and Hispanic foundation comes together, everyone above has to adjust. We are not the bottom of this society where things end up. We are the foundation – where everything begins.'[21]

God's option for the poor and marginal people, the homeless nobodies, sends us to look among those poeple to find how God's power is at work in the world. We discover that the bottom line for a new household of freedom is those who are not free. Welcoming them into the household causes a major shift in the way that we see reality. It causes a paradigm shift towards an inclusive authority of partnership or *koinōnia*. In solidarity with those at the bottom we join in expectant action, knowing that the first signs of God's household are already among us as we welcome one another.

Coming home again

The black women's ensemble Sweet Honey in the Rock sings a song that begins, 'We all, every one of us, have to come home again.'[22] Of course it attracted my attention because I have been thinking a lot about household metaphors. This one seemed to contradict the metaphor of Nelle Morton's book *The Journey Is Home*, not even to mention the familiar words from Thomas Wolfe that you can't go home again.[23] It most certainly is true that we can't go home again as long as the home we left is still part of the old relationships of patriarchy. I thought perhaps that going home in the song might refer to God's home in a manner similar to the spiritual 'Oh, Freedom!' which ends with the words: 'And before I'd be a slave, I'll be buried in my grave, and go home to my Lord and be free.'

As I continued to listen to the women of Sweet Honey in the Rock, I heard another theme, however. They were singing of those who 'were born on the bottom . . . lived on the bottom . . . grew up from the bottom' and declared that they'd never return to the bottom. And it seemed to me that they were singing about the foundation of the household of freedom. Only by coming home again to the bottom and building up the household in solidarity with all the wretched of the earth can we create all manner of different styles, types and sizes of houses in which God's people will be free.

Clues to good housekeeping

Beginning from the bottom may provide us with some clues for the work of good housekeeping as we reinterpret the various ways described in Chapter 1 that authority operates in our lives. We have already seen that it is not the feminist theologians who changed the paradigm. The paradigm was changed long ago through God's liberating activity in the exodus and resurrection. But the new reality of following a servant/Lord and a God who suffers in solidarity with the people has always been transformed back into a pyramid with God stuck up on the top, no longer allowed to share with Christ in the story of the suffering people of God's world house.

The authority that comes to those who have the knowledge of the tradition was also locked up in the old house of domination. If the paradigm shifts, then that *authority through knowledge* can again be accessible to all those who want to participate in naming and changing their world. By using the 'tools of the master' in the service of the oppressed, academic research and social analysis will become involved with reconstructing their 'invisible past' as well as in analysing ways to both fit and not fit into the dominant structure. The authority of knowledge will have a new source as well as a new task. As the words of the Sophia/Christ are heard with new ears, we turn to learn about the household of freedom from those who have discovered God in their midst in all ages.

From the perspective of the bottom, those whose cultural wisdom has been denied, ignored or stolen from them find that they can still live out of the vision of God's new household. The memory of that future comes to them from such sources as Mary's Magnificat in Luke 1:46–55, which declares that human life was not created for domination. It also comes to them out of their own stories, told and retold, about a past of holding on against tyranny and of a Housekeeper who intends the world to be otherwise. Those who believe this memory and this future will be maladjusted with the present as they join Mary's song about God's messianic politics. The *authority of wisdom* in this perspective becomes an authority that is born out of the experience of struggle, a wisdom at the disposal of the people as they cope with the present out of their living memories and hopes.

Those at the bottom must still cope with established forms of *structural authority* that justify their position at the bottom of the social, economic and political structures of the world. Yet the basis of the new household of freedom is the refusal to worship these powers of domination and to worship God alone. Thus Jesus refused the temptation to jump from the pinnacle of the temple as a display of power and chose the way of obedient solidarity with the outcasts (Luke 4.9–13). In the same way, those who follow him find that they must reject the temptation of the 'pinnacle complex' and work not to reverse the pyramid, so that they are on top, but rather to transform the pyramid so more persons gain access to the structures of decision-making.

When many persons have access to participation in the structures of decision-making, there is often an explosion of energy that makes it possible to build new households. This is what happened among the followers of Jesus. As poor and unorganized as they were, they discovered that it was possible to share together in feeding one another and in discovering new gifts for ministry. The charismatic authority of Jesus that enabled him to preach, heal and work among the people was not something he kept to himself. Thus, for instance, in the story of the five thousand we hear that he involved the disciples and the people in the feeding (Mark 6:30–44). In a household of freedom the charisma of God's Spirit is recognized is one of *diakonos*, servant, and the job description is to work themselves out of a job. Charisma becomes a gift of empowerment for others rather than one for dominating and manipulating others.

On Maundy Thursday we do not have much trouble remembering what it means for at least one charismatic leader to work himself out of a job. Yet even here our congregations often avoid much of the meaning of that sacrifice by omitting John's powerful story of Mary anointing Jesus for his role as servant/housekeeper, and of Jesus acting out the meaning of that service in the washing of feet (John 12–13). In East Harlem we used to try to keep the liturgy as close to home as possible, so we celebrated the supper as a potluck with wine, fish and bread, and invited all the neighbourhood. (Some of our street friends were regular attenders because of the abundant wine!) During the liturgy the pastors acted out the foot washing by becoming 'shoeshine boys and girls', carefully polishing each person's shoes with a shoe-rag stole.

Recently some of us at Yale Divinity School who had read Elisabeth Fiorenza's powerful account of the anointing story as an act of 'solidarity from below' wanted to celebrate 'in memory of her' as part of the story of Maundy Thursday (Mark 14.9).[24] In the service we used dishcloths for the foot washing and put perfume on the cloths as a symbol of the anointing. Thus we celebrated the Last Supper as a domestic scene in which women and men gathered together and enacted the meaning of discipleship: 'In memory of Jesus who washed the disciples' feet, and of Mary who anointed him as Messiah.' The One who is the God's anointed continues to be with us among the poor, and the invitation to remember him, to remember her, to remember them is real.

In a discussion with Nicaraguan peasants about John 12.8, Ernesto Cardenal says in *The Gospel in Solentiname*: 'I think [Jesus] is saying that he's going away but that in place of him the poor are left. What that woman was doing with him, they'd have to do later with the poor, because he wasn't going to be there any longer, or rather, we are going to have his presence in the poor.'[25]

That presence is a dangerous memory of the future. But it is offered to all who want to share in the good housekeeping chores of God's household.

☐ We now turn to the intractable and controversial set of issues that cluster round the topic of artificially assisted human reproduction.[15] Margaret Farley's essay is particularly helpful at this point because it deliberately and successfully reminds us of some of the basic contours of feminist theology, and the way these may contribute to discussion of reproduction – all too obviously central to the whole enterprise of loving and life-giving which some continue to find possible within the Christian tradition.

20   MARGARET A. FARLEY
Feminist Theology and Bioethics

The aim of this essay is to explore the connections between feminist theology and issues in the field of bioethics. I shall try to indicate basic contours of feminist theology and some ways its values bear on the vast network of ethical issues related to the biological sciences, technology and medicine. In order to press the question of possible contributions by feminist theology to bioethics, I shall focus on the implications of feminist theology for reproductive technology.

To some extent, the connection between the concerns of feminist theology and bioethics is obvious. Feminist theology proceeds from a methodological focus on the experience of women, and feminist ethics begins with a central concern for the well-being of women. Medical ethics (as a part of bioethics) can be expected to share this focus and this concern, if for no other reason than that women constitute the majority of those who receive and provide health care.[1] Beyond this, however, traditional religious views of women associate them symbolically and literally with nature, with the body, with human relationships, with reproduction – all themes for feminist theological critique, all foci for major concerns for bioethics. Three caveats are in order. It is helpful to identify some forms of relation that we should *not* expect to find.

First, we should not expect to find feminist theology articulating for bioethics fundamental values or moral principles which are in every way unique. Few contemporary theological ethicists claim for their theologies exclusive access to moral insight in the formulation of commonly held norms.[2] It is not only religious belief, or theology, or a particular theology that can ground, for example, a requirement to respect persons, or a principle of equality, or a rational system of distributive justice. Likewise, it is not only feminist theology that can ground a view of human persons as fundamentally interpersonal and social, or that can formulate a view of nature that requires human stewardship rather than exploitation. Still, the critical function of feminist theology may provide a new perspective on some issues in bioethics.

Second, there is no one definitive form of feminist theology. Theology in general is pluralistic on many levels. Feminist theology is one among many options in theology, but it is itself as pluralistic as is theology generally. Thus, there are feminist theologies centred in goddess worship, and others that locate themselves in the Jewish and Christian biblical traditions, and still others that move beyond any historical traditions at all. So clear have the differences in feminist theologies become that typologies abound in a growing effort to compare and contrast them.[5] This divergence must be kept in mind while we explore the convergence of basic ethical concerns, values, and norms for action.

Third, feminist theology is at beginning points in its systematic formulation. While monumental strides have been taken by feminist biblical scholars, theologians, and historians,[4] sustained theological synthesis is new on the horizon, at least for the Christian tradition.[5] Even newer is a systematic comprehensiveness and depth on the ethical side of feminist theology.[6] There is no easy route from the sources of religious faith to the specific insights needed for the radically new questions generated by scientific and medical capabilities. This conviction is mirrored in the reservations that many feminist theologians and ethicists express regarding some technologies of reproduction.[7] It is also mirrored in the recognition of the necessity of collaboration with disciplines other than theology and ethics for the gradual forging of moral perspectives on the multitude of issues which a comprehensive bioethics may address.

There are limits, then, to the connections presently discernible between feminist theology and bioethics. Within those limits, however, lie meeting points, challenges, resources, of potential critical importance to both disciplines. We turn first to the methods, sources, and relevant themes of feminist theology.

Feminist theology

Three themes in feminist theology can be raised up for central consideration: (1) relational patterns among human persons (2) human embodiment, and (3) human assessment of the meaning and value of the world of 'nature'. Feminist theology's development of these themes includes an articulation of basic ethical perceptions and leads to the formulation of some ethical action-guides. Moreover, these themes illuminate important methodological decisions which constitute not only central commitments for feminist theology, but possible warrants for ethical arguments in bioethics.

Patterns of relation

Feminism, in its most fundamental sense, is opposed to discrimination on the basis of sex. This opposition has the ultimate aim of equality among persons regardless of gender. To achieve this aim, feminism is necessarily pro-woman. Since discrimination on the basis of sex remains pervasively discrimination against women, feminism aims to correct this bias by a bias for women, however temporary or prolonged that bias must be. A bias for women includes a focal concern for the well-being of women and a taking of account of women's experience in coming to understand what well-being demands for women and men.

Feminist theology perceives profound discrimination against women in traditions of religious patriarchy. There are massive tendencies in religious traditions to justify patterns of relationship in which men dominate women. Within the history of Christianity, for example, the major pattern of relationship between women and men has been one of dominance and subjugation, sustained through beliefs about the essential inferiority of women to men and the need for a hierarchical order in social arrangements. Theological assessments of woman's nature were based on a fundamental dualism within humanity. Women and men are distinguished as polar opposites, representing body or mind, emotion or reason, passivity or activity, dependence or autonomy. The female-identified pole is always inferior to the male. More than this, women are often symbolically associated with evil, perceived as temptresses, feared as the threat of chaos to order, carnality to spirituality, weakness to strength. Even when women are exalted as symbols of virtue rather than vice, they bear the liabilities of imposed expectations and the burden of mediating 'femininity' to men.[8]

Feminist theology's critique of religious tradition extends to the central symbols of faith. Christianity's traditional formulations of a doctrine of God have often served as sexist warrants for discrimination against women. Personal metaphors for God are strongly masculine in the biblical tradition, as well as in theological formulations of the Trinity. Moreover, Christian faith is centred in a Saviour who is male. Hence, there is a strong tendency in this tradition to consider men more appropriate as representatives of God in the human family, society, and the Church. Indeed, traditional Christian theology has often granted the fullness of the *imago dei* to men, yielding it only derivatively and partially to women. But more than this, characterizations of the Christian God as a sovereign, transcendent, requiring submission from human persons,[9] have offered a model of relationship (dominance and submission) on which human relationships are then patterned. Along with this goes a view of the human self in which the height of Christian virtue is patient suffering and self-sacrificial love, and the only mode of Christian action is humble servanthood. Women are socialized into these ideals in a way that men are not, for men can imitate the autonomy and agency of God in their role as God's representatives. Doctrines of sin that stress the evil of prideful self-assertion only reinforce the submissiveness that already characterizes women.[10]

What emerges in feminist theology is an analysis of oppressive patterns of relationship and ideologies that foster them. These patterns of oppression are identified in every human relation where the pattern is one of domination and subjugation on the basis of sex or race or class. Given the radical nature of a critique which reaches every major doctrine, feminist theologians either move away from Christianity altogether, or take up the task of critical reconstruction of Christian theology. In either case, they have by and large moved to develop a view of human relations characterized by equality and mutuality, in which both autonomy and relationality are respected.

Feminist theologians who seek to reconstruct Christian theology 'beyond the feminist critique' argue that there are fundamental resources within the tradition which are not ultimately sexist and which can be brought to bear precisely as a challenge to sexism. With feminist hermeneutical methods, biblical resources reveal a God who does not need to compete with human beings for sovereignty, who comes forth with freedom in order to call forth freedom from human persons; a God who is able to be imagined in feminine as well as masculine terms,[11] for whom 'friend' or 'partner' are more apt metaphors than 'king' or 'logos'.[12] Historical and theological resources yield a view of human community that challenges the domination of one group over another, one class of persons over another.[13]

It has not been open to feminist theology simply to appropriate a view of the human person which makes autonomy paramount as the ground of respect or the primary principle to be protected in social relations. Relationality has pressed itself on feminist theologians from the experience of women. It is this that has demanded continued analysis of the nature of human relations and has led to historical and biblical studies of, for example, Christian communities, and to theological studies of the very nature of God (as relational). But if feminist theology cannot ignore relationality, neither has it been able to let go of autonomy as an essential feature of personhood.[14] Romantic returns to organic notions of society where relation is all, each in her place, without regard for free agency or for personal identity and worth which transcends roles – these are options that feminists judge can only repeat forms of oppression for women.

Pluralism in feminist theology, of course, leads to some profoundly different choices regarding historical forms of human relationships. Disagreements are on the level of strategy (is there any possiblity of radically transforming existing religious traditions?); or on the analysis of the cause of oppression (whether it is most fundamentally religion, or culture in a more general sense, or the conspiracy of men, or economics, etc); or on the model of relation (do exclusivity and separatism contradict the values of equality and mutuality?). Such disagreements are extremely serious, and it would be a mistake to underestimate them. Still, there is basic unanimity among feminist theologians on the values that are essential for non-oppressive human relationships – the values of equality, mutuality, and freedom.[15]

Embodiment

The second theme in feminist theology that has particular bearing on issues of bioethics is human embodiment. There is a clear history of association of ideas that we must trace if we are to see the import of this theme both for feminist theology and bioethics.

Body/spirit is in many ways the basic dualism with which historical religions have struggled since late antiquity. Women, as we have already noted, have been associated with body, men with mind. Women's physiology has been interpreted as 'closer to nature' than men's in that many areas and functions of a women's body seem to serve the human species as much or more than they serve the individual woman.[16] Women's bodies, in this interpretation, are subject to a kind of fate – more so than men's. Women are immersed in 'matter', in an inertness which has not its own agency. This is manifest not only in the determined rhythms of their bodily functions, but in a tendency to act from emotion rather than from reason, and in women's 'natural' work, which is the caring for the bodies of children and men.

Women have also been associated with the ongoing evaluations of human bodiliness and matter in general. Despite resistance from basically world-affirming attitudes in Judaism, and despite an ongoing conflict with positive Christian doctrines of creation and incarnation, both of these traditions incorporated negative views of the human body (and especially women's bodies). In late antiquity, Judaism was influenced by world-denying attitudes of Near Eastern gnosticism and mysticism. Christianity absorbed these same influences in its very foundations, along with Greek philosophical distrust of the transitoriness of bodily being.

Integral to views of the human body have been views of human sexuality. Despite traditional influences towards positive valuation (of sexuality as a part of creation, as implicated in the very covenant with God, etc), strongly negative judgements have been brought in. From ancient blood taboos, to stoic prescriptions for the control of sexual desire by reason, to Christian doctrines of the consequences of original sin, fear and suspicion regarding the evil potentialities of sex have reigned strong in the Western conscience. So great, in fact, has been the symbolic power of sex in relation to evil that there seems to have been 'from time immemorial', as Paul Ricoeur puts it, 'an indissoluble complicity between sexuality and defilement'. [17]

Women's sexuality has been seen as more 'carnal' than men's, 'closer to nature', more animal-like, less subject to rational control. Disclosure of this historical view of women's sexuality came as a surprise to many feminists whose direct learning from religious traditions had tended to be the opposite – that is, that women are less passionate than men, and hence more responsible for setting limits to sexual activity. The reversal in this regard has its roots, too, in religious traditions and reflects the tendency we have seen before to identify women with evil, on one hand, and place them on a pedestal, on the other. [18] In either case, women's identity remains closely tied to the way they relate to their bodies, and in either case, women have learned to devalue their bodies. For women themselves, Freud's comment on beliefs about menstruation, pregnancy, and childbirth held true: ' . . . it might almost be said that women are altogether taboo'. [19]

The rise of feminist consciousness called into question all past interpretations of the meaning of women's bodies. Women's turn to their own experience for new interpretations of embodiment was not a simple process. A beginning feminist response was a rejection of this association. Anatomy was *not* destiny; women were not to be identified with their bodies any more than were men; women could transcend their bodies through rational choices. Such a response paradoxically freed women, however, to take their bodies more seriously. Women soon moved to 'reclaim' their bodies – to claim them as their own, as integral to their selfhood and their womanhood. This entailed new practical and theoretical approaches. Reflecting on their experiences, women shared insights and interpretation, formulated new symbols, expanded and revised understandings of human embodiment as such. [20]

Feminist philosophers and theologians used a phenomenological method to describe what it means to *be* a body as well as *have* a body, to understand their own bodies as ways of being inserted into the world, as structured centres of personal activity, as body-subjects not just body-objects. [21] From an understanding of themselves as embodied subjects, women 'reclaim' their bodies not just by taking them seriously and 'living' them integrally, but by refusing to yield control of them to men. New intimate self-understandings and new philosophical and theological anthropologies yield new personal and political decisions.

The world of nature

The third theme in feminist theology relevant to bioethics is the meaning and value of the world of nature. Feminist theologians' concern for this theme is directly influenced by their concern for patterns of human relations and for the world as the place of human embodiment.

Just as women have been thought of in religious and cultural traditions as 'close to nature', so the world of nature has been symbolized as female. This is a clue to the difficulties that feminist theologians have with past beliefs and attitudes regarding nature. They find, in fact, a correlation between patterns of domination over women and efforts at domination over nature.[22]

Perceptions of nature change through history, of course. Nature has been exalted beyond the being and culture of humans, or reduced to a tool for humans; it has been viewed as the cosmic source of life and goodness, or a mysterious force to be feared and fled or controlled. All of these interpretations of nature mirror similar identifications of the essence of woman.

Despite the fact that a Christian worldview and specific Christian teachings have supported 'sacramental' views of the whole of creation, Christianity has also tended to trivialize nature. Ascetic theologies sometimes reduced nature to a transitory illusion, a distraction from 'higher things'. Christian leaders sometimes forbade the study of nature as dangerous or a waste of time. When nature and culture were paired among traditional dualisms, nature was assigned the value of the negative pole. Similarly, while there is a strong tradition in Christian thought requiring reverence for and stewardship of nature, there is also strong support for a way of relating to nature which sees it only as something to be used, dominated, controlled by human persons.[23]

Rosemary Ruether traces a history of Western attitudes towards nature from an early ascetical 'flight' from nature to a modern 'return' to nature.[24] The rise of scientific research in the seventeenth century helped secularize nature, fostered a perception of it as intrinsically rational, penetrable, manageable. Unintended negative consequences of scientific and technological development produced romantic reactions calling for a different return to nature

– a restoration of 'pure' nature, uncontaminated and unalienated by human intervention. All of these attitudes towards nature represented the pattern of hierarchical domination and subjugation – domination through possession and control, whether through denigration, or exploitation, or the expectation of mediated happiness and identity through 'keeping' nature as a haven for some (despite the suffering this in turn might cause for others).[25]

Feminist theology argues, alternatively, for a view of nature consonant with a view of a God who takes not see creation seriously and a view of creation which does the whole of predatory hierarchy as the basis of order. Nature, in this view, is valuable according to its concrete reality, which includes an interdependence with embodied humanity. It is limited in its possibilities, which precludes its moral use as the battleground for the ultimate challenge to human freedom. Human intelligence and freedom are not barred from addressing nature, but measures for understanding and just use are lodged both in nature itself and in ethical requirements for relations among persons.

Feminist theological ethics

We have seen enough of feminist theology to draw some conclusions regarding the *methods* likely to characterize any ethics that derive from it. First in this regard, there is a sense in which feminist theology and ethics can be said to be concerned with objective reality, and hence to presuppose methodologically some access to an intelligible reality. Like feminism in general, feminist theology had its origins in women's growing awareness of the disparity between received traditional interpretations of their identity and function within the human community and their own experience of themselves and their lives. The corresponding claim that gender role-differentiation and gender-specific limitations on opportunities for education, political participation, economic parity, etc., are discriminatory was based on the argument that past interpretations of women's reality were simply wrong. That is, past theories failed to discover the concrete reality of women and represented, in fact, distorted perceptions of that reality.

It would be a mistake, however, to label feminist theology and ethics in any simple sense 'naturalistic'. Feminist theology does not, obviously, reduce to a natural or behavioural science. Nor does it rely for its access to reality on human reason alone. And while feminist theological ethics searches for and proposes universally valid norms, it does so in a way that acknowledges the historical nature of human knowledge and the social nature of the interpretation of human experience. The fact that present insights may be superseded by future ones, and that present formulations of specific principles may change, does not contradict either the methodological requirement of attending to concrete reality or the methodological presupposition that the accuracy and adequacy of theories can be tested against that reality.

Closely aligned with all of this is the methodological commitment to begin with and continue a primary focus on the experience of women.[26] This is often coupled with the qualification that no claims are made for the universality of women's experience in relation to human experience. There is a claim made, however, that until a theology based on women's experience is developed, traditionally assumed universal claims for a theology based on men's experience will continue to render inadequate if not inaccurate the major formulations of religious belief.

A methodological commitment to the primacy of women's experience as a source for theology and ethics yields, in addition, a feminist hermeneutical principle which functions in the selection and interpretation of all other sources. While not every feminist theologian articulates this principle in exactly the same way, it can be expressed as strongly as, 'Whatever diminishes or denies the full humanity of women must be presumed not to reflect the divine or an authentic relation to the divine, or to reflect the authentic nature of things, or to be the message or work of an authentic redeemer or a community of redemption.'[27] This principle functions in different ways in different feminist theologies. In some, it leads to the rejection of the authority of the Bible altogether;[28] in others it allows the relativization of the authority of some texts;[29] in still others, it leaves all texts standing as a part of an authoritative revelation, but renders their meaning transformed under a new feminist paradigm.[30] The same is true for theological doctrines, historical events, and for other sources of theology and ethics.

A focus on women's experience, the use of a feminist hermeneutical principle, and a concern for the lived experience of women precisely as disadvantaged, constitute for feminist theological ethics the bias for women which is the earmark of feminism in general. If this is chosen as a strategic priority, feminist theological ethics can be methodologically oriented ultimately as an ethic whose concerns include the well-being of both women and men, both humanity and the world of nature. Its theological centre will depend on its ultimate warrants for these concerns.

Finally, feminist theological ethics has been open to both deontological and teleological patterns of reasoning.[31] On one hand, the very notion of 'strategic-priority', as well as a strongly 'ecological' view of reality, imply a concern for consequences, an ethical evaluation of means in relation to ends and parts in relation to wholes, a relativization of values in situations of conflict. On the other hand, demands of the concrete reality of persons are such that some attitudes and actions can be judged unethical precisely because they contradict values intrinsic to that reality. Neither of these modes of reasoning is ruled out for feminist theological ethics.

When we turn from method to *substance* in feminist theological ethics, we need only summarize the ethical import of feminist theological themes. Thus, an ethic derived from feminist theology understands the well-being of persons in a way that takes account of their reality as *embodied* subjects, in relation to an historical world. This ethic also gives important status to equality and mutuality. It holds together autonomy and relationality. It gives ethical priority to models of relationship characterized by collaboration rather than competition or hierarchical gradation. Finally, it does not isolate an ethic of human relations from ethical obligations to the whole of nature.

Some test of this ethic can be made by turning now to issues in bioethics.

Feminist theology and bioethics

Feminist theology offers a distinctive perspective on many issues under bioethics, because women's lives are deeply implicated in personal medical care, public health, and the development and use of biomedical technologies. Here the lived experience of women reveals some of the central opportunities and limitations of the human condition. Here it is that 'reflection upon the goals, practices, and theories of medicine validates philosophical reflection upon many issues that have traditionally been of concern to women', but ignored by the traditional disciplines of philosophy and theology.[32]

We can explore the interrelation between feminist theology and bioethics in a number of ways. From a feminist perspective, we can examine general principles of bioethics, such as autonomy, beneficence, and justice; and specific issues such as abortion, medical care of the elderly, psychiatric biases in the treatment of women, hierarchical ordering of medical professions. Let me focus upon the issue of the development and use of reproductive technologies.[33] A feminist theological approach to this issue may show some of the implications of feminist theology for understanding both context and principles in the area of bioethics.

The potentialities of reproductive technology have for some time caught the attention of feminists, though without unanimity of analysis. Some feminists have argued that the ultimate source of women's oppression is their physiological capability of bearing children. While physical motherhood can constitute individual and social power, it also renders women powerless – before nature, before men, before their children, before society (which judges and determines the conditions under which their children must grow). In the face of this powerlessness, and the suffering it entails, technology offers a solution. Indeed, in an extreme view, women's liberation can only be achieved with a revolution not only against forms of society, but against nature itself. Thus, Shulamith Firestone argued for the 'freeing of women from the tyranny of their reproductive biology by every means available', including technology that could separate women once and for all from a gender-identified responsibility for reproduction.[34]

This was a relatively early position, however, and strong disagreement came from other feminists on a variety of grounds. Many consider the analysis of the causes of oppression to be wrong.[35] Others see in the development of reproductive technologies a new means of devaluing women, rendering them 'expendable in the procreative process'.[36] Still others argue that some uses of technology, such as amniocentesis for the purpose of gender selection, will pit women against themselves.[37]

Feminists agree, however, on at least two things in regard to these questions. First, the history of women's experience in relation to the power and process of reproduction is a history of great pain. While fertility, pregnancy and childbirth have been a source of women's happiness and fulfilment, and occasions for powerful expressions of great human love and enduring fidelity to duty, they have also been the locus of a cumulative burden of immense oppression and suffering. The twentieth-century incursion of technology into reproduction (the 'medicalization' of pregnancy and childbirth) has often added to this suffering, extended this oppression.

Secondly, feminists agree that the development and use of reproductive technology cannot be evaluated apart from its concrete, sociocultural context. This context remains an 'historically specific social order in which positions of power and privilege are disproportionately occupied by men'.[38] As long as sexism continues to characterize the lived world that women know, technology will have different consequences for women and for men. Far from freeing women from unnecessary burdens in reproduction, further technological development may result in greater bondage.

Neither feminism in general nor feminist theology render wholly negative judgements on reproductive technology. One obvious reason is that such technology can take many forms. Evaluations of developments of contraceptives, childbirth procedures, methods of abortion, artificial insemination, *in vitro* fertilization, foetal diagnosis, cloning, and many other technologies can hardly be lumped together in a single comprehensive judgement. Generally, despite deep ambivalence towards reproductive technologies, feminists can affirm that 'natural-scientific breakthroughs represent genuine gains in human self-understanding. The widespread social irresponsibility of medical practice, exacerbated by male monopoly of the medical profession that is only now changing, must not be confused with the value of scientific discoveries.'[39] Science and technology have been instruments for reform at times, even in regard to sexism.[40]

It will be helpful to narrow our focus still more to one form of reproductive technology. The form that I will consider is *in vitro* fertilization for the purpose of producing a child. As a technology, it raises the issue of profound change in human modes of reproduction.

One place to begin a feminist analysis of *in vitro* fertilization (with embryo transfer or some other form of providing for gestation) is with women's experience to date of technology in the area of pregnancy and birth. As we have already noted, in many respects this is not a happy experience. Recent studies have helped to make visible the difficulties women have had.[41] Recalling these difficulties can help us to formulate the questions that need to be asked of *in vitro* fertilization. The use of medical technology in relation to childbirth has contributed to the alienation of women from their bodies, their partners, and their children (by, for example, moving childbirth into settings appropriate primarily for the treatment of disease, isolating mothers both from 'women's culture' and their spouses, regimenting the presence of mothers with their babies, etc.);[42] and it has placed women in a network of professional relations which unjustifiably limit their autonomy (as 'patient'). Does the development and use of *in vitro* fertilization hold this same potential for alienation, albeit in different ways? Does *in vitro* fertilization violate (or is it in accord with) feminist understandings of embodiment, norms for relationships, and concerns for the common good?

For many feminists the sundering of the power and process of reproduction from the bodies of women constitutes a loss of major proportions. Hence, the notion of moving the whole process to the laboratory (using not only *in vitro* fertilization but artificial placentas, etc.) is not one that receives much enthusiasm. On the other hand, *in vitro* fertilization does not necessarily violate the essential embodying of reproduction. If its purpose is to enable women who would otherwise be infertile to conceive a child, it becomes a means precisely to mediate embodiment. Feminists generally oppose the sacralization of womens' reproductive organs and functions that would prohibit all technological intervention. In fact, desacralization in this regard is a necessary step in the breaking of feminine stereotypes and the falsification of anatomy as destiny. Moreover, feminist interpretations are very clear on the validity of separating sexuality from reproduction. Without contradiction, however, they also affirm reproduction as a significant potential dimension of sexuality. Yet feminists do not give an absolute value to a series of 'natural' physical connections between sexual intercourse and the fertilization of an ovum by male sperm. It is a failure of imagination which sees this as the only way in which integrated sexuality can be related to reproduction. All in all, then, while human embodiment remains a central concern in a feminist analysis of *in vitro* fertilization, it does not thereby rule out the ethical use of this technology.

Feminists are generally clear on the need to understand and experience childbearing in an active way. Pregnancy and childbirth are not events in relation to which women should be wholly passive.[43] Part of taking active control and responsibility regarding their reproductive power can include a willingness to use technology in so far as it makes childbearing more responsible, less painful, and more safe. Sometimes discernment of just these consequences for technology is difficult, but the fact that it is called for indicates, again, that *in vitro* fertilization is not ruled out in principle.

Perhaps the most troubling aspect of *in vitro* fertilization, and other technologies that actually empower reproduction, is the question of primary agency and responsibility. Women's previous experience with reproductive technology suggests that women's own agency is likely to be submerged in the network of multiple experts needed to achieve *in vitro* fertilization. Far from this accomplishing a liberation of women from childbearing responsibilities, it can entail 'further alienation of our life processes'.[44] Moreover, efforts to restrict and share the agency of professionals often move only in the direction of what some feminists fear as collectivism or state control, the 'total alienation of one's life to institutions external to one's own control and governed by a managerial elite'.[45] Without a drastic change in the composition of society and the professions, widespread use of *in vitro* fertilization could make it difficult for women to achieve or sustain control of human reproduction.

Does it matter whether women or men, parents or scientists, control reproduction? Feminists argue that those who will bear the responsibility for childrearing should have primary agency in decisions about childbearing – not just because it is their right if they are to bear the burden of such responsibility, but because this is required for the well-being of offspring. 'Only those who are deeply realistic about what it takes to nourish human life *from birth onward* have the wisdom to evaluate procreative choice.'[46] Reproductive technologies that divorce decisions for childbearing from childrearing fail to take seriously the basic needs of children for not only material resources but personal relation and support, in contexts that allow the awakening of basic trust and the development of fundamental autonomy.[47] It is not only women who, in principle, can make these choices,[48] but it is 'parents', not just 'scientific facilitators' or society at large or any persons unprepared to take responsibility at an intimate and comprehensive level for our children. Such problems of agency are complex and sobering in the face of technological capabilities such as *in vitro* fertilization. They are not, in principle, intractable, perhaps not even in practice. They need not rule out the ethical use of *in vitro* fertilization. But they occasion grave moral caution.

Yet another consideration regards the developing capability for 'selection' of offspring from among many candidates (differentiated by gender, bodily health, intellectual capacity, etc.). The problem of 'discards' in *in vitro* fertilization is larger than the discernment of grave embryonic anomalies. For some feminists this capability can erode moral and religious obligation to accept all sorts of persons into the human community. In so doing, it undermines basic feminist principles of equality, inclusiveness, mutuality, and toleration of difference and of 'imperfection'.[49] *In vitro* fertilization need not, of course, be used in this way. But once again, a voice of caution is raised.

Underlying all of these considerations is the need to measure *in vitro* fertilization according to norms of justice. If justice in its deepest sense can be understood as treating persons in truthful accordance with their concrete reality, then all the issues of embodiment, non-discrimination, agency, responsibility, inclusive care, are issues of justice. They are not focused only on individuals, but on the human community. They converge in the fundamental question, 'How are we to reproduce ourselves as human persons?' They press us to new theories of justice which extend a requirement for 'just parenting' in relation to all human children. They include, too, questions of the meaning and value of *in vitro* fertilization in a world threatened by overpopulation, in countries where not every existing child is yet cared for, in communities where grave needs of children require the resources of science and technology. Questions of macroallocation of scarce goods and services may finally be unresolvable, but they cannot be ignored. At the very least, in this instance, they preclude justifications of *in vitro* fertilization on the basis of any absolute right to procreate.

A feminist analysis of *in vitro* fertilization remains, then, provisional. It yields, however, the following position. Negatively, there are not grounds for an absolute prohibition of the development and use of technology such as *in vitro* fertilization. Positively, such technology may aid just and responsible human reproduction. The presence of certain circumstances, or certain conditions, sets limits to its ethical development and use – circumstances such as (1) high risk of injury to the well-being of either parent or child (2) a context unconducive to the growth and development of any child produced (unconducive because, for example, no one is prepared to offer the child a basic human personal relationship) (3) an intention to produce a child to be used as a means only, in relation to the producers' ends (as, for example, if the child is produced merely for the sake of the advance of scientific research, or for the duplication of one's own self without regard for the child's development into an autonomous self) (4) failure to meet criteria of distributive justice (when it is determined that other basic human needs place legitimate prior claims on the resources involved). Such conditions rule out spectres of human laboratory 'farms'. They also tell us something about the conditions for any ethical decisions regarding human reproduction, not just decisions made in the context of reproductive technology.

With this, then, we have one example of the relation between feminist theology and an issue of bioethics. My development of the issue is more suggestive than exhaustive of the particular ethical values and ultimate theological warrants that feminist theologians may offer. Future work in bioethics will bring careful reflection on questions that I have not addressed at all – questions, for example, of women's interpretation not only of birth but of death, and women's evaluation of the strength of 'quality of life' claims in relation to sanctity of life principles. Whatever lines along which a feminist bioethics may develop, however, it will never be far from central concerns for human embodiment, for the well-being of women-persons on a par with the well-being of men-persons, for newly just patterns of relationship among all persons, and for the balanced care of the whole world of both non-personal and personal beings.

☐ Beyond Margaret Farley's concerns are those of a rather different kind of feminist theologian, Sallie McFague, who, as it were, has her eyes on large horizons in her book *Models of God: Theology for an Ecological, Nuclear Age* (London, SCM, 1987). She has written a theological treatment of language about God which is in its way quintessentially North American. She signals this by her own analogy for theology, as a house to live in for a while, windows partly open and door ajar, which becomes a prison if it does not allow us to come and go, add a room or take one away, or even move out and rebuild. And she is scrupulously careful to acknowledge her own standpoint as white, middle class in a social context in which some few control resources as fundamental as food and shelter for so very many others. Being female by sex and feminist in perspective is relevant precisely because it provides her with sufficient disorientation from the dominant symbol system of Christianity. For McFague, theology is a human construct for which we must take responsibility. We must be sensitive to the 'cracks' that lie between the *little* we know, learn to live with the *via negativa* (the negative way), and learn to endure uncertainty, partiality and relativity. We need to resist closure, coherence, identity and totality, and the identification of divine reality with our theological constructions.

Theology *for our time* needs to work with an inclusive, non-hierarchical vision, stressing relationship and interdependence, transformation and openness, care and creativity, thinking about human responsibility for the post-double-holocaust world *we* have made. After explaining her method, the crucial move she makes is to explore the metaphor of the world as God's body, a body to which 'God is present as mother, lover, and friend of the last and least in all of creation' (p. 87). The very phrasing of this summary (which leads to the separate expositions of each metaphor and the sorts of love and activity characteristic of each, hence to the conduct of human existence) immediately suggests an area of tension, which a metaphorical, but not a systematic, theology can tolerate. Metaphors, as 'naming', name by catching all sorts of strands of association in a text or cluster of texts, as Sallie McFague does for herself in her imaginative, inventive experiment naming God as mother, lover and friend, edging us away from the idolatry which issues from viewing certain metaphors as descriptions. Well worth attention here is her association of 'mothering' with the pursuit of justice, 'loving' with the work of healing, and 'being a friend' with the enjoyment of companionship. These three sections on ethics are of central importance in exploring relationships which are essential expressions of the life-giving instincts of our species.

21 SALLIE McFAGUE
The Ethic of God as Mother, Lover and Friend

The Ethic of God as Mother: Justice

We all know, some by heart, the two great commandments: we are commanded to love God with all our heart, soul, and mind, and our neighbour as ourselves (Mark 12.28–31; Matt. 22.34–40; Luke 10.25–28). Many Christians, especially Protestants, have felt uneasy about these commandments, for not only are sinners unable to love God genuinely, that is, with 'giving' (agapic) love, but they ought not to love the neighbour with love based on *self*-love.[1] But in the context of the doctrine of the created world as the body of our mother-God in which we all live and have our being, the commands take on a very different complexion. In this context it is impossible to consider loving God apart from loving the others (human and otherwise) that constitute the body of the world, and love toward the others, the agapic love of creation, is a very basic love: the affirmation of existence. In an ecological, nuclear world, the 'as ourselves' of the commandment is first of all the affirmation of existence for the others as we also, and most fundamentally, affirm it for ourselves. Loving others 'as yourself' means – whatever else it may also mean – willing for others the existence, the right to birth, nurture, and fulfilment, that one wills for oneself. Not to wish this for oneself is to wish for death, but in the context of our doctrine of creation, the commandment to love others is to wish for them what one, unless suicidal, wishes for oneself: life.

As simple as that sounds, the fulfilment of the command is complex and 'impossible' – but then the fulfilment of the commandments, on any interpretation, has always been considered impossible. What is important, however, is the direction they give for human living. The direction suggested by the present interpretation is toward bedrock justice: the establishment of the conditions of a just order in which the necessities of existence are shared. God as mother-judge condemns those who selfishly refuse to share. When judgement is connected to the mother-creator, it is different from when it is connected to the king-redeemer. In the picture of the king-redeemer, individuals are condemned who rebel against the power and the glory of the monarch, assigning to themselves the status that only the king deserves. The king judges the guilty and metes out punishment, or as the Christian story happily concludes, takes the punishment upon himself and thus absolves those condemned. In the picture of the mother-creator, however, the goal is neither the condemnation nor the rescue of the guilty but the just ordering of the cosmic household in a fashion beneficial to all. God as mother-creator is primarily involved not in the negative business of judging wayward individuals but in the positive business of creating with our help a just ecological enonomy for the well-being of all her creatures.[2] God as the mother-judge is the one who establishes justice, not the one who hands out sentences.[3] She is concerned with establishing justice now, not with condemning in the future.

But how, more specifically, can such an ethic of justice be pertinent in our day? Before answering this question, we must recall that our experiment is not meant to suggest a life style for individual Christians so much as it is meant to suggest a framework, a heuristic picture, for interpreting Christian faith in a holistic, nuclear age. It is not expected that human beings can bring about a just order for all life, for such a vision is utopian and apocalyptic – a way of expressing what the tradition has meant by the 'kingdom of God'. Nonetheless, the picture that one holds of utopia makes a difference in the way one conducts daily business. If one thinks of it as individual election to an eternal otherworld, one will act differently than if one thinks of it as a just order for all in this world: both are utopian in the sense that fulfilment is always partial, but each serves as a goal and a goad, as an attraction and a critique.

According to some liberation theologies, the establishment of a just social, political, and economic order is the gospel of the Christian faith. And this, we agree, is the heart of the ethic of justice implicit in God as mother-creator. But even within most liberation theologies the right to existence and the basics necessary to live and live decently have been narrowly allocated. They have been allotted to human beings, with little regard for the rights of other levels of being and little concern with these other levels apart from their support of the human population. At a still deeper level little attention has been given to the right to existence of unborn generations of our own as well as other species, a right that we as the creatures who have the power to cut off birth, to extinguish ourselves and all others, can withhold. In most liberation theologies, the justice issue has not been joined with the ecological and nuclear issues but has been dealt with largely as a human, historical, economic problem. Therefore, Marxism has seemed adequate for analyzing the situation and, with ancillary insights from the Christian tradition, for dealing with it. But if one considers the justice issue in an ecological, nuclear context, there is no way to separate history from nature in this way, and though one can rightfully speak of liberation from oppressive structures, one must also speak of caring for the world that provides all the necessities that we would distribute justly.

As we have indicated earlier, an ethic of justice in a holistic, nuclear world implies an ethic of care, for with the shift of power from nature to human beings there is no way we can deal justly with other orders of beings, either in recognition of their intrinsic worth or as the necessary support for our existence, unless we become caretakers.[4] It is here that the model of parent, mother and father, becomes especially relevant as a way to envision human behaviour that is concerned to bring about justice through care. We should become mothers and fathers to our world, extending those natural instincts we all have, whether or not we have children of our bodies (or adopted children), to what Jonathan Schell calls 'universal parenthood'.[5] Schell uses the term in regard to the nuclear threat of extinction, in which birth would become extinct. In this context, universal parenthood is the will to allow others to come into existence, the desire for the renewal of life which birth always brings. It appeals to that level deep within all of us that links death and birth: we can stand the thought of the one because of the link with the other. Even though each of us must die, others will be born: this, up to now, one could always count on. But, says Schell, there is now the possibility of a 'second death'. The first death is our own individual death, which, difficult as it is to face, we can and do face, because we know that birth will bring others who will succeed us: life will be passed on. The second death, however, is the death of life itself: extinction. It is the death of birth, for none will be born, but it is also the death of death, for there will be none to die. The second death we can scarcely imagine, but once imagined, it is too revolting and appalling to dwell on, especially when we know that we are responsible. It is at this level, and nothing short of it, that we must ask, in such a situation, how should we model our behaviour?

If we were to see ourselves as universal parents, as profoundly desiring not our own lives to go on forever but the lives of others to come into being, we would have a model highly appropriate to our time. Schell limits the model to the human species and to birth (or the simple willing of others into existence); I, on the other hand, would extend it both to other species and to nurturing activities beyond birth and feeding. Before amplifying these two points, however, I would stress that the power of the model rests on the base Schell has given it: the will deep within all of us which could be called the parental instinct, the will not to save ourselves but to bring others into existence. Most broadly, whether or not one is a biological or adoptive parent, the parental instinct says to others, 'It is good that you exist!' even if this involves a diminishment and, in some cases, the demise of the self. Or to put it a little differently, we realize, if we contemplate the possible death of our species (or worse still, the extinction of all life), that it is not our own individual end that is most appalling to us but the death of birth. We all want to be life givers, to pass life on, and when we do we can

face our own deaths more easily. Therefore, to suggest universal
parenthood as a model to help bring about justice through care calls
upon our deepest instincts, where life and death mingle and where
the preservation of life for others takes precedence over concern for
the self.

Universal parenthood, however, cannot be limited to our species
or to birth. To limit it to our species displays the anthropocentric
focus that fails to appreciate the interdependence and interrelatedness of all levels of life. Since human beings are the only 'conscious'
parents – that is the only ones who can, both for their own species
and as surrogate parents for other species, will to help birth take
place – we have the special responsibility to help administer the
process: to join God the creator-mother in so arranging the cosmic
household that the birth and growth of other species will take place
in an ecologically balanced way, both for our own well-being and
for the well-being of other species.[6] We must become the gardeners
and caretakers of our Eden, our beautiful, bountiful garden, not
taming and ruling it, let alone despoiling and desecrating it, as we
so often do, but being to it as a universal parent, willing the
existence of all species and, as a good householder, ordering the
just distribution of the necessities of existence. We are, of course,
speaking here of an attitude, of a role model that, if assumed, can
begin to change both how one sees the world and how one acts in
and toward it. If one thought of oneself as parent to the world, that
is, if one moved oneself inside that model and walked around in it,
acting the role of parent, what changes might come about in, say,
how one spent one's time, one's money, one's vote? The univer-
salizing of our most basic loves, extending them beyond the
confines of our immediate families and primary communities and
even beyond our own species, is, I believe, the necessary direction
in our search for models for behaviour in an ecological, nuclear age.

The other direction in which we must universalize parenthood is
in extending it beyond birth and an attention to basic nurture, to an
attention to the entire well-being of our successors. As creator, God
the mother is concerned not only with birth and nourishment but
also with fulfilment. We have noted that female deities in other
religious traditions and female attributes or personas of God in ours
were not limited to bearing and caring for new life but were also
pictured as involved in the fulfilment of life through the ordering of
justice, the impartation of wisdom, the invitation to the oppressed,
the transformation of life, and so forth. Parenthood is not limited
to birth and nurture but includes all creative activities supporting

the next generation – and by implication, the weak and vulnerable as well.[7] This, of course, once again undercuts the split between nature and history, for in the human species at least, nurture and fulfilment involves all ranges of the body, mind, and spirit. All people, therefore, who engage in work, paid or unpaid, that helps to sustain the present and coming generations are universal parents. The agapic, just love that we have designated as parental, the love that gives without calculating the return, that wills the existence and fulfilment of other beings – this love is manifest in ways beyond counting. It is found in the teacher who gives extra time to the slow or gifted student, in the social worker whose clients are drug-addicted pregnant women, in the librarian who lovingly restores old books, in the specialist in world population control whose days are spent on planes and in board meetings, in the zoologist who patiently studies the behaviour of the great apes in the wild, in the owner of the local supermarket who employs ex-juvenile delinquents, in the politician who supports more funds for public education, in the botanist who catalogues new strains of plants, in rock stars who give their talents to famine relief. All of these are examples of universal parenthood: the examples are independent both of gender and of biological parenthood and are not limited to our own species. Nor are they unusual. In fact, much paid work in any society and almost all volunteer work have potential parental dimensions. It is these dimensions that need to be uncovered and encouraged in order to work within the ethic of God as mother-creator, the ethic of justice.

Needless to say, individual examples alone will not accomplish revolution. Is it possible to think of governments modeling themselves as universal parents? The model in most capitalist democracies is a mechanical one, balancing the rights and responsibilities of various constituencies while focusing on the freedom of the individual. In such a model the vulnerable and the weak, including children and the natural world, tend to do poorly, since they do not have a voice strong enough – if they have any voice at all – to sway the balance of power or to protect themselves against rapacious individualism. Some forms of socialism do approach the parental model more closely, both in understanding the political order in organic rather than mechanistic terms and in providing better support for the necessities of life to the young, the sick, and the vulnerable.

The intention of these remarks on the ethic of God the mother-creator as justice is not, however, to provide a blueprint for the reconstitution of society but to sketch the change in attitude, the conversion of consciousness, that could come about were we to begin to live inside the model and allow it to become a lens through which we looked out on the world. We would no longer see a world we named and ruled or, like the artist God, made: mothers and fathers to the world do not rule or fashion it. Our positive role in creation is as preservers, those who pass life along and who care for all forms of life so they may prosper. Our role as preservers is a very high calling, our peculiar calling as human beings, the calling implied in the model of God as mother.

In closing this chapter on God as mother we return to our opening prayer 'Father-Mother God, loving me, guard me while I sleep . . .' God as mother does not mean that God is mother (or father). We imagine God as both mother and father, but we realize how inadequate these and any other metaphors are to express the creative love of God, the love that gives, without calculating the return, the gift of the universe. Nevertheless, we speak of this love in language that is familiar and dear to us, the language of mothers and fathers who give us life, from whose bodies we come and upon whose care we depend. We in turn pass on that life, and in this model of birth, nurture, and fulfilment, we dimly perceive a pattern of giving and receiving in which to speak of God as creator. It is partial at best, inadequate and false at places, and in need of other balancing models. Yet this bit of nonsense is, I believe, also an illuminating expression of an inclusive Christian vision of fulfilment appropriate to a holistic, nuclear age . . .

The Ethic of God as Lover: Healing

The link between salvation and healing is an obvious one: if salvation is the making whole again of the ruptured body of the world, then healing is the way to bring it about.[8] What belongs together but has been broken and estranged in innumerable ways must be pieced and sewn together again. At best, it is makeshift work; there is no quick fix, no miraculous cure, and often the healers will become wounded in their work. Not all parts of the body will survive, and the burdens of those who engage in this work will often seem greater than they can bear. It is at such times that the revelation of God in the paradigmatic figure of Jesus of Nazareth empowers them to continue – the revelation that the source of all being in the universe is on the side of the lovers of the world and healers of the body of the world. As we do not suffer alone in defeat, neither do we work alone: the source of healing power comes from God, the lover of the world.

There are several characteristics of healing that make it an obvious image for the work of God as lover as well as the work of the followers of this God.[9] First, and of great importance, the model of healing undercuts the body/spirit split in traditional views of redemption. Classical treatments of redemption, in spite of affirming the resurrection of the body, tend to separate the whole person into two parts – primarily spirit, incidentally body – and of course the body of the world (nonhuman, physical matter) receives no attention. The healing model, however, is based in the physical, and only by extension, as in holistic medicine and psychotherapy, are the mental and spiritual dimensions included.[10] As with other models we have considered, the power of the healing model is its grounding in life and death: healers are those who are able to give and take away life.[11]

It is a model, then, that emphasizes the importance of bodies, and this is critical in our time in at least two respects. First, it brings out that reunification of our disordered world is primarily, whatever more it might be, attention to the basics that human (and other kinds of) bodies need in order to survive. In other words, God as lover and healer is at one with God as mother and judge in insisting on the health of bodies as the condition for other kinds of well-being.[12] A second, related point is that the healing model in its concern for bodies undercuts the heavy anthropocentrism of traditional Christian theories of redemption. If we are spirits who have bodies and other creatures are bodies who have spirits, an understanding of salvation as healing tips the balance in favour of what we share with all the rest of creation, rather than what is primarily ours. It is worth noting, finally, that although the body/spirit split is usual in most classical views of atonement, it is remarkably absent from the healing ministry of Jesus of Nazareth. Unlike some of his contemporaries, he never appeared to claim that sickness was divine punishment for sin; rather, he saw a proportionality between physical and spiritual health.[13] He appeared to see human beings as a unity of body and soul such that sin and evil could produce an imbalance in both. He had great sympathy for those in physical pain, and the healings, like the teachings, were signs of the kingdom.

A second important feature of the healing model is its appropriateness for imaging salvation in an ecological, evolutionary context. If one of the characteristics of health is a balanced integration of all parts of the organism, the health (or salvation) of the body of the world involves redressing the imbalances that have occurred in part through inordinate human desire to devour the whole rather than to be part of it. Inordinate human desire is sin, and the acceptance of limits, the willingness to share basic necessities, and the desire to bring order out of disorder are all aspects of the salvation our world needs. The health of the entire organism depends on an intricate balance not unlike the balance necessary in a much smaller but marvelously intricate organ, our own bodies.

An ecological understanding of the world, in viewing the world on an organic rather than a machine model, implies that what is wrong cannot be fixed by a technician; rather, the causes of the disorder, and its solution, are internal and involve a redress of imbalances. The role of the healer in this view will necessarily be somewhat indirect; it will not be of the miracle worker intervening to cure one diseased part but of a helper working to restore right relationships, proper balance among the parts. Finally, healing in an ecological, evolutionary context implies that there is no cure, only better or worse health, greater or lesser imbalances. Salvation or health in the complex world we inhabit is a relative concept and must be so if it is to be at all inclusive and if salvation and health are to attend to basic needs of the many beings who inhabit the universe. For some to be in 'perfect health', given our limited resources, means for others to die. Moreover, the disorder, the imbalances – the evil, if you will – is so great that a cure is not realistic.[14] To love the world and to wish to alleviate the pain in its torn body is not to expect miraculous results; this view of salvation is a modest one, conscious of the great power of sin and its tragic consequences. At times it is only possible to refuse to join those who spread the disease.[15]

A third feature of the healing model which recommends it as a way to understand salvation is its dual emphasis on resistance and identification: resistance to disease, disorder, and chaos, in the fighting to overcome the ruptures in the wounded body, and identification with the sufferers in their pain.[16] The first, active phase has close connections with the model of liberator: God as lover of the world desires the beloved to be whole and free. As healer of the divisions in the body and liberator of those oppressed by others, God as lover of the world works actively to bring well-being to the beloved. It is no mere coincidence that the active phase of Jesus' ministry is well expressed in the metaphors of healing to the sick and liberation to the oppressed (Luke 4.18–19), for to be whole and free is what lovers want for their beloved, and one must work actively and relentlessly to help bring such conditions about. Healers and liberators must be tireless in their battle against the forces that bring disorder to the body, that enslave the spirit. The military imagery here, repugnant as it may be to some, is necessary in order to express the anger that God as lover feels toward those who wound the body and oppress the spirit of the beloved. God as mother-creator feels the same anger and judges those harshly who deny life and nourishment to her children. Those who join the healing and liberating work of God are invited, then, into a fighting unit that does not easily accept defeat. But two qualifications must be added immediately, lest misunderstanding occur. First, to fight does not necessarily mean to commit violence – as for instance, the relentless fight for India's independence led by Mohandas Gandhi illustrates. Second, to accept some inevitable personal injury (to 'turn the other cheek') in the battle for wholeness and freedom does not entail passive acceptance of defeat – again, a point well illustrated by Gandhi.

The second, passive phase of the healing model – identification with the sufferers in their pain – is an inevitable dimension of the model if salvation is seen as involving God as lover.[17] The reason that God as lover wants the beloved world healed and made whole is his great love for it. A lover feels the pain of the beloved deep within himself and would undergo any sacrifice to relieve the pain.[18] One way to understand the passion of Jesus of Nazareth is as the suffering that inevitably came to him in his fight against the divisions separating people from God and one another – the hierarchies, dualisms, and existence of outcasts. The passion or death is the passive side of his active ministry as healer of the sick, prophet of inclusive love, liberator of the oppressed. The passive side witnesses to solidarity of each with all: in the model of God as lover there are no healers that do not feel wounded, no liberators that do not experience oppression.[19] This second, passive side must be seen as second: solidarity with the sufferings of the beloved is a permanent feature of the kind of love for the world implicit in the model of God as lover; nevertheless, if it is conceived as the primary feature of salvation, acceptance of the status quo and a romanticizing of suffering occur. In our model, suffering is not salvific but it is inevitable: it is a risk incurred by all who confront evil by siding with those who suffer and are oppressed.

Who, then, are the healers and the liberators – the 'saviours' of the world? The tradition says there is only one, Jesus Christ, who does all the work. This position made sense in a time that understood the one thing needful to be atonement for sins, ransom from the devil, or reconciliation with an angry God, but if the one thing needful is reunification of the shattered, divided world, there must be many saviours. Jesus of Nazareth, as paradigmatic of God as lover, reveals God's passionate, valuing love for the world. In his teachings, healings, and death he seeks to make the beloved whole and free through overcoming hierarchies and dualisms, healing bodies and spirits, suffering in solidarity with the outcast and the oppressed. But as revelatory and powerful as that life was and continues to be, it cannot stand alone as accomplishing salvation if salvation is seen as the piecing together of the fragmented body of the world in one's own time and place. That work must be done and done again, by many minds, hearts, hands, and feet.

One sees from time to time other paradigmatic figures who reveal in their own lives and often deaths the same passionate, valuing, inclusive love for the world that we see in the figure of Jesus. Often they are disciples of Jesus, but they need not be. If such inclusive love is in any sense revelatory of reality, why should it be limited to one historical community? In the Christian tradition this passionate, inclusive love has centred on overcoming divisions among human beings; in Eastern and native American traditions the cosmos and other forms of life are often included.[20] In an ecological, evolutionary era our inclusive, valuing love needs to extend beyond our own species; nonetheless, those within our tradition who manifest this love to our own kind are paradigmatic healers of the divisions that separate people. There are several qualities that many of these people share, but two of the most outstanding are the inclusive and the *radical* character of their love for others.[21]

One thinks, for instance, of John Woolman, the eighteenth-century Quaker abolitionist, who not only spent life fighting slavery as an itinerant crusader walking hundreds of miles (to protest the enslavement of the post boys who cared for the carriage horses) and wearing undyed clothing (to protest the slave-manned dye ships from the West Indies) but who also reasoned endlessly with the slaverholders whom he included in his ministry.[22] Or the case of Dietrich Bonhoeffer comes to mind: a brilliant young theologian in Nazi Germany, who as part of an assassination plot on Hitler's life was imprisoned and hanged but during his imprisonment not only held services for his guards, but also came to a new understanding of Christianity as secular, contemporary suffering with *all* who suffer – a view far from his early, sectarian 'Christian' theology.[23] One is also reminded of Sojourner Truth, an illiterate slave and mother of twelve children, all but one sold away from her, who was emancipated in 1827 to begin an itinerant ministry after a religious experience in which she responded, 'Oh God, I did not know you were so big!': a ministry of abolitionism and women's rights, the overcoming of the divisions of slave and slave-holder, women and men.[24] One remembers also Dorothy Day, American journalist, member of the Communist Party, who as a convert to Roman Catholicism left her lover and the father of her child to spend a life founding hospitality houses in New York and other cities across the country for the most destitute outcasts, houses where she herself lived and worked to create an alternative society free of war and exploitation.[25] Another example is Mohandas Gandhi, Hindu and sometime Christian, peacemaker and healer of the enmity between Indian and South African, Indian and British, finally giving his life in his fight to unify Hindu and Muslim.[26]

There are many others like these, of course, and many whose lives of inclusive, radical love have passed largely unnoticed and usually unrecorded; nonetheless, all help to fill out the paradigm of saving love as willing to go to the limit to heal the wounds dividing people. These lives reveal once again the inclusive, nonhierarchical love of God, and they do so with the passion and intensity of those who find others, all others, valuable and worthy. None of these people, however, is a 'saint': they are not miracle workers, and they did not reach their vision of inclusive love and and their willingness to practice the healing ministry of this vision easily or quickly. In the stories of their lives which they themselves tell, all the warts show: they are at one level very ordinary human beings battling their own desire for money and comfort, afraid for their families, lonely in prison and frightened of death, discouraged by the slight gains they make against the forces of discrimination, fear, and prejudice that divide people. Nonetheless, they are, in our model of God as lover, illustrative of the many saviours of the world: their stories flesh out the paradigmatic story of Jesus of Nazareth.

Is the world going to be saved by these special but also very weak, ordinary human beings? Obviously not. Their lives, as reflections of life and death of Jesus of Nazareth, are revelatory of God's love: to have faith in the God whom the lives of Jesus and these others reveal is to believe that the universe is neither malevolent nor indifferent but is on the side of life and its fulfilment. In our day this love must be imagined and conceived in a way that takes into account the ecological, evolutionary network in which we actually live, the incredibly complex natural, historical, and cultural web of existence, which includes ourselves and other beings. Moreover, we have become conscious of the deterioration of this web of life as well as of our power to extinguish it. In this situation, what can salvation mean except working along with the power who is on the side of life to heal the divisions that tear the world apart? We do not work alone, but the work cannot be done without us.

But is this not asking too much? In the traditional view of redemption, something is done for us; here we are asked to join the work. Moreover, we are asked to love others, all others, and to find them valuable. Is this not impossible? Two things must be said here. First, it is important not to water down the passionate love of God for the valuable world, which is the paradigm, whether fulfilled or not, of human love for the world. We recall that, however interpreted, the great commandments of love to God and neighbour have always been considered impossible. The traditional view that Christian love, following God's love, should be agapic – totally giving love with no thought of return – is no easier to live up to than the view that our love should value the world, finding it attractive and precious. Second, however, just as we extended the notion of parenthood beyond actual, physical parenting, so also we extend the lover model beyond the passionate, valuing love that is its base.

There is the obvious extension to include all whose work liberates and heals; that is to say, the work of salvation in this model is not done solely or even principally by the special, paradigmatic people. The healers and liberators of the world are many and diverse: all those whose work, whether paid or unpaid, brings together those who belong together and frees the oppressed are participating in salvation. The peacemakers on a city block or at an international negotiating table; the reformers of economic injustice, racial conflict, or sexual discrimination, whether at the personal, familial, or public level; the healers of torn bodies and broken spirits, whether of those at hand or treated by institutions we support; the ecological planners, whether of a backyard garden, a model town, or the world community – all these and many more participate in the work of salvation. Such work need not be seen as special or religious; rather, it is ordinary secular work oriented toward healing the world's divisions and freeing the world's oppressed. The ways such work can be done are limitless; the need for such work is equally limitless.

But there is another less obvious but equally important extension of the lover model. This extension involves a kind of empathy or sympathy, an identification, with all that lives, which, though not as intense as love, derives from the same base of desire for unity with everything else that is. It could be called fellow feeling (understanding 'fellow' in neither a male- nor species-specific way), which unites all life at a deep level of affirmation based on the shared adventure in which we all participate, and on our imaginative ability to enter empathetically into the pain and pleasure of other beings, including nonhumans.[27] This is not agapic love, love that gives quite apart from the merits of the object, but it derives from a sense of relationship with other beings. It assumes that relationship, unity with others, is more basic than individuality, separation from others, and that although human beings differ enormously from one another and our species differs in untold ways from other species, there is a shared substratum that provides a basis for imaginative and sympathetic identification with others. Thus, to take two extreme examples, we can sympathize with the mortal terror of a bird or share 'Jesus' despair in Gethsemane . . . regardless of our historical, racial and even human limitations'.[28] This fellow feeling is the basis of a morality that, if not as radical as love for the valuable, is kin to it, for it desires healing for the wounded and liberty for the captive, on the basis of a common bond in suffering and joy. It is to this fellow feeling that appeals to feed starving peoples, support welfare programs for the young and the old, and end segregation of people by race can be made, for even if we have never experienced starvation, deprivation, or discrimination, we can imagine what it feels like and experience pain for such suffering. Likewise, it is possible to appeal to fellow feeling to avert actions that would be harmful to others even if these have not yet taken place, as in the case of further ecological deterioration and, most especially, a nuclear holocaust. We can imagine the disaster these events would bring to all with whom we share life, and we can will and work toward averting them.

As with universal parenthood, fellow feeling takes many forms and, were it to become part of our daily, operating sensibility, would have a powerful and at times revolutionary effect. It is not only those whose lives are totally and radically dedicated to inclusive love that do the healing work of love but also those whose sensibilities have been converted from an individualistic, divisive, dualistic way of thinking to a relational, unitive, holistic way. As one sees things differently, one begins to act differently, whatever one's position, influence, or occupation might be.

The attempt here to suggest the changed sensibility linked to the model of God as lover is not a *plan* for the systemic reformation of the institutions in our society that oppress human beings and divide them from one another and human life from other kinds of life. These institutions are many, wicked, and powerful, and working to reform if not to revolutionize them is a task demanding great ingenuity, intelligence, technical expertise, and dedication. But the will, the desire, to do that work comes from a sensibility that believes such work is worthwhile, necessary, and possible. Heuristic, metaphorical theology is not directly in the business of reforming or revolutionizing society. Its work is at the deep level where the most basic feelings about God and the world are formed: feelings of fear, alienation, estrangement, exclusion, divisiveness, separation, or of attraction, caring, valuing, inclusion, belonging, relatedness. Western Christianity has been part of and has contributed to the former sensibility regarding God and the world. But what if the inclusive sensibility became dominant? Such a sensibility is one that finds the world, its rich and varied life, valuable, and one that is enabled to work for its well-being, its salvation, in the knowledge and by the power of God, the lover of the world. A large part of such salvation would be systematizing the inclusive vision in economic, political, and social institutions. Thus, in this sense, metaphorical theology is in the business of reforming and revolutionizing society . . .

The Ethic of God as Friend: Companionship

One of the traditional images for the Christian church is as the body of Christ.[29] But throughout these pages we have spoken of the world, the cosmos, as God's body, finding that this metaphor brought out the inclusive character of God's presence both to all human beings and to all forms of life. Thus, when we turn to the specific community and the mode of existence intrinsic to it that are identified with Jesus of Nazareth, the limitations of the image of the church as the body of Christ must be acknowledged. The community of Jesus' followers is not the body of God, it is not the universal community implicitly embracing all, but it is rather one way that this body, our world, is cared for and loved. This particular way is characterized by a vision of destabilizing, nonhierarchical, inclusive fulfilment, epitomized in the shared meal in which hospitality is extended to all outsiders. This is a specific vision of salvation, the characteristic notes of which suggest that an appropriate way to speak of those united by this vision is as a 'community of friends' or, more precisely, a 'fellowship of the friends of Jesus'.[30] Such a community is obviously modeled not on the elitist, separatist view of friendship, as suggested by the church as the 'communion of saints', but on the solidarity view, as epitomized in Jesus' table fellowship. To be friends of Jesus, in this sense, means to stand with him and with all others united by and committed to the common vision embodied in the shared meal extended to the outsider. It means choosing, freely and out of a sense of joy, to be friends of the world one likes and wishes to see fulfilled. It means being willing, as an adult, to join in mutual responsibility with God and others for the well-being of this world. It means being to it as a mother and father, a lover, and a friend. It means welcoming different others and many others into the community, for such a friendship is not limited to the like-minded few: it invites and needs all who share the vision.[31]

What creates this friendship is the common vision: in this model of fellowship, God and human beings are both friends of the world. In an ecological, nuclear era, salvation must mean this; hence, the friendship is not between two – God and individual human beings – but between all those who are united by love for the world.[32] As with the models of God as mother and lover, so with the model of friend, what appear to be individualistic images for the relationship between God and the world become universalized when the world, and not specific human beings, is seen as the focus of divine love.

Let us now look more specifically at two ways in which this fellowship of the friends of Jesus, this companionship of those who share meals with all, is especially pertinent as a mode of existence in an ecological, nuclear time. The first is in respect of what we shall call fear of others; the second, care for others. As to the first: One way to characterize the mentality promoting the escalation of nuclear weapons is as extreme xenophobia, a fear of the stranger, the other, the outsider.[33] That such fear is deep within all of us, human and nonhuman, is well illustrated by animal territorial patterns and by our national boundaries. If friendly feelings are intrinsic to human beings, unfriendly ones certainly are as well. Many in fact believe that unfriendly feelings are more intrinsic, since a case can be made that evolutionary survival depends not on cooperation but on superiority of various kinds.[34] Whatever may be the case with this hotly debated issue, it is difficult to think of a more precise symbol for xenophobia than a nuclear holocaust. In such an occurrence, all others would be extinguished, including, ironically, the like-minded who feared the others. It is suicidal xenophobia: such fear of the stranger that one wills the end of all existence, including one's own. The seriousness of xenophobia in our time can scarcely be overstated: the fact that we live in a global village and must accept that fact if we are to survive does not, unfortunately, mean that we will accept it or even that we know how to accept it in significant ways. It is not the task of a heuristic theology to deal with the complex technical, economic, political, and social dimensions of reducing xenophobia, but it is its task to offer contrary models. The inclusive character of the Christian vision, epitomized in the shared meal with the outcast and stranger – the image of the church as the community of friends – is a powerful countermodel to xenophobia. It focuses on exclusion as the heart of the problem, insisting that what we fear most and apparently are willing to kill and die for, namely, the outside, is not necessarily the enemy but is rather only the stranger. What Greek culture recognized in the reversal of host and guest (that we all are potential strangers) and what Christian culture claims in befriending the stranger (that God is also present in such occurrences) suggest that the willingness to risk such encounters is central to overcoming xenophobia.[35] Openness to the different, the unexpected, the strange, an openness that identifies with the outsider as embodying a condition common to all and that is receptive to possible value in such encounters, can be seen as the negative side of our model to counter xenophobia. It merely suggests that strangers need not be enemies, that in a sense we are all strangers, and that when we risk encounters with strangers, surprising things can happen. In its negative work, the model raises the question whether exclusion is necessary or beneficial.

The positive side of the model of the community of friends concerns care for others. In an ecological, nuclear age, the decline of xenophobia is not sufficient; in addition, a new kind of community needs to be built, and the work of heuristic theology in this task is at the level of helping to form the sensibility necessary for the task. The sensibility is an inclusive one, and the term 'companionship', which embraces many levels of friendly fellowship, including advocacy and partnership, is a good one for the range of care for others needed in the new kind of community. The shared meal of friends with outsiders of the Christian community is one form of an inclusive sensibility, but an inclusive sensibility is by no means solely the possession of Christians. Many cultures, especially those modeled on an organic image, have a version of it. An interesting case is found in the notion of civic friendship in Greek political life.[36] According to Aristotle, there is political bonding that is mutual well-wishing and well-doing by and for all citizens. There is reciprocal benefit in such civic bonding, to be sure, but it emerges out of warmth and attachment and not just from a sense of cold justice. In fact, in Aristotle's view, if friendship is present among citizens, the claims of justice become greater, for citizens who live in mutual well-wishing are not satisfied with a notion of justice as mere fairness and legality but insist on much more for a truly just society.[37] Thus, friendship has been called the 'soul of socialism', giving the inside to justice, and justice has been seen as the outside of friendship, insuring that neither special interests nor preferential treatment dominates.[38] In a truly socialized society the assumption is that citizens should conduct themselves toward one another not just in terms of rectitude but also in terms of friendship. One can see in civic friendship expansion of the host-guest bond: 'The city which forgets how to care for the stranger has forgotten how to care for itself.'[39]

Our model of the church as a community of friends united by a common vision of fulfilment for all can also be seen as the product of an inclusive sensibility. Beginning with the image of a shared meal open to outsiders, it expands to include the entire cosmos in its circle of care. What is evident in both the Greek and Christian instances is a deprivatization of friendship: what is usually seen as a personal relationship between two (or a few) is politicized and becomes a model for public policy. Although some would prefer to keep friendship as a private and indeed romantic relationship, unconcerned and uninvolved with public matters, the qualities that we have found to be present in solidarity friendship are far too important to be relegated to the fringes of life.[40] Of all human loves, philia is the most free, the most reciprocal, the most adult, the most joyful, the most inclusive. Its range, from best friend to partner, as well as the depths we uncovered through an analysis of its paradoxes, reveals it to be eminently suited to participate in the formation of a new sensibility for the conduct of our public life and not just for our private pleasure. Thus, when we speak of the kind of care for the world that our model suggests, we extend the model (as we did with the mother model, in elaborating the idea of universal parenthood, and with the lover model, in elaborating the idea of fellow feeling) and suggest that to befriend the world is to be its companion – its advocate and partner.[41] In the solidarity view of friendship which we have promoted, private versus public is not a relevant division, for hospitality to the stranger, though ostensibly a private event, is in both its Greek and Christian forms implicitly and intrinsically public. For, once the door has been opened to the other, the different, the stranger one does not know, it has been opened to the world. All can become companions together, sharing the bread of life with one another in an atmosphere of both justice and concern. Both justice and friendship, both advocacy and partnership, then, are aspects of companionship. To participate in the ongoing, sustaining work of God as friend of the world means, as the word 'sustain' suggests, to support the world, to be its companion, both as advocate for its needs and as partner in its joys and sufferings. What we are suggesting, therefore, is that the notion of companion of the world, modeled on God as the sustaining friend of the world, comprises being with the world in two ways: as an advocate fighting for just treatment for the world's many forms of life, and as a partner identifying with all the others. Both aspects of this public model of a 'companionable sensibility' are extensions of hospitality to the stranger: they represent the just provision of necessities, epitomized in the shared meal, in an atmosphere of fellowship and concern.

Is such a sensibility possible as our public stance toward others? Or is it simple naive sentimentality to suggest something other than the xenophobic sensibility that fuels nuclear escalation and that not only denies to others what is justly theirs but does so in cold blood? A companionable sensibility is certainly needed in our time: one that accentuates neither dependence nor independence but interdependence. A companionable sensibility stresses, as no other model can, the reciprocity of all life, the mutual give-and-take, that is central to an ecological, evolutionary perspective. Is this sensibility an utter absurdity? It does not seem that it should be. One need not be a Christian or an adherent of any religion to be converted to a companionable sensibility. As we have seen, the awareness of divine oppression (or absence) as well as of divine presence can be the occasion for the development of a companionable attitude toward others. And there are innumerable ways that advocacy of and partnership with strangers and outsiders can take place; again, Christians have no corner on that market. What they do have, however, is a very powerful model of God as friend to sustain them as they go about the work of sustaining the world. In the model of the church we have sketched, God is present as our friend in all our companionable encounters with the world. For the Christian community, companionship is not necessary because of divine oppression; rather, it is possible because of divine presence. The model of God as friend says that we are not our own, but also that we are not on our own: as friends of the Friend of the world, we do not belong to ourselves nor are we left to ourselves.

It is in this context of God as present with us as we work together to feed, heal, and liberate the world that prayer becomes both natural and necessary. We ask God, as one would a friend, to be present in the joy of our shared meals and in the suffering of the strangers; to give us courage and stamina for the work we do together; to forgive us for lack of fidelity to the common vision and lack of trust in divine trustfulness. Finally, we ask God the friend to support, forgive, and comfort us as we struggle together to save our beleaguered planet, our beautiful earth, our blue and green marble in a universe of silent rock and fire. Just as betrayal is the sin of friendship in which one hands over the friend to the enemy, so intercessory prayer is the rite of friendship in which one hands over the friend to God.[42] When we pray for our friend the earth, for whose future we fear, we hand it over not to the enemy but to the Friend who is freely, joyfully, and permanently bonded to this, our beloved world. The model of God as friend defies despair.

☐ Finally, I want to conclude this *Reader* by citing part of a lecture by Ursula King. Towards the end of my Introduction, I noted her expertise in thinking about women, world religions and spirituality, finely represented by her latest book, *Women and Spirituality: Voices of Protest and Promise* (London, Macmillan, 1989). The whole of the lecture, of which part is reproduced here as a concluding statement, as it were, was the seventh Cardinal Heenan Memorial Lecture, delivered at Heythrop College, University of London, in November 1984. If she is correct in what she says, far from feminist theology and spirituality being a threat to Christian institutions and their theology, the whole movement may in fact be the very source of their renewal. If so, the churches may become better equipped to render to the world the true service that they allege is their vocation.

22 URSULA KING
Women in Dialogue: A New Vision of Ecumenism

Women's *OIKUMENE*: What is women's dialogue about?

We hear a great deal about the Third World and its suffering, about the need for development, justice and peace and for a more equitable distribution of the world's resources. Perhaps few are aware that there exists also a 'Fourth World' of deprivation, injustice, subordination and suffering – and that is the world of women who experience themselves as the alienated 'other' in Church and society.[1]

In many parts of the world Christian reflection has created a vigorous liberation theology born out of the experience of the suffering and struggle of the poor and oppressed. Some consider liberation theology as a new point of ecumenical convergence for different traditions, experiences and struggles. In trying to overcome their oppression, women have created another liberation movement. This is not only concerned with their own liberation, but that of all people by affirming the full humanity of all women.[2] Christian women see this as a genuine possibility to express an authentic Christian universalism. It is significant that a recent theological consultation organized by women was entitled 'Called to Full Humanity: Women's Responsibilities as Members of the Church Today'.

The roots of the women's liberation movement go deep into history – a history of struggle for equality, justice and human rights. In the nineteenth century the women's movement was closely interwoven with the fight to abolish slavery while the new feminism born in the 1960s grew out of the campaign for equal rights and against racism. If we adopt an inclusive definition of feminism, then every person who recognizes the subordination of women and aims to overcome it, is a feminist, whether woman or man. Feminism is not a unitary, but diverse, movement, not without its internal contradictions and tensions. Yet over the last twenty years women have spoken out with ever increasing strength and entered into a new dialogue. They have discovered themselves and each other; they have learnt to perceive and criticize the deep injustices done to them; they have also developed an amazing ability to envisage alternatives.

Through sharing their experiences women have discovered consciousness-raising as an adventure and systematic method. By working together in small, non-hierarchical groups, women have deliberately fostered a change in awareness. This has sometimes led to a radical conversion experience of such intensity, that it can only be likened to the profound *metanoia* of a religious experience. It may be difficult for men – and some women – to realize what it means when women experience their own strength and power by learning to speak out, to name and define themselves and make independent decisions in a newly found freedom.

This ecstatic self-discovery has also led to a new celebration of community, of the bonding among women. Sisterhood, vividly described in poems, songs and other art forms, is the term used to express the solidarity of all women – their relatedness in suffering, in giving birth and life, in nurturing and caring, in joy and ecstasy. Sisterhood is an experience and powerful symbol among women today against which many of the vague references to the general 'brotherhood of man' pale into insignificance. Sisterhood can of course be used in an exclusive all-female sense, but it has the potential of widening out into larger circles of community. It implies the vision of a new, more equal and just community of partnership between women and men, a newly found wholeness. As Sheila Collins has written: 'The wholeness that feminists are proposing is a wholeness based on a multi-dimensional vision of the world, rather than on the single vision which has dominated Western culture and most theological thought. Such a multi-dimensional vision means the ability to grasp complexity, to live with ambiguity, and to enjoy the great variety that exists in the world. Wholeness does not imply the eradication of differences . . . or . . . the fear of a monotonous unisexual creature. . . . On the contrary, wholeness of vision may lead to a multiplication of differences, as people are able to choose freely the person they want to be rather than following a pattern of one they are *expected* to be. Only through an affirmation and celebration of our differences can we come to an understanding of the ties that bind the total creation together.'[3] This it not only a vision of a 'New Woman – New Earth' (as Rosemary Ruether entitled her book) but for Christians it includes the vision of a 'new woman – new Church'.

Several feminist theologians have pointed to the elements of prophecy and revelation in modern feminism, to its implicit religious dimension. Anyone who has close contact with women's groups will recognize this. Here a spirit is alive which is vibrant, joyous, loving, caring and compassionate; a warmth of human feeling, a sincerity of purpose and existential commitment, a sharpness of vision rarely found elsewhere. Sometimes I think this experience must be like the joy of the early Christians, their love and fellowship, their sense of belonging together and sharing all things.

These positive, life-enhancing and community-strengthening aspects of feminism are probably less well known than the negative aspects of feminist anger, protest and critique, much publicized by biased reporting in the media. Feminism challenges the structures of sexism, androcentrism and patriarchy embedded in our institutions, our language, our thought. Its critique addresses all religions as presently practised; it is a critique which also applies to ecumenical and interfaith dialogue.

Sexism has been defined as a way of ordering life by gender, as 'any kind of subordination or devaluing of a person or group solely on the ground of sex'. In Christian terms sexism can be understood as a collective form of sin, a social oppression which exists in society and church. It is the particular merit of the World Council of Churches to have called as early as 1974 a consultation of 170 women from different countries and churches, including the Roman Catholic Church, to discuss 'Sexism in the 1970's'.[4] Pauline Webb introduced that consultation by saying that sexism is not just a matter of acknowledging the physical difference between men and women, but rather:

> Recognizing that alongside this difference there have been different histories, different expectations, a different sense of identity, and an association with the structures of power that have created a male-dominated order in almost all human society and certainly within the Church, making it impossible for the Church to foreshadow the truly human community. So it is for the sake of that community that we Christian women come now to examine the heresy of sexism and to explore ways of overcoming it that will liberate both men and women for a new partnership in the gospel.[5]

Androcentrism takes male examples and practices as the basic norm for everything human without taking into account the view of women. In order to be fully human we have to be truly inclusive, and bring together the insights of both men and women. Many men do not realize that their understanding of humanity is one-sided because it is only male-defined. Feminists uncover this androcentric perspective in all areas of our culture. For Christian feminists it is particularly important to read the androcentric passages of the Bible in a new light, to examine the language of liturgy and prayer and to uncover the androcentrism of many theological premises.

The strongest feminist critique is addressed to patriarchy, the exclusively male-dominated structures and powers that have shaped all aspects of society. A growing number of Christians are becoming aware of this critique, which is also exposing the patriarchal assumptions of much Christian teaching and the sexist practices of church life, language and organization. However, the greatest challenge of all posed by the dialogue of contemporary feminists is the question: Can religion, can theology and the churches still speak convincingly to women today? Can women still find the divine spirit in the churches as we know them? The history of the Church, from New Testament times onwards, seems to be shot through by a pattern of the promise and betrayal of women. In spite of their significant contribution to the life and mission of the early Church, women were soon excluded from official positions. But the history of Christianity is rich with examples of powerful 'Women of the Spirit',[6] who exercised spiritual leadership through the authority of their own experiences in searching for and discovering God.

Many voices today speak of the divine concealment in our world, the loss of transcendence. For women this is often connected with a distorted, blemished image of God and with the restrictive practices of a powerful male Church. It has been asked whether the churches are in fact destructive of religious experiences for women. In answer to this, one can point to the spiritual quality of and the spiritual quest within the women's movement which has drawn many women out of the churches, but one can also point out that womens' conversion experiences in the past have often been away from the conformity of established religious practices in search of new ways and alternative models. The medieval Beguines are a good example of this.

Today there exists a new spirituality in feminism which is rooted in women's own experience. Some even speak of a 'spiritual feminism'. It consists of a new relationship to body and nature and of a search for wholeness, integration and peace. This new feminist spirituality is mostly found outside or on the margin of official religious institutions. But it is important for Christian feminists too, as they experience how the existing church structures deny full equality and space to women and thereby restrict and dehumanize, not only women, but men too.

Many women ask themselves: can I remain at home in the traditional Church and still be a contemporary woman? The awakening to feminist consciousness has led Christian women to form subcommunities in their churches where they are in dialogue with other Christian women and with the Church – if the Church will but hear them. This is an ecumenical dialogue across denominational boundaries. Best known are perhaps the women's groups which have worked in close conjunction with the World Council of Churches, but there are other examples. Latin American women founded a group of 'Women for Dialogue' (Mujeres para el Diálogo) in 1977 at Puebla with the explicit aim 'to get the voice of women heard within the Church'.[7] They work for the liberation of Latin American women and strive to develop a feminist theology within the Latin American context. Many different Christian feminist groups exist in England. To name but a few, there is 'Christian Women's Information and Resources' at Oxford; the 'Catholic Women's Network'; 'Women in Theology' as well as the 'Movement for the Ordination of Women', focused on a particular issue. There is also 'The Society for the Ministry of Women in the Church', founded as long ago as 1929 and, in the Catholic Church, St Joan's International Alliance, which dates from the beginning of this century.

Women of today have developed a newly sharpened awareness which challenges the sexist and patriarchal assumptions of religious and social institutions, and proclaims the vision of an alternative community and world. For Christians it is important that the feminist movement is not seen at the fringes of the Church, but as the central embodiment of the vision and incarnation of the Church as the people of God. Feminists have discovered a new sense of divine immanence and transcendence closely related to the experience of the wholeness of body-spirit, of the closeness to nature to which we all belong and of the bonds of community. In seeking new paths of spirituality, women are drawing on old and new sources commensurate to their own renewed experience of self, world and divine. In this sense the dialogue and *oikumene* of women bears the potential for transforming spiritual and theological thinking, including the thinking on ecumenism.

Notes

The Notes to Ann Loades's editorial commentaries are numbered consecutively from Note 1 throughout each Part.

Introduction

1 A. Yarbro Collins, *The Gospel and Women:* The 1987 Fred O. Francis Memorial Lectures in Religion, September 1987 (Chapman College, Orange CA, Department of Religion, 1988), p. 1, following R. Radford Ruether's *Sexism and God-Talk* (Boston, Beacon Press, 1983), but primarily concerned with feminist interpretation of the Bible; and E. Storkey, *What's Right with Feminism* (London, SPCK, 1985).
2 G. Lerner, *The Creation of Patriarchy* (New York, OUP, 1986), pp. 236–7.
3 ibid., p. 220
4 See also R. Eisler, *The Chalice and the Blade: Our History, Our Future* (San Francisco, Harper & Row, 1987) p. 206, n.10, on the 'equalitarianism' which would describe social relations in a partnership society where women and men (and 'masculine' and 'feminine') are accorded equal value.
5 See M. R. Miles, *Image as Insight: Visual Understanding in Western Culture and Secular Culture* (Boston, Beacon Press, 1985), p. 152.
6 See P. Webb, 'Gender as an Issue', *The Ecumenical Review*, 40:1 (1988), pp. 4–15.
7 Lerner, *The Creation of Patriarchy*, op.cit., p. 217; and see S. Brooks Thistlethwaite, 'Every Two Minutes: Battered Women and Feminist Interpretation', in L. M. Russell (ed.), *Feminist Interpretation of the Bible* (Oxford, Basil Blackwell, 1985), pp. 96–107; and reprinted in J. Plaskow and C. P. Christ, *Weaving the Visions: New Patterns in Feminist Spirituality* (San Francisco, Harper & Row, 1989).
8 D. Pearce, 'The Feminization of Poverty: Women, Work and Welfare', *Urban and Social Change Review*, 2:1–2 (1978), pp. 28–36; P. Washbourn, 'Women in the Workplace', *Word and World*, 4:2(1984), pp. 159–64; M. Alperin, 'The Feminization of Poverty', in V. Ramey Mollenkott (ed.), *Women of Faith in Dialogue* (New York, Crossroad, 1987), pp. 170–6; A. Borrowdale, 'The Church as an Equal Opportunities Employer', *Crucible* (April–June 1988), pp. 62–9; and her *A Woman's Work: Changing Christian Attitudes* (London, SPCK, 1989); A. O'Hara Graff, 'Women and Dignity: Vision and Practice', in C. R. Strain (ed.), *Prophetic Visions and Economics and Economic Realities: Protestants, Jews, Catholics Confront the Bishops' Letter on the Economy* (Grand Rapids, Eerdmans, 1989), pp. 216–28.

9 Lerner, *The Creation of Patriarchy*, op.cit., p. 216.
10 E. Springstead, *Who Will Make us Wise? How the Churches are Failing Higher Education* (Cambridge, MA, Cowley, 1988), p. 42.
11 N. Morton, *The Journey is Home* (Boston, Beacon Press, 1985), pp. 21–2; see also B. A. Thompson, 'Nelle Morton: Journeying Home', *Christian Century* (26 Aug – 2 Sept 1987), pp. 711–12.
12 A. Wilson Schaef, *Co-Dependence: Misunderstood-Mistreated* (New York, Harper & Row, 1986).
13 M. A. Farley, 'Sexism', *New Catholic Encyclopaedia* (Supplement) (Washington DC, Publishers' Guild, 1979), 17, p. 604. And see her essay, 'Sources of Sexual Inequality in the History of Christian Thought', *The Journal of Religion*, 56:2(1976), pp. 162–96.
14 C. Delaney, 'The Meaning of Paternity and the Virgin Birth Debate', *Man*, 21:3(1986), pp. 454–513.
15 Springstead, *Who Will Make Us Wise?*, op. cit., pp. 11 and 18.
16 H. T. Kerr and C. Dykstra, 'A Brief Statement of Reformed Faith', *Theology Today*, 14:2(1989), pp. 151–8.
17 A. K. Hammar, 'After Forty Years – Churches in Solidarity with Women?' *Ecumenical Review*, 40:3–4(1988), pp. 528–38. The *Ecumenical Review* seems to have begun publishing feminist theology from 1975 onwards.
18 M. K. Hellwig, *The Role of the Theologian* (Kansas, Sheed & Ward, 1987), p. 13.
19 M. Amba Oduyoye, 'Feminism: A Precondition for a Christian Anthropology', in *Hearing and Knowing: Theological Reflections on Christianity in Africa* (Maryknoll, NY, Orbis, 1986), pp. 120–37.
20 V. Fabella, MM, and M. Amba Oduyoye, *With Passion and Compassion: Third World Women doing Theology* (Marykoll, NY, Orbis, 1988).
21 A. M. Isasi-Díaz, 'A Hispanic Garden in a Foreign Land', in L. M. Russell (ed.), *Inheriting our Mother's Gardens: Feminist Theology in Third World Perspective* (Philadelphia, Westminster, 1988), pp. 97–8; Mud Flower Collective, *God's Fierce Whimsy: Christian Feminism and Theological Education* (New York, Pilgrim, 1985).
22 For instance, essays by D. S. Williams are to be found in *Weaving the Visions* as in n. 7 above; and see 'Black Women's Literature and the Task of Feminist Theology', in C. W. Atkinson, C. H. Buchanan and M. R. Miles (eds.), *Immaculate and Powerful: The Female in Sacred Image and Social Reality* (Boston, Beacon Press, 1985), pp. 88–110; and 'The Color of Feminism: or Speaking the Black Woman's Tongue', *Journal of Religious Thought*, 43(1986), pp. 42–58. K. G. Cannon's *Black Womanist Ethics* (Atlanta, Scholars, 1988) is another excellent example; and see *The Christian Century*, 1988 Fall Book Issue, 105:34(1988), on the work of Alice Walker, Toni Morrison, Zora Neale Hurston and Maya Angelou.
23 R. J. Weems, *Just a Sister Away: A Womanist Vision of Women's Relationships in the Bible* (San Diego, Lura Media, 1988); and a brilliant reading by S. Briggs of Pauline language about slavery and marriage, especially the language of Eph.5, in 'Sexual Justice and the "Right-

eousness" of God', in L. Hurcombe (ed.), *Sex and God: Some Varieties of Women's Religious Experience* (London, Routledge & Kegan Paul, 1987), pp. 251–77. The latest response to womanist theology is S. Brooks Thistlethwaite, *Sex, Race and God: Christian Feminism in Black and White* (New York, Crossroad, 1989).

24 N. Slee, 'Parables and Women's Experience', *Modern Churchman* (published by the Modern Churchpeople's Union and *MC* rather than *MCP* for short), 26:2 (1984), pp. 20–31.

25 R. D. Kahoe, 'Social Science of Gender Differences: Ideological Battleground', *Religious Studies Review*, 11:3(1985), pp. 223–7.

26 See, for instance, the book edited by V. Ramey Mollenkott in n. 8 above; also, the excellent bibliography in U. King, *Women and Spirituality: Voices of Protest and Promise* (London, Macmillan, 1989); and C. Erricker and V. Barnett (eds.) (on behalf of the Shap Working Party on World Religions in Education) *Women in Religion: World Religions in Education* (London, Commission for Racial Equality, 1988).

Part One: Biblical Tradition and Interpretation

1 As just one example, see P. Dronke, *Women Writers of the Middle Ages: A Critical Study of Texts from Perpetua (+203) to Marguerite Porete (+1310)* (Cambridge, CUP, 1984); and see also K. M. Wilson, *Medieval Women Writers* (Athens, GA, Georgia University Press, 1984) for further reference.

2 E. Griffith, *In Her Own Right: The Life of Elizabeth Cady Stanton* (Oxford, OUP, 1984), p. 54.

3 E. Cady Stanton, S. B. Anthony, *Correspondence, Writing, Speeches*, ed. with a critical commentary by E. C. Dubois (New York, Schocken Books, 1981), p. 33. See also Z. Eisenstein, 'Elizabeth Cady Stanton: Radical-Feminist Analysis and Liberal-Feminist Strategy', in A. Phillips (ed.), *Feminism and Equality* (Oxford, Basil Blackwell, 1987), pp. 77–102; E. Flexner, *Century of Struggle* (Cambridge, MA, Belknap Press of Harvard University Press, 1959); and E. Rice Hays, *Morning Star: A Biography of Lucy Stone* (New York, Octagon, 1978).

4 Reprinted from F. D. Gage's *Reminiscences* in L. K. Kerber and J. De Hart-Mathews (eds.), *Women's America: Refocusing the Past* (New York, OUP, 1987), pp. 213–14.

5 Griffith, *In Her Own Right*, op.cit., p. 209.

6 See also E. Schüssler Fiorenza's assessment of Elizabeth Cady Stanton in *In Memory of Her* (London, SCM, 1983), pp. 7–14.

7 K. Doob Sakenfeld, 'In the Wilderness, Awaiting the Land: The Daughters of Zelophedad and Feminist Interpretation', *Princeton Seminary Bulletin*, 9:3 (1988), pp. 179–96.

8 See B. Wildung Harrison, *Our Right to Choose: Toward a New Ethic of Abortion* (Boston, Beacon Press, 1983), especially pp. 96–118 on feminist theology/spirituality in relation to this topic; and 'Feminist Approaches', in P. Beattie Jung and T. A. Shannon (eds.), *Abortion*

and Catholicism: The American Debate (New York, Crossroad, 1988), pp. 99–180.

9 See, for instance, L. Dawson Scanzoni and N. A. Hardesty, *All We're Meant To Be: Biblical Feminism for Today* (Nashville, Abingdon, 1974[1], 1986[2]).

10 R. Coggins, 'The Contribution of Women's Studies to Old Testament Studies: A Male Reaction', *Theology*, 91(1988), pp. 5–16.

11 P. Trible, 'Women in the Old Testament', *The Interpreter's Dictionary of the Bible*, Supplementary Volume, (Nashville, Abingdon, 1976), pp. 963–6; and see her article on 'God, Nature Of', in the Old Testament' in the same volume.

12 P. Trible, 'Depatriarchalizing in Biblical Interpretation', *Journal of the American Academy of Religion*, 41:1(1973), pp. 30–48. See also A. L. Laffey, *An Introduction to the Old Testament: A Feminist Perspective* (Philadelphia, Fortress Press, 1988); P. Bird, 'The Place of Women in the Israelite Cultus', in P. D. Miller Jr, P. D. Hanson, S. Dean McBride (eds), *Ancient Israelite Religion* (Philadelphia, Fortress Press, 1987), pp. 397–419; C. Meyers, *Discovering Eve: Ancient Israelite Women in Context* (New York, OUP, 1988).

13 M.I. Gruber, 'The Motherhood of God in Second Isaiah', *Revue Biblique*, 90(1983), pp. 351–9. See also F. Young, 'The Woman In Travail', in her book, *Can These Dry Bones Live?* (London, SCM, 1982), pp. 43–53.

14 See one of the very rare pictures of this incident in E. Moltmann-Wendel, *The Women Around Jesus* (London, SCM, 1982), p. 92.

15 This section has been reprinted in Joann Wolski Conn (ed.), *Women's Spirituality: Resources for Christian Development* (New York, Paulist, 1986), which also includes an essay, 'The Incomprehensibility of God and the Image of God Male and Female' by E. A. Johnson, and an essay by B. Cooke on 'Non-patriarchal Salvation', which argues that in acknowledging and continuing to name God as 'God the Father of our Lord Jesus Christ' as the God experienced by Jesus, is to relate us to 'a God who demands the rejection in both men and women of those humanly-demeaning prejudices and injustices which have marked patriarchal cultures historically.' See also S. Cady, M. Ronan, H. Taussig, *Sophia: The Future of Feminist Spirituality* (San Francisco, Harper & Row, 1986); D. Tennis, 'The Loss of the Father God: Why Women Rage and Grieve', *Christianity and Crisis*, 41:9(1981), pp. 164–70; and her *Is God the Only Reliable Father?* (Philadelphia, Westminster, 1985).

16 Another essay by Elisabeth Schüssler Fiorenza is 'The "Quilting" of Women's History: Phoebe of Cenchreae', in P. M. Cooey, S. A. Farmer and M. E. Ross (eds), *Embodied Love: Sensuality and Relationship as Feminist Values* (San Francisco, Harper & Row, 1987), pp. 35–49; and someone who displays the greatest sensitivity to the women as well as the men in the biblical material is Paul Edwards SJ, for instance in his *The People of the Book* (Springfield, Templegate, 1987).

1 Ruth Page: Elizabeth Cady Stanton's *The Woman's Bible*

1 E. Griffith, *In Her Own Right: The Life of Elizabeth Cady Stanton* (Oxford, OUP, 1984), p. 159.
2 ibid., p. 209
3 ibid., p. 210
4 ibid.
5 E. Stanton, *The Women's Bible* (Edinburgh, Polygon, 1985), Preface, p. 5.
6 ibid., part I, p. 18.
7 ibid., part II, p. 95.
8 ibid., part III, p. 88.
9 ibid., part I, p. 138.
10 ibid., part II, p. 154.
11 ibid., part II, p. 123.
12 ibid., part II, p. 126.
13 P.L. Lehmann, *Ethics in a Christian Context* (London, SCM, 1963), p. 29.

3 Toni Craven: Tradition and Convention in the Book of Judith

1 In D. A. Knight (ed.), *Tradition and Theology in the Old Testament* (Philadelphia, Fortress Press, 1977), pp. 11–30.
2 ibid., p. 23.
3 See esp. Harrelson's discussion of the revolutionary character of tradition, ibid., pp. 25–7.
4 While Ruth and Esther are found in the Masoretic Text, Judith and an expanded version of Esther appear only in the LXX. Judith is designated as a deuterocanonical book by Roman Catholics and as an apocryphal book by Jews and Protestants. For a recent treatment of these three books, see J. F. Craghan, 'Esther, Judith, and Ruth: Paradigms for Human Liberation', *Biblical Theology Bulletin*, 12 (1982), pp. 11–19.
5 For demonstration, see esp. P. Trible, 'A Human Comedy', in *God and the Rhetoric of Sexuality* (Philadelphia, Fortress Press, 1978), pp. 166–99: S. B. Berg, *The Book of Esther, Motifs, Themes and Structures* (SBL Dissertation Series 44; Missoula, Scholars, 1979); I. Alonso-Schökel, 'Narrative Structures in the Book of Judith', in *The Center for Hermeneutical Studies in Hellenistic and Modern Culture*, Colloquy 11 (Berkeley, Graduate Theological Union, 1975), pp. 1–20; and T. Craven, *Artistry and Faith in the Book of Judith* (SBL, Dissertation Series, Chico, Scholars, 1983).
6 Since incongruity, irony, and happy endings mark each of these books, they are appropriately designated as 'comedies'. See Trible, op. cit., Craven, op. cit., pp. 219–21. Cf. also W. C. Booth, *A Rhetoric of Irony* (Chicago, University of Chicago, 1975) and E. M. Good, *Irony in the Old Testament* (Philadelphia, Westminster, 1965), pp. 14ff.
7 Though part of a comment on the book of Ruth, these words are equally true of the books of Esther and Judith: 'All together they are

women in culture, women against culture, and women transforming culture. What they reflect, they challenge. And that challenge is a legacy of faith to this day for all who have ears to hear the stories of women in a man's world.' Trible, op.cit., p. 196.

8 In the most practical of senses, these women work at maintaining and shaping the traditious of Israel. On 'practical tradition', see D. A. Knight, *Rediscovering the Traditions of Israel* (SBL, Dissertation Series 9, rev. edn., Missoula, Scholars, 1975), p. 1.

9 On the religious significance and theology of the book of Esther, see Berg, *Book of Esther*, op. cit., pp. 173–87.

10 See R. M. Hals, 'Analysis of References to God', in *The Theology of the Book of Ruth* (Facet Books, Biblical Series 23; Philadelphia, Fortress Press, 1969), pp. 3–19, esp. p. 16.

11 Judith exercises the role of theologian and interpreter. As such, she joins the prophetic company of those like Elijah and Jeremiah who declared the religious understandings of their day wanting. Judith shows that such roles are for women as well as for men.

12 Because the Book of Judith is more religious than the Book of Esther and because Judith 'tried to beguile Holofernes, but did not have an affair with him, whereas Esther lived with Ahasuerus', S. Zeitlin postulates that the story of Judith 'was written to neutralize the book of Esther' (*The Book of Judith* (Philadelphia, Dropsie, 1972), pp. 13–14). J. F. Craghan takes issue with this assessment and suggests that: 'It would seem more accurate to say that both books are deeply religious, but in different ways' ('Judith Revisited', *Biblical Theology Bulletin*, 12 (1982),p. 50).

13 For specifics, see T. Craven, 'Artistry and Faith in the Book of Judith, *Semeia*, 8 (1977), pp. 75–101.

14 Elsewhere I have demonstrated the details of the intricate compositional patterns which give balance and proportion to this book as a whole. For particulars, see the references in n.5 and n. 13.

15 Whereas subjects of the scenes in Part I alternate between the Assyrians and the Israelites, in Part II Judith literally dominates every scene. Once she appears in ch. 8, she shares the stage with others but surrenders it to no one. For details, see Craven, *Artistry and Faith*. op. cit., pp. 109–20.

16 For other examples of narratives that contain lament elements, see the story of Hannah (1 Sam. 1.1–18) and the Book of Job.

17 Of these components, only the word of assurance and the vow do not appear with complete regularity. For examples of assurances, see Pss. 12.5; 60.6–8; 81.6–7; 85.8–13; 91.14–16; and 108.7–9). For examples of vows in which the community pledges a future action of praise, see Pss. 14.8; 79.13; 80.18; 106.47. For discussion, see C. Westermann, *The Psalms: Structure, Content and Message* (Minneapolis, Augsburg, 1980), pp. 36–45; and J. H. Hayes, *Understanding the Psalms* (Valley Forge, Judson, 1976), p. 63.

18 The penitential use of sackcloth in Judith 4.9–15 is extreme. Sackcloth is put on the men, women, and children of Israel; and on their cattle,

every resident alien, hired labourer, and purchased slave (4.10); and
even on the altar itself (4.11). More regularly, only the community of
Israel itself would be involved, though in Jonah 3.8 the beasts and
people of Nineveh repent by covering themselves with sackcloth and
crying aloud to the Lord. For additional comment, see H. Gunkel, *The
Psalms* (Facet Books, Biblical Series, 19; Philadelphia, Fortress Press
1967), pp. 13–15; S. Mowinckel, *The Psalms in Israel's Worship* (trans.
D. R. Ap-Thomas; New York, Abingdon, 1967), pp. 193–5; and W.L.
Reed, 'Sackcloth', *Interpreter's Dictionary of the Bible*, 4 (ed. G. A.
Buttrick; New York, Abingdon, 1962), pp. 146–7.

19 John Craghan calls this prayer 'a communal lament' in which 'Judith
prays for herself only as God's instrument' (*Esther, Judith, Tobit,
Jonah, Ruth* (Old Testament Message 16; ed. C. Stuhlmeuller and M.
McNamara (Wilmington, Glazier, 1982) p. 83). For the compositional
details of this intricate prayer and for additional bibliography, see
Craven, *Artistry and Faith*, op. cit., pp. 162–79.

20 The author is untroubled by the ethical senstivities expressed by many
modern commentators about Judith's plan. Judith expressly sets out 'to
deceive' the enemy. The story has been called 'somewhat shocking' (R.
C. Dentan, *The Apocrypha, Bridge of the Testaments* (New York,
Seabury, 1964), p. 61), 'fierce and almost vindictive' (B. M. Metzger,
An Introduction to the Apocrypha (New York, OUP, 1957), p. 52), and
has been accused of containing 'some distinctly revolting passages'
(W. O. E. Osterley, *An Introduction to the Apocrypha* (London, SPCK,
1935), p. 176). For another defence of Judith's actions, see A. M.
Dubarle's discussion 'Légitimité de la ruse de Judith', *Judith: Formes et
sens des diverse traditions, Tome I: Etudes* (Rome, Institut Biblique
Pontifical, 1966), pp. 166–9.

21 The defeat here executed by Judith is an ignominious one; she 'breaks
in pieces their high estate by the hand of a female' (9.10). In 9.10,
13.15, and 16.6, the author uses the word θήλεια in place of the more
regularly employed λυνή. In all three cases, the author emphasizes that
'by the hand of a female' Yahweh triumphs. For additional comment,
see Enslin and Zeitlin, *Judith*, op. cit., p. 125, n. 10; and P. W.
Skehan, 'The Hand of Judith', *Catholic Biblical Quarterly*, 25 (1963),
pp. 94–109.

22 See Craven, *Artistry and Faith*. op. cit., pp. 200–13.

23 I take my title from a talk which Pope John Paul II gave to 4,000
priests' housekeepers in which he commented: 'My first impression is:
women do have their place in the Church. Be happy that you can keep
the residence of the priest clean and free him from material tasks which
would absorb part of the time he so needs for his apostolic labours.'
Such material tasks, the Pope said, 'are more suited to the female
charisms . . . you could never thank God enough for giving you the
grace of choosing to serve the clergy'. See 'No Comment Department',
Christian Century, 588 (12 May 1982); 'Clergy Housekeepers Praised',
National Catholic Reporter, 8 (7 May 1982); R. J. McClery, 'Speech to
Housekeepers Sparks Claim of Sexism', *National Catholic Reporter*, 6

(28 May 1982). Using Scripture as my guide, I here submit an opposing impression about the place of women in the community of faith.

24 cf. the maternal language in 16.5.

25 For a description of three feminist approaches to the study of women in Scripture, see P. Trible, 'Feminist Hermeneutics and Biblical Studies', *Christian Century* (3–10 February 1982), pp. 116–18.

4 Nicola Slee: Parables and Women's Experience

1 S. Mosteller, 'Living with', in J. Vanier (ed.), *The Challenge of L'Arche* (London, Darton, Longman & Todd, 1982), pp. 14–15.

2 L.W. Reese, 'I Never Talk of Hunger', in L. Bernikow (ed.), *The Word Split Open: Four Centuries of Women Poets in England and America 1552–1950* (London, Women's Press, 1979), p. 223.

5 Sharon Ringe: A Gentile Woman's Story

1 P. Trible, 'Feminist Hermeneutics and Biblical Studies', (see pp. 23–9 of this *Reader*); E. Schüssler Fiorenza, *In Memory of Her* (London, SCM, 1983).

2 Luke does not tell the woman's story at all. If he knew the story from Mark's Gospel, he apparently chose not to repeat it. In fact, Luke's Gospel does not contain a series of accounts clustered at this point in Mark (Mark 6.45–7.26), all of which deal with Jesus' relationship to Gentiles. Thus it may be that the omission of this story was part of a broader decision.

3 In Matthew the woman speaks of dogs receiving crumbs from 'the master's table', whereas in Mark she responds in a way more directly parallel to Jesus' words to her (JESUS: Children's bread not thrown to dogs; WOMAN: Dogs under the table eat the children's crumbs [Ringe]). The saying in verse 27 of Mark ('Let the children first be fed') appears to be an editorial addition to the story, since there is no suggestion in the narrative that the woman has forced herself on to Jesus' agenda ahead of anyone else. Note also similar sayings in Romans 1.6 and 2.10.

4 That coherence is evident despite some variation in wording in the account. The cause of the daughter's distress is called an 'unclean spirit' in verse 25 but a 'demon' elsewhere. It must be noted that the different word occurs only in the setting, which was probably supplied by Mark. That same introductory verse also contains the only instance where the daughter is called by the diminutive word 'little daughter'; elsewhere she is called 'daughter', except in the concluding verse, where she is called a 'child'. That last term echoes the one used in the woman's reply to Jesus in verse 28. In a sense, then, the variations interweave even more tightly the components of the story.

5 R. Bultmann, *The History of the Synoptic Tradition* (New York, Harper & Row, 1963), p. 38. This view is held by many scholars, including E. Schweizer, *The Good News According to Mark* (Atlanta, John Knox Press, 1970), p. 151; V. Taylor, *The Gospel According to St Mark* (New York, Macmillan, 1957), p. 347; W. Marxsen, *Mark the Evangelist* (Nashville, Abingdon Press, 1969), p. 60.

6 Taylor, *The Gospel, According to St Mark*, op. cit., p. 350.
7 H. Clark Kee, *Community of the New Age* (Philadelphia, Westminster, 1977), p. 83.
8 The conclusion that the issue of Jewish–Gentile relations represents a later interpretation of the story is further supported by details in Matthew's version. First, there the woman is identified not by the political or geographic designation of 'Greek' or 'Syrophoenician', but rather as a 'Canaanite', the term common in Hewbrew scriptures to refer to those most clearly not part of the chosen people. Second, Jesus' initial response to the woman's request sets her apart from the 'lost sheep of the house of Israel' to whom he has been sent. Finally, Matthew breaks the homely metaphor of the Markan account, so that the 'dogs' no longer simply get to eat up the crumbs that the children drop, but rather are entitled to the leftovers from the master's table.
9 T. A. Burkill, 'The Story of the Syrophoenician Woman', *Novum Testamentum*, 9:173 (1967).
10 J. D. M. Derett ('Law in the New Testament: The Syrophoenician Woman and the Centurion of Capernaum', *Novum Testamentum*, 15:162 (1973)) points out that this is a common resolution by both the Church and the scholarly community to the unnacceptable portrait of Jesus that is presented here.
11 Taylor, *The Gospel According to St Mark*, op. cit., p. 350.
12 See the discussion of laws and customs affecting women in first-century Palestine in chapter XVIII ('Appendix: The Social Position of Women') of J. Jeremias, *Jerusalem in the Time of Jesus* (Philadelphia, Fortress Press, 1969), pp. 359–76.

6 Elisabeth Schüssler Fiorenza: Missionaries, Apostles, Co-workers: Romans 16 and the Reconstruction of Women's Early Christian History

1 For a review of the discussion, see J. J. MacDonald, 'Was Romans XVI a Separate Letter?', *New Testament Studies*, 16 (1969/70), pp. 369–72; K. P. Donfried, 'A Short Note on Romans 16', *Journal of Biblical Literature*, 89 (1970), pp. 441–9; W. H. Ollrog, 'Die Abfass-ungsverhältnisse von Röm 16', in D. Lührmann and G. Strecker (eds.), *Kirche: Festschrift Bornkamm* (Tubingen, Mohr/Siebeck, 1980), pp. 221–44; E. Käsemann, *Commentary on Romans* (Grand Rapids, Eerdmans, 1980); P. Achtemeier, *Romans* (Atlanta, John Knox, 1985).
2 G. Theissen, *The Social Setting of Pauline Christianity* (Philadelphia, Fortress Press, 1982); cf. E. Troeltsch, *The Social Teaching of the Christian Churches*, 2 vols (New York, Macmillan, 1931), 1.78.
3 cf. G. Leff, *History and Social Theory* (Garden City, Doubleday, 1971); P. Hernadi, 'Clio's Cousins: Historiography as Translation, Fiction and Criticism', *New Literary History*, 7 (1975/76), pp. 247–57; R. S. Humphreys. 'The Historian, His(sic) Documents, and the Elementary Modes of Historical Thought', *History and Theory*, 19 (1980), pp. 1–20; S. Bann, 'Towards a Critical Historiography', *Philosophy*, 56 (1981), pp. 365–85.

4 cf. T. S. Kuhn, *The Structure of Scientific Revolutions* (Chicago, University of Chicago, 1962); I. G. Barbour, *Myth, Models, and Paradigms* (New York, Harper & Row, 1974).

5 J. Kelly-Gadol, 'The Social Relations of the Sexes: Methodological Implications of Women's History', *Signs*, 1 (1976), p. 809. See for this whole section, B. A. Caroll, *Liberating Women's History: Theoretical and Critical Essays* (Urbana, University of Illinois, 1976); D. Spender (ed.), *Men's Studies Modified: The Impact of Feminism on the Academic Disciplines* (New York, Pergamon, 1981); S. Harding and M. B. Hintikka (eds), *Discovering Reality* (Boston), D. Reidel, 1983); J. Kelly, *Women, History and Theory* (Chicago, University of Chicago, 1986); G. Lerner, *The Creation of Patriarchy* (New York, OUP, 1986).

6 For such a proposal, see my book, *In Memory of Her: A Feminist Theological Reconstruction of Christian Origins* (New York, Crossroad, 1983).

7 See my book, *Bread Not Stone: The Challenge of Feminist Biblical Interpretation* (Boston, Beacon Press, 1984).

8 E. Goodspeed, 'Phoebe's Letter of Introduction', *Harvard Theological Review*, 44 (1951), p. 56.

9 For examples, see H. Gamble, *The Textual History of the Letter to the Romans* (Grand Rapids, Eerdmans, 1977), pp. 84–7.

10 See, for example the reasoning of C. K. Barrett, *A Commentary on the Epistle to the Romans* (New York, Harper & Row, 1962), p. 282: 'The word itself (*diakonos*) does appear to have been on the way to technical use by the time this epistle was written (xii.7), but whether it was so used of women is not certain.'

11 H. Lietzmann, *Geschichte der Alten Kirche*, 4 vols (Berlin, De Gruyter, 1961), 1.149. See, however, W. H. Ollrog, *Paulus und Seine Mitarbeiter* (Neukirchen-Vluyn, Neukirchener Verlag, 1979), p. 31, who argues that such interpretations originated in the mind of privileged men. He points out that the participle *ousan* speaks for a institutionalization of the *diakonia* function. However, he understands then *prostatis* in terms of 'protectress, assistant, or helper' and understands then Phoebe's ministry in terms of financial or social assistance. Since Phoebe's ministry depended on her personal financial situation, it is particular to her and cannot be generalized.

12 W. A. Meeks, *The First Urban Christians. The Social World of the Apostle Paul* (New Haven, Yale University, 1983), p. 60, accepts the understanding of the term in the sense of the Latin *patrona*, but argues that such an understanding excludes that of 'leader, president'. However, his argument is not convincing, since both meanings are not exclusive of each other.

13 Käsemann, *Commentary on Romans*, op. cit., p. 411.

14 H. J. Klauck, *Hausgemeinde und Hauskirche im frühen Christentum* (Stuttgart, Katholisches Bibelwerk, 1981), p. 31, argues that the ministry of Phoebe consisted in her function as hostess for the community at Cenchreae, to whom she opened her house. However, the text does not refer to a house church.

15 cf. D. Georgi, *Die Gegner des Paulus im 2. Korintherbrief* (Neukirchen-Vluyn, Neukirchener Verlag, 1964); V. P. Furnish, *II Corinthians* (Garden City, Doubleday, 1984).
16 cf. A. Lemaire, 'The Ministries in the New Testament', *Biblical Theology Bulletin*, 3 (1973), pp. 133–66.
17 S. C. Mott, 'The Power of Giving and Receiving: Reciprocity in Hellenistic Benevolence', *Current Issues in Biblical and Patristic Interpretation*, G. E. Hawthorne, (ed.) (Grand Rapids, Eerdmans, 1975), pp. 133–66.
18 For the literature and interpretation, cf. *In Memory of Her*, op. cit., pp. 205–41.
19 Meeks, *The First Urban Christians*, op. cit., p. 60.
20 S. Pomeroy, *Goddesses, Whores, Wives, and Slaves: Women in Classical Antiquity* (New York, Shocken, 1975), pp. 191–7.
21 Ollrog, 'Die Abfassungsverhältnisse von Röm 16', op. cit., p. 236.
22 Meeks, *The First Urban Christians*, op. cit., p. 59. See also A. V. Harnack, 'Probabilia über die Adresse und den Verfasser des Hebräerbriefes', *Zeitschrift für die neutestamentliche Wissenschaft*, 1 (1900), pp. 35–41.
23 F. J. Foakes Jackson and K. Lake, *The Beginnings of Christianity. The Acts of the Apostles* 5 vols. (London, Macmillan, 1920–1933; reprinted, Grand Rapids, Baker Book House, 1965), 4.222.
24 M. A. Getty, 'God's Fellow Worker and Apostleship', in L. S. Swidler and A. Swidler (eds) *Women Priests* (New York, Paulist, 1977), pp. 176–82; E. E. Ellis, 'Paul and His Co-Workers', *New Testament Studies*, 17 (1970/71), pp. 437–52.
25 See my article, 'Die Rolle der Frau in der urchristlichen Bewegung', *Konzilium*, 12 (1976), pp. 3–9, in which I pointed out that Roman Catholic exegesis followed the lead of the 'Fathers' in understanding Junias as a woman's name. cf. M. J. Lagrange, *Saint Paul, Epitre aux Romains* (Paris, Lecoffre, 1916), p. 366. B. Brooten subsequently explored this reference in an unpublished MA thesis. cf. her summary 'Junia . . . Outstanding Among the Apostles', in *Women Priests*, op. cit., pp. 141–4; the correction finds its way slowly into the standard commentaries and introductions to the New Testament. See, for example, H. Koester, *Introduction in the New Testament*, 2 vols. (Philadelphia, Fortress Press, 1982), 2.139.
26 P. Lampe, 'Junia/Junias: Sklavenherkunft im Kreise der vorpaulinischen Apostel (Röm 16:7)', *Zeitschrift für die neutestamentliche Wissenschaft*, 76 (1985), pp. 132–3.
27 For a review of the problem, see my articles, 'The Apostleship of Women in Early Christianity', and 'The Twelve', in Swidler and Swidler, *Women Priests*, op. cit., pp. 135–40 and 114–23.
28 For such an understanding, cf. already Clement of Alexandria, *Stromateis*, 3.6.53.3f: ' . . .and took their wives with them not as women with whom they had marriage relations but as sisters that they might be their co-missionaries (*syndiakonous*) in dealing with housewives'.
29 A. J. Malherbe, *Social Aspects of Early Christianity* (Barton Rouge,

Louisiana State University, 1977)); R. Banks, *Paul's Idea of Community: The Early House Churches in Their Historical Setting* (Grand Rapids, Eerdmans, 1980); Klauck, *Hausgemeinde und Hauskirche,* op. cit.

30 Pomeroy, *Goddesses, Whores, Wives, and Slaves,* op. cit., pp. 176–89; R. MacMullen, 'Women in Public in the Roman Empire', *Historia,* 29 (1980), pp. 208–18.

7 Angela West: Sex and Salvation: A Christian Feminist Bible Study on 1 Corinthians 6.12–7.39

1 S. Griffin, *Pornography and Silence* (London, Women's Press, 1981).
2 W. E. Phipps, 'Is Paul's Attitude to Sex Relations Contained in 1 Corinthians 7.1?', *New Testament Studies,* 1 (1982), pp. 126–8.
3 D. Wiesen, *St Jerome as a Satirist* (Ithaca, NY, Cornell University Press, 1964), pp. 115–16, quoted in ibid.
4 J. M. O'Connor, *I. Corinthians,* New Testament Message 10 (Dublin, Veritas Publications, 1979), p. 63.
5 ibid.
6 Phipps, 'Is Paul's Atitude to Sex Relations contained in 1 Corinthians 7.1?', op. cit., p. 128.

Part Two: Christian History and Tradition

1 Appropriately, Valerie Saiving's essay was reprinted as the first selection in C. P. Christ and J. Plaskow (eds), *Womanspirit Rising: A Feminist Reader in Religion* (San Francisco, Harper & Row, 1979).
2 See L. Broughton's 'Find the Lady', *Modern Theology,* 4:3 (1988), pp. 267–81, which takes its starting point from the lively and neglected essays by Dorothy Sayers published in *Unpopular Opinions* (London, Gollancz, 1946).
3 O. L. Arnal, 'Theology and Commitment: Marie-Dominique Chenu', *Cross Currents,* 28:1(1988), p. 69.
4 The year 1988 has seen some remarkable documents produced under Roman Catholic auspices, as it were. The Apostolic Letter of 15 August 1988, by John Paul 11, *On the Dignity and Vocation of Women* (Washington DC, United States Catholic Conference, 1988), is a fascinating example of gender construction. The appeal for women's equality was heard from all quarters of the Church at 'The Synod of Great Expectations' (see the article of that title by Gerard O'Connell, in *The Month,* 21:2(1988), pp. 530–9. The National Conference of Catholic Bishops also produced the first draft of *Partners in the Mystery of Redemption: A Pastoral Response to Women's Concerns for Church and Society* 23 March 1988, discussed in *Partners Against Sexism: The Priests for Equality Response to the US Bishops' Pastoral Letter on Women's Concerns* (W. Hyattsville MD, Priests for Equality, 1988). Bishop Victor Balke of Crookston, Minnesota and Bishop Raymond Lucker of New

Ulm, Minnesota, issued a pastoral letter, 'Male and Female God Created Them', on 23 March 1988, published in *Origins*, (23 March 1988), pp. 333–8. A range of essays that are informative about the Roman Catholic Church in the USA is the result of the Women in the Church Conference, Washington DC, 10–12 October 1986, in M. Kolbenschlag (ed.), *Women in the Church 1* (Washington, Pastoral Press, 1987).

5 See also R. Radford Ruether, 'Patristic Spirituality and the Experience of Women in the Early Church', in M. Fox (ed.), *Western Spirituality: Historical Routes, Ecumenical Routes* (Santa Fe, Bear & Company, 1981), pp. 140–63.

6 See E. Pagels, *The Gnostic Gospels* (New York, Vintage, 1981), especially pp. 57–83 on 'God the Father/God the Mother'; and *Adam, Eve and the Serpent* (New York, Random, 1988).

7 C. Stewart OSB, 'The Portrayal of Women in the Sayings and Stories of the Desert', *Vox Benedictina*, 2:1(1985), pp. 5–23; and *The World of the Desert Fathers* (Oxford, SLG, 1986), especially pp. 14–16. Also see Sister Benedicta Ward SLG, *Harlots of the Desert: A Study of Repentance in Early Monastic Sources* (London, Mowbray, 1987); S. P. Brock and S. Ashbrook Harvey (trans. and introd.), *Holy Women of the Syrian Orient* (Berkeley, University of California, 1987). Most recently, see R. S. Kraemer (ed.), *Maenads, Martyrs, Matrons, Monastics: A Sourcebook on Women's Religions in the Greco-Roman World* (Philadelphia, Fortress Press, 1988), pp. 117–24, which gives us sayings of the ascetic desert mothers Sarah, Syncletica and Theodora, as well as many other valuable sources in translation, and with a bibliography. Finally, L. Leloir OSB, 'Woman and the Desert Fathers', *Vox Benedictina*, 3:3 (1986), pp. 207–27.

8 See G. Bonner, 'Augustine's Attitude to Women and "Amicitia"', in C. Mayer (ed.), *Homo Spiritalis: Festgabe für Luc Verheijen OSA* (Würzburg, Augustinus-Verlag, 1987), pp. 259–75; A. M. Wilson, 'Augustine on the Status of Women' and discussion, in *Milltown Studies* 19–20 (1987), pp. 87–122. And see E. A. Clark, *Women in the Early Church*, Message of the Fathers of the Church 13 (Wilmington, Glazier, 1983), and her *Ascetic Piety and Women's Faith: Essays on Late Ancient Christianity*, Studies in Women and Religion 20 (Lewiston, Mellen, 1984).

9 G. Lloyd, *The Man of Reason: 'Male' and 'Female' in Western Philosophy* (Minneapolis, University of Minnesota, 1984), pp. 28–37.

10 Compare M. Cline Horowitz, 'The Image of God in Man – is Woman Included?', *Harvard Theological Review*, 72:3–4(1979), pp. 175–206.

11 C. Walker Bynum, *Jesus as Mother: Studies in the Spirituality of the High Middle Ages* (Berkeley, University of California, 1982).

12 P. Allen RSM, 'Two Medieval Views on Woman's Identity: Hildegard of Bingen and Thomas Aquinas', *Studies in Religion/Sciences Religieuses*, 16:1 (1967), pp. 21–36; and see her *The Concept of Woman: The Aristotelian Revolution (750 BC–1250 AD)* (Montreal, Eden Press, 1985); and I. MacLean, *The Renaissance Notion of Woman* (Cambridge,

CUP, 1980); and K. M. Wilson (ed.), *Women Writers of the Renaissance and Reformation* (Athens, GA, University of Georgia, 1987). Flourishing about the same time as Thomas Aquinas was a beguine and mystic, Hadewijch, whose work is now available translated by Mother Columba Hart OSB in The Classics of Western Spirituality Series (London, SPCK, 1980). And see P. Mommaers, 'Hadewijch: A Feminist in Conflict', *Louvain Studies*, 13(1988), pp. 58–81. Important too is E. W. McDonnell, *The Beguines and Beghards in Medieval Culture: With Special Emphasis on the Belgian Scene* (New York, Octagon, 1960), pp. 299–319 on Juliana of Cornillon and devotion to the Eucharist; and C. Walker Bynum, *Holy Feast and Holy Fast: The Religious Significance of Food to Medieval Women* (Berkeley, University of California, 1987).

13 E. McLaughlin, 'Women, Power and the Pursuit of Holiness in Medieval Christianity', in R. Radford Ruether and E. McLaughlin, *Women of Spirit: Female Leadership in the Jewish and Christian Traditions* (New York, Simon & Schuster, 1979), pp. 99–130.

14 J. Bethke Elshtain, *Public Man, Private Woman: Women in Social and Political Thought* (Oxford, Robertson, 1981), on 'Early Christianity to Machiavelli', pp. 55–99; 'Luther *Sic* – Luther *Non!*', *Theology Today*, 43:2(1986), pp. 155–68 (reprinted in her *Meditations on Modern Political Thought: Masculine/Feminine Themes from Luther to Arendt* (New York, Praeger, 1986). See also 'Luther and the Protestant Reformation: From Nun to Parson's Wife', in E. Clark and H. Richardson (eds), *Women and Religion: A Feminist Sourcebook of Christian Thought* (San Francisco, Harper & Row, 1977), pp. 131–48, which quotes original sources in translation; and P. R. Hinlicky, 'Luther Against the Contempt of Women', *Lutheran Quarterly*, 2:8(1988), pp. 515–30.

15 Elshtain, *Public Man, Private Woman*, op. cit., p. 87.

16 M. Wiesner, 'Luther and Women; The Death of two Marys', in J. Obelkevich, L. Roper, R. Samuel (eds), *Disciplines of Faith: Studies in Religion, Politics and Patriarchy* (London, Routledge & Kegan Paul, 1987), pp. 295–308.

17 See 'The Triumph of Patriarchalism in the Theology of Karl Barth: Selections from *Church Dogmatics*, 3/4("The Doctrine of Creation")', in Clark and Richardson, *Women and Religion*, op. cit., pp. 239–58.

18 C. Green, 'Liberation Theology? Karl Barth on Women and Men', *Union Seminary Quarterly Review*, 19 (1974), pp. 221–31.

19 M. Tardiff OP, 'Bibliography: Rosemary Radford Ruether', MC, 30:1 (1988), pp. 50–5. *Religious Studies Review*, 15:1 (1989), pp. 1–11, is a 'Retrospective' on her work, with her own account of 'The Development of My Theology'.

20 See R. Radford Ruether and E. McLaughlin (eds), *Women of Spirit: Female Leadership in the Jewish and Christian Traditions* (New York, Simon & Schuster, 1979); H. Barbour, 'Quaker Prophetesses and Mothers in Israel', in C. and J. Stoneburner (eds), *The Influence of Quaker Women on American History*, Studies in Women and Religion 21 (Lewiston, Mellen, 1986), pp. 57–80. In the collection edited by L.

Irwin, *Womanhood in Radical Protestantism, 1525–1675* (New York, Mellen, 1979), of particular interest is 'The Examination of Mrs. Anne Hutchinson at the Court at Newtown', pp. 225–35; also to be found in D. D. Hall (ed.), *The Antinomian Controversy 1636–1638: A Documentary History* (Middletown CT, Wesleyan University Press, 1968), pp. 311–95. And see also E. Battis, *Saints and Sectaries* (Chapel Hill, University of North Carolina, 1962); S. R. Williams, *Divine Rebel* (New York, Holt, Rinehart & Winston, 1981); A. Schrager Lang, *Prophetic Woman: Anne Hutchinson and the Problem of Dissent in the Literature of New England* (Berkeley, University of California, 1987).

21 See also R. Radford Ruether, 'Christian Quest for Redemptive Community', *Cross Currents*, 38:1(1988), pp. 3–16.

22 R. Radford Ruether, 'The Liberation of Christology from Patriarchy', *New Blackfriars*, 66 (1985), pp. 324–35; and see her response to Edmund Hill OP in 67 (1986), pp. 92–3. And see M. Hembrow Snyder, *The Christology of Rosemary Radford Ruether* (Mystic CT, Twenty-Third Publications, 1988); G. R. Lilburne, 'Christology: in Dialogue with Feminism', *Horizons*, 11:1(1984), pp. 7–27.

23 A. E. Carr, *Transforming Grace: Christian Tradition and Women's Experience* (San Francisco, Harper & Row, 1988), especially chs. 7 and 8, 'Feminist Reflections on God' and 'Feminism and Christology'. D. Lardner Carmody, *Feminism and Christianity: a Two-Way Reflection* (Nashville, Abingdon, 1982); S. McFague, *Models of God: Theology for an Ecological, Nuclear Age* (London, SCM, 1987), from which extracts are reproduced in Part Three, has material on God as mother, lover and friend. Sarah Coakley has a devastating analysis of how *not* to proceed in '"Femininity" and the Holy Spirit', in M. Furlong (ed.), *Mirror to the Church: Reflections on Sexism* (London, SPCK, 1988), pp. 124–35.

24 See also J. Morley's essay, 'Liturgy and Danger', in *Mirror to the Church*, pp. 24–38; and her '"The Faltering Words of men": Exclusive Language in the Liturgy', in M. Furlong (ed.), *Feminine in the Church* (London, SPCK, 1984), pp. 56–70.

25 See G. Ramshaw, *Christ in Sacred Speech: the Meaning of Liturgical Language* (Philadelphia, Fortress Press, 1986); and B. Wren, *What Language Shall I Borrow? God-Talk in Worship: A Male Response to Feminist Theology* (London, SCM, 1989). There are now three volumes of the Inclusive Language Lectionary available, for years A, B, C, prepared by a committee appointed by the Division of Education and Ministry, National Council of the Churches of Christ in the USA (an ecumenical committee, however), published for The Cooperative Publication Association, John Knox, Pilgrim and Westminster Presses, 1985–1987. Some of the articles published by members of the committee are as follows: P. D. Miller, Jr, 'The Inclusive Language Lectionary', *Theology Today*, 41:1(1984), pp. 26–33; and a Symposium on the subject included S. Brooks Thistlethwaite, 'Inclusive Language and Linguistic Blindness', P. D. Miller, 'The Translation Task', R. A. Bennett, 'The Power of Language in Worship', and S. H. Ringe,

'Standing Toward the Text', in *Theology Today*, 43:4 (1987), pp. 533–57. There is also *Making Women Visible: The Use of Inclusive Language with the ASB* (London, Church House Publishing, 1989). For someone like Rosemary Radford Ruether, this does not go nearly far enough. See her assessment in 'Feminism and Jewish–Christian Dialogue: Particularism and Universalism in the Search for Religious Truth', in J. Hick and P. F. Knitter (eds), *The Myth of Christian Uniqueness: Towards a Pluralistic Theology of Religions* (New York, Orbis, 1987), pp. 137–48, especially p. 147, on why the feminist challenge to Christianity 'cannot find sufficient response in the recovery of neglected texts in the Bible or in inclusive translation. Women must be able to speak out of their own experiences of agony and victimization, survival, empowerment, and new life, as places of divine presence and, out of these revelatory experiences, write new stories. Feminists must create a new midrash on scripture or a "Third Testament" that can can tell stories of God's presence in experiences where God's presence was never allowed or imagined before in a religious culture controlled by men and defined by male experience'. So see Rosemary Radford Ruether, *Womanguides: Readings Towards a Feminist Theology* (Boston, Beacon Press, 1985).

9 Genevieve Lloyd: Augustine and Aquinas

1 See especially, Augustine, *Confessions*, XIII, chs 32 and 34, trans. V. J. Bourke, in *The Fathers of the Church: A New Translation* vol. XXI (Washington, Catholic University of America Press, 1953); and *The Trinity*, XII, trans. S. McKenna, in *The Fathers of the Church: A New Translation*, vol. XLV (Washington, Catholic University of America Press, 1963).

2 Augustine, *Confessions*, XIII, ch. 32, in Bourke, *The Fathers of the Church*, op. cit., p. 452.

3 Augustine, *De Trinitate*, XII, ch. 3, in McKenna, *The Fathers of the Church*, op. cit., p. 345.

4 ibid., XII, ch. 7, in ibid., pp. 351–5.

5 ibid., in ibid., p. 355.

6 ibid., XII, ch. 8, in ibid., p. 355.

7 ibid., X, ch. 8, in ibid., p. 305.

8 Augustine, *City of God*, XIV, ch. 23, trans. G.G. Walsh and G. Monahan, in *The Fathers of the Church: A New Translation*, vol. XIV (Washington, Catholic University of America Press, 1952), p. 401.

9 Augustine, *On Continence*, ch. 9, sec. 23, trans. Sr. M. F. McDonald, 'Treatises on various subjects', in *The Fathers of the Church: A New Translation*, vol. XVI, (Washington, Catholic Unitersity of America Press, 1952), pp. 215–18.

10 Aquinas, *Summa Theologica*, I, Q.76. art, 4, trans. Fathers of the English Dominican Province (London, Burns, Oates & Washbourne, 1922), vol. IV, pp. 39–43.

11 ibid., I, Q.92, art. 2, vol. IV, p. 277.

12 ibid., I, Q.93, art. 4, reply to obj. 1, vol. IV, p. 289.

13 ibid., I, Q.92, art. 1, vol. IV, p. 275.
14 ibid., p. 276.
15 ibid., II, Q.156, art. 1, vol. XIII, p. 173.
16 ibid., II, Q.70, art. 3, vol. XI.
17 ibid., I, Q.92,art. 1, vol. IV, pp. 275–6.

10 Eleanor McLaughlin: Women, Power and the Pursuit of Holiness

1 H. Cox, *Turning East: The Promise and Peril of the New Orientalism* (New York, 1977), pp. 99–100.
2 See J. Morris, *The Lady Was a Bishop* (New York, 1973).
3 See M. C. Facinger, 'A Study of Medieval Queenship: Capetian France, 987–1237', *Studies in Medieval and Renaissance History*, V (1968), pp. 3–48.
4 M. de Fantette, *Les Religieuses à l'âge classique du droit canon, recherches sur les structures juridiques de branches féminines des ordres* (Paris, 1967).
5 M. K. Dale, 'The London Silkwomen of the 15th Century', *Economic History Review*, IV (1933), p. 329.
6 P. F. Chambers, *Juliana of Norwich* (London, 1955), p. 53.
7 F. du Plessix Gray, 'Nature as the Nunnery', quoting Margaret Atwood, *Surfacing*, in *New York Times Book Review* (10 July 1977), p. 3.
8 See K. Thomas, *Religion and the Decline of Magic* (New York, 1971).
9 Especially useful on this topic are O. Barfield, *Saving the Appearances: A Study in Idolatry* (New York, n.d.); J. S. Dunne, *A Search for God in Time and Memory* (New York, 1967); P. Ricoeur, *The Symbolism of Evil* (Boston, 1967).
10 *Life of Saint Leoba*, by Rudolf, monk of Fulda, trans. and ed. C. H. Talbot, *The Anglo-Saxon Missionaries in Germany* (New York, 1954), pp. 205–26.
11 *Life of Saint Leoba*, op. cit., p. 211.
12 ibid., p. 214: 'holding her in great affection not so much because she was related to him on his mother's side as because he knew that by her holiness and wisdom she would confer many benefits by her word and example'.
13 ibid., p. 211.
14 ibid. p. 215.
15 *Letters of Saint Boniface*, trans. and ed. C.H. Talbot, *The Anglo-Saxon Missionaries in Germany* (New York, 1954), no. 17 (Tangl. 29), p. 88.
16 Rudolf, *Life of Saint Leoba*, op. cit., p. 215.
17 ibid., pp. 207–8.
18 ibid., pp. 219–20.
19 ibid., p. 223.
20 ibid.
21 ibid., p. 222.
22 ibid., p. 223.
23 For the impact of evolving English political institutions on the role of noblewomen, see B. Bandel, 'English Chronicles Attitude Towards Women', *Journal of the History of Ideas*, XVI (1955), pp. 113–18; see

also J. A. McNamara and S. Wemple, 'The Power of Women Through the Family in Medieval Europe, 500–1100', in M. Hartman and L. W. Banner (eds), *Clio's Consciousness Raised* (New York, 1974), pp. 103–18.

24 C. H. Talbot (ed. and trans.), *The Life of Christina of Markyate, a Twelfth Century Recluse* (Oxford, 1959), p. 6.

25 ibid., p. 35.

26 ibid., p. 47.

27 ibid., p. 51.

28 ibid., pp. 51–3.

29 ibid. p. 59.

30 ibid., p. 65.

31 ibid. pp. 65–7.

32 ibid., pp. 73–5.

33 ibid. p. 93. Once again we see this aspect of the anthropology of sainthood for women, in which the specifically female was left behind; to be holy is to regain the image God, to become more fully human and therefore, in this inheritance of patristic anthropology, to become male. See R. R. Ruether, 'Misogynism and Virginal Feminism in the Fathers of the Church', *Religion and Sexism* (New York, 1974), p. 160.

34 ibid., p. 103.

35 Aelred of Rievaulx, *Spiritual Friendship*, trans. M. E. Laker, Cistercian Fathers Series, no. 5 (Washington DC, 1974).

36 Talbot, *Life of Christina*, op. cit., p. 151.

37 ibid., p. 143.

38 ibid., pp. 165–7.

39 ibid., p. 169.

40 ibid., p. 91.

41 ibid., p. 133.

42 ibid., p. 107.

43 She is referred to as a 'lover of Christ', ibid., p. 173.

44 ibid., p. 119.

45 See A. Curtayne, *Saint Catherine of Siena* (London, 1929); S. Undset, *Catherine of Siena*, trans. K. Austin-Lund (London/New York, 1954).

46 Saint Raymond of Capua, *The Life of St Catherine of Siena*, trans. G. Lands (London, 1965). Citations of her letters here are from Vida D. Scudder (ed. and trans.), *Saint Catherine of Siena as Seen in Her Letters* (New York, 1911).

47 Curtayne, *Saint Catherine*, op. cit., pp. 196–8.

48 ibid., p. 202.

49 ibid., p. 184.

50 Scudder, *Letters*, op. cit., p. 297.

51 ibid., p. 305.

52 ibid., p. 298.

53 ibid., p. 234.

54 *The Dialogue of Saint Catherine of Siena*, trans. Algar Thorold (Rockford, Ill., 1974), pp. 65–6.

55 ibid., p. 185.

56 Scudder, *Letters,* op. cit., pp. 285–6.
57 ibid., p. 283.
58 ibid.
59 Scudder, *Letters,* op. cit., p. 289.
60 *Dialogue,* trans. Thorold, op. cit., p. 27.
61 Scudder, *Letters,* op. cit., p. 345.
62 *Dialogue,* trans. Thorold, op. cit., p. 284.
63 ibid., p. 69.
64 R. Grossetest to the Papal Notary (1253), in M. Baldwin, *Christianity Through the Thirteenth Century* (New York, 1970), p. 383.
65 E. McLaughlin, 'Women and Medieval Heresy', *Concilium,* CXI (1976), pp. 73–90.
66 Julian of Norwich, *Revelations of Divine Love,* ed. C. Wolters (Baltimore, 1973), ch. 59, p. 167.
67 New books on the significance for Christian anthropology of the cult of the Virgin are numerous. A. Greeley, *The Mary Myth: On the Femininity of God* (New York, 1977), or J. de Satgé, *Down to Earth: The New Protestant Vision of the Virgin Mary* (Wilmington, NC, 1976), need to be read with reference to basic research, as, for example, K. E. Børresen, *Anthropologie médiévale et théologie mariale* (Oslo, 1971).
68 V. Saxer, *Le Culte de Marie Magdelène en occident des origines à la fin du moyen âge* (Paris, 1959).
69 'André Cabassut, une dévotion médiévale peu connue: La dévotion à Jesus notre mère', *Revue d'ascétique et de mystique,* XXV (1949), pp. 234–45; E. Pagels, 'What Became of God the Mother? Conflicting Images of God in Early Christianity', *Signs,* II (1976), pp. 293–303; E. McLaughlin, 'Christ My Mother: Feminine Naming and Metaphor in Medieval Spirituality', *Nashotah Review,* XV (1975), pp. 228–48; C. Walker Bynum, 'Maternal Imagery in Twelfth Century Cistercian Writing', 7th Cistercian Conference, Kalamazoo, MI, 5–8 May 1977.
70 For what I believe to be a controversial discussion of the issue of 'female piety', see J. Bugge, *Virginitas: An Essay in the History of a Medieval Ideal* (The Hague, 1975).
71 Julian of Norwich, *Revelations,* op. cit., ch. 58, p. 166. See also K. E. Børresen, 'Christ notre mère, la théologie de Julienne de Norwich', *Mitteilungen und Forschungsbeiträge der Cusanus-Gesellschaft,* 13 (Mainz, 1978).

11 Merry Wiesner: Luther and Women: The Death of Two Marys

Abbreviations
Erl.: *D.Martin Luthers sämmtiliche Werke.* Erlangen and Frankfurt, 1826–57.
WA: *D. Martin Luthers Werke.* Kritische Gesamtausgabe, Weimar, 1883–
WA, TR: *D. Martin Luthers Werke.* Tischreden, Weimar, 1912–21.
LW: *Luther's Works,* American edition, Philadelphia, 1955–

1 Erl. 61, 125.
2 Erl. 20, 84.

3   Erl. 61, 212.
4   WA, TR 4, 4786.
5   K. Bücher, *Die Frauenfrage im Mittelalter* (Tübingen, 1910), pp. 68ff; W. Kamerau, *Die Reformation und die Ehe* (Verein für Reformationsgeschichte, 1892); E. W. Cocke, Jr, 'Luther's View of Marriage and Family'. *Religion in Life*, 42 (Spring 1973), pp. 103–16.
6   W. Lazareth, *Luther on the Christian Home* (Philadelphia, Muhlenberg Press, 1960), p. vii.
7   E. Ahme, 'Wertung und Bedeutung der Frau bei Martin Luther', *Luther*, vol. 35, pp. 63–4.
8   S. Baranowski, *Luthers Lehre von der Ehe* (Münster, 1913), pp. 198–9.
9   M. Behrens, 'Martin Luther's View of Women', MA thesis, (North Texas State, 1973), pp. 34 and 95.
10   J. Yost, 'Changing Attitudes toward Married Life in Civic and Christian Humanism', *ASRR Occasional Papers*, vol. 1 (Dec. 1977), p. 164. Similar ideas also in Yost, 'The Value of Married Life for the Social Order in the Early English Renaissance', *Societas*, VI/i (Winter 1976), pp. 25–37.
11   K. Davies, 'Continuity and Change in Literary Advice on Marriage', in *Marriage and Society: Studies in the Social History of Marriage,* ed. R. B. Outhwaite (New York, 1981).
12   L W 5, 331.
13   Erl. 33, 112.
14   WA, TR 1, 1046; WA 15, 419; 16, 218.
15   Erl. 51, 431.
16   Erl. 51, 46–7.
17   LW 1, 203.
18   LW 15, 130.
19   Erl. 51, 428.
20   O. Lahteenmaki, *Sexus und Ehe bei Luther*, Schriften der Luther–Agricola Gesellschaft, nr 10, Turku, 1955. Lilly Zarncke, 'Die Naturhafte Eheanschauung Luthers', *Archiv für Kulturgeschichte*, 25 (1935), pp. 281–305.
21   WA 20, 149.
22   WA 17, 1, 25.
23   M. Heinsius, *Das unüberwindliche Wort: Frauen der Reformationszeit* (Munich, 1953), pp. 45–57.
24   It is interesting to speculate on how much effect this ideal had on Catholic Counter-Reformation leaders. As Ruth Liebowitz has pointed out, women in the late sixteenth century wanted to form active orders, working out in the world (comparable to the Jesuits), but were generally blocked by the Church, which wanted them strictly cloistered ('Virgins in the Service of Christ', in R. R. Reuther and E. McLaughlin (eds), *Women of Spirit* (New York, Simon & Schuster, 1979), pp. 132–52). Thus although Catholic women still had the option of remaining unmarried, they were to be cloistered in the convent in the same way that Lutheran women were to be cloistered in their own homes. The ideal woman in all religions became increasingly similar, a

woman who was 'chaste, silent and obedient' (Suzanne Hull, *Chaste, Silent and Obedient: English Books for Women 1475–1640* (San Marino, 1982).
25 LW 1, 202–3; WA 42, 51.
26 LW 29, 56; WA 25, 45.
27 WA 25, 46; LW 29, 56.
28 Ahme, op. cit., p. 67. Even Luther did not go as far as Henry VIII in this matter, however. He did encourage his wife to read the Bible, while an Act passed in England in 1543 forbade Bible reading by 'Women, artificers, prentices, journeymen, husbandmen and labourers . . . for the advancement of the true religion. Noblemen, gentlemen and merchants might read the Bible in their own families: noblewomen and gentlewomen might read it privately, but not to others.' This Act was repealed in 1547 when Henry's more enlightened son assumed the kingship (Hull, op. cit., p. xii).
29 Heinsius, *Das unüberwindliche*, op. cit., pp. 20 and 24.
30 WA, TR 1, 1046.
31 WA 1, 431–5.
32 WA 10, 1, 208.
33 Erl. 61, 272.
34 WA, Tr 4, 4786; LW 7, 76.
35 D. Kelley, *The Beginning of Ideology* (Cambridge, 1981), p. 75.
36 Er. 16, 142.
37 E. Midelfort, *Witchhunting in Southwestern Germany 1562–1684* (Stanford, 1972), pp. 184–6.
38 I. MacLean, *The Renaissance Notion of Woman* (Cambridge, 1980), p. 88.
39 G. Strauss, *Luther's House of Learning* (Johns Hopkins, 1978), p. 307.
40 WA, TR, 3, 2807b.
41 LW 1, 256–7.
42 WA 10/1/1, 280.
43 WA 7, 547, 549, 550.
44 WA 10/3, 285; WA 42, 452.
45 I. Siggins, *Martin Luther's Doctrine of Christ* (New Haven, 1970), *passim*.
46 E. L. McLaughlin, 'Male and Female in the Christian Tradition', in R. T. Barnhouse and U. T. Holmes III (eds) *Male and Female: Christian Approaches to Sexuality* (New York, 1976), pp. 43–4.
47 C. Bynum, *Jesus as Mother: Studies in the Spirituality of the High Middle Ages* (University of California Press, 1982).
48 ibid., p. 185.
49 McLaughlin, Male/Female, op. cit., p. 46.
50 Bynum, *Jesus as Mother*, op. cit., p. 185.
51 ibid., p. 255.
52 Kelley, *The Beginning of Ideology*, op. cit., p. 74.
53 MacLean, *The Renaissance Notion of Women*, op. cit.
54 Joan Kelley, 'Early Feminist Theory and the Querelle des Femmes, 1400–1789', *SIGNS*, 8/1 (Autumn 1982), p. 8.

55 Kelley, *The Beginning of Ideology*, op. cit., pp. 75–6.
56 M. Daly, *Beyond God the Father*, (Boston, 1973). Quote is from A. Douglas, *Feminization* (New York, 1977), p. 167.
57 MacLean, *The Rennaissance Notion of Women*, op. cit., p. 85.
58 K. Barth, *Church Dogmatics: A Selection*, trans. and ed. G. W. Bromiley (New York, 1962), pp. 218–20.

12 Rosemary Radford Ruether: The Liberation of Christology from Patriarchy

1 For the development of Logos Christology in the New Testament, particularly the Gospel of John, see C. H. Dodd, *The Interpretation of the Fourth Gospel* (Cambridge and New York, CUP, 1963), pp. 263–85. For Logos Christianity in second-century Christianity, especially the theology of Justin Martyr, see E. Goodenough, *The Theology of Justin Martyr* (Amsterdam, Philo Press, 1968), pp.139–75.
2 P. Bird, 'Male and Female He Created Them: Gen. 1:27b in the Context of the Priestly Account of Creation', *Harvard Theological Review*, 74:2 (1981), pp. 129–59.
3 G. Nyssa, *De Opif, Hom*. 16.7; see R. Radford Ruether, 'Misogynism and Virginal Feminism in the Fathers of the Church', in R. Radford Ruether (ed) *Religion and Sexism: Images of Women in the Jewish and Christian Traditions* (New York, Simon & Schuster), 1974, pp. 153–5.
4 K. Børresen, 'God's Image: Man's Image; Female Metaphors Describing God in the Christian Tradition', *Temenos* 19 (Helsinki, 1983), pp. 17–32.
5 Augustine, *De Trinitate*, 7.7.10.
6 Aristotle, *Gen An.*, 729b. pp. 737–8.
7 T. Aquinas, *Summa Theologica*, pt 1, q. 92, art. 1.
8 This is the view taken by post-Christian feminists such as Naomi Goldenberg, in *The Changing of the Gods* (Boston, Beacon Press, 1979).
9 For example, Isa. 42.13, 14 and Isa. 49. 14–15. See L. Swidler, *Biblical Affirmations of Women* (Philadelphia, Westminster, 1979), pp. 21–50.
10 Swidler, ibid., pp. 36–48.
11 Luke 11.49, Matt. 11.18–19: See J. M. Robinson, 'Jesus as Sophos and Sophia: Wisdom and Tradition in the Gospels', and E. Schüssler Fiorenza, 'Wisdom Mythology and the Christological Hymns of the New Testament', in R. L. Wilkin (ed.) *Aspects of Wisdom in Judaism and Early Christianity* (South Bend, Indiana, Notre Dame University Press, 1975), pp. 35ff.
12 See entry on 'Son of Man' in *An Inclusive Language Lectionary: Readings for Year A*, by the Inclusive Language Lectionary Committee, appointed by the Division of Education and Ministry, National Council of Churches of Christ in the USA (Philadelphia, Westminster, 1983), appendix.
13 Luke 1.46–55.
14 Matt. 27.56; Mark 15.40; Luke 23.49, John 19.25. John alone has the tradition of the mother of Jesus at the cross, as well as the disciple

John, but he too affirms the presence of Mary Magdalene there. In the resurrection traditions, Matthew says that the angel told the women to announce it to the disciples. Luke says only that they told it to the 'eleven and to all the others', and Mark says that they told no one of their experience. John has the most extended account of Mary Magdalene's presence, saying that first she told Peter and John of the empty tomb and then later she spoke to the risen Lord and was told by him to impart her revelation to the brethren: Matt. 28.1–8; Mark 16.1–8; Luke 24.1–9; John 20.1–18. The gnostics elaborated the Gospel stories of Mary Magdalene's role in the resurrection, and made her a key figure in interpreting the message of the resurrection to the male apostles. For the gnostics, this also affirms women's place in apostolic ministry and teaching. See the Gospel of Mary, in the *Nag Hammadi Library in English*, J. Robinson *et al.* (San Francisco, Harper & Row, 1977), pp. 471–4.

15 See E. Schillebeeckx, *Jesus, an Experiment in Christology* (New York, Seabury, 1979), p. 703, ns 31–33.

16 Joel 2.28–32; Acts 2. 17–21.

17 See E. Schüssler Fiorenza, 'Word, Spirit and Power: Women in Early Christian Communities', in *Women of Spirit: Female Leadership in the Jewish and Christian Traditions* (New York, Simon & Schuster, 1979), pp. 39–44.

18 Didache 11.3–13.7.

19 1 Cor. 7.25–31.

20 1 Tim. 3.1–12.

21 See D. R. MacDonald, *The Legend and the Apostle: The Battle for Paul in Story and Canon* (Philadelphia, Westminster, 1983), who argues that 1 Timothy was written by a second-generation Christian representing a patriarchal view of Paul, to combat an alternative view of Paul found in the oral traditions of the story of Paul and Thecla.

22 The Montanist women prophets were accused of abandoning their husbands, which suggests that they shared the view of the *Acts of Paul and Thecla* that women converts to Christ transcend their marital obligations. Gnostic women also believed that spiritual rebirth transcended marriage and procreation in a new state of androgynous existence. Both groups supported women in leadership, following the early Christian traditions of a leadership of apostle, prophets and teachers. See Fiorenza, 'Word, Spirit and Power', op. cit., p. 42, and E. Pagels, *The Gnostic Gospels* (New York, Random House, 1979), pp. 48–69.

23 It became formulaic for the fourth-century advocates of asceticism, such as St Jerome and St Athanasius, to affirm the three levels of blessings on states of life: thirtyfold for marriage, sixtyfold for continent widowhood and one hundredfold for virginity, in order to both affirm the superiority of chastity to marriage and yet also separate themselves from groups that forbade marriage altogether to the baptized. See Athanasius, Ep. 48 and Jerome, Ep. 48.2.

24 S. Laeuchli, *Power and Sexuality: The Emergence of Canon Law at the*

Council of Elvira (Philadelphia, Temple University Press, 1972). The Council of Elvira in AD 400 was the first to mandate continence for the clergy, and shows the emerging connection between clerical celibacy and an obsession with control over female sexuality.

25 See R. R. Ruether, 'Women in Utopian Movements', in R. Radford Ruether and R. S. Keller, *Women and Religion in America: The Nineteenth Century* (New York, Harper & Row, 1981), pp. 46–100.

26 Eusebius, *Oration on Constantine*, 10.7.

27 The fullest development of the union of mystical and millennialist theology, together with the affirmation of sexual equality, is found in the theology of the Anglo-American sect, the Shakers, or the United Society of Christ's Second Appearing. See especially their bible, *The Testimony of Christ's Second Appearing* (United Society, 1856).

28 On the Leveller party in the Puritan Civil War, see especially W. Haller, *Liberty and Reformation in the Puritan Revolution* (New York, Columbia University Press, 1955), pp. 254–358; also C. Hill, *The World Turned Upside Down: radical ideas during the English Revolution* (London, Temple Smith, 1972).

29 A secularized millennialism is typical of much of Enlightenment writing. See, for example A.-N. de Condorcet, *Sketch for a Historical Picture of the Progress of the Human Mind*, trans. June Barraclough (London, Weidenfeld & Nicolson, 1955).

30 Acts of the Martyrs of Lyons and Vienne, in H. Musurillo, *The Acts of the Christian Martyrs* (Oxford, Clarendon, 1972), p. 75.

13 Sara Maitland: Ways of Relating

1 B. Campbell, Alla, 'Transfiguration/full moon' for *Women Listening*. Alla Bozarth Campbell lent me this essay in 1979; at that point the book, a collection of women writing about their prayer life, had not been published. I do not know if it has been now and, if so, who edited or published it. I would be grateful if anyone could supply the full reference.

2 Quoted from C. Miller and K. Swift, *Words and Women* (London, Penguin, 1979), an invaluable source text for this whole issue.

3 R. R. Ruether, in an interview with the author, August 1979. Evanston, Ill., and quoted in S. Maitland, *A Map of the New Country* (London, Routledge, 1983).

4 cf. C. M. Warner, *Alone of All Her Sex: The Myth and Cult of the Virgin Mary* (London, Weidenfeld and Nicolson, 1976), for a detailed study of how such images change in affectual value through the historical process.

5 Prov. 8. 30–31; rendered into non-sexist language rather unprofessionally by myself.

6 B. Campbell, Alla, *Womanpriest* (New York, 1978), p. 209.

15(ii) Gail Ramshaw: The Gender of God

1 T. Aquinas, *Summa Theologiae*, 1a. 13.1.

2 H. Ott, *God*. trans. I. and U. Nicol (Atlanta, John Knox, 1974).

3 For example, *God as Father?* J.-Baptist Metz and E. Schillebeeckx, *Concilium*, 143 (New York, Seabury 1981), and K. Stendahl, 'Enrichment or Threat? When the Eves Come Marching in', in A. Hageman (ed.), *Sexist Religion and Women in the Church: No More Silence!* (New York, Association, 1974), pp. 117–23.

4 L. Russell, 'Changing Language and the Church', in *The Liberating Word* (Philadelphia, Westminster, 1976), pp. 92–3; M. Sawicki, *Faith and Sexism: Guidelines for Religious Educators* (New York, Seabury, 1979), pp. 19–23.

5 S. D. Collins, *A Different Heaven and Earth* (Valley Forge, Penn., Judson, 1974), p. 217.

6 Aquinas, *Summa*, la.1,9.

7 M. Searle, 'Liturgy as Metaphor', *Worship*, 55 (1981), pp. 98–120; G. Ramshaw Schmidt, 'Liturgy as Poetry: Implications of a Definition', *Living Worship*, 15 (October 1979), no. 8.

8 Aquinas, *Summa*, la. 13.1.

9 Aquinas, *Summa*, la. 13.4.

10 T.S. Eliot, 'The Hollow Men', in *The Complete Poems and Plays 1909–1950* (New York, Harcourt, Brace and World, 1958) p. 60.

11 R. M. Gross, 'Steps Toward Feminine Imagery of Deity in Jewish Theology', *Judaism*, 30 (1981), pp. 190–92.

12 Aquinas, *Summa*, la. 13.2.

13 W. Pannenberg, 'Analogy and Doxology', *Basic Questions in Theology*, trans. G. H. Kehm (Philadelphia, Fortress Press, 1972), I, p. 215.

14 E. Schillebeeckx, *Interim Report on the Books* Jesus *and* Christ (New York, Crossroad, 1981), p. 24, *passim*.

15 I. Ramsey, *Religious Language* (New York, Macmillan, 1963), pp. 203–5.

16 L. Swidler, *Biblical Affirmations of Women* (Philadelphia, Westminster, 1979), pp. 21–73.

17 For example, P. D. Hanson. 'Masculine Metaphors for God and Sex-Discrimination in the Old Testament', *the Ecumenical Review*, 27 (1975), pp. 317–21. and E. H. Pagels, 'What Became of God the Mother? Conflicting Images of God in Early Christianity', in C. P. Christ and J. Plaskow (eds.), *Womanspirit Rising: A Feminist Reader in Religion* (New York, Harper & Row, 1979), pp. 107–19.

18 Gregory of Nazianzus. 'The Fifth Theological Oration: On the Spirit,' in E. R. Hardy and C. C. Richardson (eds), *Christology of the Later Fathers*. The Library of Christian Classics vol. 3. (Philadelphia, Westminster, 1954), p. 198.

19 Aquinas, *Summa*, la. 13.11.

20 Ott, *God*, 42.

21 Pannenberg, *Basic Questions*, op. cit., I, p. 232.

22 U. T. Holmes, 'The Feminine Priestly Symbol and the Meaning of God', *The Saint Luke's Journal of Theology*, 17 (1974), p. 7.

23 R. A. Norris, Jr, 'Priesthood and the "Maleness" of Christ: Trinity and Christology in the Fathers', *Pro and con on Ordination of Women*. Report and Papers from the Anglican-Catholic Consultation, pp. 75–6.

24 'Guidelines for Equal Treatment of the Sexes in the McGraw-Hill Book Company Publications', McGraw-Hill, 1974: 'Guidelines for Creating Positive Sexual and Racial Images in Educational Materials', Macmillan, 1975: 'Eliminating Stereotypes', Houghton Mifflin, 1981; and 'Guidelines for Improving the Images of Women in Textbooks', Scott, Foresman & Co., 1974.

25 A. Pace Nilsen, *et al.*, *Sexism and Language* (Urban, Ill. National Council of Teachers of English, 1977).

26 C. Miller and K. Swift, *Words and Women: New Language in New Time* (Garden City, New York, Doubleday, Anchor, 1977), pp. 116–19.

27 For example, J. G. Williams, 'Yahweh, Women, and the Trinity', *Theology Today*, 32 (1975), p. 240.

28 A. Bodine, 'Androcentrism in Prescriptive Grammar: singular "they", sex-indefinite "he", and "he or she"', *Language in Society*, 4 (1975), p. 141.

29 For example, J. F. White, *Introduction to Christian Worship* (Nashville, Abingdon, 1980), pp. 12.18, *passim*.

Part Three: Practical Consequences

1 G. Kennedy Neville, 'Religious Socialization of Women within US Subcultures', in A. L. Hageman (ed.), *Sexist Religion and Women in the Church: No More Silence* (New York, Association Press, 1974), pp. 77–91.

2 B. Wildung Harrison, 'Sexism and the Contemporary Church: When Evasion Becomes Complicity', in Hageman, *Sexist Religion*, op. cit., p. 200.

3 As in L. Russell, *Household of Freedom: Authority in Feminist Theology* (Philadelphia, Westminster, 1987).

4 I. Woodward, *The Catholic Sisters of the United States: Signs of Contradiction or Signs of the Times?* Pro Mundi Vita: Dossiers 4/1986; and see M. E. Hines, 'Women Religious in Transition', *New Theology Review*, 1:1(1988), pp. 93–106.

5 And see J. Schaberg, *The Illegitimacy of Jesus: A Feminist Theological Interpretation of the Infancy Narratives* (San Francisco, Harper & Row, 1987).

6 For an example of 'liberation theology' transferred to the North American scene, see S. D. Welch, *Communities of Resistance and Solidarity: A Feminist Theology of Liberation* (Maryknoll, Orbis, 1985).

7 See M. A. Stenger, 'A Critical Analysis of the Influence of Paul Tillich on Mary Daly's Feminist Theology', *Encounter*, 43:3(1982), pp. 219–38; and 'Male over Female or Female over Male: a Critique of Idolatry', *Encounter*, 47:4 (1986), pp. 464–78. In view of the fact that St Teresa of Avila is such an important example for Mary Daly in *The Church and the Second Sex*, compare C. Garside Allen, 'Self-Creation

and Loss of Self: Mary Daly and St Teresa of Avila', *Studies in Religion/Sciences Religieuses*, 6:1(1976), pp. 67–72.

8 See J. Rowan, *The Horned God: Feminism and Men as Wounding and Healing* (London, Routledge & Kegan Paul, 1987).

9 Quoted in ibid., pp. 42–3. See also J. Pohier, *God in Fragments* trans. J. Bowden (London, SCM, 1985), p. 188.

10 M. Daly, 'Theology after the Demise of God the Father: A Call for the Castration of Sexist Religion', in J. Plaskow and J. Arnold Romero (eds), *Women and Religion* (Chico, Ca, Scholars, 1974), pp. 3–19.

11 Hageman, *Sexist Religion*, op. cit., p. 197.

12 Important too here, I believe, is the work of writer in theological ethics, Helen Oppenheimer. See her sermon, 'Life after Death', *Theology*, 82(1979), pp. 328–35; *The Hope of Happiness: a Sketch for a Christian Humanism* (London, SCM, 1983); and her most recent book, *Looking Before and After* (London, Collins, 1988). In *The Hope of Happiness*, there are two brilliant chapters on 'Liking' and 'Attending'. See the options examined by S. F. Parsons on 'The Intersection of Feminism and Theological Ethics', *Modern Theology*, 4:3(1988), pp. 250–66.

13 From the Orthodox tradition, see T. Hopko (ed.) *Women and the Priesthood* (Crestwood, NY, St Vladimir's Seminary Press, 1983). The best discussion of the biblical material is probably M. Hayter, *The New Eve in Christ: The Use and Abuse of the Bible in the Debate about Women in the Church* (London, SPCK, 1987). See the way the issues connect with abortion in D. Larner Carmody, *The Double Cross: Ordination, Abortion and Catholic Feminism*, (New York, Crossroad, 1986); and with spirituality, in M. Ross, *Pillars of Flame: Power, Priesthood, and Spiritual Maturity* (London, SCM, 1988).

14 Alternatives are represented by D. Lardner Carmody, *Seizing the Apple: A Feminist Spirituality of Personal Growth* (New York, Crossroad, 1984); M. E. Giles (ed.), *The Feminist Mystic: And Other Essays on Women and Spirituality* (New York, Crossroad, 1987); K. Fischer, *Women at the Well: Feminist Perspectives on Spiritual Direction* (London, SPCK, 1989).

15 See the valuable chapter, 'What Some Women are Saying about IVF', in K. Kelly's *Life and Love: Towards a Christian Dialogue on Bioethical Questions* (London, Collins, 1987), pp. 83–104.

17 Beverly Wildung Harrison: The Power of Anger in the Work of Love

1 Mary Daly, *Gyn/Ecology: The Metaethics of Radical Feminism* (Boston, Beacon Press, 1978), pp. 30ff. Mary Daly's work rightly has shaped most discussion and debate among women in theological and religious studies. Few, if any, male scholars seem to appreciate the importance of Daly's critique of Christian theology as exemplary patriarchy, perhaps because it is easier to ignore her claims than to offer a serious rejoinder. I have chosen to take public issue with Daly here not to give aid and comfort to those who think her work 'too angry' and 'too man-hating' but because, with the publication of *Gyn/Ecology*, Daly

enters directly into 'metaethics', or a discussion of the foundations of particular moral claims. It will not do, as Rebecca Porper did in *Union Seminary Quarterly Review* 35, nos. 1 and 2 (Fall, Winter 1979–80), pp. 126–8, simply to treat the book as 'beyond academic categories'. Many of Daly's complaints about 'methodolatry' in academia are on target, but she is also developing a substantive conceptual position herself, so her own method (consisting of operative assumptions and appeals for justification) deserves scrutiny. Daly is concerned about anti-intellectualism among women. It would be an exemplification of such anti-intellectualism not to hold her accountable for the factual and moral claims she makes or for her explicit or implicit methodological moves.

2 Daly, *Gyn/Ecology*, pp. 27–31.

3 My differences with Daly are numerous and beyond full classification here. Methodologically, I believe Daly has not repudiated adequately the extreme abstract rationalism of her Roman Catholic philosophical background, nor has she completed the shift from static ontic categories to the process categories she often celebrates. Carter Heyward is correct in claiming that Daly remains philosophically a subjective idealist (Carter Heyward, 'Speaking and Sparking; Building and Burning', *Christianity and Crisis* 39: 5 (2 April 1979), p. 69). I assume a connection between subjective idealism and the body/mind dualism of the western tradition. The test of one's philosophical epistemology always becomes clear at the level of action. Idealism produces a critique of concepts, but it does not produce a historically concrete critique of institutions (that is, collective practice) or an alternative strategy for action. Even when Daly is correct about the depth of misogyny, her historical analysis of it lacks concreteness, nuance, and accuracy, and the book does not open the way to a strategy of change for a real, material world. It is not surprising that many begin to connect Daly's position with the ancient Gnostic movements, which in their developed form became dualistic.

4 As noted above, the quality of Daly's historical scholarship leaves much to be desired, especially in light of the growing amount of competent feminist research available on some of the historical periods about which she writes. Daly seems unwilling to draw on the work of distinguished women colleagues whose training is in historical scholarship and who are better able to do historical analysis. The record of women's oppression is powerful enough, when carefully reconstructed, to ground Daly's claims without recourse to casual and noncontextual historical judgments. Daly often rips historical materials out of their cultural context, as for example in condemning the practices of 'African genital mutilation' without noting that male subincision rites are part of the same cultural practice, or in condemning *both sides* of the sometimes contradictory treatment women in the United States receive at the hands of gynecologists. The result of this has been that many of Daly's critics have dismissed her substantive claims because of easily disputable historical overgeneralization.

5 Daly, *Gyn/Ecology*, pp. 413ff. As this manuscript was going to press, Mary Daly's *Pure Lust* (Boston, Beacon Press, 1984) appeared. A perusal suggests that Daly has shifted her position somewhat from some of the views criticized here. The analysis was, of course focused on Daly's work through *Gyn/Ecology*.

6 I am assuming here that a 'feminist moral theology' arises from the indepth experience of women's struggle for life and from the consciousness that emerges through that struggle to live and to maintain a culture that expresses our lives. Such experience produces a critique of dominant, male-articulated Christian and secular theological, philosophical, and moral assumptions. I want to stress that for me *biological gender does not ground this point of view;* women's *historical* struggle for life grounds it. I agree with Mary Daly that a feminist perspective – in this case a feminist moral theology – cannot assume the adequacy of any male notions of 'reason' or 'revelation'. However, since I am philosophically a dialectical materialist, I believe that critique of tradition equals transformation of tradition. The goal of a feminist moral theology, then, as Daly suggests, is to expose the death-dealing assumptions in the male-articulated tradition. However, contrary to Daly, I insist that women's culture has also been alive and concretely implicated in the real historical past of existing religious communities. The goal is to break the male monopoly on past and present interpretation so as to thereby displace patriarchal (that is, idolatrous) tradition with a humanly inclusive one.

7 I want to stress the similarity of hermeneutical assumptions made by feminists and by other liberation theologians even though many male-articulated liberation theologies often relish misogynist and masculinist idolatrous assumptions. See, for example, Juan Luis Segundo, *The Liberation of Theology* (Maryknoll, N.Y., Orbis Press, 1976), pp. 37–8, n. 55. Segundo would reserve the term 'Christian' for the male element in revelation. From the standpoint of the method of feminist theology, it is well to remember that women are not a minority. This means that the liberation theologies of all communities and groups must be transformed by the experience of women in those groups. If the world survives at all, all theologies will be forced to the feminist assumption since women are the underclass within every historical group. However, this also means, as noted here, that the liberation of women is 'the longest revolution'.

8 Roman Catholic theologian Matthew Fox has particularly stressed this theme of sensuality and spirituality. Happily, he notes the connection between feminist theology and the recovery of a spirituality of sensuliaty (M. Fox, *On Becoming a Musical Mystical Bear* (New York, Paulist Press, 1972), pp. ix–xxvi). He pursues this theme in other books, including *A Spirituality Named Compassion* (Minneapolis, Winston Press, 1979).

9 Sojourner Truth's speech was recorded in *History of the Women's Suffrage Movement*, vol. 1, reprinted in *The Feminist Papers*, ed. A. Rossi (New York, Bantam, 1973), pp. 426–29.

0 Mary Daly, *Beyond God the Father* (Boston: Beacon Press, 1973), pp. 35, *passim*.
11 Susanne Langer, *Mind: An Essay on Human Feeling*, Vol. 1 (Baltimore: Johns Hopkins University Press, 1967). Langer traces in minute detail the evolution of organic structure from invariant process to motivated act as the major transition point between mind and the rest of nature.
12 See 'Sexism and the Language of Christian Ethics' in this book, [*Making the Connections*].
13 The best available study of the values and virtues intrinsic to a feminist ethic, which also stresses this nurturance theme, is E. H. Haney, 'What Is Feminist Ethics: A Proposal for Continuing Discussion', *Journal of Religious Ethics* 8: 1 (Spring 1980), pp. 115–24.
14 N. Morton, 'The Rising of Women's Consciousness in a Male Language Structure', *Andover Newton Quarterly* 12: 4 (March 1972), pp. 177–90.
15 The phraseology is from the Boston Women's Health Collective, *Our Bodies, Ourselves* (New York, Simon and Schuster, 1973). This work has been one of the most powerful influences in transforming women's self-understanding during the past decade.
16 An important work that elaborates this theme is J. B. Nelson, *Embodiment: An Approach to Sexuality and Christian Theology* (Minneapolis, Augsburg Press, 1979).
17 See especially R. Radford Ruether, *New Woman: New Earth* (New York: Seabury Press, 1975).
18 See especially T. F. Driver, *Patterns of Grace: Human Experience As Word of God* (New York, Harper and Row, 1977). Recognition of the problem is also receiving attention in the works of theologians such as Charles Davis and Harvey Cox and, as noted above, Matthew Fox.
19 Happily, a few recent works by male colleagues in Christian ethics stress the importance of body and feeling in moral epistemology in a way consonant with my thesis here. See *Embodiment*, J. B. Nelson and D. Maguire, *The Moral Choice* (New York, Doubleday, 1978).
20 See Haney, 'What Is Feminist Ethics', and A. K. Rush, *Getting Clear: Body Work for Women* (New York, Random House, 1972).
21 M. Buber, *I and Thou*, trans. W. Kaufmann (New York, Scribner's 1970), pp. 67f.
22 See, for example, B. Commoner, *The Closing Circle* (New York, Knopf, 1971).
23 Carter Heyward, *The Redemption of God: A Theology of Mutual Relation* (Washington, DC, University Press of America, 1982).
24 J. R. Wikse, *About Possession: The Self as Private Property* (University Park, Pa. The Pennsylvania University Press, 1977).
25 Wikse, *About Possession*, pp. 44–45.
26 Wikse, *About Possession*, pp. 12–13.
27 A major source for the deprecation of mutuality in Protestant Christian ethics was A. Nygren's study *Agape and Eros* (Philadelphia, Westminster Press, 1953). Among those who followed Nygren was Reinhold Niebuhr. See G. Outka, *Agape: An Ethical Analysis* (New Haven, Yale

University Press, 1972), pp. 7–92. An early critique of Nygren never adequately appropriated was D. D. Williams, *The Spirit and Forms of Love* (New York, Harper and Row, 1968). Roman Catholic writers have usually included a more positive role for mutuality in ethics than have Protestants, but the critique of sacrifice proposed here is relevant to Roman Catholic writers.

28 For an excellent critique of orthodox christologies see Carter Heyward, *The Redemption of God*, and D.Sölle, *Christ the Representative*, (Philadelphia, Fortress Press, 1967) and *Political Theology* (Philadelphia, Fortress Press, 1974).

29 A. Rich, *Lies, Secrets and Silence* (New York, Norton, 1979).

30 J. Girardi, 'Class Struggle and the Excluded Ones,' trans. and distributed by New York Circus, from *Amoe Christiano Y Lucha De Classes*.

31 Thomas Aquinas argued, following Aristotle, that male and female 'natures' differed because biological structure differed. This two natures idea runs deep in Christian theology. Daly has, of course, reversed the traditional argument, making women alone expressive of full rationality. She continues the traditional dualism, however.

32 Within a liberation theology method, 'thinking' or 'reflection' is, of course, a moment *within* praxis. We 'do' theology, which includes our naming, interpretation, and analysis of our world, in the process of acting to change it in a life-giving direction.

18 Daphne Hampson: Luther on the Self: A Feminist Critique

1 'The Freedom of a Christian', in J. Dillenberger (ed.), *Martin Luther Selections* (New York, Garden City, 1961), p. 80.

2 'Ideo theologica est certa, quia ponit nos extra nos.' WA 40, I.589.8 (1531 Galatians lectures), quoted by G. Ebeling, *Luther* (ET London, Fontana, 1972), p. 174. The chapter of Ebeling's book 'Faith and Love', in which he quotes this line, is, I think, the best exposition of this theme in English. The major work in the field is Wilfried Joest *Ontologie der Person bei Luther* (Göttingen: Vandenhoeck & Ruprecht, 1987).

3 'Freedom and the Lutheran Reformation', *Theology Today*, 38:3 (Oct. 1981).

4 WA 56.422, 17(1515–16); WA 4.350.15f(1513–15). Quoted by Ebeling, op. cit. p. 162.

5 WA 56.281.11.

6 I explore this in 'Kierkegaard on the Self', in J. Watkin (ed.), *Kierkegaard at Sunderland* (Copenhagen, C A Reitzels Forlag, 1988). Kierkegaard's analysis of the structure of the self is found in particular in *The Sickness Unto Death* (1849), from which the quotation is taken (ET Princeton University Press, 1941), p. 213.

7 'The New Testament and Mythology' (1941), in H.W. Bartsch (ed.), *Kerygma and Myth*, vol. i (London, SPCK, 1953), p. 21.

8 'Church and Teaching in the New Testament', in *Faith and Understanding* (Princton University Press, 1966), p. 200.

9 It may be an interesting gloss to suggest that the transcendent God, before whom one cannot stand, represents 'the Father'. Luther indeed seems to have been much afraid of his Father. When he speaks of living by God's righteousness, his picture of God is in contrast motherly. Thus: 'The person who believes in Christ is righteous and holy through divine imputation. He already sees himself, and is, in heaven, being surrounded by the heaven of mercy . . . we are lifted up into the bosom of the Father . . . We dwell under the shadow of the wings of our mother hen' (WA 39, I;521.5–522.3.; Ebeling, op. cit., pp. 162–3). Unable to face the Father directly (and having cast aside the female intercessor in the form of the Virgin Mary), Luther overcomes his fear by making the Father God into a Mother who protects him.

10 *Philosophical Fragments* (1844; Princeton University Press, 1967), p. 37. Kierkegaard's major discussion of the inability of the individual – an entirely isolated individual – to exist before God is however found in *The Concluding Unscientific Postscript* (1846). cf. pp. 410–11, 432–3.

11 'Between Man and Man', *Between Man and Man* (London, Fontana, 1961), pp. 167–81.

12 See my 'Reinhold Niebuhr on Sin: A Critique', in R. Harries (ed.), *Reinhold Niebuhr and the Issues of Our Time* (Oxford, Mowbray, 1986).

13 I cannot here discuss the feminist literature that has developed round these themes in recent years. Carol Gilligan's *In A Different Voice* (Harvard University Press, 1982), to which I allude, has been influential. Nancy Chodorow *The Reproduction of Mothering* (Berkeley, University of California Press, 1978) suggests that the more relational sense of women, and individuated sense of men, owes to the fact that in all societies women perform the task of mothering; thus the female child learns relationality, while the male child has to gain a sense of himself in apposition to the mother.

14 There has been considerable feminist writing on this theme. For bibliography, see my 'Reinhold Niebuhr', in Harries (ed.) op. cit.

15 'What is Feminist Ethics?' *Journal of Religious Ethics*, 8 (1980), pp. 115–24. Quotation on p. 123.

16 See S. Collin's discussion of this theme, *A Different Heaven and Earth* (Valley Forge, Pennsylvania, Judson Press, 1974), pp. 202–5.

17 See my discussion in *Theology and Feminism* (Oxford, Basil Blackwell, 1990) ch. 5.

19 Letty M. Russell: Good Housekeeping

1 Some of the material in this chapter was published as 'Authority in Mutual Ministry', *Quarterly Review*, 6:1 (Spring 1986), pp. 10–23, and is reprinted in modified form, with permission.

2 'Minutes of the Standing Commission on Faith and Order', World Council of Churches, Crete, 1984, Faith and Order, Paper no.121, pp. 33–52.

3 L. M. Russell, 'Women and Unity: Problem or Possibility?' *Mid-Stream* 21:3 (July 1982), pp. 298–304.

4 See also L. Russell, *The Future of Partnership* (Philadelphia, Westminster Press, 1979).

5 R. Sennett, *Authority* (New York, Random House, 1981), pp. 16–27.

6 M. Marshall Fortune, *Sexual Violence: The Unmentionable Sin* (Pilgrim Press, 1983). cf. R. Radford Ruether, 'Politics and the Family: Recapturing a Lost Issue', *Christianity and Crisis*, 40:15 (29 Sept 1980), pp. 261–6.

7 Sennett, *Authority*, op. cit., pp. 50–83.

8 ibid., pp. 84–124.

9 C. Gilligan, *In a Different Voice* (Harvard University Press, 1982), p. 74.

10 Russell, *Growth in Partnership* (Philadelphia, Westminster, 1981) pp. 22–9.

11 R. Radford Ruether, 'Family, in a Dim Light', *Christianity and Crisis*, 43:11 (27 June, 1983), pp. 263–6.

12 See G. S. Wilmore, 'Religion and American Politics: Beyond the Veil', in W. K. Tabb (ed.), *Churches in Struggle: Liberation Theologies and Social Change in North America* (New York, Monthly Review Press, 1986), pp. 321–5.

13 Sennett, Authority, pp. 165–90.

14 ibid., pp. 175–90, cf. L. M. Russell, 'Women and Ministry: Problem or Possibility?', in J.L. Weidman (ed.), *Christian Feminism* (San Francisco, Harper & Row), pp. 75–94.

15 A helpful book for analysing social issues is J. Holland and P. Henriot, *Social Analysis: Linking Faith and Justice*, rev. and enl. edn (Mary Knoll, NY, Orbis Books, 1984).

16 W. K. Tabb (ed.), *Churches in Struggle: Liberation Theologies and Social Change in North America*, pt 5, 'Political Action and the Mission of the Church', pp. 268–325.

17 J. H. Elliott, *A Home for the Homeless* (Philadelphia, Fortress Press, 1981), pp. 102–6. Elliott is discussing 'sect' characteristics in 1 Pet.

18 E. Schüssler Fiorenza, *Bread Not Stone*, (Boston, Beacon Press, 1986), pp. 7–8.

19 M. Buhrig, 'The Role of Women in the Ecumenical Dialogue', *Concilium*, 182 (June 1985): *Feminist Theology*, p. 97. Buhrig says, 'A growing number of women within and outside the churches are no longer content to accept office in an unchanged and patriarchally structured Church. They are looking for new models (e.g. the "Church of Women") summed up in expressions such as "participatory", "communicative", "partnership", "non-hierarchical", and "reciprocity of ministries".' See also The Mud Flower Collective, *God's Fierce Whimsy: Christian Feminism and Theological Education* (New York, Pilgrim Press, 1985).

20 R. Radford Ruether, *Womanguides: Readings Toward a Feminist Theology; Women-Church: Theology and Practice of Feminist Liturgical Communities* (New York, Harper & Row, 1986).

21 J. Jackson, 'Converging Interests and a New Direction', speech delivered on 16 April 1984, quoted in 'Somewhere Over the Rainbow'

by S. D. Collins, in Tabb, *Churches in Struggle*, op. cit., p. 315.

22 B. Johnson Reagon, Song Talk Pub. Co., *Sweet Honey in the Rock: 'We all . . . Every One of Us'* (Chicago, Flying Fish Records, 1983).

23 N. Morton, *The Journey Is Home* (Boston, Beacon Press, 1985), pp. xviii–xix.

24 E. Schüssler Fiorenza, *In Memory of Her: A Feminist Theological Reconstruction of Christian Origins* (New York, Crossroad, 1983), pp. 153, xiii–xiv. cf. S. H. Ringe, *Jesus Liberation and the Biblical Jubilee: Image for Ethics and Christology* (Philadelphia, Fortress Press), pp. 63–71.

25 P. and S. Scharper (eds), *The Gospel in Art by the Peasants of Solentiname* (Maryknoll, NY, Orbis Books, 1984), p. 44.

20 Margaret A. Farley: Feminist Theology and Bioethics

1 C. Whitbeck, 'Women and Medicine: An Introduction', *The Journal of Medicine and Philosophy*, 7 (1983), pp. 119, 125; and B.K. Rothman, 'Women, Health and Medicine', in J. Freeman (ed.), *Women: A Feminist Perspective* (Palo Alto, Mayfield, 1979), pp. 27–40.

2 R. A. McCormick, *How Brave a New World? Dilemmas in Bioethics*, (Garden City, NY, Doubleday, 1981), p. 9; and 'Bioethics in the Public Forum', *Milbank Memorial Fund Quarterly*, 61 (1983), p. 119; B. Wildung Harrison, *Our Right to Choose: Toward a New Ethic of Abortion* (Boston, Beacon Press, 1983), pp. 84–90; J. M. Gustafson, *The Contributions of Theology to Medical Ethics* (Milwaukee, Marquette University Press, 1975), p. 26. For a contrary emphasis, see S. Hauerwas, 'Can Ethics Be Theological?', *Hastings Center Report*, 8 (1978), p. 48.

3 R. Radford Ruether, *Sexism and God-Talk: Toward A Feminist Theology* (Boston, Beacon Press, 1983), pp. 214–34; E. Schüssler Fiorenza, *In Memory of Her: A Feminist Reconstruction of Christian Origins* (New York, Crossroad, 1983), pp. 7–36; and C. S. Robb, 'A Framework for Feminist Ethics', [*Women's Consciousness, Women's Conscience*], supra.

4 M. Daly, *Beyond God the Father* (Boston, Becon Press, 1973); Ruether, *Sexism*, op. cit.; L. Russell, *The Future of Partnership* (Philadelphia, Westminster, 1979); Schüssler Fiorenza, *In Memory of Her*, op. cit., and P. Trible, *God and the Rhetoric of Sexuality* (Philadelphia, Fortress Press, 1978).

5 See Ruether's *Sexism and God-Talk*, op. cit.

6 Harrison, *Our Right to Choose*, op. cit.

7 ibid., p. 37; and R. Radford Ruether, *Sexism and God-Talk*, op. cit., p. 226.

8 R. Radford Ruether (ed.), *Religion and Sexism: Images of Women in the Jewish and Christian Traditions* (New York, Simon & Schuster, 1974).

9 C. P. Christ, 'The New Feminist Literature: A Review of Literature', *Religious Studies Review*, 3 (1977), pp. 203–12, and Daly, *Beyond God the Father*, op. cit.

10 J. Plaskow, *Sex, Sin and Grace* (Washington, DC, University Press of America, 1980).

11 Trible, *God and the Rhetoric of Sexuality*, op. cit.
12 S. McFague, *Metaphorical Theology* (Philadelphia, Fortress Press, 1982), and Russell, *The Future of Partnership*, op. cit.
13 R. Radford Ruether, *Sexism and God-Talk*, op. cit., p. 23; Schüssler Fiorenza, *In Memory of Her*, op. cit.
14 V. Saiving, 'Androgynous Life: A Feminist Appropriation of Process Thought', in S. G. Davaney (ed.), *Feminism and Process Thought* (New York, Edwin Mellon Press, 1981).
15 To the argument that separatist feminist movements do indeed contradict these values (by affirming a new form of elitism, by simply 'reversing' the order in the hierarchy of men and women, etc.), the response is sometimes give that separation does not entail domination, and that elitism is no more a necessarily substantial charge against separatist feminism than it is against any religious sectarianism. It is more difficult for some separatists to answer the criticism that they are duplicating oppressive patterns of 'identifying an enemy'.
16 S. B. Ortner, 'Is Female to Male as Nature Is to Culture?' in M. Zimbalist Rosaldo and L. Lamphere (eds), *Woman Culture and Society*, (Stanford, Stanford University Press, 1974).
17 P. Ricoeur, *The Symbolism of Evil* (New York, Harper & Row, 1967), p. 28.
18 N. F. Cott, 'Passionlessness', *Signs* 4 (1978), pp. 227–8.
19 S. Freud, 'The Taboo of Virginity', *Collected Papers*, 8:75.
20 P. Washbourn, *Becoming Woman: The Quest for Spiritual Wholeness in Female Experience* (New York, Harper & Row, 1979).
21 M. Crenshaw Rawlinson, 'Psychiatric Discourse and the Feminine Voice', *Journal of Medicine and Philosophy*, 7 (1982), pp. 153–77.
22 R. Radford Ruether in *Sexism and God-Talk*, op. cit., pp. 72–85, and in *To Change the World* (New York, Crossroad, 1981), pp. 57–70, Griscom, [*Women's Consciousness, Women's Conscience*] supra.
23 McCormick, *How Brave a World?* op. cit., p. 7.
24 R. Radford Ruether, *Sexism and God-Talk*, op. cit., p. 82.
25 R. Radford Ruether, *Sexism and God-Talk*, op. cit., p. 85, and in *To Change the World*, op. cit.
26 Plaskow, *Sex, Sin and Grace*, op. cit.; and R. Radford Ruether, *Sexism and God-Talk*, op. cit., pp. 12–13.
27 R. Radford Ruether, *Sexism and God-Talk*, op. cit., p. 19.
28 E. Cady Stanton, (ed.), *The Original Feminist Attack on the Bible: The Woman's Bible* (New York, Arno Press, 1974).
29 Schüssler Fiorenza, *In Memory of Her*, op. cit.
30 Trible, *The Rhetoric of Sexuality*, op. cit.
31 Harrison, *Our Right to Choose*, op. cit., pp. 12–13.
32 Whitbeck, *'Women and Medicine'*, op. cit., p. 120.
33 Reproductive technologies include all those technologies which relate to human reproduction. They are sometimes differentiated from technologies of genetic engineering, though I do not in this essay maintain a sharp separation. For some helpful distinctions, see President's Commission for the Study of Ethical Problems in Medicine and

316   Notes

Biomedical and Behavioral Research, *Splicing Life* (Washington, DC, US Government Printing Office, 1982), pp. 8–10.

34 S. Firestone, *The Dialectic of Sex: The Case for Feminist Revolution* (New York, Bantam Books, 1971), p. 238.

35 J. Mitchell, *Woman's Estate* (New York, Vintage Books, 1971), pp. 87–91.

36 Harrison, *Our Right to Choose*, op. cit., p. 37.

37 T. M. Powledge, 'Unnatural Selection: On Choosing Children's Sex', in Holmes, Hoskins and Gross (eds), *The Custom-Made Child: Women Centered Perspectives* (Clifton, NJ Humana Press, 1981), pp. 193–9.

38 J. Bethke Elshtain, 'A Feminist Agenda on Reproductive Technology', *Hastings Center Report*, 12 (1982), p. 41.

39 Harrison, *Our Right to Choose*, op. cit., pp. 169–70.

40 R. Rosenberg, *Beyond Separate Spheres: Intellectual Roots of Modern Feminism* (New Haven, Yale University Press, 1982), pp. 22, 83, 136.

41 R. W. Wertz and D. C. Wertz, *Lying-In: A History of Childbirth in America* (New York, Free Press, 1977); A. Oakley, 'A Case of Maternity', *Signs*, 4 (1979), pp. 606–31; A. Rich, *Of Woman Born: Motherhood as Experience and Institution* (Buffalo, Prometheus, 1976); K. Lebacqz, 'Reproductive Research and the Image of Woman', in C.B. Fisher (ed.), *Women in a Strange Land* (Philadelphia, Fortress Press, 1975); and M. Daly, *Gyn/Ecology: The Metaethics of Radical Feminism* (Boston, Beacon Press, 1978).

42 'Tales of horror' are told more and more in recent sociological studies in this regard. However, it should be noted that very recently there have come significant changes – changes, for example, such as an increase in home birthing, the provision of birthing rooms in hospitals, the rise once again of the profession of midwifery, etc. Some feminists express concern that some new movements, such as natural childbirth, incorporate an alienating technology just as previous methods did (Wertz and Wertz, *Lying-In*, op. cit., pp. 183–98, and Oakley, 'A Case of Maternity', op. cit., pp. 628–30).

43 Harrison, *Our Right to Choose*, op. cit., pp. 169, 246–7.

44 R. Radford Ruether, *Sexism and God-Talk*, op. cit., p. 227.

45 R. Radford Ruether, *Sexism and God-Talk*, op. cit., p. 226.

46 Harrison, *Our Right to Choose*, op. cit., p. 173. I am not, here, focusing on the grounds for women's right to procreative choice which are often central to feminist arguments – that is, a right to bodily integrity or a right to privacy. One reason I am not focusing on those grounds is that *in vitro* fertilization *can* be understood to prescind from women's bodies in a way that, for example, abortion cannot.

47 S. Ruddick, 'Maternal Thinking', *Signs*, 6 (1980), p. 358 and President's Commission, *Splicing Life*, op. cit., p. 65. This can be maintained without conflicting with contemporary concerns for 'too much mothering', etc.

48 Ruddick, 'Maternal Thinking', op. cit., p. 262. Nor should it be the exclusive prerogative of women. When it is this, it justifies a male dismissal of obligation regarding childrearing – something feminists have long been concerned to oppose.

49 Elshtain, A Feminist Agenda, op. cit., p. 42.

21 Sallie McFague: The Ethic of God as Mother, Lover and Friend

1 In the debate between eros and agape, the thought that Christian love is based on self-regard in any form has been anathema to Nygren and his followers. For some it has resulted in a decision to avoid the language of love entirely. Joseph Fletcher, for instance, insists that Christian 'love' is a matter of will, not of the emotions, and accuses the Gospel of John of confusing philia (friendship with God and other beings) with agape (justice, with no emotional involvement): '*The best practice is never to use the word "love"* in Christian ethical discourse. Every time we think "love" we should say "justice"' (*Moral Responsibility: Situation Ethics at Work* [Philadelphia: Westminster Press, 1967], p. 57).

2 The background of this view of God's justice is so evident in the Hebrew Scriptures that it probably does not need mentioning. The emphasis is decidedly on the side of a communal order of well-being in this world, which includes the poor (as well as concern for animals), rather than on punishment for rebellious individuals, though that is also present.

3 I am indebted to my students Vicki Matson and Doug Gastelum for these thoughts.

4 See *Models of God*, chap. 1, pp. 12–13.

5 J. Schell, *The Fate of the Earth* (New York: Avon Books, 1982), 174ff.

6 Needless to say, this is a vast, complex process involving high-level technical knowledge and planning. If one considers the complexity of international business and finance, however, or of current military technology and deployment, it is evident that human beings have the capacity to handle massive problems, when the will is there to do it. The issue before us now is whether we will put human intelligence, resources, and our natural instincts for the preservation of life to work on the side of life.

7 Rita Gross makes the point in regard to God as mother that as a model for human behaviour, it should extend beyond what mothers literally do, to include any woman who performs an act that gives positive, creative results. She notes that 'father' language is used in this way—'father of the country' or 'founding fathers'. To call God father, she says, does not mean God is the 'cosmic universal inseminator', so why limit God the mother to birth and nurturing ('Hindu Female Deities', p. 255)?

8 Throughout this essay we have used the term 'salvation' rather than 'redemption' for the work of God as lover. Redemption implies a recovering by effort or payment, a ransom or rescue—all of which fit the classical sacrificial, substitutionary atonement theories—but salvation implies the healing of divisions, making whole what has been torn apart.

9 The literature on the model of healing is extensive; a few important sources are W. Clebsch and C. Jaekle, *Pastoral Care in Historic Perspective* (Englewood Cliffs, N.J.: Prentice-Hall, 1964), chap. 3; Thomas A. Droege, 'The Religious Roots of Wholistic Health Care', in

Theological Roots of Wholistic Health Care, G.E. Westberg (ed.) (Hinsdale, Ill.: Wholistic Health Centers, 1979), pp. 5–47; R.K. Harrison, 'Health and Healing', in *Interpreter's Dictionary of the Bible*; J.N. Lapsley, *Salvation and Health: The Inter-locking Processes of Life* (Philadelphia: Westminster Press, 1972); R.E. Miller, 'Christ the Healer', in *Health and Healing*, H.L. Letterman (ed.) (Chicago: What Ridge Foundation, 1980), pp. 15–40; W.F. May, *The Physician's Covenant: Images of the Healer in Medical Ethics* (Philadelphia: Westminster Press, 1983); H. Nouwen, *The Wounded Healer* (New York: Image Books, 1979); P. Tillich, 'The Relation of Religion and Health', in *Healing: Human and Devine*, Simon Doniger (ed.) (New York: Association Press, 1957), and 'The Meaning of Health', in *Religion and Medicine*, David R. Belgum (ed.) (Iowa State University Press, 1967).

10 See esp. Droege, 'The Religious Roots of Wholistic Health Care', and Tillich, 'The Relation of Religion and Health'.

11 Needless to say, this power over life and death can be misused by the medical profession. Thus, doctors appear as 'gods' who can perform miracles, usually on essential parts of individuals, often elderly and wealthy ones. Less often, however, is the connection made between the health of the body and the rest of the person, or of even greater importance, rarely are basic nutritional and medical needs of the population, especially the young, given comparable attention as aspects of the healing profession.

12 E. Schüssler Fiorenza puts it directly when she says that just as oppressive ideologies are not abstract but concrete in being social-economic-political systems, so liberation from these systems must be equally concrete: 'Being human and being Christian is essentially a social, historical, and cultural process' (*In Memory of Her: A Feminist Theological Reconstruction of Christian Origins* [New York: Crossroad, 1983], p. 30).

13 See Harrison, 'Health and Healing'.

14 Albert Camus's novel *The Plague* deals with the issue of evil as 'the plague' in an allegorical and highly complex way. The plague cannot be 'cured', for 'it can lie dormant for years and years in furniture and linen-chests', only one day to 'rouse up its rats again and send them forth to die in a happy city' (New York: Alfred A. Knopf, 1964, p. 278).

15 Camus notes that no one is innocent; all persons participate actively or passively in passing death sentences on others, being indifferent to the suffering of others. As one character remarks, 'There are pestilences and there are victims, and it is up to us, so far as possible, not to join forces with the pestilences' (ibid., p. 229).

16 I owe this insight to a paper by Nancy Victorin, a Vanderbilt student.

17 The treatment here of the active and passive phases owes much to P. Teilhard de Chardin's *The Divine Milieu*.

18 Norman Pittenger expresses it in the following way: 'Very likely [Jesus] came to the conviction that only in this way, through obedience to the point of death, could he disclose and impart the reality which

evidently possessed him completely: the reality of God as loving Parent, we might even say as cosmic Lover, whose care for his people would go to any lengths and would accept suffering, anguish, even death, if this would bring to his children a full and abundant life, *shalom* or harmonious and truly human existence in and under his loving yet demanding care' (*The Divine Triunity*, p. 26).

19 See Nouwen, *The Wounded Healer* for expansion of this point.

20 One impressive example is Black Elk of the Sioux nation, who reports a vision of inclusive love: 'And while I stood there I saw more than I can tell and understood more than I saw; for I was seeing in a sacred manner the shape of all shapes as they must live together like one being. And I saw that the sacred hoop of my people was one of many hoops that made one circle, wide as daylight and as starlight, and in the center grew one mighty flowering tree to shelter all the children of one mother and one father. And I saw that it was holy' *Black Elk Speaks*, John Neilhardt (ed.) [Lincoln: University of Nebraska Press, 1961], p. 43).

21 In teaching a course on religious autobiography for some years, I have noted a number of characteristics shared by a type of religious autobiography that I call vocational; that is, a type that links the personal and public in such a way that the personal life is in the service of a commitment to public issues, such as issues of peace, abolitionism, women's rights, and poverty, within a religious context. Some of these characteristics are a profound, ongoing practice of meditation and prayer; a concern with the uses of money and often the adoption of a very simple lifestyle, combined with a monetary discipline; a relinquishment of the nuclear family or at least an enlargement of it to include many others in a communal family; a wrestling with sexuality, either as a problem to conquer or as a freedom to achieve a more inclusive kind of love; and a gradual movement toward a more and more inclusive love, as barrier after barrier of race, creed, sex, class and religion falls.

22 See *The Journal of John Woolman* (New York: Corinth Books, 1961).

23 See D. Bonhoeffer, *Letters and Papers from Prison*, rev. ed. (New York: Macmillan Co., 1967).

24 See *Narrative of Sojourner Truth* (Battle Creek, Michigan, 1878).

25 See Dorothy Day's autobiography, *The Long Loneliness* (New York: Harper & Bros., 1952).

26 See Mohandas K. Ghandi, *An Autobiography: The Story of My Experiments with Truth* (Boston: Beacon Press, 1957).

27 This notion of fellow feeling is expanded in D.L. Norton and M.F. Kille, *Philosophies of Love*, (London, Rowman and Allanheld, 1983), p. 263, though the authors restrict it to human beings. Max Scheler, however, in *The Nature of Sympathy* (London: Routledge & Kegan Paul, 1954), extends it to other species.

28 Scheler, *The Nature of Sympathy*, p. 281.

29 See treatment of this image and others in P.C. Hodgson and R.C. Williams, 'The Church', in *Christian Theology*, ed. P.C. Hodgson and

R.H. King (London, SPCK; Philadelphia, Fortress Press, 1982), pp. 249–73.

30 See Moltmann, 'Open Friendship', in *The Passion for Life: A Messianic Lifestyle*, trans. M.D. Meeks (Philadelphia, Fortress Press, 1977), p. 60.

31 My understanding of the church is similar to the following definition but differs from it mainly in its inclusion of nonhuman life: 'Ecclesia is a transfigured mode of human community, comprised of a plurality of peoples and cultural traditions, founded upon the life, death, and resurrection of Christ, constituted by the redemptive presence of God as Spirit, in which privatistic, provincial, and hierarchical modes of existence are overcome, and in which is actualized a universal reconciling love that liberates from sin, alienation, and oppression' (Hodgson and Williams, 'The Church', p. 271).

32 Hodgson and Williams note, ' . . . the characteristic perversion of ecclesia in our time is no longer institutionalism but individualism; that is, the notion that Christian faith exists for the sake of the salvation of individuals' (ibid., p. 264).

33 See the fine work by T.W. Ogletree, *Hospitality to the Stranger: Dimensions of Moral Understanding* (Philadelphia: Fortress Press, 1985), esp. pp. 41–3.

34 This very complex issue is dealt with by C. Birch and J.B. Cobb, Jr, in a way compatible with the view presented in these pages, namely, that an ecological, evolutionary model of living demands a 'symbiosis of desirable goals' rather than one species or individual's winning out over others. See their *The Liberation of Life: From the Cell to the Community* (Cambridge University Press, 1981), pp. 273–5

35 It is interesting to note that human beings – at least in the popular media, such as the television series 'Star Trek' or the film *Close Encounters of the Third Kind* – seem more interested in meeting aliens than mere (human) strangers. The alien from outer space appears fascinating, but the foreigner (from Russia?) is *dangerous*. Hence, the value in retaining reversal of roles is that we keep the stranger 'close to home'.

36 See the fine analysis of this concept in Aristotle by J.M. Cooper, 'Aristotle on the Forms of Friendship', in *Review of Metaphysics* 30 (1971), pp. 645ff.

37 ibid., 646–7. One sees this clearly in a number of democratic nations that have achieved a 'compassionate society' based on both justice and care or friendship. These societies, such as England and the Scandinavian countries, insist from a sense of justice on narrowing the distance between the wealthy and the poor in order to provide basic medical, educational, and nutritional assistance to all.

38 Moltmann, 'Open Friendship', p. 53.

39 Meagher's introduction to *Albert Camus*, p. 22.

40 Moltmann, for example, regrets the split that keeps 'enemy' as a public term while relegating 'friend' to the private realm ('Open Friendship', pp. 61–2). On the other hand, G. Meilaender finds obligation, and

hence justice, alone appropriate for the public sphere, fearing sentimentality should philia be allowed into matters of governance (*Friendship: A Study in Theological Ethics* (Notre Dame, Ind.: University of Notre Dame Press, 1981), chap. 4).

41 See Letty M. Russell's development of the concepts of advocate and partner in her books *The Future of Partnership* and *Growth in Partnership*.

42 W.F. May makes this point in his essay 'The Sin against the Friend: Betrayal', *Cross Currents* 17 (1967), p. 169

22 Ursula King: Women in Dialogue: A New Vision of Ecumenism

1 This theme has been movingly explored by the Indonesian woman theologian Marianne Katoppo. See her book, *Compassionate and Free: An Asian Woman's Theology, World Council of Churches* (Geneva, WCC, 1979).

2 The insights of liberation theology and feminist theology are brought together in L. M. Russell, *Human Liberation in a Feminist Perspective – A Theology* (Philadelphia, Westminster, 1974).

3 S. D. Collins, 'The Personal is Political', in C. Spretnak (ed.), *The Politics of Women's Spirituality* (New York, Anchor, 1982), pp. 362–7. The quotation is from p. 366.

4 *Sexism in the 1970s. Discrimination Against Women. A Report of a World Council of Churches Consultation, West Berlin 1974, WCC* (Geneva, WCC, 1975).

5 ibid., p. 10.

6 See R. Radford Ruether and E. McLaughlin (eds), *Women of Spirit, Female Leadership in the Jewish and Christian Traditions* (New York, Simon and Schuster, 1979).

7 *Pro Mundi Vita Bulletin*, 'The Situation of Women in the Catholic Church. Developments since International Women's Year', no. 83, Brussels, (October 1980), p. 27.

Bibliography

ACHTEMEIER, P.J. (ed.) 'The Bible, Theology and Feminist Approaches', *Interpretation* January (1988) pp. 5–72.

ALLEN, C.G. 'Self-Creation and Loss of Self: Mary Daly and St. Theresa of Avila', *Studies in Religion/Sciences Religieuses* 6:1 (1976) pp. 67–72.

ALLEN, P. *The Concept of Woman: the Aristotelian Revolution* (750BC–1250AD), Cheektowaga, NY, Eden Press, 1985.

ALLEN, P. 'Two Medieval Views on Woman's Identity: Hildegard of Bingen and Thomas Aquinas', *Studies in Religion/Sciences Religieuses* 16:1 (1967) pp. 21–36.

ALPERIN, M. 'The Feminisation of Poverty', pp. 170–6 of Mollenkott, V.R. (ed.) *Women of Faith in Dialogue,* New York, Crossroad, 1987.

ANDOLSEN, B.H., GUDORF, C.G. and PELLAUER, M.D. (eds.) *Women's Consciousness, Women's Conscience: A Reader in Feminist Ethics,* New York, Harper & Row, 1985.

ARMSTRONG, K. *The Gospel According to Woman,* London, Elm Tree; New York, Anchor Pr., Doubleday, 1986.

ARNAL, O.L. 'Theology and Commitment: Marie-Dominique Chenu', *Cross Currents* 28:1 (1988) pp. 64–75.

ATKINSON, C.W., BUCHANAN, C.H. and MILES, M.R. (eds.) *Immaculate and Powerful: The Female in Sacred Image and Social Reality,* Boston, Beacon, 1987.

BAKER, D. (ed.) *Medieval Women,* Oxford and Cambridge, MA, Basil Blackwell, 1978.

BALKE, V. and LUCKER, R. 'Male and Female God Created Them', *Origins,* 23 (1988) pp. 333–8.

BARBOUR, H. 'Quaker Prophetesses and Mothers in Israel', pp. 57–80 of Stoneburner, C. and J. (eds.) *The Influence of Quaker Women on American Society: Biographical Studies,* Lewiston, NY, Edwin Mellen, 1986.

BASS, D.C. 'Women's Studies and Biblical Studies', *Journal for the Study of the Old Testament* 22 (1982) pp. 6–12.

BATTIS, E. *Saints and Sectaries,* Chapel Hill, NC, University of North Carolina Press, 1962.

BIRD, P. 'The Place of Women in the Israelite Cultus', pp.397–419 of Miller, P.D., Hanson P.D. and McBride, S.D. (eds.), *Ancient Israelite Religion: Essays in Honor of Frank Moore Cross,* Philadelphia, Augsburg Fortress, 1987.

BISHOPS' CONFERENCE OF ENGLAND AND WALES 'Ministry and Mission: Proposals for a National Policy for Lifelong Priestly Formation', *Briefing* 17:7 (1987).

BOFF, L. *The Maternal Face of God: The Feminine and its Religious Expressions*, San Francisco, Harper & Row, 1987.

BONNER, G. 'Augustine's Attitude to Women and "Amicitia"', pp. 259–75 of Mayer, C. (ed.) *Homo Spiritalis*, Würtzburg, Augustinus-Verlag, 1987.

BORROWDALE, A. 'The Church as an Equal Opportunities Employer', *Crucible* April–June (1988) pp. 62–9.

BORROWDALE, A. *A Woman's Work: Changing Christian Attitudes*, London, SPCK, 1989.

BOWIE, F. (ed.) *Beguine Spirituality*, London, SPCK; New York, Crossroad, 1989.

BRIGGS, S. 'Sexual Justice and the Righteousness of God', pp. 251–77 of Hurcombe, L. (ed.) *Sex and God: Some Varieties of Women's Religious Experience*, London, Routledge and Kegan Paul; New York, Routledge, Chapman & Hall, 1987.

BROCK, S.P. and HARVEY, S.A. (trans. and eds.) *Holy Women of the Syrian Orient*, Berkeley, CA, University of California Press, 1987.

BROUGHTON, L. 'Find the Lady', *Modern Theology* 4:3 (1988) pp. 267–81.

BROWN, M.J.P. 'The Liberation and Ministry of Women and Laity', pp. 89–106 of Miller, A.O. (ed.) *Christian Declaration on Human Rights*, Grand Rapids, MI, Eerdmans, 1977.

BYNUM, C.W. *Jesus as Mother: Studies in the Spirituality of the High Middle Ages*, Berkeley, CA, University of California Press, 1982.

BYNUM, C.W. *Holy Feast and Holy Fast: The Religious Significance of Food to Medieval Women*, Berkeley, CA, University of California Press, 1987.

BYRNE, L. *Women Before God*, London, SPCK; Mystic, CT, Twenty-Third Publications, 1988.

CADY, S., RONAN, M. and TAUSSIG, H. *Sophia: The Future of Feminist Spirituality*, New York, Harper & Row, 1986.

CAMERON, A. and KUHRT, A. *Images of Women in Antiquity*, London, Croom Helm; Detroit, MI, Wayne State University Press, 1983.

CANNON, K.G. *Black Womanist Ethics*, Decatur, GA, Scholars, 1988.

CARMODY, D.L. *Feminism and Christianity: a Two-Way Reflection*, Nashville, Abingdon, 1982.

CARMODY, D.L. *Seizing the Apple: a Feminist Spirituality of Personal Growth*, New York, Crossroad, 1984.

CARMODY, D.L. *The Double Cross: Ordination, Abortion and Catholic Feminism*, New York, Crossroad, 1986.

CARMODY, D.L. *Biblical Women: Contemporary Reflections on Scriptural Texts*, New York, Crossroad, 1988.

CARR, A.E. *Transforming Grace: Christian Tradition and Women's Experience*, New York, Harper & Row, 1988.

CARR, A. and FIORENZA, E.S. *Motherhood: Experience, Institution, Theology*, Edinburgh, T. & T. Clark, 1989.

CHRIST, C.P. and PLASKOW, J. (eds.) *Womanspirit Rising: A Feminist Reader in Religion*, New York, Harper & Row, 1979.

CLARK, E.A. *Ascetic Piety and Women's Faith: Essays on Late Ancient Christianity*, Lewiston, NY, Edwin Mellen, 1984.

CLARK, E.A. *Women in the Early Church*, Wilmington, DE, Michael Glazier, 1983.

CLARK, E.A. and RICHARDSON, H. (eds.) *Women and Religion: A Feminist Sourcebook of Christian Thought*, New York, Harper & Row, 1977.

CLARK, S.R.L. 'Household, Sex and Gender', pp. 180–95 of his *The Mysteries of Religion*, Oxford and Cambridge, MA, Basil Blackwell, 1986.

COAKLEY, S. '"Femininity" and the Holy Spirit', pp. 124–35 of Furlong, M. (ed.) *Mirror to the Church: Reflections on Sexism*, London, SPCK, 1988.

COGGINS, R. 'The Contribution of Women's Studies to Old Testament Studies: a Male Reaction', *Theology* 91 (1988) pp. 5–16.

COLL, R. (ed.) *Women and Religion: a Reader for the Clergy*, Mahwah, NJ, Paulist Press, 1982.

COLLINS, A.Y. *Feminist Perspectives on Biblical Scholarship*, Decatur, GA, Scholars, 1985.

COLLINS, A.Y. *The Gospel and Women*, Chapman College, Orange, CA, 1988.

CONN, J.W. *Women's Spirituality: Resources for Christian Development*, Mahwah, NJ, Paulist, 1986.

CONN, J.W. and others *Horizons 9* 14:2 (1987), an issue by and about women.

COOEY, P.M., FARMER, S.A. and ROSS, M.E. (eds.) *Embodied Love: Sensuality and Relationship as Feminist Values*, New York, Harper & Row, 1987.

CRAVEN, T. 'Tradition and Interpretation in the Book of Judith', pp. 49–61 of Tolbert, M.A. (ed.) *The Bible and Feminist Hermeneutics*, Decatur, GA, Scholars, 1983.

CRAWFORD J. 'Faith and Feminism: An Introduction to Feminist Theology', pp. 1–10 of Pratt, D. (ed.) *Signposts: Theological Reflections in a New Zealand Context* , Yorktown Heights, NY, Meyer Stone Books, 1987.

DALY, M. 'The Forgotten Sex: a Built In Bias', *Commonweal* 15 January (1965) pp. 508–11.

DALY, M. 'After the Death of God the Father', *Commonweal* 12 March (1971) pp. 7–11.

DALY, M. 'Theology after the Demise of God the Father: a Call for the Castration of Sexist Religion', pp. 3–19 of Plaskow, J. and Romero, J.A. (eds.) *Women and Religion*, Decatur, GA, Scholars, 1974.

DALY, M. *Beyond God the Father*, Boston, Beacon, 1973; London, Women's Press, 1986.

DALY, M. *Gyn/Ecology*, Boston, Beacon, 1978; London, Women's Press, 1979.

DALY, M. *Pure Lust*, Boston, Beacon, 1984; London, Women's Press, 1984.

DALY, M. *The Church and the Second Sex*, Boston, Beacon, 1985 ed.

DALY, M. CHRIST, C.P. and GEARHART, S., pp. 197–228 of Pearsall, M. (ed.) *Women and Values: Readings in Recent Feminist Philosophy*, Belmont, CA, Wadsworth, 1986.

DELANEY, C. 'The Meaning of Paternity and the Virgin Birth Debate', *Man* 21:3 (1986) pp. 454–513.

DOUGLASS, J.D. *Women, Freedom and Calvin*, Philadelphia, Westminster, 1985.

DOWELL, S. and HURCOMBE, L. *Dispossessed Daughters of Eve: Faith and Feminism*, London, SPCK, 1987.

DRONKE, P. *Women Writers of the Middle Ages: A Critical Study of Texts from Perpetua (+ 203) to Marguerite Porete (+ 1310)*, Cambridge University Press, 1984.

ECUMENICAL PATRIARCHATE *The Place of Women in the Orthodox Church and the Question of the Ordination of Women*, The Ecumenical Patriarchate, 1988.

EDWARDS, P. *The People of the Book*, Springfield, IL, Templegate, 1987.

EDWARDS, R.B. 'What is the Theology of Women's Ministry?' *Scottish Journal of Theology* 40 (1987) pp. 421–36.

EDWARDS, R.B. *The Case for Women's Ministry*, London SPCK, 1989

EISENSTEIN, Z. 'Elizabeth Cady Stanton: Radical-Feminist Analysis and Liberal Feminist Strategy', pp. 77–102 of Phillips, A. (ed.) *Feminism and Equality*, Oxford, Blackwell; New York, New York University Press, 1987.

EISLER, R. *The Chalice and the Blade*, New York, Harper & Row, 1987.

ELSHTAIN, J.B. *Public Man, Private Woman: Women in Social and Political Thought*, Oxford, Robertson; Princeton, NJ, Princeton University Press, 1981.

ELSHTAIN, J.B. 'Luther Sic-Luther Non', *Theology Today* 43:2 (1986) pp. 155–68.

ELSHTAIN, J.B. *Meditations on Modern Political Thought: Masculine/Feminine Themes from Luther to Arendt*, New York, Praeger, 1986.

ERRICKER, C. and BARNETT, V. (eds). *Women in Religion: World Religions in Education*, London, Commission for Racial Equality, 1988.

EVANS, M. *Woman in the Bible: an overview of all the crucial passages on women's roles*, Exeter, Paternoster; Downer's Grove, IL, InterVarsity Press, 1984.

EXUM, J.C. and BOS, J.W.H. (eds.) 'Reasoning with the Foxes: Female Wit in a World of Male Power', *Semeia* 42 (1988) pp.1–156.

FABELLA, V. and ODUYOYE, M.A. *With Passion and Compassion: Third World Women Doing Theology*, Maryknoll, NY, Orbis, 1988.

FALK, N.A. and GROSS, R.M. (eds.) *Unspoken Worlds: Women's Religious Lives*, Belmont, CA, Wadsworth, 1989.

FARLEY, M.A. 'Sources of Sexual Inequality in the History of Christian Thought', *The Journal of Religion* 56:2 (1976) pp. 162–96.

FARLEY, M.A. 'Sexism', p. 604 of *New Catholic Encyclopaedia (Supplement)*, Palatine, IL, Publishers' Guild, 1981.

FARLEY, M.A. 'Theology and Bioethics', pp. 163–85 of Shelp, E.E. (ed.) *Theology and Bioethics: Exploring the Foundations and Frontiers*, Dordrecht, Holland, D. Reidel Publishing Co.; Norwell, MA, Kluwer Academic, 1985.

FINGER, R.H. (ed.) 'Your Daughters Shall Prophesy: A Christian Feminist Critiques Feminist Theology', *The Other Side*, October (1988) pp. 28–41.

FINGER, R.H. (ed.) 'Feminist Biblical Interpretation', *Daughters of Sarah*, 15, May-June (1989) pp. 4–21.

FIORENZA, E.S. *In Memory of Her: A Feminist Theological Reconstruction of Christian Origins*, London, SCM; New York, Crossroad, 1984.

FIORENZA, E.S. 'Missionaries, Apostles, Co-workers: Romans 16 and the Reconstruction of Women's Early Christian History', *Word and World*, 6:4 (1986) pp. 420–33.

FIORENZA, E.S. 'The "Quilting" of Women's History: Phoebe of Cenchreae', pp. 35–49 of Cooey, P.M., Farmer, S.A. and Ross, M.E. (eds.) *Embodied Love, Sensuality and Relationship as Feminist Values*, New York, Harper & Row, 1987.

FIORENZA, E.S. and CARR, A. (eds.) *Women, Work and Poverty*, Edinburgh, T. & T. Clark, 1987.

FISCHER, K. *Women at the Well: Feminist Perspectives on Spiritual Direction*, Mahwah, NJ, Paulist; London, SPCK, 1989.

FLANAGAN, S. *Hildegard of Bingen 1098–1179: A Visionary Life*, London, Routledge & Kegan Paul; New York, Routledge, 1989.

FLEXNER, E. *Century of Struggle*, Cambridge, MA, Belknap Press (Harvard University Press), 1975.

FRYE, R.M. *Language for God and Feminist Language: Problems and Principles*, Princeton, NJ, Center of Theological Enquiry, 1988

FURLONG, M. (ed.) *Feminine in the Church*, London, SPCK, 1984.

FURLONG, M. (ed.) *Mirror to the Church: Reflections on Sexism*, London, SPCK 1988.

GARCIA, J. and MAITLAND, S. (eds) *Walking on the Water: Women Talk About Spirituality*, London, Virago, 1983.

GILES, M.E. (ed.) *The Feminist Mystic: and Other Essays on Women and Spirituality*, New York, Crossroad, 1987.

GOULD, C.G. (ed.) *Beyond Domination: New Perspectives on Women and Philosophy*, Totowa, NY, Rowman & Littlefield, 1984.

GRAFF, ANN O'H. 'Women and Dignity: Vision and Practice', pp. 216–28 of Strain, C.R. (ed.) *Prophetic Visions and Economics and Economic Realities: Protestants, Jews, Catholics Confront the Bishops' Letter on the Economy*, Grand Rapids, MI, Eerdmans, 1989.

GREAVES, R.L. (ed.) *Triumph Over Silence: Women in Protestant History*, Westport, CT, Greenwood, 1985.

GREEN, C. 'Liberation Theology? Karl Barth on Women and Men', *Union Seminary Quarterly Review* 19 (1974) pp. 221–31.

GREY, M. *Redeeming the Dream: Feminism, Redemption and Christian Tradition*, London, SPCK, 1989; Mystic, CT, Twenty-Third Publications, 1990.

GRIFFITH, E. *In Her Own Right: The Life of Elizabeth Cady Stanton*, New York, Oxford University Press, 1984.

GROSS, R.M. (ed.) *Beyond Androcentrism: New Essays on Women and Religion*, Decatur, GA, Scholars, 1977.

GRUBER, M.I. 'The Motherhood of God in Second Isaiah', *Revue Biblique 90* (1983) pp. 351–59.

HADEWIJCH, *The Complete Works*, trans. Hart, C., *Classics of Western Spirituality*, Mahwah, NJ, Paulist; London, SPCK, 1980.

HAGEMAN, A.L. (ed.) *Sexist Religion and Women in the Church: No More Silence*, New York, Association Press, 1974.

HALL, D.C. (ed.) *The Antinomian Controversy 1636–1638: A Documentary History*, Wesleyan University Press, 1968.

HAMMACK, M.L. *A Dictionary of Women in Church History*, Chicago, Moody Press, 1984.

HAMMER, A.K. 'After Forty Years – Churches in Solidarity with Women?' *Ecumenical Review* 40:3–4 (1988) pp. 528–38.

HAMPSON, D. 'Luther on the Self: a Feminist Critique', *Word and World* 7:4 (1988) pp. 334–42.

HAMPSON, D. *Theology and Feminism*, Oxford and Cambridge, MA, Basil Blackwell, 1990.

HAMPSON, D. and RUETHER, R.R. 'Is there a Place for Feminists in a Christian Church?', *New Blackfriars* 68:801 (1987) and reprinted as a separate pamphlet.

HANNAY, M.P. *Silent but for the Word: Tudor Women as Patrons, Translators, and Writers of Religious Works*, Kent State University Press, 1985.

HARDESTY, N.A. *Great Women of Faith*, Nashville, TN, Abingdon, 1980.

HARDESTY, N.A. *Women Called to Witness: Evangelical Feminism in the Nineteenth Century*, Nashville, TN, Abingdon, 1984.

HARDESTY, N.A. *Inclusive Language in the Church*, Philadelphia, Westminster, 1987.

HARRIS, K. *Sex, Ideology and Religion: The Representation of Women in the Bible*, Brighton, Wheatsheaf; Totowa, NJ, Barnes & Noble, 1984.

HARRISON, B.W. 'Sexism and the Contemporary Church: When Evasion Becomes Complicity', pp. 195–216 of Hageman, A.L. (ed.) *Sexist Religion and Women in the Church: No More Silence*, New York, Association Press, 1974.

HARRISON, B.W. *Our Right to Choose: Toward a New Ethic of Abortion*, Boston, Beacon, 1983.

HARRISON, B.W. (ed. ROBB, C.S.) *Making the Connections: Essays in Feminist Social Ethics*, Boston, Beacon, 1985.

HAYS, E.R. *Morning Star: A Biography of Lucy Stone*, New York, Octagon, 1978.

HAYTER, M. *The New Eve in Christ: the Use and Abuse of the Bible in the Debate about Women in the Church*, London, SPCK; Grand Rapids, MI, Eerdmans, 1987.

HEARN, V. 'Christian Feminists in North America: The Experience of Evangelical Women', *Dialogue and Alliance*, 2, Fall (1988) pp. 57–75.

HEINE, S. *Women and Early Christianity: A Reappraisal*, London, SCM; Minneapolis, Augsburg Fortress, 1988.

HELLWIG, M.K. *The Role of the Theologian in Today's Church*, London, Sheed & Ward; Kansas City, Sheed & Ward, 1987.

HICK, J. and KNITTER, P.F. (eds) *The Myth of Christian Uniqueness: Towards a Pluralistic Theology of Religions*, Maryknoll, NJ, Orbis: London, SCM, 1987.

Hildegard of Bingen: An Anthology, BOWIE, F. and DAVIES, O. (eds), London, SPCK; New York, Crossroad, 1990.

HINES, M.E. 'Women Religious in Transition', *New Theology Review* 1:1 (1988) pp. 93–106.

HINLICKY, P.R. 'Luther Against the Contempt of Women' *Lutheran Quarterly* 2:8 (1988) pp. 515–30.

HODGSON, P. and KING, R. (eds.) *Christian Theology: An Introduction to its Traditions and Tasks*, Philadelphia, Fortress, 1982; London, SPCK, 1983.

HOPKO, T. (ed.) *Women and the Priesthood*, Crestwood, NJ, St. Vladimir's Seminary Press, 1983.

HOROWITZ, M.C. 'The Image of God in Man – is Woman Included?', *Harvard Theological Review* 72:3–4 (1974) pp. 175–206.

HURCOMBE, L. (ed.) *Sex and God: Some Varieties of Women's Religious Experience*, London, Routledge & Kegan Paul; New York, Routledge, Chapman & Hall, 1987.

HURLEY, J.B. *Man and Woman in Biblical Perspective*, Leicester, Inter-Varsity Press; Grand Rapids, MI, Zondervan, 1981.

IRWIN, L. (ed.) *Womanhood in Radical Protestantism, 1525–1675*, Lewiston, NY, Edwin Mellen, 1979.

ISASI-DIAZ, A.M., 'A Hispanic Garden in a Foreign Land', pp. 97–8 of Russell, L.M. (ed.) *Inheriting Our Mother's Gardens: Feminist Theology in Third World Perspective*, Philadelphia, Westminster, 1988.

JAKOBSEN, W. and others, *Special Issue: Feminist Theology, Journal of Theology For Southern Africa* 66 (1989).

JANTZEN, G. *Julian of Norwich: Mystic and Theologian*, London, SPCK, 1987; Mahwah, NJ, Paulist, 1988.

JEWETT, P.K. *Man as Male and Female*, Grand Rapids, MI, Eerdmans, 1975.

JEWETT, P.K. *The Ordination of Women*, Grand Rapids, MI, Eerdmans, 1980.

JOHN PAUL II, POPE, *Mulieris Dignitatem: On the Dignity and Vocation of Women*, Washington, DC, United States Catholic Conference; London, Catholic Truth Society, 1988.

JOSEPH, A. (ed.) *Through the Devil's Gateway: Women, Religion and Taboo*, London, SPCK, 1990.

JUNG, P.B. and SHANNON, T.A. (eds) *Abortion and Catholicism: The American Debate*, New York, Crossroad NY, 1988.

KAHOE, R.D. 'Social Science of Gender Differences: Ideological Battleground', *Religious Studies Review* 11:3 (1985) pp. 223–27.

KEE, A. *Domination or Liberation*, London, SCM, 1986; Minneapolis, Augsburg Fortress, 1988.

KELLY, K. *Life and Love: Towards a Christian Dialogue on Bioethics*, London, Collins; New York, Harper & Row, 1987.

KERBER, L.K. and DE HART-MATHEWS (eds) *Women's America: Refocusing the Past*, New York, Oxford University Press, 1987.

KERR, H.T. and DYKSTRA, C. 'A Brief Statement of Reformed Faith', *Theology Today* 14:2 (1989) pp. 151–8.

KING, U. 'Women in Dialogue: a New Vision of Ecumenism', *The Heythrop Journal* 26 (1985) pp. 125–42.

KING, U. (ed.)*Women in the World's Religions, Past and Present*, New York, Paragon House, 1987.

KING, U. *Women and Spirituality: Voices of Protest and Promise*, London, Macmillan; New York, New Amsterdam Books, 1989.

KIRSHNER, J. and WEMPLE, S.F. (eds) *Women of the Medieval World*, Oxford and Cambridge, MA, Basil Blackwell, 1985.

KOLBENSCHLAG, M. (ed.) *Women in the Church 1* Westminster, DC, Pastoral Press, 1987.

KRAEMER, R.S. (ed.) *Maenads, Martyrs, Matrons, Monastics: A Sourcebook on Women's Religions in the Greco-Roman World*, Philadelphia, Fortress, 1988.

LAFFEY, A.L. *An Introduction to the Old Testament: A Feminist Perspective*, Philadelphia, Fortress, 1988; London, SPCK (as *Wives, Harlots and Concubines*), 1990.

LANG, A.S. *Prophetic Woman: Anne Hutchinson and the Problem of Dissent in the Literature of New England*, University of California Press, 1987.

LANGLEY, M. *Equal Woman: A Christian Feminist Perspective*, Basingstoke, Marshall, Morgan & Scott, 1983.

LEECH, K. 'God the Mother', pp. 350–78 of his *True God: An Exploration in Spiritual Theology*, London, Sheldon, 1985.

LELOIR, L. 'Woman and the Desert Fathers', *Vox Benedictina* 3:3 (1986) pp. 207–27.

LERNER, G. *The Creation of Patriarchy*, New York, Oxford University Press, 1986.

LILBURNE, G.R. 'Christology: In Dialogue with Feminism', *Horizons* 11:1 (1984), pp. 7–27.

LITURGICAL COMMISSION, *Making Women Visible: The Use of Inclusive Language with the ASB*, London, Church House, 1989.

LIVEZEY, L.G. 'Women, Power and Politics: Feminist Theology in Process Perspective', *Process Studies* 17, Summer (1988) pp. 67–77.

LLOYD, G. *The Man of Reason: "Male" and "Female" in Western Philosophy*, University of Minnesota Press, 1984.

McDONNELL, E.W. *The Beguines and Beghards in Medieval Culture*, New York, Octagon, 1960.

McFAGUE, S. 'An Epilogue: The Christian Paradigm', pp. 323–36 of Hodgson, P., and King, R. (eds.) *Christian Theology: An Introduction to its Traditions and Tasks*, London, SPCK, 1983; Minneapolis, Augsburg Press, 1985.

McFAGUE, S. *Models of God: Theology for an Ecological, Nuclear Age*, London, SCM, 1987; Minneapolis, Augsburg Fortress, 1987.

MacHAFFIE, B.J. *Her Story: Women in Christian Tradition*, Philadelphia, Fortress, 1986.

MacLEAN, I. *The Renaissance Notion of Woman*, Cambridge, MA, Cambridge University Press, 1980.

MAGUIRE, D.C. 'The Exclusion of Women from Orders: a Moral Evaluation', pp. 130–40 of his *The Moral Revolution*, New York, Harper & Row, 1986.

MAGUIRE, M.R. 'Catholic Women and the Theological Enclave', *Christian Century* February 3–10 (1982) pp. 109–11.

MAGUIRE, M.R. 'Personhood, Covenant and Abortion'; Kolbenschlag, M., 'Abortion and Moral Consensus: Beyond Solomon's Choice'; Callahan, S., 'Abortion and the Sexual Agenda: A Case for Prolife Feminism'; Jung, P.B., 'Abortion and Organ Donation: Christian Reflection on Bodily Life Support'; Patrick, A.E., 'Dimensions of the Abortion Debate', pp. 99–180 of Jung, P.B., and Shannon, T.A. (eds). *Abortion and Catholicism: the American Debate*, New York, Crossroad, 1988.

MAITLAND, S. *A Map of the New Country: Women and Christianity*, London, Routledge & Kegan Paul; New York, Routledge, Chapman & Hall, 1983.

MAITLAND, S. 'Ways of Relating', *The Way* 26:2 (1986) pp. 124–33.

MAITLAND, S. 'A Case History of Structural Oppression', pp. 18–21 of General Synod Board of Education, *All are Called: Towards a Theology of the Laity*, London, Church House Publishing, 1986.

MALMGREEN, G. *Religion in the Lives of English Women*, 1760–1930, London, Croom Helm; Bloomington, Indiana University Press, 1986.

MARRIAGE, A. *Life-Giving Spirit: Responding to the Feminine in God*, London, SPCK, 1989.

MASSEY, M.C. *Feminine Soul: The Fate of an Ideal*, Boston, Beacon, 1985.

MAYER, C. (ed.) *Homo Spiritalis: Festgabe fur Luc Verheijen OSA*, Würtzburg, Augustinus-Verlag, 1987.

MEYERS, C. *Discovering Eve: Ancient Israelite Women in Context*, New York, Oxford University Press, 1988.

MIDDLETON, D.F. 'God as Mother: a Necessary Debate', *New Blackfriars* 65:679 (1984) pp. 319–22.

MILES, M.R. *Image as Insight: Visual Understanding in Western Culture and Secular Culture*, Boston, Beacon, 1985.

MILLER, O.A. (ed.) *Christian Declaration on Human Rights*, Grand Rapids, MI, Eerdmans, 1977.

MILLER, P.D. 'The Inclusive Language Lectionary', *Theology Today* 41:1 (1984) pp. 26–33.

MOLLENKOTT, V.R. (ed.) *Women of Faith in Dialogue*, New York, Crossroad, 1987.

MOLLENKOTT, V.R. *Women, Men and the Bible*, New York, Crossroad, 1988.

MOLLENKOTT, V.R. and BARRY C. *Views from the Intersection: Poems and Meditations*, New York, Crossroad, 1984.

MOLONEY, F.J. *Woman: First Among the Faithful*, London, Darton, Longman & Todd, 1985; Notre Dame, IN, Ave Maria, 1986.

MOLTMANN-WENDEL, E. *The Women Around Jesus*, London, SCM; New York, Crossroad, 1982.

MOLTMANN-WENDEL, E. *A Land Flowing with Milk and Honey*, London, SCM, 1986; New York, Crossroad, 1988.

MOLTMANN-WENDEL, E. and J. *Humanity in God*, London, SCM; New York, Pilgrim, 1983.

MOMMAERS, P. 'Hadewijch: A Feminist in Conflict', *Louvain Studies* 13 (1988) pp. 58–81.

MORLEY, J. '"The Faltering Words of Man": Exclusive Language in the Liturgy', pp. 56–70 of Furlong, M. (ed.) *Feminine in the Church*, London, SPCK, 1984.

MORLEY, J. *All Desires Known*, London, Women in Theology, 1988; Wilton, CT, Morehouse, 1989.

MORLEY, J. 'I Desire Her with My Whole Heart', *The Month* 21:2 (1988) pp. 541–4

MORLEY, J. 'Liturgy and Danger', pp. 24–38 of Furlong, M. (ed.) *Mirror to the Church: Reflections on Sexism*, London, SPCK, 1988.

MORTON, N. *The Journey is Home*, Boston, Beacon, 1985.

MUD FLOWER COLLECTIVE, *God's Fierce Whimsy: Christian Feminism and Theological Education*, New York, Pilgrim, 1985.

NATIONAL CONFERENCE OF CATHOLIC BISHOPS, *Partners in the Mystery of Redemption: A Pastoral Response to Women's Concerns for Church and Society*, Washington, DC, United States Catholic Conference, 1988.

NEVILLE, G.K., 'Religious Socialization of Women within US Subcultures', pp. 77–91 of Hageman. A. (ed.) *Sexist Religion and Women in the Church: No More Silence*, New York, Association Press, 1974.

NEWMAN, B. *Sister of Wisdom: St Hildegard's Theology of the Feminine*, University of California Press, 1987.

NICHOLS, J.A. and SHANK, L.T. (eds.) *Distant Echoes: Medieval Religious Women 1*, Kalamazoo, MI, Cistercian Publications, 1984.

NORRIS, R.A. 'The Ordination of Women and the "Maleness of the Christ"', pp. 71–85 of Furlong, M. (ed.) *Feminine in the Church*, London, SPCK, 1984.

OBELKEVICH, J., ROPER, L. and SAMUEL, R. (eds), *Disciplines of Faith: Studies in Religion, Politics and Patriarchy*, London, Routledge & Kegan Paul; New York, Routledge, Chapman & Hall, 1987.

OCHS, C. *Women and Spirituality*, Lanham, MD, Rowman & Allanheld, 1983.

O'CONNELL, G. 'The Synod of Great Expectations', *The Month* 21:2 (1988) pp. 530–9.

O'CONNOR, J. and others 'Symposium: Toward a Theology of Feminism?, with a special focus on *Beyond God the Father* by Mary Daly', *Horizons* 2:1 (1975) pp. 103–24.

ODUYOYE, M.A. *Hearing and Knowing: Theological Reflections on Christianity in Africa*, Maryknoll, NJ, Orbis, 1986.

O'FAOLAIN, J. and MARTINES, L. (eds.) *Not in God's Image*, New York, Harper & Row, 1973.

OPPENHEIMER, H. 'Life After Death', *Theology* 82 (1979) pp. 328–35.

OPPENHEIMER, H. *The Hope of Happiness: a Sketch for a Christian Humanism*, London, SCM, 1983; Minneapolis, Augsburg Fortress, 1989.

OPPENHEIMER, H. *Looking Before and After*, London, Collins, 1988.

OSIEK, C. *Beyond Anger: On Being a Feminist in the Church*, Dublin, Gill & Macmillan; Mahwah, NJ, Paulist Press, 1986.

OTWELL, J.H. *And Sarah Laughed: The Status of Woman in the Old Testament*, Philadelphia, Westminster, 1977.

PAGE, R. 'Re-Review: Elizabeth Cady Stanton's *The Woman's Bible*', MC 29:4 (1987) pp. 37–41.

PAGELS, E. *The Gnostic Gospels*, New York, Random, 1989.

PAGELS, E. *Adam, Eve and the Serpent*, New York, Random, 1988.

PAPE, D. *God and Women: A Fresh Look at What the New Testament says about Women*, Oxford, Mowbray, 1977.

PARSONS, S.F. 'The Intersection of Feminism and Theological Ethics', *Modern Theology* 4:3 (1988) pp. 250–66.

Partners Against Sexism: The Priests for Equality Response to the US Bishops' Pastoral Letter on Women's Concerns, West Hyattsville, MD, Priests for Equality, 1988.

PEARCE, D., 'The Feminization of Poverty: Women, Work and Welfare', *Urban and Social Change Review* 2:1–2 (1978) pp. 28–36.

PEARSALL, M. (ed.) *Women and Values: Readings in Recent Feminist Philosophy*, Belmont, CA, Wadsworth, 1986.

PELPHREY, B. *Christ Our Mother: Julian of Norwich*, London, Darton, Longman & Todd; Wilmington, DE, Michael Glazier, 1989.

PHILLIPS, A. (ed.) *Feminism and Equality*, Oxford, Blackwell; New York, New York University Press, 1987.

PLASKOW, J. *Sex, Sin and Grace: Women's Experience and the Theologies of Reinhold Niebuhr and Paul Tillich*, Lanham, MD, University Press of America, 1980.

PLASKOW, J. and CHRIST, C.P. (eds) *Weaving the Visions: New Patterns in Feminist Spirituality*, New York, Harper & Row, 1989.

PLASKOW, J. 'Religion and Gender: The Critical and Constructive Tasks', *Iliff Review* 45, Autumn (1989) pp. 3–13.

PLASKOW, J. *Standing Again at Sinai: Judaism from a Feminist Perspective*, New York, Harper & Row, 1990.

PLASKOW, J. and FIORENZA, E.S. (eds) 'Feminist Scholarship in Religion: Reformist or Revolutionary?', *Journal of Feminist Studies in Religion* 5, Spring (1989) pp. 7–142.

POHIER, J. *God in Fragments*, London, SCM, 1985; New York, Crossroad, 1986.

RAMSHAW, G. 'De Divinis Nominibus: the Gender of God', *Worship* 56 (1982) pp. 117–31.

RAMSHAW, G. *Letters for God's Name*, Seabury/Winston; New York, Harper & Row, 1984.

RAMSHAW-SCHMIDT, G. *Christ in Sacred Speech: the Meaning of Liturgical Language*, Philadelphia, Fortress, 1986.

RAMSHAW, G., *Worship: The Search for Liturgical Language*, Washington, DC, Pastoral Press, 1988.

RHODES, L.N. *Co-Creating: A Feminist Vision of Ministry*, Philadelphia, Westminster, 1987.

RINGE, S., "A Gentile Woman's Story", pp.65–72 of Russell, L.M. (ed), *Feminist Interpretation of the Bible*, Oxford, Blackwell; Philadelphia, Westminster, 1985.

ROBINS, W.S. (ed.) *Through the Eyes of a Woman: Bible Studies on the Experience of Women*, New York, World YWCA, 1986.

ROMERO, J.A. (comp.) *Women and Religion, 1983: pre-printed papers for the working group on women and religion*, Tallahassee, FL, American Academy of Religion, 1973.

ROSS, M, *Pillars of Flame: Power, Priesthood, and Spiritual Maturity*, New York, Harper & Row, 1988.

ROWAN, J. *The Horned God: Feminism and Men as Wounding and Healing*, London, Routledge & Kegan Paul; New York, Routledge, Chapman & Hall, 1987.

RUETHER, R.R. *Religion and Sexism: Images of Woman in the Jewish and Christian Traditions*, New York, Simon and Schuster, 1974.

RUETHER, R.R. *To Change the World: Christology and Cultural Criticism*, London, SCM, 1981; New York, Crossroad, 1983.

RUETHER, R.R. 'Patristic Spirituality and the Experience of Women in the Early Church', pp. 140–63 of Fox, M. (ed.) *Western Spirituality: Historical Routes, Ecumenical Routes*, Santa Fe, NM, Bear & Co, 1981.

RUETHER, R.R. 'Feminism and Patriarchal Religion: Principles of Ideological Critique of the Bible', *Journal for the Study of the Old Testament* 22 (1982) pp. 54–66.

RUETHER, R.R. *Sexism and God-Talk: Towards a Feminist Theology*, London, SCM; Boston, Beacon, 1984.

RUETHER, R.R. 'Sexism, Religion, and the Social and Spiritual Liberation of Women Today', pp. 107–22 of Gould, C.G. (ed.) *Beyond Domination: New Perspectives on Women and Philosophy*, Totowa, NJ, Rowman & Littlefield, 1984.

RUETHER, R.R. *Women-Church: Theology and Practice of Feminist Liturgical Communities*, New York, Harper & Row, 1985.

RUETHER, R.R. *Womanguides: Readings Toward a Feminist Theology*, Boston, Beacon, 1985.

RUETHER, R.R. 'The Liberation of Christology from Patriarchy', *New Blackfriars* 66 (1985) pp. 324–35 and 67 (1986) pp. 92–3.

RUETHER, R.R. 'Feminism and Jewish-Christian Dialogue: Particularism and Universalism in the Search for Religious Truth', pp. 137–48 of Hick, J., and Knitter, P.F. (eds) *The Myth of Christian Uniqueness: Towards a Pluralistic Theology of Religions*, Maryknoll, NJ, Orbis, 1987.

RUETHER, R.R. 'Christian Quest for Redemptive Community', *Cross Currents* 38:1 (1988) pp. 3–16.

RUETHER, R.R. 'The Development of My Theology', *Religious Studies Review* 15:1 (1989) pp. 1–11.

RUETHER, R.R. and KELLER, R.S. (eds) *Women and Religion in America*, 3 vols, San Francisco, Harper & Row, 1981.

RUETHER R. and McLAUGHLIN, E. (eds) *Women of Spirit: Female Leadership in the Jewish and Christian Traditions*, New York, Simon & Schuster, 1979.

RUSSELL, L.M. *Human Liberation in a Feminist Perspective*, Philadelphia, Westminster, 1974.

RUSSELL, L.M. *The Future of Partnership*, Philadelphia, Westminster, 1979.

RUSSELL, L.M. *Growth in Partnership*, Philadelphia, Westminster, 1981.

RUSSELL, L.M. *Becoming Human*, Philadelphia, Westminster, 1982.

RUSSELL, L.M. (ed.) *Feminist Interpretation of the Bible*, Oxford, Blackwell; Philadelphia, Westminster, 1985.

RUSSELL, L.M. *Household of Freedom: Authority in Feminist Theology*, Philadelphia, Westminster, 1987.

RUSSELL, L.M. *Household of Freedom: Authority in Feminist Theology*, Philadelphia, Westminster, 1987.

RUSSELL, L.M. (ed.) *Inheriting our Mother's Gardens: Feminist Theology in Third World Perspective*, Philadelphia, Westminster, 1988.

RUSSEL, L.M. 'Unity and Renewal in Feminist Perspective', *Mid-Stream: An Ecumenical Journal* 27, January (1989) pp.55–6.

SAKENFELD, K.D. 'In the Wilderness, Awaiting the Land: The Daughters of Zelophedad and Feminist Interpretation', *Princeton Seminary Bulletin* 9:3 (1988) pp. 179–96.

SAKENFELD, K.D. 'Feminist Biblical Interpretation', *Theology Today* 46, July (1989) pp.154–68.

SAIVING, V. 'The Human Situation: a Feminine View', *Journal of Religion* 40 (1960) pp. 100–12.

SAXONHOUSE, A.W. *Women in the History of Political Thought: Ancient Greece to Machiavelli*, New York, Praeger, 1985.

SAYERS, D. *Unpopular Opinions: twenty-one essays*, London, Gollancz, 1946; New York, Harcourt, Brace, 1947.

SCANZONI, L.D. and HARDESTY, N.A. *All We're Meant to Be: Biblical Feminism for Today*, Nashville, TN, Abingdon, 1986.

SCHABERG, J. *The Illegitimacy of Jesus: A Feminist Theological Interpretation of the Infancy Narratives*, New York, Harper & Row, 1987.

SCHAEF, A.W. *Co-Dependence: Misunderstood, Mistreated*, New York, Harper & Row, 1986.

SHELP, E.E. *Theology and Bioethics*, Dordrecht, Holland, D. Reidel Publishing Co.; Norwell, MA, Kluwer Academic, 1985.

SLEE, N. 'Parables and Women's Experience', *MC* 26:2 (1984) pp. 20–31.

SMITH, C. *Weaving the Sermon: Preaching in a Feminist Perspective*, Louisville, KY, Westminster/ John Knox Press, 1989.

SMITH, J.M. *Women, Faith and Economic Justice*, Philadelphia, Westminster, 1985.

SNYDER, M.H. *The Christology of Rosemary Radford Ruether*, Mystic, CT, Twenty-Third Publications, 1988.

SPRINGSTEAD, E. *Who Will Make Us Wise? How the Churches are Failing Higher Education*, Cambridge, MA, Cowley, 1988.

STANTON, E.C. and ANTHONY, S.B. (ed. Dubois, E.C.) *Correspondence, Writing, Speeches* New York, Shocken, 1981.

STENGER, M.A. 'A Critical Analysis of the Influence of Paul Tillich on Mary Daly's Feminist Theology', *Encounter* 43:3 (1982) pp. 219–38.

STENGER, M.A. 'Male over Female or Female over Male: a Critique of Idolatry', *Encounter* 47:4 (1986) pp. 464–78.

STEWART, C. 'The Portrayal of Women in the Sayings and Stories of the Desert', *Vox Benedictina* 2:1 (1985) pp. 5–23.

STEWART, C. *The World of the Desert Fathers*, Oxford, SLG, 1986.

SCHELKLE, K.H. *The Spirit and the Bride: Woman in the Bible*, Collegeville, MN, Liturgical Press, 1979.

STONEBURNER, C. and J. (eds.) *The Influence of Quaker Women on American History*, Lewiston, NY, Edwin Mellen, 1986.

STORKEY, E. *What's Right with Feminism*, London, SPCK, 1985; Grand Rapids, MI, Eerdmans, 1986.

STRAIN, C.R. (ed.) *Prophetic Visions and Economics and Economic Realities: Protestants, Jews, Catholics Confront the Bishops' Letter on the Economy*, Grand Rapids, MI, Eerdmans, 1989.

TARDIFF, M. 'Bibliography: Rosemary Radford Ruether', *MC* 30:1 (1988) pp. 50–5.

TENNIS, D. 'The Loss of the Father God: Why Women Rage and Grieve', *Christianity and Crisis* 41:9 (1981) pp. 165–70.

TENNIS, D. *Is God the Only Reliable Father?* Philadelphia, Westminster, 1985.

THISTLETHWAITE, S.B. 'Every Two Minutes: Battered Women and Feminist Interpretation', pp. 96–107 of Russell, L.M. (ed.) *Feminist Interpretation of the Bible*, Oxford, Blackwell, 1985.

THISTLETHWAITE, S.B. *Sex, Race and God: Christian Feminism in Black and White*, New York, Crossroad, 1989.

THOMPSON, B.A. 'Nelle Morton: Journeying Home', *Christian Century*, August 26–Sept 2 (1987) pp. 711–12.

TOLBERT, M.A. (ed.) *The Bible and Feminist Hermeneutics* Decatur, GA, Scholars, 1983.

TREVETT, C. (ed.) *Womens Speaking Justified: and Other Seventeenth-Century Quaker Writings About Women*, Quaker Home Service, 1989.

TRIBLE, P. 'Depatriarchalizing in Biblical Interpretation', *Journal of the American Academy of Religion* 41:1 (1973) pp. 30–48.

TRIBLE, P. 'Woman in the Old Testament', pp. 963–6 of *The Interpreter's Dictionary of the Bible*, Supplementary Volume, Nashville, TN, Abingdon, 1976.

TRIBLE, P. *God and the Rhetoric of Sexuality*, Philadelphia, Fortress, 1978.

TRIBLE, P. *Tests of Terror*, Philadelphia, Fortress, 1984.

TRIBLE, P. 'Feminist Hermeneutics and Biblical Studies', *The Christian Century* February 3–10 (1982) pp. 116–18.

VALENZE, D.B. *Prophetic Sons and Daughters: Female Preaching and*

Popular Religion in Industrial England, Princeton University Press, 1985.

WARD, B. *Harlots of the Desert*, Oxford, Mowbray; Kalamazoo, MI, Cistercian Publications, 1987.

WASHBOURN, P. 'Women in the Workplace', *Word and World* 4:2 (1984) pp. 159–64.

WEAVER, M.J. *New Catholic Women: a contemporary challenge to traditional religious authority*, San Francisco, Harper & Row, 1986.

WEBB, P. 'Gender as an Issue', *The Ecumenical Review* 40:1 (1988) pp. 4–15.

WEEMS, R.J. *Just a Sister Away: A Womanist Vision of Women's Relationships in the Bible*, San Diego, CA, Lura Media, 1988.

WEIDMAN, J.L. (ed.) *Christian Feminism: Visions of a New Humanity*, New York, Harper & Row, 1984.

WEIDMAN, J.L. (ed.) *Women Ministers*, New York, Harper & Row, 1985.

WELCH, S.D. *Communities of Resistance and Solidarity: A Feminist Theology of Liberation*, Maryknoll, NY, Orbis, 1985.

WEST, A. 'Sex and Salvation: a Christian Femininst Bible Study on 1 Cor. 6, 12–7, 39', *MC* 39:3 (1987) pp. 17–24.

WIESNER, M. 'Luther and Women: the Death of Two Marys', pp. 295–308 of Obelkevich, J. Roper L., Samuel, R. (eds.) *Disciplines of Faith: Studies in Religion, Politics and Patriarchy*, London, Routledge & Kegan Paul; New York, Routledge, Chapman & Hall, 1987.

WILLIAMS D.S. 'Black Women's Literature and the Task of Feminist Theology', pp. 88–110 of Atkinson, C.W., Buchanan, C.H., and Miles, M.R. (eds) *Immaculate and Powerful: The Female in Sacred Image and Social Reality*, Boston, Beacon, 1985.

WILLIAMS, D.S. 'The Color of Feminism: or, Speaking the Black Woman's Tongue', *Journal of Religious Thought* 43 (1986) pp. 42–58.

WILLIAMS, S.R. *Divine Rebel*, New York, Holt, Rinehart & Winston, 1981.

WILSON, A.M. 'Augustine on the Status of Women', *Milltown Studies* 19–20 (1987) pp. 87–122.

WILSON, K.M. (ed.) *Medieval Women Writers*, University of Georgia Press, 1984.

WILSON, K.M. (ed.) *Women Writers of the Renaissance and Reformation*, University of Georgia Press, 1987.

WILSON-KASTNER, P. *Faith, Feminism, and the Christ*, Philadelphia, Fortress, 1983.

WITHERINGTON, B. *Women in the Ministry of Jesus*, Cambridge, MA, Cambridge University Press, 1984.

WOODWARD, I. *The Catholic Sisters of the United States: Signs of Contradiction or Signs of the Times?* Pro Mundi Vita: Dossiers 4/1986.

WREN, B. *What Language Shall I Borrow? God-Talk in Worship: a Male Response to Femininst Theology*, London, SCM; New York, Crossroad, 1989.

YOUNG, F. *Can These Dry Bones Live?*, London, SCM, 1982.

Select Index of Names